Psychotherapy for a Democratic Mind

Psychotherapy for a Democratic Mind

Treating Intimacy, Tragedy, Violence, and Evil

Israel W. Charny

Foreword by Douglas Sprenkle

LEXINGTON BOOKS
Lanham • Boulder • New York • London

Published by Lexington Books
An imprint of The Rowman & Littlefield Publishing Group, Inc.
4501 Forbes Boulevard, Suite 200, Lanham, Maryland 20706
www.rowman.com

Unit A, Whitacre Mews, 26-34 Stannary Street, London SE11 4AB

British Library Cataloguing in Publication Information Available

Library of Congress Cataloging-in-Publication Data

Names: Charny, Israel W., author.
Title: Psychotherapy for a democratic mind : treating intimacy, tragedy, violence, and evil / Israel W. Charny ; foreword by Douglas Sprenkle.
Description: Lanham : Lexington Books, [2017] | Includes bibliographical references and index.
Identifiers: LCCN 2017031966 (print) | LCCN 2017030073 (ebook) | ISBN 9781498566988 (electronic) | ISBN 9781498566971 (cloth : alk. paper)
Subjects: | MESH: Psychotherapeutic Processes | Mental Disorders—therapy | Theory of Mind | Violence—prevention & control | Existentialism
Classification: LCC RC480 (print) | LCC RC480 (ebook) | NLM WM 420 | DDC 616.89/14—dc23
LC record available at https://lccn.loc.gov/2017031966

∞™ The paper used in this publication meets the minimum requirements of American National Standard for Information Sciences—Permanence of Paper for Printed Library Materials, ANSI/NISO Z39.48-1992.

Printed in the United States of America

I have a dear close friend in my life, my wife, Judy.
And we have six children, and from them thirteen beautiful grandchildren:

Children
ADAM
RENA
ANNA
MICHELLE
DAVID
AVIV

Grandchildren
ZACHARY
YUVAL
TAL
MAAYAN
MATAN
HALLEL
ORI
RONI
TAMAR
SHIRA
LIA
ANNA
NATHAN

With much love is this book about life dedicated to each of your lives.
Your husband-friend/father/grandfather or step-grandfather,
"Sababa"
Israel W. Charny

Contents

Foreword

This is a wonderful book. It is the most provocative—very much in a positive sense—book I have read on psychotherapy in the past decade.

The author, Israel Charny, throws down the gauntlet on many aspects of traditional psychiatric diagnosis as represented by the *DSM*. All the chapters are enlivened with case studies that reflect the author's exceptional wisdom, sensitivity, and courage. It is rare to read a book that offers a synergy of theory, research, and practice in a way that is so scholarly, compelling, and practical. I felt that it was a privilege to be drawn into the consulting room of a master clinician who handles very difficult cases with such sensitivity and brutal honesty. Few clinical writers are also so open about their failures as well as their triumphs, and this shows that Charny is willing to practice what he preaches—since he himself is not afraid of ambiguity and less than tidy solutions (the stuff of life).

Without denying some role for biology, he offers an alternative that relies far less on the biological etiology of dysfunctions and is much more skeptical of the (over) medicalization of treatment. He offers an alternative that gives considerably greater attention to the systemic (interpersonal) nature of dysfunctional and healthy functioning. His alternative also places much more emphasis on psychological processes and how people organize their lives. His approach is also adaptive to the changing ways in which culture and context produce new syndromes that he believes appear too late, or not at all, in the *DSM*.

The basic metaphor for both Charny's approach to diagnosis and treatment is what he calls the Democratic Mind and the Fascist Mind. He argues persuasively that democracy and fascism are not only political systems but ways of organizing the mind. This guiding metaphor arose undoubtedly from the author's life work as an internationally renowned genocide/Holocaust scholar as well as a psychotherapist.

His life work convinced Charny that humans are both good and evil; that both constructing and destroying life are innate drives rooted in evolutionary survival. While some people naively believe that all cruelty, human destruction, and mass murder are carried out by people who are grossly abnormal/dysfunctional, the data, Charny argues convincingly, clearly show that many "normal" people get co-opted into becoming perpetrators or accomplices of barbaric acts, or they become bystanders who do not stand up and oppose evil, or they become passive victims (who should not be blamed for these crimes but who make themselves too available) to those who hurt them. Charny asserts that the common thread is that these "normal" human beings do not sufficiently work to value and cherish life and protect it at all costs.

For this reason Charny proposes that all diagnoses of emotional and mental problems should be based on two critical questions. First, to what extent is a person dysfunctional and/or doing significant harm to him/her self? Second, to what extent is a person doing significant harm to others? Again, the common denominator is doing, or not doing, harm to life. The Fascist (organized) Mind is the internal "software or program" that leads to dysfunction and self-harm as well as harm to others. Self-harm includes acts like cutting one's body, or imposing impossible "shoulds" or "oughts" on oneself, or a million others ways of hurting oneself or doing violence against oneself. These acts are the counterparts of doing harm to others. The Democratic (organized) Mind is structured to provide appropriate self-care; even when a person is appropriately or inappropriately angry, one resists bodily harm toward others and strives to find constructive alternatives. Charny believes that traditional psychiatric diagnosis, with its emphasis on internal mental processes within the individual (self-adjustment), has not given sufficient attention to the impact that the acts of the person being diagnosed have on others. Overall, I found the aforementioned two questions to be a very parsimonious yet elegant model of diagnosis that became a very useful lens for the cases with which I have worked.

One of the key aspects to the Fascist Mind is that it seeks and demands absolute truth and certainly. This is why otherwise "normal" people may revert to this "software" installed in us at birth during times of high stress (like economic hardship), and how it can be reinforced by even well-meaning institutions like churches and schools (as was the case in Nazi Germany). It is our inner defense against uncertainty, complexity, and the existential anxiety of the human condition. Many of us "good" people revert back to this programming when we demand simplistic answers to complicated questions, are rigid and uncompromising (say, as parents), or seek to over-control others (say, in our workplace). It is certainly evident when we engage in extreme or self-destructive behaviors such as anorexia or compulsive extramarital affairs.

The Democratic Mind does the opposite. It not only tolerates uncertainty/ambiguity but seeks out diversity and welcomes the free exchange of ideas. The Democratic Mind values flexibility and eschews rigidity and extremism—even if well intentioned or politically correct. In sum, the Democratic Mind values and cherishes life.

For most of the book, Charny dissects and elaborates the ways in which rigid and extreme patterns are behind most mental disorders. As for my own particular area of expertise, marriage and family relations, I was deeply impressed with his application of the Democratic-Fascist Mind metaphor to marital and parental tensions, and to such diverse problems as sexual abuse, emotional abandonment, and sexual dysfunctions (areas that are generally underdeveloped in the *DSM* since relationship disorders are given short shrift). He demonstrates how all of these are rooted in rigid and extreme attempts to impose control on life's vicissitudes and ambiguities, or conversely, represent the failure of responsibility. His lens for viewing intimate relationships alone are worth the price of the book. As in most of his chapters, he takes on syndromes that some might view positively given their ostensible "goodness." For example, "the perfect marriage" (which is inevitably imperfect even if partners are afraid to talk about it) or "unquestionable loyalty to one's family" (which may become the basis for being abused).

Interestingly, Charny restores the term "neurosis," which had been abandoned by the *DSM*, since he thinks the term is more broad based and descriptive than some of the now accepted *DSM* "disorders." In keeping with his model, he creatively explains neurosis as the patient being in the grips of some rigid underlying paradigm of mind that he/she cannot shake off. "There is an unquestionable obedience to a guiding thought or model, which dictates the way they must live, achieve, be, or appear. Some condition of life must be fulfilled." Again, this pattern sucks life out of the patient and/or those around him/her. At the same time, like Rollo May, he credits anxiety itself with often being a positive call from within to emotional growth and fulfillment of one's potential.

For me this concept of Fascist Mind programming versus Democratic Mind processing is not only an apt way of describing people in my caseload, but it also points to avenues for treating them.

Charny clearly does not ignore the *DMS* entirely, as he includes chapters on the personality disorders (although he also adds the discontinued term "character disorders," since he believes, in spite of being politically incorrect, that these disorders often reflect deficiencies in "character"). Oher chapters also treat major mental illnesses of psychotic disorders including schizophrenia, and mood disorders like major depression and mania. As noted previously, however, while not denying a biological basis for many major mental illnesses, and the value of some medications used conservatively, he stresses the psychological processes that are at work.

Emotional processes emphasized in this volume include choosing major goals in one's life mistakenly. Some organize their lives to escape responsibility. Others orient their lives to escape the violence that is inside themselves or around them. Yet another life theme is excessive striving for power over other people. These ways of life, whether chosen consciously or unconsciously, bypass more productive and constructive ways of facing our difficult human condition.

Where the book is most creative, and perhaps makes its greatest contribution, is in Charny's descriptions of the diagnoses and treatment of syndromes ignored or underemphasized in the *DSM*. These include, as examples, what he calls the "orphan syndrome" of successful self-made people who are sometimes not only literal orphans but also emotional orphans who did not enjoy the support of their original family, and now with their own families either cannot accept family members who are unwilling to be like themselves or are incapable or unwilling to forge strong emotional bonds with their family members. He describes the syndrome of grown kids who live at home forever and sometimes rule their parents absolutely. Another is the syndrome of criminal behavior for "the thrill of it all." Not surprisingly, given Charny's background, he describes the syndrome of suicide killers of our era, including some "quiet good guys and women" who became suicide killer terrorists. Related is the "American Way" of mass killers like Columbine, and the movie theater and school shooters, nightclub killers, and those who terrorize other public places.

A whole chapter is devoted to the aforementioned theme of "treating disorders of doing harm to others and techniques for psychotherapy of emotional violence." Again, he faults psychiatry for paying too much attention to emotional hurt or inner unhappiness and not enough attention to the impact of dysfunctional behavior on others. The guiding and major principle for this treatment is to confirm that clients' violent *emotions* are acceptable and natural, and will be listened to respectfully, but that violent *actions* that cause bodily harm to others "are inhuman, unethical, immoral, and wrong." Charny does not shy away from terms that some might consider moralistic, value laden, and judgmental, but he is not apologetic. He agrees with William Doherty that psychotherapy is "a moral laboratory," and that one of the most important tasks of this discipline is to develop a social consciousness. I personally agree.

Since he unabashedly believes there are evil forces in people and systems, he offers techniques for the "psychotherapeutic engagement of evil," including how to respond to it with firmness and power. Not surprisingly, Charny is a much more confrontational therapist than most—although I was impressed with the respectful ways in which he challenged clients—and he offers vivid examples of giving people alternative positive ways to act. Frequently he would accept the natural nature of anger and help clients to harness the potential constructive energy of anger.

This is a volume that will generate controversy, since, although his position is not extreme, many are more convinced than Charny that especially serious mental illness is rooted in genetic causation—for which there is some fairly strong evidence from studies of identical twins reared apart. Thus the correlation between twin pairs is about 50 percent—if one twin has schizophrenia, there is a 50 percent chance the other twin will be schizophrenic. Although this is far above chance, there is a lot of variance to be explained by other factors, including psychological processes such as those emphasized by Charny. As previously mentioned, he takes many value stances that some will consider overly moralistic. Some readers, especially those who believe human nature is basically good, may not like the way that evil is presented as real as well as an inherent potential within the makeup of virtually all of us. Our critical choice is whether we channel these impulses through our Democratic or Fascist Minds.

Lastly, the book is almost eerily timely. Our headlines are dominated by fascist-minded terrorists and dictators. Many are worried about the appeal of candidates and newly elected ultra-nationalist leaders in the West who many consider potential threats to democracy—including the most recently elected president of the United States. Only time will tell if these fears are justified. Charny warns that although democracies have many more checks and balances, and that strong democracies make it easier for more citizens to cultivate Democratic Minds, all democracies are vulnerable to fascist leaders. They may weaken and destroy these checks and balances. They may even become perpetrators and others will join them as accomplices, or citizens will fail to protest and be bystanders, or they themselves will become overly willing victims under the "right" set of circumstances. Given these beliefs and Charny's intimate knowledge of history, he urges us to stand up and fight for caring for life. In fact, "This should be the ultimate goal of education, culture, religions, also science, in fact all pursuits of life."

I sincerely hope this book will be adopted and discussed widely in graduate programs where psychotherapy is taught. It is that important. I also hope that practicing psychotherapists as well as educated non-therapists will have the courage to read it through to the end. Not only is the future of psychotherapy at stake, but also perhaps the future of this planet.

Douglas H. Sprenkle
Professor Emeritus, Purdue University,
former director of doctoral program in marriage and family therapy,
former editor of the Journal of Marriage and Family Therapy

Preface

Applying a Concept of a Democratic Mind to Psychological Diagnosis and Therapy

Psychotherapy for a Democratic Mind applies the concepts developed in two previous books: *Fascism and Democracy in the Human Mind* (which was awarded "Outstanding Academic Book of the Year" by the American Library Association) and, very recently, *A Democratic Mind: Psychology and Psychiatry with Fewer Meds and More Soul.*

In all three books we are laying a groundwork for a psychology and politics of a free mind that does no harm.

In the present book we go on to *apply* the concept of a Democratic Mind to the actual diagnosis and treatment of many relationship disorders and psychiatric conditions—both to traditionally defined conditions with their relatively familiar names in the language of *DSM* psychiatry, as well as to new, unrecognized syndromes.

Note particularly that we address intimacy and relationship disorders such as those in marriage, parenting, and family life in the same language that we use for identifying and treating psychiatric disorders. Usually these two subjects are treated as separate from one another, addressed in different books and different courses in academic and professional training curricula. Here the two subjects are not segregated as if they were the provinces of different professions. In both relationship disorders and the recognizable psychiatric disorders of a person, we draw from a single concept of mental health that is defined essentially by how well or poorly a person is treating *both* themselves and/or others.

Further, in our considerations both of relationship disorders and bona fide conditions of mental disturbance, we identify in relationship disorders not only familiar and recognizable symptomatic complaints and conditions such as marital conflict and family dysfunction, and in psychiatric conditions syndromes such as various neuroses, psychoses, and personality disorders, but in both cases also focus on a variety of mistaken and ill-chosen ways of life and the conditions they bring on; and we propose that a good number of these largely unrecognized conditions be recognized as bona fide mental health problems. As stated, the key in our approach is whether a person is harming their own life and/or the lives of others.

We propose that all psychiatric-psychological diagnosis be based first of all on two "back to back" (like two views of DNA) questions:

Is the person harming his/her own life significantly?

Is the person doing significant harm to the life opportunities of others?

Either is a basis for diagnosing bona fide disturbance, and this means that at last we also have a conceptual basis for defining top-functioning people who are ruining other people's lives as disturbed, including what M. Scott Peck identified in his best seller as "People of the Lie."[1]

We then go on to name a variety of unrecognized syndromes as proper subjects of psychological and psychiatric treatment, no less than traditional syndromes of mental suffering and dysfunction. Beyond the tradition in mental health of treating symptoms of mental pain and disorder, we call for a psychotherapy that also treats other situations where a person does harm either to their own life or to the lives of others, including conditions brought on by human evil.

Psychotherapy strives to cultivate a free and democratic mind that embraces life and does no harm to others.

Thus, in our consideration of relationship disorders, we identify the following processes and conditions that are not recognized in formal psychiatric diagnosis, and often enough also are not named in categories of family disturbances despite the fact that many of these concepts were pioneered by family therapists:

- Family enmeshment and disengagement: reasonable ideas for family life taken too far
- The inevitable imperfection of "perfect marriages"
- Victimization in families in everyday life: violence and sexual abuse, abandoning, exploiting, scapegoating, and sacrificing members of one's family
- "I'm alright Jack personalities": people who seemingly don't have any problems and assign all the burden to someone else in the family
- A need to give to others but not to receive for oneself: big givers who take away the others' strength
- Unquestioning loyalty to one's family as a basis for being abused
- Sexual dysfunctions: how certainties can get in the way of making love well
- Genuine communication for genuine relationships: the give-and-take of real clarification of needs, criticism, anger, and love

Following, in our consideration of old and new psychiatric disorders, we address the following processes and conditions, many of which are not recognized in formal psychiatric diagnosis, including some unrecognized bedeviling syndromes and disorders of evil in our age of extremisms:

- Paranoid thinking in a political context
- A newer "hit" disorder of our time: anorexia

Table P.1. Psychotherapy for a Democratic Mind: Intimacy, Tragedy, Violence, and Evil

• Upsets the applecart of a 'symptom-cataloging psychiatry' (which then sells meds) • Proposes a basic diagnostic test for mental and relationship disorders: the extent to which a person is doing harm to themselves *and* the harm they are doing to others—the common denominator is how one is harming Life? • Looks at disorders that are nowhere in *DSM* because it is so busy with symptoms, and doesn't understand real underlying process of escape from Being, including kids who don't leave their parent's home (and often take over as dictators),	Sudden Death Syndrome (migrant workers from Asia in particular), violent killing in Columbines, and "People of the Lie" who look fine while driving someone else into a bad place in life • Uses a lens of a "Democratic Mind" to see relationship disorders along with mental disorders as akin and deriving from the same kind of "fascist thinking" that makes for terrifying destruction also on the societal level • Seeks first and foremost possibilities of inspiration, relearning, and coaching in individual and family therapy (with meds assisting on a selective basis)

- The "Orphan Syndrome," or self-made person
- A new syndrome of grown kids who live at home forever and often rule their parents absolutely
- Strange, crazy criminal behaviors including "for the thrill of it all" cases of "perfect" and "normal" kids who murder someone—sometimes their parents—unexpectedly
- The unsavory suicide-killers of our era, including some cases of nice and quiet "good guys"—or women—who become suicide-killer terrorists
- Sudden Unexpected Nocturnal Death Syndrome (SUNDS)
- The new "American Way" of mass killing at Columbines, shopping centers, and other public places
- People of the Lie—invisible destroyers of others' lives

Note that when it comes to major destruction of human life, we have broken with professional tradition to look also at political behaviors as psychological and behavioral roles and not only political choices. The subjects of terrorism and genocide are referred to often as huge extensions of the everyday psychological issues of how a person treats *life*.

We also note how psychiatric symptoms change dramatically over time within a given culture and even differ strikingly from one culture to another. (Oh, where are you wonderful Viennese hysterias? In our times we are stuck more with anorexias, borderline personality disorders, and suicide bombers.)

We then address the treatment of tragedy, violence, and evil, and here too we advance a positive ethic of the sanctity of human life, and it is this categorical imperative that is the basis for thinking about methods of treatment of these terrible situations. In the face of tragedy, we of course look to psychotherapists for their helpful traditions of understanding, support, and encouragement, but we also have therapists urge even *Job*-like figures who have been "wiped out" to fight back as much as possible. In the case of emotionally based violence, we propose that the therapist say explicitly and simultaneously that he/she will help the violent person with their anger but that said violent person knows that doing actual harm to others is wrong. What is critical to this technique is that both messages need to be delivered simultaneously—and also very passionately—in what begins as a passion-overflowing situation. As I report, I have used this method a fair number of times, including instances where I retrieved knives and a gun and helped stop mayhem without being personally injured. In the case of evil persons and evildoing, we advise therapists to counsel their patients/clients to recognize evil as early as possible and to take active steps to attempt to contain it. In all of these we act as if responding to a Call from Life as much as humanly possible.

Finally, it should be noted that we are also guided by a conception that features of fascist or totalitarian thinking are at work both on a societal level and in people's personal spaces. There is a considerable parallel between the use of totalitarian thinking in the organization of human experience by the individual and the phenomena of fascism we know so well and too often on the level of society.

In sum, the book proposes that the optimal goal of psychotherapy, and also the potential contribution of the mental health professions to society at large, lies in a cultivation of free minds with integrity that seek not to do major harm to their own lives or to the lives of others.

The unifying principle is as simple and obvious as life itself: that when individuals do harm either to their own lives or to the lives of others (or both), they are emotionally disturbed.

Frances Allen, MD, who was no less than the editor of *DSM-IV*, honored this alternative way of addressing mental health in his foreword to *A Democratic Mind*, where our underlying conceptions of psychotherapy were spelled out more fully. Even as Allen expressed his differences with our approach, he wrote that it is "fascinating . . . expressing noble and spectacularly ambitious aims" based on a "hope to perfect humanity and improve society by reducing our inborn tendency to dogmatic, selfish, authoritarian thinking. The premise is that our species is limited by a fairly primitive mental apparatus that needs a 'software upgrade' to provide us with the tools to live more at peace with ourselves and with each other."

Dr. Allen continues respectfully:

> To accomplish this, Dr. Charny would widely expand the purview of psychiatric diagnosis and treatment. Whenever possible, psychotherapy is given the new and grand purpose of promoting a "free and nonviolent Democratic Mind that enters into basically respectful and egalitarian relations with others." No longer should therapists be satisfied with helping patients reduce symptoms and mental suffering; they should now also identify and remediate the hurtful and even evil tendencies that cause suffering in others. Diagnosis and treatment must also extend beyond the individual to encompass

Table P.2. Overview: Sequence of Procedures in Psychotherapy for a Democratic Mind

1. Symptom Narrative	Interview and "active listening" to patient stories, complaints, symptoms, and requests.
2. Psychoethical Analysis—Treatment of Self and Others	Redirecting focus to how a person cares for their life or harms it, and how a person cares about the lives of others or harms them.
3. Acceptance of *All* Human Emotions	Identification, respect, empathy, and acceptance of major emotions (and their dialectical contradictions)—often including intense anger and/or intense yearning for relationship comfort—*but* together with number 4.
4. Redirection toward Life Building	Definition of needed corrections of acting out of emotions in destructive behavior, extremism and totalitarian thinking, and corrections of failures to honor the "gods of life."
5. Instruction and Enactment for Arresting Destructiveness	Instruction, enactments, and takeaway experiential and behavior exercises in stopping destructive behaviors (e.g., self-injury, overt violence, humiliation and insult, deprivation and neglect to others).
6. Instruction and Enactment of Life-Building Behaviors	Instruction, enactments, and takeaway experiential and behavior exercises in mindfulness, caring for and honoring oneself, and caring for and honoring others.
7. Psychodynamic Processing	Psychodynamic processing that is possible to the extent of the client's ego strength, flexibility, and readiness, including free-association, dream work, transference, and counter-transference (intrasubjectivity) interactions.
8. Relationship Therapy	Direct treatment of relationships in marital, parent child, and family therapies as made possible by the clients' caring and commitment to stay together and love one another, and to the extent made possible by the emotional strengths of the participants.
9. Celebration of Growth	Celebration of growth with the patients and therapist sharing pleasure in the patients' happiness, pride, and self-assurance about living well, and their readiness to cope with inevitable adversity in the future.
10. Separation and Individuation	Empowering separation by the client with the therapist's encouragement and celebration of independent living.

Source: Created and compiled by the author.

> relational problems at the family and societal level. We must not be satisfied with treating pathology; instead, we must strive to create goodness where once there was evil.
>
> Dr. Charny's original contribution to diagnosing mental health problems is his proposal that all psychiatric diagnosis revolve around the two sides of a human being's functioning, a person's disabilities and whether they are doing harm to their lives, and Dr. Allen indeed goes on to doubt, also respectfully, that much of the above is at all possible with our human species as it is—he writes that he has major doubts about "human perfectibility"—but he certainly warmly wishes us good luck for the trying.

To conclude, the basic principle applied to understanding and treatment of psychopathology and relationship disorders in this book is the cultivation of what we call a "Democratic Mind." I believe that emotional and relationship health and satisfaction are best served by a commitment to love of life—both for oneself and for others.

Elie Wiesel summed up how we are obligated to protect life wherever it is in our world: "Once you bring life into the work, you must protect it. We must protect it by changing the world."[2] Martin Luther King spoke of the importance of being concerned about others thus: "Life's most persistent and urgent question is, 'What are you doing for others?'"[3]

NOTES

1. Peck, Scott M. (1983). *People of the Lie: The Hope for Healing Human Evil. New York:* Simon & Schuster.
2. Wiesel, Elie (date unknown). The late Nobel Prize Laureate Elie Wiesel, who was a moving and profound witness to the Holocaust, is cited very widely as the author of this statement, but we have not been able to identify a specific source. For the reader's interest, Elie Wiesel was a cofounder of the Institute on the Holocaust and Genocide in Jerusalem together with the writer of this book and the late Shamai Davidson, MD.
3. In 1957 Martin Luther King made this statement to an audience in Montgomery, Alabama, and it has since been very widely cited. See, for example, *Huffington Post* (updated January 20, 2015). MLK, Jr. Asked Us 'What Are You Doing For Others?' Here's How We Answered. http://www.huffingtonpost.com/2015/01/19/mlk-day-serving-others_n_6489236.html. See also a tweet on January 16, 2017, Martin Luther King Day, by former president of the United States Bill Clinton. Tweet https://twitter.com/billclinton/status/820998131668160512.

Acknowledgments

"How shall I thank thee?

It is always a great pleasure when sending a book on to publication to stand back and say a very warm and even loving thanks to people who have accompanied and supported the journey.

Judy, dear (my wife), thanks once again for so very much in our lives together, including your growing appreciation over the years that when I go off to my world of writing I am not simply escaping family time and house maintenance responsibilities (although of course I am getting a bonus of some such relief). You are my best friend and sounding board in my endless search for new understanding of all that is incomprehensible in our existence. Moreover, as a well-experienced and excellent therapist yourself, your authentic reactions (including our periodic disagreements) help me a great deal to sort out my ideas. Finally, my gratitude for our "just" being together—it makes all the difference in everything I do.

Thanks very much also to my good assistant and friend, Karen Wolberger, MPH, obviously for your management of the computerization and word processing of the emerging manuscript from start to finish, but no less for your thoughtfulness and wisdom as a reviewer and very helpful critic as the project flowed forward. It is a pleasure to share working together in an atmosphere that combines a spirit of fun with the seriousness of task completion.

To my colleague of many years, Marc I Sherman, MLS, Director of Information Services at our Institute on the Holocaust and Genocide Jerusalem, thanks for the preparation of the comprehensive and genuinely useful index that you know so well how to prepare, and for your assistance in compiling information throughout the progress of the work.

I am also deeply grateful to Douglas Sprenkle, PhD, for his stirring and thoughtful Foreword. Doug was for many years the very successful editor of the prestigious

Journal of Marriage and Family Psychotherapy of the American Association of Marriage and Family Therapy (AAMFT) and, in addition to directing a department at Purdue University, remained an actively practicing clinician over the years. It is a great honor to me to have him hailing this book as "wonderful" and "enlivened with case studies that reflect . . . wisdom, sensitivity, and courage."

In addition, once again I am deeply grateful to Allen Frances, MD, who was the editor of the vaunted *DSM-IV*, for his very special foreword to *A Democratic Mind*, in which much of the theoretical basis for this more applied book was laid out.

Along with Drs. Sprenkle and Frances, I have heartfelt thanks to give to my additional colleagues who wrote warm endorsements of the book: Robert Krell, MD, Bill Doherty, PhD, Peter Suedfeld, PhD, and Samuel Karff, DHL. As these endorsements came in, my excitement grew with the realization that no one was extending to me simply a conventional courtesy about still another "interesting" book for the field of mental health. The genuine respect and enthusiasm for the very new ideas in this book is much appreciated.

THE CASE HISTORIES IN THIS BOOK

There are many clinical illustrations in this book, which are preceded by the diamond symbol (❖) and set off in indented extracts. Needless to say, no identifying information is given about the people in these cases. The clinical illustrations presented have been purposely chosen to also include cases where the treatment was *not* helpful, or worse, had a bad outcome. I have always felt uncomfortable as well as critical of a kind of hucksterism in the many books that present testimonials only to successes in psychotherapy. *It ain't so*, no matter what wonderful technique of therapy is used, and no matter how capable the therapist.

I love psychotherapy and take joy in the fact that we help many, many people, but it is far from a cure-all, and there are regrettably many poor outcomes. Certainly this book, which is about not pandering to certainties and not suppressing information that is disagreeable, needs to project relatively authentic pictures of people and the outcomes of therapy. Besides, failed cases of therapy, like many of the mistakes we make in our own lives and the failures we all rack up, also are opportunities for much constructive learning.

TO THE EDITORIAL TEAM AT LEXINGTON BOOKS

I also want to express my respectful appreciations to the editorial team headed by Kasey Beduhn at Lexington Books. You were earnest and hardworking, more than responsive in a timely fashion as we worked along, and impressively as well as annoyingly tough. I trust your "tough editing" will pay off like good "tough love" does, and we will proudly see a fine book that is good for people.

I

SOME OLD-FASHIONED PLUS SOME NEWLY FASHIONABLE PSYCHIATRIC SYNDROMES AND RELATIONSHIP DISORDERS

1

Some Old and New Psychiatric Disorders

INTRODUCTION TO SOME OLD AND SOME NEW PSYCHIATRIC DISORDERS, INCLUDING SOME CONDITIONS OF EVIL

Coming up are four chapters on a variety of relationship and psychiatric disorders: disorders in intimacy and relationships in marriage, parenting, and family life (Chapter 2); neurosis, depression, and suicide (Chapter 3); the widespread, baffling, and so often hard to treat personality disorders (Chapter 4); and psychoses, anorexia, and a whole host of new "bedeviling syndromes" that have not yet qualified for recognition by official psychiatry (Chapter 5).

These chapters are *not* intended to offer a comprehensive textbook of psychopathology. However, they are intended to introduce a meaningful kaleidoscopic picture of a good number of psychiatric disorders from a new perspective that is not generally recognized by the Establishment in mental health.

We propose that *all* diagnosis of emotional and mental problems be based on two critical questions:

1. To what extent is a person dysfunctional and/or doing significant harm to themselves?
2. To what extent is a person doing significant harm to others?

Either or both ways of doing harm to life are the critical ingredients of a psychiatric or psychological diagnosis, and it is important to understand also that both can alternate with each other dramatically and seemingly unexpectedly. The common denominator is *doing harm to life*.

Mental Disorders and Relationship Problems Are All Cut from the Same Cloth of Problems in Living

We look at mental disorders through a conception of a Democratic Mind that fundamentally calls for nonviolence, conflict resolution, and seeking peace, as well as acceptance of responsibility for whatever harms we do to ourselves and/or to others.

- We look at relationship problems both within ourselves and in relation to others through the lens of a Democratic Mind. We look for open-mindedness and respect for differences and disagreement; basic equality with others with checks and balances against excessive power; an ability to use constructive anger and aggression without cancelling out love and caring; and an overall orientation to life as pleasure and security both for oneself and for others. We lay the groundwork for a unified psychotherapeutic approach to all of the above as a process intending to overcome what we have called in previous books a Fascist Mind (see the summary of major characteristics of Democratic and Fascist Minds in Table 1.1).
- Democratic Mind refers *both* to the ways in which we treat *ourselves* in our minds *and* to the ways in which we treat *others*. Thus, insisting of ourselves one overriding way of thinking and feeling is fascism at work in a person's own mind just as we recognize in relationships to others when we demand total love, loyalty, or attention. Ways of hurting oneself, such as in today's common symptom of cutting one's body, or imposing on oneself a horrible mood, or a million other ways of hurting oneself, are violences against one's self that are counterparts to harms done to others. In contrast, being open to the flow of both positive and negative feelings toward ourselves and toward others is an expression of a healthier, more Democratic Mind.

The Democratic Mind and Fascist Mind are models of ways of experiencing our personal lives inside our minds as well as in our relationships to others. They are our own "personal politics" of life that correspond to fascist and democratic processes in society. A Fascist Mind punishes and hurts us personally just as fascist regimes do so much violence to many people. Democratic regimes protect freedom of rights, speech, and choices on a societal level, and a Democratic Mind is a freedom to be authentic and decent, first in our minds, bodies, and spirits and then in relationships too.

Disorders in Intimate Relationships in Marriage and the Family (Chapter 2)

In the following chapter we report on several prominent disorders in intimate relationships, including enmeshed relationships and rejecting relationships, the inevitable problematique of "perfect" marriages, excessive loyalty to family, sexual dysfunctions; on the nature of communication in healthy relationships and how

Table 1.1. Table Summarizing Major Characteristics of Democratic and Fascist Minds

Democratic Mind	Fascist Mind
Processes and organizes contradiction, diversity, and complexity and tests different possible solutions to life problems. Life is understood to be complex and full of contradictions.	Insists on total and final solutions, denies complexity, and emphasizes purity or holiness of purpose. There is a disavowal of complexity and often zealot-like convictions.
Accepts uncertainty, tension, and anxiety—in fact values them as potential sources of one's creative potential.	Devotes itself rigidly to authoritarian, ritualistic extremes and seeks to escape from uncertainty, vulnerability, and anxiety.
Is open-minded to new information, including welcoming contradictions and corrections of existing beliefs. Understanding of reality is sought largely through the use of the scientific method for testing reality.	Suppresses—even viciously—undesirable information and refuses to accept contradictions of its absolute values. Science is used to advance one's unquestionable goals more than to banish the darkness of ignorance.
Believes in freedom, respect for dissent, and the rights of people to make many choices in their lives.	Believes in obedience and conformity and is intolerant of dissent—often viciously. Absolute obedience is required to the values and choices made by authority.
Shares power and seeks a basic equality with others with checks and balances against excessive power or domination. Power is respected for self-expression and fulfillment, but not to abuse others.	Advocates superiority, allows excessive power over others, and is intolerant and dehumanizing of others.
Holds unwaveringly to nonviolence—except in objectively justified self-defense, strives to resolve conflicts, and seeks peace.	Engages in violence against oneself and/or others—retaliation and destruction Doing harm to life may even be celebrated as a "higher state of being."
Accepts responsibility for doing harm to oneself and/or others, and is ready to correct such harms.	Denies destructiveness and doing harm to oneself and/or others by denying the facts outright, or by minimizing, relativizing, or otherwise sanitizing the harm being done.

Source: Charny, Israel W. (2006). *Fascism and Democracy in the Human Mind.* Lincoln, NE: University of Nebraska Press.

they very much need to include criticism and anger communicated constructively and enrichingly; and on sexual abuse or violent abuse of members' of one's family.

The Democratic Mind does not tolerate violence or a host of other noxious styles of relating, including punitive coercion, demands for obedience and conformity, and claims of superiority over others. It also rejects insistence on absolute perfection or absolute compliance to prescribed models of emotional experience and to suppression of individuality. These are all expressions of what we call fascist ways of organization human experience, and they are destructive in personal life just as they are on the societal level. A Democratic Mind shapes a happier and more respectful way of life.

Good Old Neuroses and Depression and Suicide (Chapter 3)

In this chapter we write first of all about classic neurotic disorders followed by discussions of depression and suicide. In regard to all three subjects, we are "bad guys" in respect to Establishment psychiatry.

First, we discuss further[1] the drumming out of the classic concept of neuroses by the psychiatric Establishment—almost like a public banishment—from the *DSM*. We reiterate a point of view that our not knowing how to live our humanness and failing to experience and express one's real self are at the heart of neurotic suffering.

Second, we are adamant that depression in most cases is exactly what the word says—a person feels down about themselves and some major aspects of their life, and the job of mental health professionals is to help bring out the sadness and address it. Is the depression a hereditary or otherwise physiological illness (like the Establishment says)? In most cases we dare say, *No*. We do say that depression is a psychosomatic condition where emotions trigger physiological processes that in their own right contribute further to depression; hence medication *can* help break the cycle of symptoms, but woe, woe unto those who do so without going on to heal their inner sadness.

Third, the subject of suicide has not been banished from the *DSM*. It simply does not exist and never has! In this section we discover this unbelievable omission and learn that suicide is regarded "simply" as an aspect of depression and doesn't warrant a discussion in its own right of how and why people decide on a finite destiny for themselves, and how to treat what we call suicidality. Ironically, people continue to stream to psychiatrists and psychologists in grave suicidal situations when this is officially an unrecognized condition. Indeed, we have plenty of other conditions for which people understandably seek the help of mental health professionals that at best are given a name of "conditions for which people go to psychiatrists," but they are not really "psychiatric disorders." It is depressing.

A New View of Personality and Character Disorders (Chapter 4)

In this chapter, we propose a new view of what we call personality and character disorders. The term "character disorders" was standard for many years but then was dropped—heaven forbid that psychiatry express any value judgment, and besides, behaviors are so relative to different cultures. Our view overrides such relativism and does not flee from making judgments about a universal *good* and therefore *desirable* behavior (on behalf of life) versus undesirable behavior (destructive of life).

We look at personality and character disorders overall as disorders of self-centeredness, self-serving, and excessive claims of power over other people, and dare to believe that it is a task of Western mental health to characterize such behaviors as undesirable.

The classification we use of personality and character disorders is broken into three groups.

- Group 1 involves self-defeating and self-restricting personalities, and the awe-provoking borderline personalities—although today there are a few reports such as from Marsha Linehan and Otto Kernberg's group that do report at long last advances in treating this disorder, which for so many therapists has long been a sad graveyard of untreatability.[2] The self-limiting personality disorders are often more limiting, sad, and tragic than ostensibly self-serving, although the cases that involve addicting oneself unnecessarily to weakness and dependency also involve elements of self-serving and exploitativeness.
- Group 2 involves narcissistic, self-indulgent, and addictive personalities—also not very happy turfs for traditional psychotherapy and often susceptible only to methods of control of behavior.
- Group 3 includes people seeking excessive power, and paranoid personality disorders and full-blown antisocial personalities. If Group 1 emphasized disorders of hurting oneself and Group 2 indulging oneself, the emphasis in Group 3 is on taking it out on others and causing harm to others.

Personality disorders can also involve mixtures of several disturbing traits that are prominent in several different conditions, and can also be the infrastructure for another more prominent condition of mental illness such as bipolar disorder or a paranoid psychotic condition.

❖ He bragged unendingly that he could do many things far better than any other person (narcissistic). With this he indulged himself shamelessly in grabbing others coercively to satisfy his sexual appetites (self-indulgent). He displayed himself as being bigger and better and above all others over and over again (excessive power strivings). Never would he take responsibility for his attitudes or actions, but instead he would blame, demonize, and scorch others—in many cases attributing to others with certainty a plot against him (paranoid).

Who are we talking about? This is not the kind of person who is likely to come to therapy. As we will later learn, such people will have to be stopped in their tracks as early as possible by others who are not afraid to see the truths of their disturbances and harmful actions. The most prominent, easy-for-us-to-see case examples await in a frightening number of national leaders. Try choosing at least three for starters.

Here are several more interesting questions:

- Were these people "that way" before assuming political office?
- Did the cluster of these traits serve them in their quest to climb to high office?
- How much did these personality traits develop and expand in response to the power they gained à la the ancient dictum that power corrupts (a subject we will examine in greater detail later)?

In some cases the answers to these questions are obvious; in others it is more of a puzzle; in all cases there is a likely interaction between the preexisting personality and the sickening grandiosity of power.

It is not hard to see how all three basic groups of personality and character disorders are far from what we call the methods of experiencing that characterize a Democratic Mind. It is striking that many of these conditions involve—directly or indirectly—people who are making themselves superior to others, whether by overuse of weakness or excessive use of power. People with personality disorders characteristically do not respond to calls or even pleas by those close to them to take responsibility for their harming others. Overall, our treatment techniques for these problems are still primitive and limited.

Some Psychoses, but Also Other "Crazy" Conditions that are Bedeviling to Understand (Chapter 5)

Here we write about a variety of psychotic conditions, but with a new twist. Without being know-it-alls—as if we know everything about the origins of madness—we write about the disturbances not simply as serious "illnesses" or "dysfunctions" that in some cases possibly are based on biological causes (we all know that you can go crazy from the side effects of drugs and some diseases), but that are most often the result of psychological processes.

"Madness" and significant mental problems of all sorts are in many cases a giving up—a retreat from reaching one's desired goals in life. This means that for each patient we want to really understand what they are seeking for themselves. Many times people are headed for trouble because what they are looking for in life to begin with is slated to get them into trouble—for example, the need to win; being nice and getting along with everybody; being admired and adored; not being criticized, embarrassed, or humiliated; an absolute need to win a certain success or a certain love; a need to be superior to others; and any number of other choices that by definition are not compatible with the realities of our human existence. These interpretations have considerable meanings for the design of therapy.

If an illness is seen as an escape from life after making bad choices about one's goals in life, then therapy should also address the patient's philosophy of their future life when this becomes possible. If the illness is an escape from too much aggression—from others or in oneself—therapy should include a good deal of training in handling aggression. If the psychiatric disturbance is seen to a significant extent as an escape from responsibility, therapy should direct and help the patient as early as possible to take and assume responsibility and how to limit undue responsibility.

The material on psychosis in this chapter will be very familiar to experienced clinicians—although I also have to observe that many of today's psychotherapists, especially in psychology and social work, do *not* know how to encounter full-blown madness and treat its soul. A great many therapists today are not trained to deal with severely ill patients in states of decompensation and regression because so much of hospital treatment is devoted to suppressing symptoms and aborting the psychological process the patient is living out in their symptoms. To my knowledge, there are many students in mental health professions who go through their training, say in family therapy, without any significant experience in a psychiatric hospital and do not really recognize regression and retreat from life when they are at their peak.

Additionally, many of today's therapists in all the mental health professions are trained primarily or even solely in here-and-now techniques—not only of psychopharmacology to halt symptoms, but also in psychotherapy techniques of support, cognitive-behavior training, renewing family communication, and other techniques that are genuinely helpful, but far less so when problems and disorders are rooted in deep unconscious feelings and ways of framing experiences. In all these instances, therapists themselves are also deprived of opportunities to meet up with their own inner "craziness" and deeper weaknesses, knowledge of which prepares therapists to be more empathic and also less frightened in dealing with regression in their patients.

While psychiatrists (as opposed to psychologists and social workers) by definition do get a meaningful exposure to hospital patients, in most cases today they are exposed to techniques for *suppressing* symptoms rather than working them through, as we learned from masters like Marguerite Sechehaye,[3] who taught us how to be present with a withdrawn psychotic; or Frieda Fromm Reichmann, who taught us how to make sense of madness as a communication and to offer a containing and comforting presence to a patient who is crazy with fears of themselves and of others;[4] or R.D. Lang's incredible understanding of the deep-down anxiety of being annihilated and his amazing readiness to accompany a psychotic patient through the natural course of their breakdown, disorganization, and possible reorganizations.[5] Thankfully, there remain a few psychiatrists in each generation who take it upon themselves to engage in a real treatment battle with madness.[6]

Still and all, the traditional psychoses are at least intellectually familiar to just about everyone in the area of mental health. What will be relatively new for many more readers are the sections that follow in the same chapter about a number of largely unrecognized or unformulated and unlabeled conditions that very much satisfy our basic definition of mental disorders as doing significant harm to oneself and/or others. Thus we describe a variety of problems including violence to life that is seemingly more present in our age of extremisms, but in fact has always been, in one form or another, around in human life and in my opinion needs to be recognized much more by mental health theory as a fundamental aspect of the human animal and not just an "add-on." We will be looking at intriguing syndromes such as:

- A syndrome of self-made people who have a very hard time handling the complexities of relationships and the weaknesses of other people in their lives
- A new syndrome of grown children who stay or come back to live at home forever, and often push their parents around unmercifully
- A condition of seemingly unexplained deathly pressure on a person's chest, which can lead to actual death, and instructs us in just how crushing emotional reactions can be
- Criminal behaviors "for the thrill of it all" as opposed to crime as a lucrative pursuit
- "Perfect kids" who murder someone—sometimes their parents
- The suicide bombers of our time who cannot really be explained away only by political considerations
- The authors of Columbine-type killings, a "popular" new way of qualifying as a psychiatric freak that American culture has "contributed" to the world
- "People of the Lie," where perfectly upstanding-looking people are very much driving someone else in their lives crazy

Are These Syndromes Psychiatric Conditions?

As always, the test of our Democratic Mind model is whether behaviors and conditions bring significant harm to the life of the person or to the lives of other human beings or both? Our judgment is, *Yes*. All of the above are sick as hell and unleash hells in human lives.

Key Psychodynamic Themes of How People Organize Their Lives

In all the chapters in this section of the book, we will be looking at the psychodynamics of psychiatric disorders from several perspectives of how a person organizes their life rather than from a point of view of the bad luck of heredity or medical conditions that somehow arise to plague us. Among the aspects of living in which many of us make errors in our choices of how to conduct our lives are selecting major goals in one's life mistakenly; panicked escapes from violence inside us and around us; escapes from responsibility, challenge, unbearable loss, and failure; excessive strivings for power; and errors in how we organize our relationships.

Selecting Major Goals in One's Life Mistakenly

The goals of a person's life obviously contribute powerfully to shaping one's emerging and ultimate fate. To take a startling extreme, a vicious dictator who kills and kills other human beings can also be "asking for it," and in many (though regrettably not all) cases will end up getting "what's coming to him" or from others; thus

Hitler, Mussolini, Tojo, Ceausescu, Gaddafi, Milosevic. Much more subtly: If one must have perfect outcomes and successes; if one's goal is to be loved and admired; if one has to be taken care of by others; if one doesn't give a damn about the welfare of others; if one wants to be in continuous hedonistic pleasure—all these factors and many others give negative odds for being emotionally healthy and happy over the years.

We want to understand what a person is looking for and saying through their madness and other symptoms: Each patient has their own version of "Stop the world, I want to get off." Some want out because they are very tired; others because they are terrified; and still others because they are furious and inclined to kill but don't want to go off such a terrible deep end, so going crazy is a safer alternative. In every psychiatric condition there is a personal message that we want to respectfully understand for the individual patient, and not just see a type of "disease."

Escapes from Violence Inside Us and Around Us

There is a surprising number of mental conditions in which one can trace back to a major role that is being played by the patient's fears of their own aggressiveness and the possibility that they could do harm to another person. (I have also seen normal people who develop a timidity or reticence in their overall personality because they grow up feeling afraid and responsible for the possible damage they could do to one or both parents if they really let loose with their full personality.)

An example of the role of fears of one's negative feelings can be found in post-partum depressions where the best explanation I have ever learned, and have found successfully applicable in therapy of these conditions, is that the new mother is deathly afraid she will reject her baby, even without knowing it or choosing to do so, just as she has known unconsciously for many years that her mother rejected her—but she has not known this consciously.[7]

In the world of full-blown psychosis, a number of psychologists and psychiatrists have dared to see that many schizophrenics are especially sensitive people who are horrified by life's brutality and/or scared stiff of their own aggression, and their psychosis is an escape hatch or defense against the ugliness of life, and often especially against the possible eruption of *their* violence.[8] If true, such escapes from the rottenness of other human beings and from having to handle one's own rottenness, meaning one's own violent urges, should be addressed not by treatments like electric shock but by a respectful psychological-philosophical cleaning up and toughening up. A therapy aiming a Democratic Mind process aims to teach patients how to handle impulses of their aggressive feelings and other emotions, and even their rottenness.

Escapes from Responsibility, Challenge, Unbearable Loss, and Failure

Mental illness is often an escape that expresses a lazy, selfish, and passive rejection of the demands of life. There are a number of psychologists and psychiatrists who dare to see psychoses through a lens of escapes from the rotten realities of human existence including responsibility, challenges, and failures and losses. Of course, the psychosis is a statement of "*I can't cope*," but from this additional point of view in any number of cases it also becomes a statement of "*I don't want to cope*." The patient is escaping life and leaving the hard work of coping with human existence to others. In its time, Soviet psychiatry—which otherwise served a totalitarian state and therefore was suspect even if it did unveil a truth that Western psychiatry was missing—identified a "vegetative psychosis" for people who chose a so-easy way of life that they didn't work or otherwise struggle to cope with various life challenges.

Is this point of view ridiculous? Aren't mental disturbances "the same as medical conditions" that in many cases just happen to people? No, it is not ridiculous *not* to see in these conditions medical illnesses. Thus see how many cases present for marital therapy that involve a spouse who is copping out from carrying their share in supporting the family. See how this is also true of some severe personality disorders as well, where people do not pull their loads—for example, the adult man or woman who could but chooses not to work in any consistent way and to remain forever dependent on others.

I also know of a surprising number of instances where middle-aged men and women are still living with their aging parents and are largely supported by them. American psychiatry is totally prejudiced on behalf of sympathy for all people afflicted with disorders, but what if the disorder to begin with is based on an escape from responsibility? The implications for treatment are that sympathy for the real suffering of the patient, and for their original hurts and trauma, which may well be playing a large role in the choice of being a freeloader, should be accompanied by calls to responsibility and a toughening up of the personality, perhaps no less than with sympathy. Treatment should involve, as early as possible, invitations to and schedules of chores, work, and responsibilities. Therapy should include major efforts to activate patients and assign them tasks of caring for themselves and contributing to the collective setting in which they are spending their lives—even when we are dealing with crazy people.

Excessive Strivings for Power Over Other People

What role does seeking excessive power play in the formation of a given psychiatric condition? The neurotic disorders seem more focused on personal stress and inadequacy, but here too cutting-edge early therapist-theorists like Alfred Adler[9] and Karen Horney[10] showed us that the drive to be superior over others played a very central role in the formation of the neurotic personality. In many of the personality disorders, there is also a bid for power via domination or exploitation of others.[11] The quest for power probably also plays a major role in senseless criminal behaviors like those of arch-extortionist Bernard Madoff. He really didn't need the money, did he?

Any number of patients are very much aware inside themselves of how much their conditions impose an enormous amount of control on the lives of others around them who must cater to them and serve them in many ways, including drawing on major economic resources for their care. A quest for too much power is often a direct goal of psychosis, and if not it nonetheless can be for the patient a welcome benefit of being crazy. Inwardly many psychotic patients feel they are running the world and forcing it to serve them. If you can't make it to a position of power in the regular world, here is another option in Alice-in-Crazy-Wonderland to run a bunch of people around. The more serious withdrawals from reality to psychosis are obviously even more tragic breakdowns of the patient, yet here too there are aspects of controlling others.

One patient described to me the glee that he experienced when the men in white coats would come with their "butterfly nets" to take him away to the psychiatric hospitals to which he was admitted a good number of times, because this clearly showed how much he was in charge of it all.

There are also many clinicians who have proposed that the worst megalomanic and destructive crazies—the brutal mass killers like Hitler and Stalin—are basically crazy to begin with. Indeed, in some cases these horrible people do move into being more obviously crazy when their powers begin to wane, and that is a kind of circumstantial evidence for seeing them as crazy from the beginning, although this is a type of retroactive thinking that is defined by logicians as fallacious. The model of a Democratic Mind does not have to wait until these monsters begin to act more explicitly crazy. The Democratic Mind has no difficulty in defining these dictators as madmen from the beginning simply on the basis of their actively seeking to destroy life—what we have defined as the prime criterion for establishing a psychiatric diagnosis.

Systemic or Relationship Problems and Errors

"Systemic" refers to the overall pattern of give-and-take "deals" we all make in our relationships with one another, and to the balancing acts and patterns of complementing one another that we design. Problems in relationships, especially with one's intimates such as spouses or partners, but also in respect of work and other relationships, play huge roles in mental problems. In so many of the emotional and personality problems, there are significant relationship hurts and disappointments and rage. There are also a whole host of explicit relationship problems that bring people to psychiatric and/or psychological treatment: rejection, divorce, violence in the family, emotional betrayal, and more.

A systemic overview is appropriate for many interactive situations such as patterns of relationships in an office or department, but they especially "touch home" in our relationships to our families—spouse, children, parents, and siblings. A very early "clinical" case of something lousy in family life is the record of Cain murdering his brother Abel. Obviously I don't know the whole story of our first human family, but I do know that Cain nurtured a competitive hatred of his brother and acted on it destructively, and that these two styles—competitiveness and manifest destructiveness—took off and are still going strong in our world today. In a number of psychiatric conditions, it has been shown that family therapy can facilitate and augment individual therapy for a patient, and also make all the difference in the outcome and the long-range durability of successful treatment.

From our beginnings in childhood, we selectively take on various roles in our families. Some believe that "psychostructurally," families need to have a representation of a number of emotional traits, so that if one child is the beauty and star, another may take a route to excellence in learning; and if one is more the tough one, another will be devoted to the emotional needs of the family and try to be a more caring person. The happy news is that, according to a number of clinical theorists, in marriage couples who are compensating and complementing one another in appositions of dialectically contradictory traits are more likely to enjoy more vivid relationships and also the possibility of surviving the long haul without being bored to death.[12] The bad news is that many, if not most, couples *do not know* how to tap the processes of dialectical tensions and get into big trouble.

See if you can identify yourself or any of your friends in the following constructs:

She is the more social one, and he is the brainier one. He gets them out into the mountains, forest, and desert for trips, and she brings an openness to music and rhythm in their home. She plays the executive in charge of finances, and he is the lovey-dovey bear to whom the children and grandchildren gravitate. He tells it pretty straight and directly, and she is the compromiser and peacemaker.

Used wisely and cooperatively, these dialectical contrasts can add up to a good and colorful marriage; but pushed combatively by struggles for power, jealousy, or not respecting the meaningfulness of the other's contribution, all hell will break loose in the marriage. It's like working with nuclear energy.

PSYCHIATRY NEEDS TO GIVE A BROAD VIEW OF WHAT HUMAN BEHAVIOR IS ALL ABOUT MORE THAN A CATALOG OF SYMPTOMS

Psychiatry could and should be one of the microscopes through which any culture sees truths about itself. Would that we were only able to look honestly at the whirlings of the minds of our many national leaders in this world through the above lenses! How much would we see that is reminiscent if not directly representational of what we have come to understand about the workings of psychiatric disorders!

Again, our overall point is that we view madness and serious mental problems not as first cousins of mumps, measles, cancer, and other biological diseases, but as ways of life chosen, however unconsciously, as alternatives to more productive and constructive ways of participating in our difficult human condition.

There is also the "happy thought" that madness and other psychological conditions are processes that can manifest in ever new ways than the old catalog of Kraeplin conditions. So the trick in diagnosis is not simply to recognize symptoms, but to understand the *process* of succumbing to an inability to carry on with normal life or making oneself ill and/or harming or disabling others.

What is more important—the symptoms a person has, or the deep-down feelings they have about themselves and about life and how they are treating other people?

Who is actually sicker—a person who suffers some anxiety or other psychiatric symptoms and deep down hates being alive or is indifferent to the extraordinary gift of life and is nasty to other people, or a person who, though plagued by even more intense anxiety, depression or other psychiatric symptoms, really wants to live and thrive and fulfill themselves and be good to others?

RESPECTING THE BRILLIANCE OF PSYCHOSOMATIC INTERACTIONS

Beyond the fact that this is hardly a formal textbook of psychopathology, we are far more concerned with the *meanings* of psychiatric disorders than with cataloging the symptoms of recognized syndromes. We understand that there is an art form to *how* to be nervously or mentally ill that is crafted by each patient, rather than that the "syndrome" exists in nature like a definable biological illness.

Of course any number of mental disorders can arise to accompany various biological disorders—for example, a hellish depression in a person who personality-wise has been anything but depressed that comes in response to a dread illness like cancer of the liver some time before the CAT scans have brought the information. Again, we note, there is no doubt that mental problems often lead to and are expressed in physiological changes, but that does not mean that these physiological features are the sole *causes* of the original basic disorder. The fascinating complication is that these physiological features in themselves become further contributors to the overall psychosomatic disorder—for example, in cases of serious depression the "drying up" you can practically see with your eyes and then the changes in the brain chemistry of serotonin that will be found. Now comes the dramatic choice. Treating the physiological processes medically indeed will impact the whole package of what is now a psychosomatic illness. It is absolutely true that the patient can get much better and the treatment will have proven to be effective. But if you have kept track of the whole process that we are describing, what in the world has happened to the original causes of the basic psychological disorder?

- Did she walk out on him?
- Was he fired from his job or passed over for promotion? (I've seen people go into tailspins and even suicide because they didn't get tenure at the college in which they were teaching, or they didn't get to be the director of the clinic or the head of the department.)
- Is their original pain of being unloved as a child getting the better of them? (One famous editor of a world-class publication had an article written about him and his lifelong suffering of high anxiety. He is quoted as saying that "there was no obvious cause for his nervousness," and yet in the same article he referred explicitly to the fact that his mother "denied him affection while at

> the same time over-protecting him while leaving him feeling at once unloved and helpless."[13]

Really? No basic cause?

Granted, once feeling better thanks to medication, some patients will be encouraged also to give up their original basic symptoms and maybe even to repair the bad mental state they were in and heal themselves inside, but in countless situations people do not and cannot become inspired enough and/or can't figure out how to go on and treat their underlying hurt, despair, and rage without further professional help.

The Considerable Dangers of Curing Symptoms without Addressing the Real Underlying Problem

As we prepare to meet up with a great variety of specific mental conditions, we want to emphasize once more that there can also be very serious limitations and at times big-time risks to the considerable improvement that psychiatric medications can bring. Thus we have seen how successful treatment with Prozac-type medications have been implicated as leading to no less than tens of thousands of cases of suicide, as well as a meaningful though much smaller number of cases of homicide. In more than one case, courts have awarded huge funds to consumers of Prozac and related SSRI medications. "By 2000, it was reported that Eli Lilly had invested at least $50 million to resolve more than 30 lawsuits, most of which involved homicide and suicide."[14]

In fact *any* treatment, very much including purely psychological treatment, that successfully repairs symptoms without working on the basic choice-making of the individual can destabilize a person or a family system seriously.

In *Fascism and Democracy in the Human Mind*,[15] I reported a case of a couple living on a kibbutz who separated for several years, during which each lived with their own new partner. Both partners had suffered difficulties in their sexual functioning with one another but reportedly enjoyed more satisfactory sex with their replacement partners. When they decided to return to one another, they turned to a talented sex therapist to help them get their sexual house in order.

The sex therapist proceeded with great skill to teach and prescribe Masters and Johnson sexual behavior exercises[16] to clear up weaknesses in sexual functioning, but did very little to clarify what the couple meant to one another, the full meaning of their separating from one another, and their emotions and thoughts upon returning to one another.[17] The couple's announced wish to be together once again and reunite their family was taken at face value. The case, which was known to me through the sex therapist coming to me for a consultation, ended tragically in the suicide of one of the partners. In the one meeting I had with the therapist, I advised him to put the sex exercises on hold and to get to work on the relationship and inner meanings, but it was too late—the suicide came a few days later.

DSM Isn't Geared to Track the Rapid Pulsation of Changes in Psychiatric Disorders

Madness and other psychiatric problems are the result of a process that can manifest in ever new ways than the old cataloged Kraeplin or *DSM* conditions. Once more we emphasize that the trick in diagnosis is not simply to recognize symptoms, but to understand the process of succumbing or making oneself unable to carry on a healthy life.

We see this process in "popular" Western syndromes such as anorexia. Until you study anorexia, you can't believe how crazy discrepant from reality the anorectic is in their perceptions of their body. They walk, talk, and look perfectly uncrazy like the rest of us, but they are really screwed up at the deepest possible level of defining the worthwhileness of their being alive. Remember how serious this madness can be—this is a condition that literally kills young people regularly.[18] Note that anorexia's "popularity" in Western countries was far less likely to be seen, say, in Japan, where eating disorders were very rare—though now more recently they are rampaging up.[19] On the other hand, in Japan we have heard for many years numerous cases of teenagers and young adults who lock themselves into an apartment and refuse to come out. I knew of one family in Japan, with whom my wife and I stayed as tourists, where the mother would deliver a daily tray of food to the door of her young adult son's apartment upstairs and had not seen him for over a year. This was a recognizable syndrome in Japan sometime before a notable number of such cases began being reported from many other countries and cultures.

One reason that a good number of new syndromes are not recognized is that the *DSM* isn't swift enough to catch up with the terrifyingly rapid pulsation of changes in psychiatric symptoms. There are in fact many existing "syndromes," meaning recognizably repeated patterns or configurations of behaviors, that qualify very much as psychiatrically or mentally troubled but are not recognized in official psychiatry. Looking at them from our point of view, we see all involve considerable harming of life. Were the *DSM* organized to identify harm to life as the prime indicator of psychological disturbance, newer conditions/forms of disturbance would be recognized much, much earlier.

Here are several reasons why *DSM* has never looked at many disturbances:

1. *DSM* does not look at disturbance from the point of view of harming one's own life and/or the lives of others.
2. *DSM* does not involve itself very much at all in expressions of social-historical-ideological forces in society.
3. Other than requirements about symptoms appearing before or after certain ages in order to qualify for whatever diagnosis, *DSM* displays a relative indifference to how normality is accompanied by many periods of characteristic mental disturbances at the different stages of a person's life journey, and to how the normal life cycle calls for different levels of skills at different stages of life.

DSM psychiatry basically looks at competence versus incompetence of a person and not at constructing and safeguarding life. The result is that all-too-competent big-time mass killers who cannot be exposed as "really" suffering from a recognizable mental illness have nowhere to get recognized and just stay "out there" as regrettable events in the turbulent human history for which our wonderful mental health professionals have no responsibility even to name as rotten and disturbed.

CONCLUSION: LOOKING AT HOW MUCH A PERSON IS DESTROYING LIFE OVERCOMES THE PROBLEM OF SYMPTOMS AND SYNDROMES THAT UNDERGO CHANGES

Mental disorders come in many, many different packages and will be shaped in a variety of still new forms in the future. Clearly, symptoms also vary dramatically from culture to culture, and without doubt symptoms undergo dramatic changes from era to era. There are many packages of behavior to which normal human beings react spontaneously that they are "crazy," or "nuts." It is tragic and shameful intellectually and philosophically that so many of these rotten behaviors are not defined as they deserve to be in psychology and psychiatry—the professional fields that implicitly provide people with normative guides to the perplexed of our society about what behavior is desirable and not.

In this book we look at a few "packages" or forms of some traditional, old-fashioned syndromes that are well named and commonly studied in conventional psychology and psychiatry textbooks, as well as at some conditions that are nowhere to be seen in those textbooks but are very much present in real life (as if waiting for "diplomatic recognition" by a new classifier of mental disorders).

If one defines in all our intellectual disciplines, including psychology and psychiatry, the valuing, safeguarding, and enhancing of healthy human life for oneself *and* others as the categorically imperative prime value in all human experience, then we not only enrich our lives with beautiful meanings, but also solve the endless problems and conundrums in mental health regarding what should and should not be diagnosed as mental problems.

> You shall love your neighbor as yourself: I am the Lord.—*Old Testament: Leviticus* 19:18

> You shall love your neighbor as yourself: I am the Lord. There is no other commandment greater.—*New Testament: John* 4:20

> That which is despicable to you, do not do to your fellow, this is the whole Torah, and the rest is commentary, go and learn it.—*Hillel* [famous Jewish religious leader in development of Talmud, c. 110 BCE, died 10 CE in Jerusalem][20]

NOTES

1. Charny, Israel W. (In Press, 2017). *A Democratic Mind: Psychology and Psychiatry with Fewer Meds and More Soul.* Lanham, MD: Rowman & Littlefield.

2. See the discussions of the work of Marsha Linehan and Otto Kernberg later in a section on "Dialectical Behavior Therapy and Structured Transference Based Therapy for Borderline Behavior Disorders."

3. Sechehaye, Marguerite (1951). *Autobiography of a Schizophrenic Girl.* New York: Grune and Stratton; Sechehaye, Marguerite (1956). *A New Psychotherapy in Schizophrenia: Relief of Frustrations by Symbolic Realization.* New York: Grune and Stratton.

4. See the beautiful semi-autobiographical novel by a patient of Frieda Fromm Reichmann, written under the patient's pen name: Green, Hannah (1992). *I Never Promised You a Rose Garden.* New York: St. Martin's Press [original publication 1964]. The book was also made into a film and a play.

5. Laing, R.D. (1960). *The Divided Self: An Existential Study in Sanity and Madness.* Harmondsworth: Penguin; Laing, R.D. (1967) *The Politics of Experience and the Bird of Paradise.* Harmondsworth: Penguin; Mullan, B. (1995). *Mad to be Normal: Conversations with R.D. Laing.* London: Free Association Books.

6. See, for example, the collections of cases published by psychiatrist Albert Honig, who directed an excellent private mental hospital in the Philadelphia area: Honig, Albert M. (2001). *Hard Boiled Eggs and Other Psychiatric Tales: The Rebirth of the Psychotherapy of Severe Mental Illness.* Doylestown, PA: North Street Publishers; Honig, Albert M. (1972). *The Awakening Nightmare: A Breakthrough in Treating the Mentally Ill.* Rockaway, NJ: American Faculty Press. [Author is at 616 North Street, Doylestown, PA 18901]

7. Rheingold, Joseph C. (1964). *The Fear of Being a Woman.* New York: Grune & Stratton. Rheingold, Joseph C. (1967) *The Mother, Anxiety, and Death.* New York: Little Brown. It upsets me a lot to see important quality studies in mental health from yesteryear completely forgotten and in their place there appear in each generation the newly politically correct formulations of that era. For me this has been especially true about the brilliant studies in psychosomatic medicine by great psychiatrists like George Engel and Franz Alexander. Thus too in respect of Rheingold's work on post-partum disorders. The neglect of his work and his key understanding of post-partum as an expression of the woman's fear of being rejecting or hostile to her baby is an excellent example of the gross neglect of wisdom accumulated in the past. Now years later, in 2014 we read in the *International New York Times* about "new research" that shows (as if for the first time) that the mother's fears of hurting her child play a major role in post-partum disturbances. See Belluck, Pam (June 15, 2014). Thinking of ways to harm her: New findings on timing and range of maternal mental illness. *International New York Times*; Belluck, Pam (June 16, 2014). After baby, an unraveling: A case study in maternal mental illness. *International New York Times.*

8. Searles, Harold Frederick (1986). *Collected Papers on Schizophrenia and Related Subjects.* London: Karnac; Clark, Robert A. (1965). *Friends and Aggression, op cit.*

9. Adler, Alfred (1917). *Study of Organ Inferiority and Its Psychical Compensation: A Contribution to Clinical Medicine.* New York: Nervous and Mental Disease Publishing; Adler, Alfred (1924). *The Practice and Theory of Individual Psychology.* New York: Harcourt Brace; Adler, Alfred (1932). *Individual Psychology and Its Results in the Practice and Theory of Individual Psychology.* New York: Harcourt Brace.

10. Horney, Karen (1937). *The Neurotic Personality of Our Time.* New York: Norton. See also Horney, Karen (1946). *Are You Considering Psychoanalysis?* New York: Norton; Horney, Karen (1942). *Self-analysis.* New York: Norton.

11. Redfield, James (1994). *The Celestine Prophecy: An Adventure.* New York: Bantam. A surprisingly gripping read about efforts to take away power from other people. Despite some historical errors and an incomplete style of writing, it has sold over 20 million copies. It has a powerfully uplifting message, including about efforts to give up control over others!

12. Charny, Israel W. (1992). *Existential/Dialectical Marital Therapy: Breaking the Secret Code of Marriage.* New York: Brunner/Mazel. For a list of works on marriage and marital conflict, see wider samples of publications on the marital process, marital therapy, and marital fighting in Chapter 2. The subject is endless.

13. Manthorpe, Rowland (January 2014). *My Age of Anxiety* by Scott Stossel, review. *Telegraph, UK.* http://www.telegraph.co.uk/culture/books/bookreviews/10558728/My-Age-of-Anxiety-by-Scott-Stossel-review.html.

14. Injury Lawyer News (2013). Prozac Lawsuit. http://injurylawyer-news.com/prozac/lawsuit/. See in Allen, Frances (2013), *Saving Normal, op cit.,* 96, a chart titled "Drug Company Hall of Shame" for a list of many cases of litigation over a variety of psychiatric medications.

15. Charny, Israel W. (2006). *Fascism and Democracy in the Human Mind, ibid.*

16. Masters, William H. and Johnson, Virginia C. (1970). *Human Sexual Inadequacy.* Boston: Little Brown.

17. Kaplan, Helen S. (1974). *The New Sex Therapy.* New York: Brunner-Mazel. As we said earlier, psychiatrist Helen Kaplan argued convincingly that although the Masters and Johnson treatment exercises, which she too continued to use, were a great contribution, they should *not* be given to a couple until there has been a full clarification of their basic relationship, the meanings of their sexual relationship, and whether any "sexual sabotage" is at play.

18. Honig, Albert M. (2001). *Hard Boiled Eggs and Other Psychiatric Tales, ibid.* The book begins with a startingly risk-filled depth therapy of an anorectic girl that was successful.

19. McNicol, Tony (2004). Japan diet risks on rise: Problems with eating disorders slip under the radar. *Japan Times.* http://www.japantimes.co.jp/community/2004/08/03/issues/japan-dietrisks-on-rise/.

20. Schechter, Solomon; Bacher, Wilhelm (1901–1906). "Hillel." In Singer, Isidore; et al. *Jewish Encyclopedia.* New York: Funk & Wagnalls Company; Herbermann, Charles, ed. (1913). Hillel. *Catholic Encyclopedia.* New York: Robert Appleton Company.

2

Intimacy and Relationship Disorders

DEMOCRATIC MIND VERSUS FASCIST MIND IN INTIMACY AND RELATIONSHIP DISORDERS IN MARRIAGE, PARENTING, AND FAMILY LIFE

The following are some bad, though well-intentioned, advice for marriage and family life that many people will fall for blindly:

- Love.
- Don't be angry. Keep a tight hold on your feelings.
- Stay all together, close to one another.
- Don't be a worrier.
- Give much more than you receive.
- Always be loyal.

Every one of these sanctimonious guidelines is going to be familiar to every one of us, because they are peddled throughout our culture, admittedly with good intentions by many decent people, including religious leaders and, regrettably, too often by professional counselors and therapists who should know better but don't. But it is not for real people in real lives.

Relationship disorders in marriage and family are generally taken to mean uncontrolled eruptions of bad emotions—the couple fight too much, they speak disparagingly to one another, the parenting of one or both is cold and brutal, and so on. Any of the above are very much problems, of course. But—perhaps even more often—relationship disorders often derive from *too much* of the "good" emotions. Better advice for marriage and the lovelorn would read more like this:

- Love and be appropriately angry when you need to be.
- Be open to and appreciative of differences in temperament, style, and values in your loved ones.
- Worry appropriately, and share the worrying and problems with your partner in marriage.
- Enjoy receiving caring and love as well as giving to the other.
- Keep your own identity and authentic personal values strong in a democratic give-and-take with your spouse and family.

In this chapter we will study:

- Integrating love and separateness-individuality in intimacy
- Identifying and intervening as early as possible in pathologies of doing harm to others in relationships in marriage and family such as violence, sexual abuse, abandonment, exploitation, scapegoating, and any kinds of sacrificing the other to one's own needs at their serious expense
- Sharing worries and *not* being so "well-adjusted" and unrattled when it's time to be naturally upset and rattled
- Receiving and giving love
- Refusing to be over-obligated
- Fun sexuality for both partners through a balance of passion and real friendship and appreciation of one another
- Authentic inner experience of ourselves including the bad, terrible, and worse, which are in fact human, but disciplining and channeling these experiences to give more power to our loving and decency
- Real communication, especially in marriage, where hurting and being hurt are welcome and necessary parts of the symphony that need to come together for very pleasing music

WHAT'S IT ALL ABOUT: BEING REAL ALONG WITH A DISCIPLINE OF DECENCY

We now turn to look at family psychopathology from the point of view of an idea or model that is taken by a family group or subgroup—most often a couple, but it also can be another subgroup, such as two siblings—where it is the inflexible, relentless adherence to a given style or paradigm of how relationships *must* be organized that plays a big role in bringing about the disturbed outcomes.

The topics that will be treated in this chapter include some basic issues in family psychiatry or psychology, beginning with two major vectors in the marvelous "circumplex model" by Sprenkle and Olson[1] (the same Douglas Sprenkle who contributed the Foreword to this book), which will be described more fully shortly: the first vector—loving too much versus being emotionally cut off from the other family member(s); the second vector—organizing family life too loosely versus organizing family life too rigidly.

There will also be a discussion of doing harm to others in one's family with violence and sexual abuse, abandoning, exploiting, scapegoating, and sacrificing the other. In addition, we will discuss some subjects that will not ordinarily be found in conventional texts on family psychopathology. These include the following:

- Cases of people who don't carry their fair share of worries in family life but leave the burden to others
- People who look marvelous in their generous giving to others but who really are playing out a power trip of dominating the other(s) by over-giving and refusing to be recipients of any emotional caring from the other(s)
- People who allow others to abuse them under the pressure of their being obligated to be loyal to their family under any and all circumstances and costs

We'll then continue with an overview of sexual dysfunctions where the guiding interpretation is that many sexual dysfunctions involve a splitting of dialectical emotional processes that need to be integrated for wholesome sexual functioning, such as experiencing a balance between sensual passion *and* deep friendship for one's sexual partner. Both together are critical to emotional potency and resonance. This is particularly interesting considering that each process—passion and friendship—in its own right is delicious and welcome. But passion without real friendship, or wonderful friendship without sufficient passion, make John or Jill or both of them dull kids. An exaggeration of either side at the expense of the other will cast a long black shadow on sexual experience.

Finally, we will look at genuine communication for genuine relationships, at straight talk about people's differences, and at criticisms, as opposed to adhering to the myths about human behavior that have sadly grown into over-certainties in our culture that intimate relationships require suppression and overcoming of anger, and that people should always be accepted uncritically as they are.

The common theme running through these subjects is that the adoption of any one given or prescribed way of being in a relationship at the expense of other natural aspects of relationship and human experience plays a major role in setting off chains of disturbances in marriage, parenting, and family relationships. In mental health in general, we see again and again that a fascist way of organizing one's relationships and life creates dysfunctions, just as we will see in later chapters how fascist ways of organizing the mind are at work in developing many cases of individual psychopathology.

FAMILY ENMESHMENT AND DISENGAGEMENT: REASONABLE IDEAS FOR FAMILY LIFE TAKEN TOO FAR

A great deal of the clinical contributions of family therapy to our understanding of individual psychopathology as well as to our understanding of family dysfunctions can be organized around the polar concepts of *enmeshment* and *disengagement*. *Enmeshment* refers to overly-connected, over-involved, invasive relationships. *Disengagement* refers to rejecting, unempathetic, uninvolved relationships.

These concepts of family systems[2] are especially interesting when applied to several psychiatric conditions whose dynamics were unclear prior to the advent of family therapy, such as cases of psychosis where social workers at psychiatric hospitals reported sincerely that the psychotic patient's family history was "normal" because the family was decent, intact, and constructive. But the social workers did not understand that there might have been overprotective symbiotic mothering, emotionally distant fathering, or a family organized around obligations or responsibility with little authentic individuality or genuine emotional expression (or other covert but powerful processes in an overall normal-looking family—see for example the excellent movie, *Ordinary People*.[3]) Only after the pioneering contributions of family therapy about the pathogenic effects of undue enmeshment in families was it possible to understand many cases of over-connection psychodynamically. (I believe strongly that understanding psychodynamics is still very much desirable as a lens for understanding mental disturbances in today's age of biologization of psychiatry.)

For those who accept the contemporary mode of psychiatry that views most if not all psychiatric conditions as essentially biological if not genetically programmed, this way of thinking will appear outmoded and passé, and will draw sneers at old-fashioned ways of thinking and, worse, at its "blaming" families and especially mothers. But I firmly continue to believe that the majority of mental illnesses are *mental* responses to loss, hurt, and disappointment in life, and an inability to cope with life stresses and challenges, to a large extent because of the adoption of regrettable and mistaken ways of thinking and living that induce disturbance. I also believe that many mental illnesses are treatable—correctable with healthy infusions of emotional skill-retraining, love, inspiration, integrity, courage, and faith.

The concept of enmeshment in particular represents a brilliant advance in our understanding of the genesis of emotional disturbance and incompetence. We have learned that *too much* family togetherness weakens the basic structure of people's personalities. It has always been clear that indifference, uncaring, rejection, and such in what the model calls disengagement are hardly the good milk of family life, and that people are going to be damaged by those family experiences. But we did not know that no less and possibly even *more* damaging experience could result where the unwritten rule is that family members are *over*-involved with one another and over-intimate. We especially did not know this about forms of togetherness that are not patently coercive or possessive or symbiotic, but where family members are truly very friendly, strongly cooperative, and agreeably devoted to one another, but nonetheless too much so.

Lyman Wynne and his colleagues created a related concept of *pseudomutuality* to describe a family that is held in the grip of a stultifying sameness, appeasement, and style of compromise that stifles individualism and creative thoughts and emotions.[4] In the pseudomutual family, there isn't necessarily over-involvement in one another's affairs or excesses of caring or love, but there is an excess of accommodating one another, or tuning in to one another to be sure to synchronize with one another, and especially to avoid conflict.

The somewhat simpler concept of *conflict-avoidant* couples or families is also a useful descriptor, found in the literatures of family therapy and family sociology that refers to a broad swath of families where there is an obvious avoidance of expressions of disagreement, conflict, and anger.[5] Studies of children of conflict-avoidant families show, for example, that they lag behind in the development of their creativity,[6] and later as adults have trouble managing conflicts in their own marriages.

Conflict-avoidant families also include families where people don't talk much to each other in general, and many where they are grumpy, growly, and unpleasant but still don't talk out their complaints and needs. The pseudomutual couples and families we referred to first are not only conflict-avoidant, but they also are very good to one another and cheerfully pleasant and cooperative, not airing tensions and differences or expressing annoyance and anger, and it becomes overwhelmingly clear that the lack of venting of differences and expression of individuality is what does them in, and not an overall unpleasantness.

Enmeshed families need more apartness and even some of the indifference, coldness, and rejection that are taken to an extreme in disengaged families; and pseudomutual families need more individuality, differences of opinion, and downright conflicts. Disengaged families need more of the accommodation, involvement, and busyness with one another of the enmeshed or pseudomutual family. *In each case, what has happened is that the family's ideal model of interpersonal relationships has been taken to an extreme.* Whatever wisdom there is in each of the basic experiential frameworks or models of closeness and separation becomes a monstrous force because it is too total—the stuff of what we are calling Fascist Mind. Togetherness and separateness are both valuable ideas, but either idea taken to its polar exaggeration and extreme becomes seriously damaging.

Sprenkle and Olson's "circumplex model," which incorporates the dynamics of enmeshment and disengagement, provides an excellent summary for a great deal of what we have learned in family therapy. The model differentiates between ranges of healthy and unhealthy family functioning based on the interaction of two factors.

Enmeshment-disengagement are the two extreme poles of one of the two key dimensions in the circumplex model. The second dimension in the model is rigidity-chaos. Families have needs both for structure and authority and for flexibility and freedom. Both are healing and building forces, but going too far with either to a point of overdoing, over-certainty, and totality of a position makes for abuse and damage to the family and its members. The circumplex model is based on the principle that it is the extremity and absoluteness of a position that breeds dysfunction and disturbance.

Pathology is seen when a family goes too far *either* in being enmeshed in closeness or too far in being coldly separate from one another; or when a family goes too far *either* in rigidly enforcing prescribed forms and contents of behavior, or in going to the other extreme of not organizing and structuring family roles and experiences sufficiently, thereby creating unduly loose organization and even chaos. In the language of our paradigm of fascist thinking, we say that any of the extreme positions is an idea taken too far. Too close is no less a problem than too distant, and a chaotic style of family life is no less inflexible than an overly rigid style of family life.

Moreover, the circumplex model combines the two dimensions of enmeshment-disengagement and rigidity-chaos *interactively*. The extremisms of *either* an overly rigid and unchanging policy of over-involvement or under-involvement with one's family members; or the opposite extreme of an overly unstructured letting-happen-what-will-happen type of under-involvement or over-involvement *both* breed family breakdown and disturbances of family members.

This model generates four—not two—configurations of emotionally troubled relationships:

- too close and too rigid
- too close and too chaotic
- too distant and too rigid
- too distant and too chaotic

The best ways to protect against family dysfunction are, first of all, *yes*, to be deeply involved, caring, and loving, and this means as a result to be vulnerable, too. Given the realities of family life, this means being subject to periodic hurt. At the same time, one needs to remain separate in one's individual identity, in charge of one's own destiny, and respectful of the independent destinies of all other family members; and to alternate flexibility, even contradictorily, between both sides of the experiences of emotional involvement and separateness.

Second, it is desirable to create modes and patterns of family life that have a certain degree of consistency and structure to them, but not overly rigid forms of family life that are imposed coercively. For example, regular family meals used as occasions for being together and as opportunities for all family members to communicate with each other have been shown to be an effective protection against the development of emotional disturbances in children, as well as a useful "glue" or "cement" for bonding family relationships. On the other hand, a pattern of family meals that is laid coercively and heavily on family members is well known to breed resentment and emotional weakness or rebellion.

❖ Well into his thirties, he struggled with feeling more manly. While his sweetness attracted women, he soon lost them as they became aware that he was too childish and unmanly. In therapy he remembered how his physician father, who always conveyed that he knew everything best, never invited him and even rejected his expressed wishes to recite the blessing over the wine at their Jewish-family Sabbath dinner. At the same time, his mother fondled and fussed over him as her beloved and forever child. Little wonder it was hard for him to feel and act manly.

In effect, family pathology is a result of any policy that is set in a fixed and extreme way, and that does not move back and forth between itself and its contradiction. Breakdown is a function of a humorless insistence on any absolute, be it love or rejection, freedom or control, even though in each case we tend to be drawn to the illusion that the positive-sounding pole can only be inherently good for people, which is not true.

THE INEVITABLE IMPERFECTION OF "PERFECT MARRIAGES"

What happens to "perfect marriages" is so sad because often the intentions of the couple are genuinely loving and good. They create a beautiful world of grace, respect, and pleasure with one another that they really mean and thoroughly enjoy. So what could be wrong?

❖ A therapist consults me about a couple in their late thirties. They began as high-school sweethearts and have continued for some twenty years to be a beautiful devoted couple, with nothing that could be called fights. They were proud and sure of themselves and were admired by all those who knew them.

As a consultant, hearing this opening description by the therapist, I knew what was coming. For given the unidimensionality of the marital style on top of such an early start to the relationship, without much if any experiences with other boyfriends and girlfriends, it was probably only a question of which one of the couple had strayed away to an alternative relationship.

Why does it "have to be" that loving and even outstanding couples will get into great difficulties? In my experience, many couples who began as young lovers have to go through a crisis of one or both later experiencing some of the variety they missed out on of another lover and another relationship. Under ideal circumstances such a "breakout" takes place on a symbolic level and plays itself out with a renewed decision to be loyal before it becomes a full-blown love affair. But there are many times, especially for nonreligious or nontraditional couples, when the crisis does reach a full form of a competing relationship, and in the more severe cases includes one of the spouses moving out to live with their new lover.

This kind of crisis is all the more likely if the original "perfect couple" have been avoiding conflicts and have been rubber stamp–approving each other pretty much unconditionally. Unknowingly, the result of this "heaven" of avoidance of tension is a slowing down, or worse, an overall cessation of needed emotional growth in the two spouses, as individual persons and as a couple. The natural dialectical process of clashes and contradictions inside each person and between the two spouses has been halted, and for all the pleasure, contentment, and official happiness of a couple with an excellent relationship, a form of stagnation and dullness lurks, because each person does not feel the tension of sufficient critical challenges from their partner. It is often the threat of such inner stagnation in one's personality that impels the need for the "breakout" of at least one of the spouses. A threat of stagnation that impels a "breakout" also issues from the marital relationship itself, where there is too little real emotional needing of one another—because the spouse's good presence is as if "guaranteed" without any question. Paradoxically, because everything is "so good," there is too little experience of really needing one another, and of helping and being helped by one another on a gut emotional level to "fill in" missing parts of one another. In the world of perfect marriages, there are few experiences of missing parts or really needing help because all is too perfect.

❖ So it came as no surprise to me in the consultation when the therapist told me that the husband had confessed to an affair. His wife was very distraught, and insisted he end the relationship with the other woman. The husband agreed, but then a few days later came back and told his wife he couldn't give up the other woman. It was at this point the couple came for therapy.

A less puzzling but still dramatic form of the inevitable imperfection of perfect marriages involves couples where one sits in the driver's seat and the other is happily and gratefully dependent until the basic inequality between the couple, and the absence of a creative process in each person, leads to a need for the "breakout." The following is another case that was brought in by a therapist seeking consultation:

❖ They were in the early forties, dashingly attractive, each highly successful in their respective professional roles. He adored her and followed her around like a puppy dog, but since he was in his own right a handsome and successful person, the basic inequality between them was seemingly masked.

Over time she became increasingly surly and explosively abusive to him, and sometimes even went so far as to hit him. She also succeeded in demanding of him to sign over to her most of his financial rights in his business. He in turn developed high blood pressure along with high cholesterol and began reporting attacks of frightening chest pains. Finally, one day she took a stick and literally beat him to a point where he was bowed over. It was at this point that he pulled himself together to walk out.

It is painful to say, but perfect marriages are, like perfect governments or perfect churches or perfect societies, expressions of fascist or too-perfect orders, and this is why the once so-successful spouses are necessarily driven toward causing great pain and downright harm to one another.

VICTIMIZATION IN FAMILIES IN EVERYDAY LIFE: VIOLENCE AND SEXUAL ABUSE, ABANDONING, EXPLOITING, SCAPEGOATING, AND SACRIFICING MEMBERS OF ONE'S FAMILY

Another area to which family therapy has contributed important insights and a basis for new treatment interventions involves the victimization of family members. *Victimization* here refers to making another person a victim. The word has also been used, even more extensively, to refer to the experiences of the people who themselves have been victimized, their physical and emotional hurts, wounds, and damages to their functioning, but here I am interested in the use of the action verb, meaning to inflict hurt and damage on another.

Violence and Sexual Abuse

The most dangerous forms of victimization are in actual violent behaviors to a family member and in sexual abuse of a family member. The physical damages of actual violence that subjugate the other and/or inflict real injuries obviously are traumatic. But what is also of the greatest significance is the trauma that is inflicted on the victim by a family member by virtue of the treachery, exploitation, and violation of trust they experience. In the case of coercive sexual abuse of a child, there is obviously a sense that the child's body has been violated or raped by the stronger party—in some cases a parent, in others a sibling. There certainly are also cases where the sexual exploitation is accompanied by physical abuse or force. But there are also many cases in which the child is sweet-talked into the sexual experience that in itself is made warm and pleasureful and is welcomed by the child, and yet there is no doubt that in these cases, too, the child's self has been invaded, violated, and cruelly damaged by an inappropriate and exploitative misuse by someone who should have had the child's interests at the fore but obviously did not.[7]

Abandoning

Victimization also takes less violent or bodily invasive forms, as in cases of abandonment of family members. Beyond the physical aspects of abandonment in which a person is left uncared for, the experience of being left, deserted, and rejected is a crushing one at all ages. Most experienced lovers know the searing pain of loss when one is rejected by one's lover. I personally believe that in the younger years of life, *some* incidents of "breaking up" and being sent away by a boyfriend/girlfriend are *desirable* developmental experiences in which one learns so much about life and about oneself. These experiences are, in effect, opportunities for a form of "immunization," or learning that being rejected is a very definite possibility in our lives for which we need to prepare, and that we need to construct our intimate relationships knowing that at some point we certainly can be rejected, and that we need to prepare ourselves to cope successfully with such heartache and loss. Among other things, we all need to know that if one behaves badly to a loved one, they can leave us. We also need to learn something about our own power to reject the other and to develop a sensitivity to the enormous pain we can inflict on the other. We also need to know that at any time the cruelties of life can take away from us any of our loved ones via illness or death, and these psychologically are also experienced as rejections, and that we need to be strong enough to survive these trials.

Notwithstanding the healthfulness of immunizations, experiences of being rejected and losing loved ones are generally painful encounters with grief and inner terror over being alone and unworthy of being loved that can be expressed in many different styles of emotional and psychosomatic breakdowns.

❖ I was nineteen. Her breaking up with me left me brooding in a pain I had never known but which was also reminiscent of the agonies of my mother's death five years earlier. I felt near madness, and also worried that people could see it on my face. I couldn't sleep nights—just as had happened to me when mother died. And I broke out with an aggravating underarm rash that brought me to the university medical clinic. One funny benefit was that I managed to figure out that this rash was part of my crying over being deserted, and then throughout my life when the same rash would recur from time to time, I would check out if I was feeling or fearing being rejected at the time. Almost always this was the case, and I had the feeling that recognizing the linkage helped make the rash go away.

Young lovers who are still in the period of dating/experimenting with a variety of partners can hurt one another so badly when they "deselect" and reject their friend. And later, being abandoned and rejected by one's already identified spouse certainly is likely to be a shattering experience. For marrieds who break up, the rejection no longer has a quality of play and rehearsal for later life. The ending of a marriage is the breaking up of the central organizing structure of one's life. For couples who have children, there is also the knowledge that the children will be seriously wounded emotionally.[8] Little wonder that so many people give up trying to love again and make no effort to remarry after divorce. Little wonder too that no small number of those who do remarry end up compromising with unpleasant marriages for fear of having to undergo once again the cataclysm of separation, loss, and divorce. Even for the mate who is the one who initiates a marital breakup, there can also be many feelings of being rejected by the other, and certainly there is also the loss of the anchor-person in their life too.

Nonetheless, all of these experiences of rejected adults pale before the abandonment of a child by a parent. This is the ultimate abandonment. A child's sense of loss is world-encompassing and goes far beyond the terrible-enough grief and pain of older persons. For the child, still so deeply dependent for emotional sustenance on the protective and loving presence of the parent, being left can be like being left to die.

By abandonment of a child, I mean first of all any and every cause of the loss of a parent—death of the parent, parental divorce and the consequent degrees of loss of the presence of one of the parents in the child's life, or outright rejection of a child by the parent.

Can we really understand what it feels like for a child to fall into a "black hole" of the dissolution of their family world? I have become personally convinced that when a parent leaves in death or divorce, *some* very young children experience the loss as the very destruction of their entire world, and at that point resolve in their tender inner minds no less than to die! My own feeling is that this decision can then even become a psychosomatic basis for a malignancy that can appear relatively immediately or some years later. Of course, this is a personal clinical observation that has not been substantiated by other observations in the professional literature to my knowledge, but the overall vulnerability of children who suffer the loss of a parent is established by the hard-fact sociological statistics we have long known: that in subsequent life they have statistically significant higher risks of a whole spate of tragic destinies, including earlier death, suicide, mental illness, emotional disturbance, addiction, and divorce. (I don't want this information to end here only as a depressing omen. For me, the implication of these facts is that people who have lost parents early in their lives deserve and need to do more to build deep and enduring love relationships into their lives. It is a matter of preventive health, let alone an optimistic way to cope with unforgettable loss.)

In the child's tender mind, even the inadvertent death of a parent away at war or who succumbs to illness is interpreted psychologically as rejection. In their primitive unconscious mind, at least at first there may be no difference between an inadvertent death of a parent and the willful choice of a parent to leave, but clearly over time there will be infinitely more painful reverberations to a parent's purposeful decision to leave a child. Of course, when the context is divorce of the parents, there is also a part of a child's brain that in time *may* be able to realize that the parents' marriage failed more than that they were personally rejected. Some children can successfully absorb such a loss to divorce, especially if the divorced parents are wise and loving, and more so if they cooperate in the continuation of their parenting.

Basic Indifference, Rejection, or Exploiting

But what in God's name happens to the children whose parents plain and simple turn on them venomously, and hate, despise, and exclude the children from their love? One of the disturbing aspects of child psychology and psychiatry for me is the reluctance of many therapists to recognize the full extent of some parents' actual rejections of their child. However well-intended, the standard treatment techniques for reducing cycles of symptoms in a child, and the seemingly reactive anger and rejection of the parents, do not work with these children because the real truth is that the parent basically has turned hatefully on the child or basically cannot love the child.

❖ The two children were enuretic. Efforts to teach the parents to show the children their love and to convey positive expectations of their overcoming their bedwetting were listened to by the mother and father tokenly but never really implemented.

The mother agreed to the therapist's invitation to come in for an individual session to discuss with her personally how she could make efforts to reach the children more effectively with messages of love and positive expectation. She took unexpected advantage of this session to reveal that, unbeknownst to her husband, both of the children were not his biological children but from a long-standing secret lover. Moreover, to the therapist it became clear that everyone, including the children and both the husband and lover, were incidental to this woman's narcissistic involvement with pleasuring her own self. Shortly after her disclosures in the above session, treatment of the children was terminated by the parents.

A year or so later, the therapist met the mother in a neighborhood market. She told him, "I sent my husband away to work [in a foreign country] for several years. He is much less of a bother this way." In a sudden burst of charm, she then surprisingly requested an appointment for the next week, but two days later she called to cancel the scheduled time and has never been seen again.

Another form of doing major harm to loved ones in family life involves emotional exploitation, such as when demands for emotional services are placed on the other in return for offering one's own emotional connection or non-dissolution of a relationship. A typical exploitative message is: *After all I have done for you, you owe me your love.* Another typical message of exploitation is: *Even though I've been a distinctly unpleasant person for you in your life, you have no right to abandon me when I'm sick and old.*

These messages are not necessarily explicitly verbal. They are also mood and silent-meaning messages that are built into the fabric of a relationship. They take advantage of an inherent niceness and sense of obligation in decent human beings, including the natural readiness of most children to be helpful to their parents. In contrast to bona fide requests for love or assistance, these are efforts to trap the other into being *obligated* to give up much of their own healthy self-interest and pleasures in living in favor of serving the other.

It has been said that the prime cause of most psychiatric problems in children is parents who, *seemingly* lovingly, expect a child to grow and function *for them*, the parents, and thereby induce major disturbances in children's functions—whether eating, learning, developing an ability to play with other children and enjoy themselves, the unfolding of sexuality for oneself, or whatever—because the child's conception of these natural functions becomes contaminated with the notion that eating, learning, and so on are not for the child himself/herself.

Emotional exploitation in families also refers to marital relationships where one mate crowds and chokes the other with demands and obligations to serve them rather than developing mutual caring and helpfulness—for example, when men are made to feel obligated to work, including at jobs they don't like at all, "in order to support my family"; or when women suppress their genuine selves and submit their identities to a traditional role of serving their men, even in distasteful ways, out of a sense of servitude rather than in a relationship of equals, friends, and lovers. (Needless to say, in all these cases, the problem includes the readiness of the second mate to be obligated to function for the other, and not only the possessive control of the dominant one.)

> To feel the difference between functioning first of all for oneself and functioning out of obligation or to serve another, run a series of experiments over a period of time of making love to your partner in order to please and satisfy them and not yourself; then on other occasions compare this way of making love with only pleasuring yourself; and finally on other occasions compare both with combining pleasuring yourself *and* enjoying giving pleasure and satisfaction to the other.

Scapegoating

Another serious major form of psychological victimization is scapegoating, which takes forms of assigning pariah psychological roles such as *the dumb one, the bad one, the disturbed or crazy one* to some person in the family.[9] What is common to the various forms of scapegoating in family life is that a family member is selected by another member of the family, generally with the concurrence of the larger family group (although sometimes other members of the family, such as a sibling, will manage to maintain a more positive relationship with the "condemned" member) as the object of this form of destructiveness.[10] The early pioneering greats of family therapy showed that a good number of psychiatric disabilities followed on such assignments of a scapegoat role in a family, and I am quite convinced that their seminal findings will stand the test of time and that they deserve to be applied regularly in current-day clinical work, especially with difficult cases.

It is inherently fascinating to see how this process works. It is a small-scale demonstration in family life of the larger horrors of prejudice and libel of a group or people on a larger level, such as antisemitism, prejudice, and hatred of blacks and persecution of Orientals (I am told that in several South Pacific societies, such as Indonesia, Malaysia, and Singapore, there is a tradition of hatred and murderous pogroms against Chinese and that some scholars have proffered that the Chinese are the "Jews" of these societies).

When the parental message is scapegoating of a child, the child is told that they are somehow seriously defective.

❖ "You crazy brat," yelled the mother sourly at her nervous and increasingly strange little boy as she swatted at him, sometimes with her hands and other times even with a belt. He grew up brooding and withdrawn. In adolescence he was on the verge of being crazy, but with the help of a loving uncle was sent for psychotherapy with an able clinician who helped him quite a lot to pull through in his functioning (but, alas, not enough to protect him for later life). With an amazing push of inner strength, he succeeded in his school work after being on the verge of failure, and even went on to graduate medical school.

As an adult physician, he was an excellent diagnostician, with great skills in emergency situations, but he largely ruined his life, first by being an alcoholic, and then by running off his mouth at colleagues, superiors, or even patients to a point where he was repeatedly fired from his medical posts. He was, in fact, at every age of his life, "a crazy brat," just like his mother had called him. His mouth was as big as hers had been.

The other side of the same coin of unfair and ultimately harmful projections onto a child is when some children are "anointed" to be great leaders by an exaggerated love and adoration by their families. While great and gifted musicians, artists, statesmen, or whatever (including psychologists) can result, they characteristically become "chosen ones" who suffer high levels of narcissism and feelings of superiority that complicate their personal lives considerably.

Doing Harm to Others and Sacrificing

Psychiatry has a built-in preference or natural interest in people who are the *objects* of being victimized or hurt by others. The field of mental health has not always liked to look at the other side of the coin of victimization as the *doing of harm to others*. I had an interesting experience in this regard some years ago when I was placed on a committee of the American Psychiatric Association for defining victimization, which the committee considered the proper word for the suffering and symptoms of the victims of trauma and destructiveness such as concentration camp survivors. (I was probably invited to be on the committee because of my work on the Holocaust and genocide). When I then proposed that *victimization* be defined in two ways—*both* as the experience of being a victim *and* as the verb describing the actions of victimizers or perpetrators of harm to others—the conveners of the committee knew that they did not want me to continue, and did not even want to discuss the subject further; the psychiatric establishment was not ready to think too much about the people who do the harm to others.

When we probe victimization as the doing of harm to others, we encounter an underlying basic mechanism that I call *sacrificing*.[11] From this point of view, much victimization is a variant on the age-old tradition of *making a sacrifice* to the gods to propitiate, expiate, and substitute a victim for oneself. Thus, in ancient times living children were literally offered up in sacrifice to the gods. Later, as "civilization" evolved, animals were substituted for the children in what is considered an enormous step forward in the psychoanthropology of the human species from the full range of our natural cruelty to a greater humanness toward our own species.

In the psychology of sacrificing, the underlying construction or program in the mind of the perpetrator says in effect, "*Better you than me.*"[12] The victim becomes a substitute solution for the problems, deprivations, and worst dreads in the mind of the victimizer. Whatever form of anxiety the victimizer himself fears—dissolution into psychic nothingness, dread of exposure as incompetent, terror of abandonment, or whatever variant of being reduced and destroyed—is projected onto the victim who is chosen as the person to suffer instead of oneself. The mechanism applies at the level of relationships between individuals, such as a cruelly ambitious father who belittles his son's manliness or talent, or a selfishly beautiful mother who ensures that her daughters will not fulfill their natural beauty; and it applies to the psychology of large group behaviors such as in "ethnic cleansing" or the genocidal destruction of a rival ethnic, religious, or national group.

The cruelty of victimization is shocking at any time, but there is an added dimension to both the cruelty and the shock when the victimization is done in one's family. What can be especially painful and incredible to an observer is that the victimizer family member is unresponsive either to logic or to the evidence of their eyes and hearts that their victim-relative is suffering terribly, and at times even that their life is endangered. The higher imperative that overcomes and rules the victimizer is the demand for a solution to *their* own selfish needs and personal problems at any cost. Thus can it be that a parent who is ostensibly rational, and who will prove to be psychiatrically "normal" on formal clinical examination, and even generally "means well" toward a child, can go blind with a rage that is projected onto a child in a severe beating because the child triggers some deep feeling of inadequacy or unfinished anger in the parent's inner mind.

There is no doubt whatsoever that, unlike people who engage in large-scale mass murders such as genocide, where there are few evidences of contrition, regret, and responsibility, in many cases of doing harm to children the victimizer-parent inwardly is genuinely regretful about the damage done to their child and guilty over doing the damage. (See the decidedly non-kosher—meaning politically incorrect—discussion of autism as a possible expression of parental hostility, but consequently of more hopeful possibilities of helping the child if the parents are enlisted in genuine efforts to care and help the child.[13] [14]) Nonetheless, the damage is done, because the basically legitimate life principle of caring for one's own survival, safety, and pleasure was allowed to become an ultimate and total point of view, which overcame and banished all other emotions of caring and responsibility for one's children.

"I'M ALRIGHT JACK PERSONALITIES": PEOPLE WHO SEEMINGLY DON'T HAVE ANY PROBLEMS AND ASSIGN ALL THE BURDEN TO SOMEONE ELSE IN THE FAMILY

One of the most fascinating discoveries of family therapy for me has been that we can also identify family structures in which some members have elected roles of being free of tensions and worries, but do so *at the expense of others* in their family.

If by definition life is replete with challenges and difficulties that are anxiety-provoking for any normal person (and I am totally convinced this is the case). And if by definition every one of us in the course of a lifetime collects a variety of "bruises" and, worse, serious blows and failures (and I am convinced this too is the case). In fact, everyone experiences in their lives periods of virtual Job-like suffering, as in the biblical figure Job who suffers it all!—see the discussion in Chapter 7, "Treating Emotional Violence and Evil"). This means there is always enough pain and hurt in our lives over which to grieve, and more than enough to fear in the unknown impending future and what it will bring us.

By definition, families are intended to divide up and share the various tasks of life, and this includes dividing and sharing the load of pain, concern, and worry about the welfares and destinies of family members. Sharing these concerns with other family members makes the burden more bearable for everyone. But in some families there are persons who refuse to carry their share of the family worries. "I'm Alright Jack Personalities" do not carry their load, and the result is that someone else, or more than one other person in the family, ends up with more than their share of worries because they have to carry more than one person's normal share.

The paradigm that guides these worry-free personalities is that one should not give away one's energy, peace of mind, strength, emotional resources, or pleasures in life for anyone else. Collecting or amassing endless supplies of personal security becomes the absolute rule by which their behaviors and emotions are formulated. They keep on conducting their own lives according to their preferred style regardless of what happens to others. Efforts to draw them into caring, worrying, or investing emotionally in another family member, such as a spouse or a child who is in some kind of serious psychological trouble or life problem, typically come to naught. These people insist on taking everything "naturally" and "unemotionally" and to deal with problems simply "realistically." They are "pseudonormals" or "supernormals" who are generally polite and *seemingly* responsible and responding, but in real emotional fact remain unmoved and unreachable even in the face of their loved ones' real anguish, and their loved ones know it and suffer all the more. They are, of course, infuriating, but since their selfishness and indifference are hidden behind a solidness and business-like attitude about life, some family members get confused and guilty about their anger at them.

Characteristically, the tension that builds around "I'm Alright Jack Personalities" in a family is very high. The troubled scenes that eventually develop between them and other family members can be dramatic, if not bizarre contrasts between seriously distraught people and an implacable person who does not lose their equanimity under any circumstances.

This pseudonormal role is frequently reserved to fathers and is consistent with cultural forms that designate men as more cool, uninvolved, stable, realistic, and tougher in battle than women, who are expected to be more fearful and worrisome. However, the role can just as easily be adopted by women, and in these cases it is the husband who becomes the sensitive and worrying person in the family. It is also a role that can be taken on by a child in the division of emotional responsibilities in a family. In the mysteries of how different people assume such different roles in their lives, we see that some children pull out and choose to feel virtually nothing about the distress of their parents or siblings, as if they are not even part of their families, while other children will practically give their whole lives away to save a parent, or the parents' marriage, or a sibling in the family.

❖ In one family therapy case that had begun around the suicidal thoughts of one of the pre-teenage boys and the chronically depressed/scowling lifestyle of the mother, nothing seemed to succeed in breaking the rational composure of the father who could not and would not understand the obvious distress of his son and wife.

This was a dignified upper-class family where mother was a senior person in the academic world, and father was the owner-executive of a very large and successful manufacturing company. In this family, natural emotions were muted to begin with and were pushed back to a second-level position behind a culture-veneer of propriety and good manners. But the father went even further in his total eschewing of natural emotions. Under all circumstances his style was to remain positive, competent, and rational. When his son spoke of suicide, the father expressed concern but showed no feeling. When his wife ached with depressive sadness, he properly wanted to get her the professional help she needed, but had nothing to offer her from his heart—neither sympathy nor anger. From his point of view, emotions such as those his son and wife displayed were obviously the indulgence of the weak and inept, as both of them were proving in the very fact that they needed psychological treatment.

One day when the father was speaking in a family therapy session, the therapist walked around the room and, without notice, hit the father sharply above the knee. True to his form of not responding with any emotion, and if possible not even taking account of problems, the father brushed away the blow and went on speaking as if nothing at all had taken place. The therapist circled the room once more and again with no comment repeated the blow. The man's wife and two children looked up and began snickering, the more so as the husband redoubled his resolve to maintain his composure, although he now asked very mildly and reasonably what the therapist was doing. It took several increasingly intense repetitions of the "meaningless blows" (administered purposely to a part of the body where there were no symbolic repercussions, such as there would be, say, to a smack on the face) before the husband became genuinely annoyed, and the point that was being illustrated could be brought home regarding his characteristic nonemotional responses and uninvolved role in family life. (This family made it to a healthier sharing, the child and mother recovered, and the father underwent a very enriching individual therapy.)

I believe that the concept of an "I'm Alright Jack Personality" helps us to understand a variety of emotional and mental disturbances in a child that develop and thrive when a parent adopts this paradigm of protecting their own personal security at any cost—even when the life of their child may be at real risk.

❖ A teenager doing compulsory army service decided that he was fed up and would get himself discharged on a psychiatric basis. To prove the point, he took a knife and cut his leg fairly severely, and then he made it clear to the doctors and officers who examined and interrogated him that unless he were discharged he would climb to the top of a tower on the base and hurl himself to his death.

The young soldier's parents were apprised by the army of what was going on, and the alarmed mother sought a private civilian psychological consultation to which she came together with her husband. The mother was hoping the consultation would show a way to get professional help organized for their son who so far had refused to be treated by the army mental health personnel, and she also wanted help for her own evident distress.

In the interview with the parents, the father was totally blasé. He stated his opinion that whatever his son did was his own business. Everyone had their own life to lead. His wife's emotionalism wasn't going to help either way. Would the father be willing to take a firm stand with his son and demand lovingly and firmly that the son stop threatening to take his life?

Not at all! The father was vehement that the recommendations of the therapist that he attempt to intervene in his son's life were stupid, meaningless, and an intrusion into his son's "freedom" to make his own decisions and lead his own life.

There is no basis in traditional psychiatric thinking for identifying the uninvolved people as problematic or troubled! There are psychiatric categories of personality disorders that recognize that people whose functioning gets them into trouble in the process will cause distress to others in their family through their symptomatic disturbances—for example, the distress that alcoholics, gamblers, or narcissists cause their families. But nowhere is there a diagnostic category or even observation about people who are as if made of iron, sterling characters of good adjustment and competence, but whose apparently good adjustment is effected at the expense of their intimates. This is a category of using, exploiting, and abusing others "without any signs of blood" on the hands of the person who does the harm.

In my opinion, along with the deficit of a lack of integrity, this style does represent a distinct condition of psychopathology. No one is actually crazy or hearing voices, but someone is driving others crazy, and that too deserves a name in formal psychiatric nomenclature.[15]

A NEED TO GIVE TO OTHERS BUT NOT TO RECEIVE FOR ONESELF: BIG GIVERS WHO TAKE AWAY THE OTHERS' STRENGTH

Another dynamic pattern, which embodies a paradigm that is adopted as a rigid way of thinking and living and is nowhere to be found in the psychiatric books as a sign of disturbance, despite the enormous emotional turmoil that this pattern brings about, involves a need of some people to give, take care of, and help others, but never to receive for themselves and never to be dependent on other people, with the result that, intentionally or unintentionally, the other person is made weaker.

This way of organizing one's life is often characteristic of highly charming and very successful people who embody admirable qualities of apparent generosity and unselfishness. Ostensibly they are the antithesis of narcissistic self-serving personalities. They will do *everything* to help others. It takes an astute observer to see how insistent they are about refusing to *receive* any caring for themselves, and that they become explicitly upset at the possibility of being put in a position of having to receive anything. Even simple gifts can upset some of them, such as merely an offer to pay for dinner at a restaurant after they have treated the other many times before. They will do everything they can to turn the tables back once again to resume the position of giving to the other.

It is in these givers' interests to have others need them. In the process of giving unendingly and, worse, their refusing to confirm the capacity of others to give in return, these seemingly generous people are likely to encourage and reinforce over-dependency, incompetence, and even serious emotional disorder in those in whom they foster dependency. I have seen such super-generous people literally become enraged if and when a person dependent on them does break out of their role as a receiving object. If the big givers are somehow forced into experiences of vulnerability and needing to receive help from others, they are likely to become very despondent.

❖ He was a generously devoted father, the leader of a large family clan who could always be counted on to be robust in his laughter and spiritedness, uplifting the spirits of all those around him. It was impossible not to appreciate what he did for all of them. He was unstinting in the financial gifts he heaped on all those who were close to him. Yet a serious and impartial reading of the record over the years would reveal that every one of the people close to him had succumbed to major patterns of incompetence. Among his children, siblings, and even his close business associates, one counted several alcoholics, regrettable divorces as a result of emotional immaturity that were also followed by a failure to remarry, several people who had adopted lifestyles that laid them open to ridicule for their pretensions at being much more than they were, and one suicide—where the victim-relative had made the devastating point of leaving his body in his "benefactor's" office.

❖ He was honest to a fault when his wife demanded to know if he had a baby with his secretary and longtime secret lover, and as a gentleman he agreed to the divorce she then insisted on getting. Now he moved in with his longtime lover and the baby and tried to institute the way of life that was familiar to him, where he was the patron and she was to be grateful for his gifts. But with the secrecy of their affair ended, she was not that kind of woman, and to his great consternation she expected him to be more sharing in spirit and activity under the same roof and to welcome her being more of a personality along with him. For him the atmosphere became excruciatingly smothering, and he soon found himself suffering from what he was convinced were "strokes," where he couldn't breathe and felt waves of panic. He soon moved out.

UNQUESTIONING LOYALTY TO ONE'S FAMILY AS A BASIS FOR BEING ABUSED

Another painful variation on paradigmatic themes of unending stuck relationships is the position that one must accept, remain loyal to, and never separate from a family member no matter what they do to you, because they are "family." Family becomes a supreme value that overrides every other consideration of self-interest, even the plain common sense that one has to fight back against somebody who kicks you maliciously.

Wives who remain dependent on abusive husbands have been described as "self-defeating personalities." This is a concept that was proposed as a diagnostic category in formal psychiatry, and although the concept was not restricted to women, feminist groups opposed adopting it as a psychiatric diagnosis on the grounds that it would likely be employed against women and add further woes to what, to begin with, they considered was the abused political position of women by psychiatry. Of course, self-defeating ways of life are seen not only in wives and female lovers but also in countless husbands and male lovers—examples include the male lover in Somerset Maugham's classic tale, *Of Human Bondage*, who could not free himself of a destructive witch of a woman; innumerable instances of parents being dominated by one or more of their children; and siblings where a brother or a sister is elected in a family to be an object of exploitation and scorn and does not know how to break loose from that role.

Submitting oneself to abuse is a way of remaining fused with and unseparated from another person, thus in a basic way being spared the anxiety of separateness and aloneness. The paradigm of over-connection and unchanging loyalty to one's kin and family as a basis for being abused has many varied expressions such as:

- One dare not attack one's family, even when one is being abused by one's relatives.
- Under no circumstances does one conceive of divorce from one's abusive spouse.
- Never does one dare to consider renouncing or sending away one's abusive child, no matter what they have done.

The abused family member is stuck and cannot change or influence the situation in any way whatsoever. This paradigmatic position is adopted and maintained in the face of every rational reason for fighting or fleeing the abuser. It is maintained notwithstanding repeated experiences of tortuous insult, pain, and even physical injury. The advice of friends or professionals to break loose, and how to do so, are typically rejected out of hand. In this locked position, the deep compulsion never to be disloyal to one's family is held as a supervalue that is absolute and inviolate; hence even continuous anguish and battering by one's relative is not enough to change the position.

❖ They were stunned. It had never dawned on them that their charming adult son could be a thief. As they looked back now, they realized that there had been several instances in which he had taken small sums of monies from their wallets, and others in which he had swindled them handily in larger family financial matters. They had allowed each of these events to pass with relatively brief and unemotional criticism, with no clear-cut anger or moral censure, and, most telltale, no demand of him to return the funds he had taken.

Now it had been revealed that he had swindled hundreds of thousands of dollars from clients in his business as well as from the business partnership with them, and he was facing serious criminal charges. As parents they were deeply concerned for him. They were also buffeted by moral indignation and emotions of contempt for his criminal behavior, which was genuinely unacceptable to their standards. They even admitted to some emotions of rage at their son who was becoming a monster in their eyes for not respecting any moral boundaries in his greed. Still, the worst for them was to picture that he would actually go to jail. They simply couldn't bear to see their beloved son there. To spare him going to jail, they were prepared themselves to repay the several hundreds of thousands of dollars that he had stolen and to make a deal that no criminal charges would be brought against him.

A therapist whom they consulted advised that although they were financially capable of providing the considerable sums of monies that would be needed to save their son from going to jail, it was nonetheless essential that they build a legal-probationary context for him that would cause him to experience the consequences of his actions. It was suggested that the parents engage an attorney who would play a judicial-like role for their son by confronting him with a severe demeanor, and insist that the son be required to sign a legal document that required him to return portions of his indebtedness from his future earnings according to a contractual schedule. The therapist advised further that the son be required to sign a formal confession of his past criminal actions, and that this document would be left with the lawyer with the understanding that it would be turned over to the police if there were any further acts of stealing or if the son did not repay his debts.

The reasoning behind these recommendations was explained to the parents. They were cautioned that there was considerable likelihood of further exploitative and criminal swindling by their son in the future, and that failure to take firm action at this time would almost certainly guarantee their son's repeating criminal behaviors in the future. Nonetheless, the parents refused to create *any* kind of disciplinary structure whatsoever. In fact, they made the statement that if their son would steal additional funds in the future, they would cover those as well. They were his parents, and it was their responsibility to protect their children under any and all circumstances. Even if he were a murderer, they concluded, they would stand behind him.

The son soon continued in his criminal activity, which now developed into fully armed robberies of a series of wealthy victims. He ended up being apprehended by the police and was sentenced to a resounding jail sentence for a good number of years. Of course the son was responsible for his behaviors, but it can also be said that his enslaved parents helped to railroad their son into a serious jail sentence because they remained in bondage and neglected their family responsibilities as parents to discipline their son in time.

SEXUAL DYSFUNCTIONS: HOW CERTAINTIES CAN GET IN THE WAY OF MAKING LOVE WELL

It seems somewhat remote to be speaking of a "fascist" way of thinking when it comes to disorders of sexual experience, but here too we see how some kind of insistent idea about sexuality can put a person out of sorts and interfere with their natural machinery for arousal, excitement, and pleasure. A rigid conception of how sex should be done demands of a person to do what they are told by that conception and only what they have been told, and not to dare stray toward any other frame or way of experiencing.

The greatest advances in recent years in the understanding and treatment of sexual disorders (male impotence, premature ejaculation, female orgasmic dysfunction, as well as other less common dysfunctions) came from the seminal (both the pun and the genuine honor are intended) contributions of Masters and Johnson.[16] These sexual behavior tasks can be conceptualized as ways of training the patient to replace a given "stuck record" or conception of making love that has been imposed on them and is inhibiting the full natural cycle of sexual arousal and consummation. Interestingly enough, Masters and Johnson first of all called on the therapist to correct the errors people were making that derived from certain fixed ideas that Masters and Johnson concluded contributed to the sexual dysfunction. (Many people do not realize that they actually insisted that these key-idea distortions be corrected *before* a therapist would undertake any of the sexual behavior tasks that are designed to retrain couples in their actual lovemaking, but in too many cases therapy with their behavioral techniques was begun without doing this prior work.)

Some of the common conceptual errors that Masters and Johnson seek to correct before entering into sexual behavior tasks are:

- A belief that one must devote one's sexual functioning first of all to serve one's partner

- Inordinate needs to please one's partner
- An inordinate insistence on being pleasured and satisfied by one's partner
- Anxious and insistent demands of oneself that one must perform "successfully"
- Fears of being censured or ridiculed

Other researchers of sexual functioning, both ancient and contemporary, have given us other pieces of the puzzle, such as Freud's seminal contributions[17] to understanding how the sexual apparatus shuts down in the face of what we shall call an inner paradigm of disavowal of one's basic right to be sexual; or the inability to separate between a parental and sexual love object, with the result that one is not allowed to make love to one's lover if the lover is taken to represent an incestuous parent object.

In effect, students of Freud were researching the impacts of wrong ideas on making love. Too few therapists today are aware, for example, of the brilliant work on premature ejaculation by early psychoanalytic pioneer Karl Abraham,[18] in which as far back as 1917 he identified dynamics of narcissism, passivity, and hostility in the male to the female as summating in premature ejaculation. In my experience to this day, this model enables effective psychotherapy of many chronic cases of premature ejaculation, including those that do not respond to treatment based on the Masters and Johnson sexual behavior tasks.

Following the pioneering work of Masters and Johnson and the remarkable sexual behavioral tasks they designed, Helen Kaplan[19] combined the sexual behavioral tasks with the psychotherapeutic tradition of psychodynamic work on the couple's relationship. In effect, she said that any attempt to make love when hostility and sabotage prevail in the relationship is a paradigmatic error (e.g., "I will use you for my sexual needs, but I don't want you as my genuine lover-friend") that then becomes a source of sexual dysfunction. Kaplan taught emphatically that the sexual therapy must *first* correct the outstanding sabotage or disconnection in the couple's relationship before proceeding to introduce specific sexual behavior treatment tasks.

In my own work on an existential/dialectical approach to marital therapy,[20] I proposed that we may understand and treat many sexual dysfunctions not only from a behavioral frame of reference of relearning sexual tasks, but also from the point of view of a specific paradigm in which the dysfunctional person has become stuck with a one-sided concept of themselves as a sexual person. The one-sidedness refers to the *splitting* of any of a number of dialectical configurations, both sides of which are vital for the creation, maintenance, consummation, and appreciation of the sexual experience.

Thus, healthy sexuality combines:

- sensuality *and* friendship-intimacy
- tenderness *and* toughness
- commitment *and* freedom from obligation
- closeness *and* independence
- activity *and* passivity

- taking *and* giving
- yielding *and* overcoming
- experiencing satisfaction *and* tolerance of frustration
- filling *and* emptying

In their oppositeness, each side of the experience in each of these dialectical pairings tones the meaning of the other, guards against excess in the other direction, and provides for some expression of hidden sides of one's personality even when a person is naturally inclined to, or is more organized around, the other or opposite side of the emotion-behavior. In each case, each polar side of the dimension of experience is a necessary correlative to the other. In developing a paradigm of over-certainty and an absolute preference for only or too much of one side of an experience, and a concomitant ruthless exclusion of the other, the sexually functioning person cuts themselves off from vital aspects of their human nature. Splitting the two sides of a dialectically integrative function leaves a person exposed to the hidden forces that nonetheless bespeak and insist on the denied side of the function. Thus, even a tough sexual man needs to feel loved, even a highly sensitive and caring person needs to feel some degree of rapacious and lustful sensuality, and so on.

The following are descriptions—as if of the internal dialogues—of some of the characteristic splits in functioning that underlie some sexual dysfunctions:

- An insistence on being aggressive and assertive and not allowing oneself to be dependent: "*I'm a tough, independent person, and I do not intend to yield or be dependent on my partner*";
- or vice versa, the opposite of the previous dynamic, a need to be dependent and an inability to experience any necessary aggression for oneself: "*I'm a gentle and loving person and wouldn't ever do anything aggressive to my partner.*"
- Needing to possess the love object as a slave while not loving the person: "*I want to discharge my sexual tension, and once I have done that I don't need or like to be with my partner*"; or vice versa, being too pure and idealistic in one's love, unable to be carnal and insistently possessive of one's sexual mate: "*My love for you is so pure, I don't need or want anything sexual to spoil it.*"
- A need to keep emotional distance from one's sexual partner and not allow softness and closeness: "*Let's have sex, but there's no need to be over-romantic, I don't like too much display of affection*"; or vice versa, a need to be so gentle and understanding of one's sexual partner that one is unable to make demands, fight back against frustration, and excite their partner through conquering them: "*I just want to make you happy, all I need is to be quietly next to you.*"

Sexual dysfunctions are hidden *I can'ts* and *I won'ts*, in which the would-be sexual person prescribes and proscribes, with absolute certainty, the boundaries of the experience they will tolerate. The inevitable appearance of the denied and disallowed emotion is met with powerful efforts to beat back and suppress intrusion of the undesired emotion.

It is the effort to stop oneself from embodying the different sides that we all inevitably have that results in the sad destruction of the capacity to function sexually, of the pleasure it offers, and of the extended invigorating meanings that healthy sexuality triggers—vitality, confidence in one's body and mind, and trust of one's relationship with one's lover. An ability to be flexible and to explore and make contact with the other side of a feeling provides a solution to the locked situations that sexual dysfunctions in effect represent.

The task of psychotherapy is to replace, as much as possible, the missing emotional functions; for example, to help a man who is too sexually aggressive to be more emotionally caring and loving, or to help a man who is too gentle and appreciatively loving to be more sexually lustful and physically "aggressive." For again, in all matters that are human, too much of any ostensibly good thing turns it into a quite bad matter. In matters of sex, it is a downer (serious pun intended).

GENUINE COMMUNICATION FOR GENUINE RELATIONSHIPS: THE GIVE-AND-TAKE OF REAL CLARIFICATION OF NEEDS, CRITICISM, ANGER, AND LOVE

To this day it seems like the great American dream is of marriages where people are consistently and forever smiling, friendly, decent, basically agree with one another, and share the same sets of correct values. Too few people realize that such a conception is not only not true to reality to begin with, but is also intrinsically not democratic—a strange-sounding remark that nonetheless should be understood now as the conception we have been developing in this book; namely, it is an uncompromisingly totalistic concept lacking a genuine freedom of each mate to their own real self, including welcome inevitable differences and clashes between the spouses.

Of course, alongside the continuation of the above myth of unconflicted and loving, peaceful marital lives, there can hardly be anyone who does not rationally know that, factually, the fate of *most* marriages is negative. Well over 50 percent of marriages in the United States and other places in the Western world end in dissolution. On the other hand, everyone knows from their own life experiences that there are an endless number of marriages that persist without divorce, where people are anything but happy and pleasured; as well as so many people who now refrain from marrying at all because it is too frequently a losing proposition. So many couples live in a state of chronic misery, emotional and sexual disloyalty, grayness, emptiness and boredom, bitterness and contempt for one another, with an affective hunger for connection, even as the busy organizational machinery of their marriage and family life moves on quasi-effectively through the routines of everyday life. Nonetheless, by the amazing quirks of the mind and social faddism, the archetypal image of the forever non-conflictual happy marriage still prevails as the desired and expected state of bliss for wedded couples.

At the same time, since the archetypal ideal can't hold out entirely by itself indefinitely against the known painful facts, an alternative supplemental archetypal image has also developed in Western life, very much spurred on by the counseling and mental health professions, and that is that couples need to communicate. This means that they need to tell each other what they think, feel, and prefer, and that an honest dialogue about each one's needs and choices, conducted in a calm and respectful manner, should result in cooperative decisions. But this truth is then channeled into the original myth: communicate with each other nicely, with full understanding and respect of one another, and then, *eureka*, the original mythological desideratum of being joined happily and respectfully to one another will have been achieved. In other words, the myth now shifts from the goal of marital happiness as a statement of continuing wholesome love without tension to a focus on proper and proven psychological methods for conducting the marriage to achieve the myth. Should the couple be unable to achieve such dialogue, they are clearly in need of education, counseling, marriage counseling, or therapy, or perhaps marital mediation (whose practitioners may take even greater pride in avoiding conflictual processes than do many marital therapists). Again, however, reality proves bigger and mightier than pat single-dimensional solutions, and the nature of man as an anger-prone, competitive, and aggressive animal comes to the fore in the marital scenes that most of us know take place even in the finest marriages. See the Ingmar Bergman films if you have any doubts about how the nicest people get into serious marital anger, intense threats and attacks on one another, and plenty of pouting and misery.[21]

The very happy news is that effective communication *does* provide a considerable constructive solution to much of the existential realities of couplehood, but the solution lies not in a romanticized communication of each person's needs and opinions to one another, but in a *genuine* give-and-take that includes telling each other naturally what one wants, and that very much also includes healthy criticism and even anger by mates to one another.

First and foremost, of course, the communication needs to be in the context of a couple's genuine commitment to one another and to their marriage. Moreover, there need to be many expressions of continuing appreciation, affection, and love. Psychologist John Gottman has shown with remarkable scientific measurement that positive statements need to predominate over negative by about 5:1 in marital communication.[22] What I like about Gottman's work is that it points all of us toward adopting a guiding philosophy for our way of being with our spouse. But beyond Gottman's admirable proof that a strong tilt to the positive keeps marriages together, I want to emphasize even more that within the boundaries of shared commitment and alongside the communication of positive feelings, there also need to be genuine criticism and periodic expressions of anger that are conveyed authentically but in good taste. Even the negative feelings we play out, and should be playing out, can be linked to our predominant positive feelings.

Genuine communication also includes an ongoing negotiating of the "sexual politics" of the couple, including issues of being attracted to other people, and the tension of jealousy as well as a healthy monitoring of one another for loyalty.[23]

❖ He was newly divorced and obviously hungry for a new relationship. Each time he would start dating a woman, he would almost immediately begin to envision marrying her. The therapist was trying to slow him down and help him avoid making a hasty marriage on the rebound.

"I recommend that you give yourself half a year in which you date several women and see how you feel in different relationships," the therapist advised.

"I can't do that," the man replied. "Once I am with a woman, I have to be loyal to her." The irony was not lost on both therapist and patient. The man's divorce had been from a woman who was chronically disloyal to him.

"Does that mean that once you're dating any lady, you can't even mention to her sometimes that you are excited by another woman, and that you have to pretend to be one hundred percent loyal to her even in your mind?"

"Yes, of course. No woman I know would agree to anything else."

"And if your flesh was weak and you did end up making love to another woman before you had married, would you tell this lady with whom you're going and face the music of the tension?"

"Are you kidding? Never!"

Unmarried as he was, this man was already enslaved rather than free to be genuinely communicative with his girlfriends.

The healthy and wholesome marital fight is a battle of ideas and feelings that takes place between friends almost as in a martial (amazingly, almost the same word as marital) art. One is happy to be present with one's partner for the sporting event. One appreciates the spiritedness and skill in battle of one's partner, and certainly their rights and need to express their real selves.

❖ A thoughtful eleven-year-old boy said to his mother after watching her fight with her second husband of some years, "Mom, the difference between the way you fight with Bob (the second husband) and the way you used to fight with Dad is that the two of you always make up, even with a kiss, but you and Dad used to stay angry at each other for days."

Obviously, many couples will need therapy to learn how to convey criticism and how to fight.[24] Couples who learn to fight well even enjoy a further intimacy that is inherent in the intense exchange of genuine ideas and feelings, and a pleasure of being with each other even in the course of the fighting exchange! They also know from life experience that a good roust of differences of opinion and feeling is a marvelous tonic for an appetite and passion for reconnection. The dance of conflict includes joy in the art form of the conflict as well as the knowledge that when done well, the conflict will be followed by embraces, caresses, and a renewed song of making love (thus, the time-honored observation that making love is all the sweeter following a lover's battle).

The actual anger that is conveyed needs to be spoken genuinely but with good control. *No insulting words or yelling are allowed*, although speaking with conviction and intensity are certainly allowed and constitute natural tools for conveying the different levels of importance of a subject to each speaker. In the tougher fights there will be a lot of tension in the air—it is one of the tasks of being grown up to be able to "contain" (handle) hefty degrees of tension about all sorts of aspects of life. The anger is to be conveyed in the context of a message that the parties are seeking to arrive at a common ground through the expression of differences rather than engaging in an all-out battle whose implied or possible goal is coercion of one party by the other, or whose possible outcome is separation or divorce if one does not give in to the other's political power and demands for one's point of view. To argue and be angry is to be *with* one another rather than to divide *from* one another. It is a reminder of the privilege and joy of all the moments of being with one another's beloved![25]

Healthy fighting is a marvelous combination of spontaneity and discipline. The feelings of anger are not suppressed, but a great deal of the feelings are purposely and naturally left to be experienced—even savored—*inside* one's mind and not expressed in words to the other. (This means one can go the whole route of "smacking," "betraying," even "murdering" the other *in the quiet of one's private imagination without saying anything about it*, and no harm is done!) In addition, *some* of the anger is expressed, not in stiff rational words that would seem to come straight from a psychological cookbook for marriages, but in genuinely emotional ways. At the same time, there is the overriding discipline not to use any words or gestures that are obscenely insulting, degrading, or incendiary. This decision to be disciplined is taken long before any given fight, and is called up in one's mind when the actual fight develops. Knowing that one can and will speak truthfully about everything that is upsetting and angering provides a strong foundation on which to lay the further decision to be disciplined.

Couples who learn that they can trust both themselves and each another to be fair, respectful, and even loving in the course of arguments and fights will have achieved a safe and happy marriage. Paradoxically, there is then also greater room for some errors and violations of courtesy in moments of fighting that "get away" from one's control, including the fact that there is greater trust in the apologies and re-resolutions to maintain better control in the future. Overall, the number of such "errors," at times including a burst of intense anger and a runaway discourtesy, have to be very "few and far between," but wrong as these are they too have an edifying and invigorating potential. For a genuinely good couple, saying "I'm sorry" is both an act of love and a sign of a personal decency that makes one more lovable. A spouse can say, "I'm sorry I was insulting. And I *really* don't want you to hurt. But I also really want you to know how deeply I feel in this matter." It's dangerous stuff, like nuclear energy, but on the good side it can stimulate a lot of growth and make a relationship more precious.

From the point of view of the model presented in this work, the ability of married people to give and take real criticism and wholesome fighting is an expression of a more democratic way of life. Differences are not swept under the carpet, but are processed successfully within formats that enable full discussion without violence and destruction. In contrast, the traditional insistence on happiness on the basis of complete unanimity and avoidance of protest, criticism, or hurting of one another is another version of the imposition of over-certainty and a totality that may achieve a temporary unity, but ultimately breeds an explosive dissension that underlies the breakup of many marriages.

❖ They were genuinely furious at each other. He felt that she was absolutely unreachable whenever he would give her information about her driving when they were together in the car and she was at the wheel. It seemed to him that she was so involved in proving her capability as a driver that she would angrily ignore any information he gave her, say about road conditions, even if it meant the possibility of an accident. She felt he was a ridiculous, insulting, backseat driver.

With billowing, bulging eyes she stared hatefully at him. Yet behind her anger he saw the flicker of her pain, and his heart went out to her. Although he couldn't stand how rigid she was, he also was genuinely worried about the possibility of a serious accident when she drove in her blind impulsive way, and he felt sorry for her deep insecurity about feeling capable and worthwhile.

He now said more quietly yet still firmly, "I'm sorry you feel so insulted. I do have to tell you what I think when you are driving if I believe there is a danger ahead of us that you are not seeing, but it really matters to me that you not feel so bad about yourself. I will try to speak to you as well as I can without insulting you." She answered, "I'm still very angry at you, but I will calm down. I appreciate very much the way you just spoke."

❖ They made little to no progress in marital therapy. Her complaints that he was selfishly involved with his own work interests and experiences had been validated by the therapist, and the lion's share of the therapy had gone to working with him in many individual sessions in addition to their couple sessions. The central goal of both their couple sessions and his individual sessions was for him to give up his insulting self-involvement and replace it with new interest, respect, and empathy for her.

But now, after he had in fact succeeded in making considerable correction of himself, a bigger problem had developed. No matter how much better he was, she was proving no less complaining and intractable than before. In effect she was insisting on her right to continue yelling her accusing despair at him as well as at their children. Repeatedly she would sweep out angrily from the couple therapy room, sometimes even before the session was over, repeating her depressing statements that he would never be a caring person.

Slowly but inexorably the clouds of potential divorce gathered intensely around the couple, and when it became obvious in the family circle that they could not create a peaceful environment, several members of their extended family—parents and siblings—were drawn into discussing concernedly whether or not the couple should break up. The husband had grown up in a home where all of the children had been considered superior beings, extensions of their mother's unduly high regard for herself. At the same time, this particular boy also had been buffeted with messages of being different and less satisfying than his siblings, so that inwardly he became genuinely confused between feeling special on the one hand and feeling disposable and rejected on the other hand. His resulting excessive self-involvement was all the more obstinate because he was also working hard to protect himself against the arrows of being unfavored and rejected by his wife.

The wife had grown up in an environment where family loyalty was the ultimate principle, and notwithstanding her brightness had barely developed a vestige of being able to see either of her parents or their family's system critically in any way. She was truly at her wits end facing the problems not only of her husband's selfishness but of many aspects of life for which she was not prepared as a sufficiently independent person, and much of her yearned to go back as a little girl to a home where all was whole and one was never subject to any criticism. The emotional dishonesties of both childhood homes were threatening to do in these two decent people in their adult marriage, where one or both were so often overly angry at one another.

OVERCOMING POLITICAL CORRECTNESS IN THE MENTAL HEALTH FIELD

A beautiful thing happened in American society some years ago when the people at large in a sense took over from the professionals defining what is considered acceptable and normal in human behavior, and applied a newly liberal standard that minimizes shaming people for being different or unattractive.

For all its good intentions, for some years the mental health field had defined pretty tightly what was "normal," "healthy," "mature," "successful," and so on—the positive adjectives of life to which all good people should aspire. It was not that many years ago that you needed to be slim, attractive, gainfully employed, successfully married—certainly not divorced—and possess other attributes of a well-ordered life in a house behind a picket fence if you wanted to be a winner in contemporary society. One certainly also had to be a heterosexual; you could forget about even trying to get into most elite circles if you had any known leanings toward being homosexual.

If you wanted to qualify for the real mental health nobility, you also needed to undergo psychoanalysis for purposes of becoming a wiser and more mature person, but this was entirely different from experiencing any manifest psychiatric disturbance or illness—certainly of the more grave psychiatric disturbances that could not be routinely treated by psychoanalysis. Thus, if you required mental hospitalization, or if you received physical kinds of treatments for your psychiatric problem, you definitely would be moved to the loser list. Naturally, millions of people didn't make it to the winner circles and were defined as "sick," "troubled," "problematic," "maladjusted," or something or other undesirable, and were treated as losers, failures, and ne'er-do-wells.

It is an understatement that people did not like being put in such a status and looked for opportunities to take the power of defining mentally healthy and unhealthy into their hands. These people protests were heartwarming in some ways insofar as they wanted to take the air out of the balloons of pretentiousness and superiority that were being worn by the ostensibly well-adjusted ones, and regain a viable status for the many millions of people who naturally want to live with basic self-respect despite imperfections and disabilities, let alone differences. Slowly but surely, peer and self-help movements developed for empowering and reconfirming the dignity, honor, and legitimacy of those who had mental problems or were different.

At first these moves remained anchored in the huge cultural transformations that had been achieved in the twentieth century, which defined mental conditions as "sicknesses" just like any other sickness, or even as "problems in living," and asserted that no shame, stigma, or devaluation was to be attached to these conditions. Fair enough, but unfortunately, over time the acceptance of people with problems was transferred into movements toward denying that there were *any* problems whatsoever in many of these conditions and ways of life. A prime example, especially in the United States, was the culture-wide insistence that there was to be no critique of obesity. Obese people were "simply" living out a natural physical course into which they were born. Besides, said many, fat people are jollier than slim people, so we have little right to criticize them. For years there were few critiques of obesity despite its obvious serious harm to health and serious price of reduced longevity. It was argued that people are as they are and what they are. Similarly destructive, fine self-help associations for different mental illnesses including schizophrenia or autism argued against most psychological causative sources, and especially against seeing sources and triggers of disturbance in families. In some areas, such as autism, there developed a virtual prohibition against citing the reports of intrepid therapists who reported significant cures or major improvement (e.g., Bruno Bettelheim,[26] Francis Tustin,[27] or Victor Sanua[28]).

Thus too, many homosexuals, male and female, including an amazing number of bisexuals who simultaneously conduct heterosexual and family lives "like everyone else" but spend some of their emotional and sexual times with homosexual partners, have become adamant that theirs are simply alternative lifestyles, and that in most cases their way of living was ordained by the mysteries of genetics and inborn dispositions and therefore cannot be faulted as wrong *choices*. This is the politically correct position in today's mental health circles. Any hint that homosexuality in some people is chosen rather than preordained will read you out of proper society. Even suggestions that for those for whom heterosexuality is a natural potential, and that learning to love the other sex is desirable for the development of a rich and mature personality—and not only for procreation (as long as this biological truth lasts, until babies become more "manufactured" than created)—will lead to tarring and feathering of the spokesman.

So, too, a once overwhelming insistence on a long-term marital status without divorce shifted not only to a progressive acceptance of divorce as a common fact of life, but in some circles of mental health practitioners there even developed a virtual insistence that unless you had been divorced at least once, you actually were remiss and lagging in your life experience and development.

In what I shall call the "new people's world," pretty much everyone is told that they should keep their heads high, that neither they nor their loved ones have anything to be ashamed of, that we are all fellow humans, and that no one is to be regarded as better than or worse than another. In my judgment, however, a constructive movement toward a greater cultural democracy replacing rigid thinking and over-certainty about attractiveness and normality with welcome changes releasing people from being shamed, humiliated, or stigmatized was now transformed into new over-certainties. Before long it had become politically incorrect to identify any of the above and other behaviors, too, as undesirable in any way whatsoever.

In fact, some of the once-disappointing conditions and ways of life now were elevated to be *more* desirable than remaining enslaved and trapped in a straight life that proceeds on a boring track of mainline conventionality (which is also translated into doing just what your mother and father and church always wanted you to do). In fact, in some communities and settings, the once deviant now became openly the favored and preferred. The once-welcome corrective movement toward greater respectful acceptance of people's differences and limitations now also invested itself with new demands for political power. Some New Age groups now demanded greater entitlement and power, and insisted on rising even to a superior position over the hapless straight and conventional persons.

Try each of the following, first of all for yourself, and secondly, take a look at how much you have encountered social consensus and even pressure in favor of each of these statements for better living:

- To be gay is more advanced and developed than to be heterosexual.
- To live in common-law relationships is more "free" than to be legally married.
- Drugs and anxiety-relieving medications will make you happier and healthier than worrying your way through life.
- Free kids from the shackles of discipline and let them be what they want to be.

- You may become an even more special person if you drop out of formal education—see Steve Jobs! Anyway it is your right not to go to school or care about grades.

The turning of the tables from rigid rights and wrongs paradoxically has brought on a new kind of fascist thinking and a political process that now casts other ways of life as the superior ways to live and lord over others. In various professional mental health circles, it has become progressively inappropriate, offensive, and for all practical purposes professionally and politically dangerous to say anything about many once-rejected behaviors as undesirable, unhealthy, or unattractive.

Another serious consideration is that the numbers of people who do live with various once-deviant conditions have been increasing very strongly. In recent years, for example, a *majority* of children in the United States are growing up in single-parent households. In many countries in Europe, the percentages of children born to unwed parents are very high—for example, already in 1999, 49 percent of all births in Norway, 62 percent in Iceland, and 38 and 41 percent, respectively, in Britain and France in 1998 were to unwed parents.[29] The actual statistics of homosexuality and bisexuality have remained unclear over the years, with widely differing reports and estimates, but there is a strong impression not only of greater openness about these ways of life but also of their increasing incidence.

With regard to weight, in the United States the number of people now defined by health authorities as *obese*—which is much more than being "overweight"—has reached the one out of three mark! At long last health authorities have become alarmed at the literal loss of years of life and the increase in deadly chronic conditions such as diabetes that result from obesity. But did it really have to take so long to recognize the ugly facts of losses of life and increasing likelihood of major illness to realize that obesity should not be ignored and should not be treated tolerantly per the protocols of political correctness? Obesity is a life-killing condition!

The fact that the incidence of any given trend may increase to the point that it is the majority can never be taken to mean that said trend is not injurious and regrettable. If obesity is associated with various illnesses such as increased risk of diabetes and a shortened life span, these facts of ill health do not change no matter if demographically obesity becomes widespread, or even the majority position in a given culture. I have often argued that the fact that most people were wiped out by a plague in whatever era did not transform that plague into a *normal* condition. If the goal of it all is to preserve and protect life, the plague remains an illness and a personal and public health problem that should certainly be labeled undesirable. Thus, any society in which AIDS becomes a condition of a majority of the people still will not transform AIDS from being what it is, a serious and life-shortening disease. A statistical "popularity" (frequency) of AIDS will not make it over into a social hit that ought to be sought out by all those who have not had the good fortune of contracting the disease.

It is sad, and to me maddening, how *a fascism of political correctness* has led mental health workers and students of the various helping disciplines of psychology, social work, medicine, counseling, psychiatry, and so on literally to be afraid to speak publicly, and then even to be afraid to think for themselves that being mentally ill, requiring biological psychiatric treatment, being obese, remaining or becoming unattached, or living a gay life if one is biologically and emotionally open to heterosexuality are *not* really desirable levels of emotional development and achievement for people. No, the above conditions are not at all equivalent. By no means are they all "illnesses." They are not all tragic or morbid. But they are all less than a desirable optimum of the safest and most mature ways of life—*especially in those cases where a healthier way of life still is within reach if efforts are made to do so.*

The above are not alternative lifestyle options that should be accepted unemotionally as tweedle-dee/tweedle-dum alternatives to good mental and physical health including a satisfying heterosexual way of life. Of course, in no way are any of these conditions "crimes," nor are they moral "failures." They should not be stigmatized, and certainly they should not lead to any suppressive "punishing" responses by governments or society. A cultural view of a way of living as less desirable does not mean shaming or oppressing individuals with such a lifestyle. Persons with different ways of life should be embraced fully with respect and encouraged, as is the case for all of us, to reach the best possible quality of life within their reach. But we should also know when a given way of life is not what we naturally seek or want to enable our children to "achieve" if there are possible alternatives.

There is a tense and as usual ever wonderfully productive dialectic between respectful acceptance of people as they are—very much including an awareness and acceptance of people who have no choice but to live a given lifestyle even if it is less than we would have hoped for them—and a capacity to keep a clear mind about the relative desirability and undesirability of different ways of living. It takes very hard work to arrive at a genuine synthesis of this dialectical tension so that one can look upon a person with acceptance and full respect and appreciation of their fine qualities while not surrendering the capacity to regret and think critically about what are indeed their limitations.

❖ "How do I respond to my twenty-year-old daughter smoking?" asks a health professional who knows what risks his daughter is incurring. "She's old enough to decide how she lives, and I know she was weakened by her mother's and my divorce when she was fourteen and that she needs the smoking, but I don't feel I am doing the right thing for her just standing by without trying to influence her to stop smoking." We agreed that the father would not allow his daughter to smoke in his home where no one else is allowed to smoke, and that he would tell her lovingly and forcefully that he strongly advises her to stop smoking, but not be harsh or make a pest out of himself.

❖ She had come a long way from her disturbed childhood in a home where mother was a brooding, worrying hawk hovering over her (especially her, but also others in the family) with a dark, despairing heaviness, and father was the sweet, distracted hanger-on to his wife who hinted of a warmer more flowing lovingness but which he could not really produce as long as he hung on to his wife being the central person in the family.

She grew up nervous, upset, with a great many dysphoric sad feelings about herself, as if slightly off-center all the time, with attacks of involuntary facial tics and relentless hair pulling that she tried to keep secret, even as she bravely was a good student and pushed herself to many moments of happiness in activities and relationships.

When she reached young adulthood, she breathed an enormous sigh of relief at finally being free to continue her life on her own away from her family. Although she cared about her family sensitively and even lovingly, she also hated them, especially mother, for the depression and self-remonstration in their family, and was very glad to be out of her childhood to continue her life on her own.

Not surprisingly, however, it wasn't all working out as well for herself as she hoped. Something "went wrong" in particular when she met young men. The only ones with whom a longer-term relationship seemed to develop turned out to be plain bastards—nasty and abusive personalities who would mock her and hold her in a bondage of being their insulted object and even sexual slave (to which she responded by never really getting pleasure out of sexual acts, which always seemed to her physically painful).

She had reached a point where she was convinced that she would never let herself get hooked up with another mean man when she met a lovely and sweet young man whom she really enjoyed. They genuinely liked each other and shared a good sense of humor and a delightful intellectual compatibility. She felt he loved her a lot, and she flourished in this experience. Her heart also went out to him with a considerable wish to nurture him. Even her experience in bed was slowly improving (although there were times when she still wished that they could spend the rest of her life just holding one another, which really gave her joy, without the penetration, which was still too painful for her though there was also a sense that the pain was lessening and might get better). The problem was that although he was very bright and even excelled in the world of his hobby activity, he disliked completing formal tasks, got bored in his studies and at work, and also was very cynical about long-term family life. In fact, he said he doubted he would ever marry, and he made an explicitly aggravating point of saying repeatedly that he never wanted children or in any other way to be "tied down." What he wanted was for the two of them "just" to continue their good experience of living together, perhaps even forever, but without saddling himself with formal marriage, the realities of family, or the responsibilities of work.

The tension in her grew, but most of all she held on to every one of the many moments of pleasure and caring between them to convince herself that someday it would all be alright. "Is it possible that the wounds you suffered in your childhood are leading you to accept less than a whole prospect for your adult life?" asked the therapist. "I know you care for him very much, and really wish to spend the rest of your life with him, but are you aware of the risk that you may never be able to be a mother with him? Unless he does a fair share of growing that you haven't been able to stimulate him to do so far, he may remain adamant about not having children. Do you think that it is in your best interest to settle for this unknown future that can very well end up being that you will never marry and never have children, and where you will always be the person who has to support the two of you?"

She broke up in wracking, despondent tears. "I didn't want to think about that," she said. "You are hurting me with your questions. I feel so confused."

"Would it be better for you if I did not ask these questions and we let the future unfold as it will, without keeping an eye on the timeline of your age, and you will make the best of whatever is?" countered the therapist. "I thought a lot about it before asking you, for I knew that I would be upsetting you very much. Was I wrong in doing so?"

CONCLUSION: ACCEPTING PEOPLE IN THEIR DIFFERENCES AND LIMITATIONS, BUT KEEPING ONE'S EYE ON TRUTH AND REALITY

Skills for personal and familial living extend across continua. There are noteworthy differences between basically irremediable limitations, failures to develop or limited development that are unlikely to improve even with today's available therapies, and other problems in development that are hopefully more accessible to correction and more complete skills development. Life calls for skills to cover a wide range of areas of human functioning, including development of one's intellectual potential, emotional potential, creativity, sexuality, emotional and mental stability, independence, leadership, and much more. The old-fashioned concepts of living in an attractively healthy body, achieving and maintaining a long-term intimate relationship with a person of the opposite sex, remaining free of manifest emotional disturbance and madness, and so on of healthy personal and family living are not wrong.

Of course, these concepts should not be taken as a basis for the creation of an elitist group. Moreover, the recognition that in the course of our lives *all of us* are prone to no small number of limitations, many of them quite major, should be a basis for humility and for a humanistic acceptance, appreciation, and respect for people in their various conditions and limitations. But the ability to talk straight and honestly to ourselves and to our children, or, for those of us who are professional therapists, to our clients, about maximizing the possibilities of development should not be lost. Our society should not suppress information about available scientific knowledge or cut off freedom of speech about the truths of our human condition. If one can sit taller and healthier in one's saddle, it is really preferable. It is important to be able to say so clearly, though also not disrespectfully, of those who ride differently.

> Before you speak, let your words pass through three gates. At the first gate, ask yourself, "Is it true?" At the second ask, "Is it necessary?" At the third gate ask, "Is it kind?"
>
> —*Sufi saying*

> Some of us think holding on makes us strong; but sometimes it is letting go.
>
> —*attributed to Herman Hesse*[30]

> A friend is one that knows you as you are, understands where you have been, accepts what you have become, and still, gently allows you to grow.
>
> —*Unknown*[31]

> The happiest moments of my life have been the few which I have passed at home in the bosom of my family.[32]
>
> —*Thomas Jefferson*

NOTES

1. Sprenkle, Douglas H. and Olson, David H. L. (1978). Circumplex model of marital systems: An empirical study of clinic and non-clinic couples. *Journal of Marriage and Family Counseling*, 4(2), 59–74; Olson, David H.; Sprenkle, Douglas H.; and Russell, Candyce S. (1979). Circumplex model of marital and family systems. 1. Cohesion and adaptability dimensions, family types, and clinical applications. *Family Process*, 18(1), 3–28.

2. Minuchin, Salvador. (1974). *Families and Family Therapy*. Cambridge MA: Harvard University Press; Minuchin, Salvador, and Fishman, H. Charles (1981). *Family Therapy Techniques*. Cambridge, MA: Harvard University Press; Minuchin, Salvador; Rosman, Bernice L.; and Baker, Lester (1978). *Psychosomatic Families: Anorexia Nervosa in Context*. Cambridge, MA: Harvard University Press.

3. Film: *Ordinary People*. Directed by Robert Redford. Written by Alvin Sargent. Based on the 1976 novel by Judith Guest. The film received six Academy Award nominations and won four awards including one for Best Picture.

4. Wynne, Lyman C.; Ryckoff, Irving M; Day, Juliana; and Hirsch, Stanley I. (1958). Pseudomutality in the family relations of schizophrenics. *Psychiatry*, 21, 205–220. Reprinted in Norman Bell and Ezra E. Vogel (Eds.) (1987). *A Modern Introduction to the Family*. New York: Free Press, 628–649. Published online by Routledge, January 8, 2015. http://www.tandfonline.com/doi/abs/10.1521/00332747.1958.11023128#.VP1r4tKUfAs. Retrieved March 9, 2015.

5. Lidz, Theoodore; Cornelison, Alice R; Fleck, Stephen; and Terry, Dorothy (1957). The intrafamilial environment of schizophrenic patients: II. Marital schism and marital skew. *American Journal of Psychiatry*, 114(3), 241–248. [Explanation—excerpted from the article: In

schismatic families the parents repeatedly threaten to separate; or one spouse seeks to coerce the other, and the parents derogate and undercut one another. In skewed couples the couples live in marriages that are badly distorted or "skewed" because serious psychopathology of the dominant parent is accepted or shared by the other.]

6. Wile, Daniel B. (1981). *Couples Therapy: A Nontraditional Approach*. New York: Wiley; Wile, Daniel B. (1988). *After the Honeymoon: How Conflict Can Improve Your Relationship*. New York: Wiley; Charny, Israel W. (1992). *Existential/Dialectical Marital Therapy, op. cit.*; Millon, Theodore (2011). *Disorders of Personality: Introducing a DSM/ICD Spectrum from Normal to Abnormal*. New York: Wiley.

7. Herman, Judith (1997). *Trauma and Recovery: The Aftermath of Violence: From Domestic Abuse to Political Terror*. Paperback New York: Basic Books; Trepper, Terry S. and Barrett, Mary Jo (1988). *Systemic Treatment of Incest: A Therapeutic Handbook*. New York: Psychology Press; Bass, Ellen and Davis, Laura (1988). *The Courage to Heal: A Guide for Women Survivors of Sexual Abuse*. Revised 20th anniversary edition 2008. New York: Collins Living.

8. Some contemporary statements minimize the bad effects of divorce on children; thus an article in *Scientific American* claims only 25 percent are damaged, subtract damages from other sources and it means "only" 15 percent are damaged. Arkowitz, Hal and Lilienfeld, Scott O. (February 14, 2013). Is Divorce Bad for Children? The breakup may be painful, but most kids adjust well over time. http://www.scientificamerican.com/article/is-divorce-bad-for-children/.

For a compilation of more painful statistics, see Children Divorce Statistics (2013). www.children-and-divorce.com/children-divorce-statistics.html. Retrieved March 3, 2015. The classic study of children of divorce was by Wallerstein, Judith S. and Kelly, Joan B. (1980). *Surviving the Breakup: How Children and Parents Cope with Divorce*. New York: Basic Books; Wallerstein, Judith S. and Blakeslee, Sandra (1989). *Second Chances: Men, Women, and Children a Decade after Divorce*. New York: Ticknor & Fields.

Personally, as a father of children of divorce and as a therapist, I have seen too much injury deep in children's hearts even when they grow up to be perfectly functioning adults to all appearances, but I also agree that some children of divorce make their way in their emotional lives successfully.

9. Vogel, Ezra F. and Bell, Norman W. (1960). The emotionally disturbed child as the family scapegoat. *Psychoanalytic Review*, 47, 21–42. Reprinted in Norman Bell and Ezra E. Vogel (Eds.) (1987). *A Modern Introduction to the Family, ibid.* Gardner, Richard A.; Sauber, S. Richard; and Lorandos, Demosthenes (Eds.) (2003). *The International Handbook of Parental Alienation Syndrome: Conceptual, Clinical and Legal Considerations*. Springfield, IL: Charles C. Thomas.

10. One of the most fascinating aspects of systemic study of families as whole units is the consideration that a family member who ostensibly does not know of the victimization of another family member may very well be knowledgeable but deny that knowledge consciously. Thus, I suggested years ago that in the biblical story of the sacrifice of Isaac by his father, Isaac's mother, Sarah, knew fully in her heart what was to transpire when Abraham went to take Isaac off to sacrifice him, and that she too carried responsibility for not intervening. *Heresy? Suspiciously anti-religious?* I found any number of legends by the rabbis in the wonderful world of Jewish legends (Midrash) that stated the very same about Sarah! Charny, Israel W. (1973). And Abraham went to slay Isaac: A parable of killer, victim and bystander in the family of man. *Journal of Ecumenical Studies*, 4(3), 304–318.

Similarly, there is a growing body of clinical literature in our time about incest, which observes that mothers often know when their husbands are having incestuous relationships with their daughters, but deny their conscious knowledge even as unconsciously they are delivering the daughter to their husband.

11. Charny, Israel W. (1982). Sacrificing others to the death we fear ourselves. In *How Can We Commit the Unthinkable? Genocide, the Human Cancer, op cit.*, 185–211.

12. *Ibid*; See also the wise probing works of R.D. Laing that were previously cited and also Laing, R.D. (1970). *Knots*. London: Penguin; and Laing, R.D. (1971). *The Politics of the Family and Other Essays*. London: Tavistock.

13. Charny, Israel W. (1980). Recovery of two (largely) autistic children through renunciation of maternal destructiveness in integrated individual and family therapy. In Lewis R. Wolberg and Marrvin. L. Aronson (Eds.), *Group and Family Therapy 1980*. New York: Brunner/Mazel, 250–281.

I am of course fully aware that interpretations of any cases of autism (there should not be a claim that it is *all* cases) that relate the condition in any way to parental influences have been roundly rejected and defined as heresy and parent bashing. My own experience says otherwise, and certainly the two cases I report—with full documentation of the original condition so that there is no doubt about the diagnosis of autism—stand on their own truthful reality. (Forty years later I am still in direct contact with one of these children and his parents. There is no doubt that there is a restriction of his personality and his need to be in a protective community, but there is also no doubt of his steady high functioning in a professional position in the world outside his community and a level of satisfaction with his life in general.) This paper was originally given in its entirety to all four of the children's parents for critical review, all of whom gave their confirmation of its accuracy and approval of publication. It was also reviewed critically by five very senior child psychiatrists—two of whom were experts in treatment of autistic children and one of whom was well known as an expert in treatment of schizophrenic children.

The following are publications by two iconic therapists from the old days who, it is important to note, used different techniques of treatment than one another, but in both cases concentrated on relationships, and both reported significant treatment successes: Bettelheim, Bruno (1967). *The Empty Fortress: Infantile Autism and the Birth of the Self*. New York: Free Press; Tustin, Frances (1992). *Autistic States in Children*. New York: Science House. Successful outcomes such as they reported should not be dismissed, but note how these publications are almost always omitted from the contemporary (politically correct) literature on autism, I believe because they convey an unacceptable message that therapists can work (agonizingly hard) at bringing about a significant degree of repair. I have never accepted the blanket condemnation of Bettelheim (whom I also knew somewhat and was aware of his tough-rough personality but respected his daring and therapeutic power) and the discrediting of all his so-meaningful work. Tustin, on the other hand, was an entirely respected and even beloved figure in UK mental health circles, and there are still continuing professional activities in her name in the UK, but she too is rarely ever cited by today's authorities on autism, certainly not in the United States.

14. Personally I have come to a conclusion-hypothesis that just about any intensive investment in helping autistic children without considering them lost causes has a possibility of bringing about beneficial growth, the more so when it is the child's two parents who carry a major role in the treatment work with their children. This is also the lens through which I view, and appreciate, reports of growth in autistic children whose parents dedicate themselves

not to psychodynamic issues but to protocols of behavior retraining, and in my view in the process quite likely convey to their child deep caring and positive expectation. I can never forget an amazing article that appeared in the *Archives of General Psychiatry* about two cases in remote places in Australia who were visited by public health nurses who reported the recovery of the children "without treatment," which meant treatment by professionals, even as they described brilliant therapeutic regimes created and implemented by the parents themselves to break up the autistic symptoms and create a holding-loving environment for the child: Gajzago, Christine and Prior, Margot (1974). Two cases of "recovery" in Kanner syndrome. *Archives General Psychiatry*, 31(2), 264–268.

15. There is perhaps a gender issue here, too, in that for many years women have been the first to initiate requests for therapy, whether for marriages or for a child, rather than their husbands. What many women were saying, in effect, is that their husbands are not carrying their fair share of the emotional work of worrying about and making a meaningful contribution to emotional relationships in the family. One psychiatrist, Joseph C. Rheingold, observed that men generally are hopeless as fathers. Rheingold, Joseph C. (1964), *The Fear of Being a Woman: A Theory of Maternal Destructiveness, op. cit.* I hope he is wrong, but I do know that whenever it is a husband/father who makes the initial request for therapy for a child, I have learned to feel more hopeful. It will be a matter of curiosity and interest in our times, when so many more divorces—at times, even a majority—are initiated by wives, and with the subsequent increasing reversals of gender roles in families, whether more requests for therapy will come from husbands/fathers.

16. Masters, William H. and Johnson, Virginia C. (1970), *Human Sexual Inadequacy, op. cit.*

17. Freud, Sigmund [1952–1974]. *The Complete Works of Sigmund Freud.* (24 volumes). London: Hogarth [reprinted in various partial and whole editions including Charleston, SC: BiblioBazaar, 2007].

18. Abraham, Karl (1957). Ejaculatio praecox, *op.cit.*

19. Kaplan, Helen (1974). *The New Sex Therapy, op. cit.* Some notable recent works on sex therapy are the following: Brotto, Lori A. and Barker, Meg (Eds.) (2015). *Mindfulness in Sexual and Relationship Therapy.* New York: Routledge; Hertlein, Katherine M.; Weeks, Gerald R.; and Gambescia, Nancy (Eds.) (2015). *Systemic Sex Therapy.* 2nd Edition. New York: Routledge; Ogden, Gina (Ed.) (2015). *Extraordinary Sex Therapy: Creative Approaches for Clinicians.* New York: Routledge.

20. Charny, Israel W. (1992). Marital sexuality: Joyful and loving sexuality versus "good marriages" with no sex and "bad marriages" with good sex. In *Existential/Dialectical Marital Therapy, op. cit.*, 199–219.

21. Bergman, Ingmar (1973). Film: *Scenes from a Marriage.* The TV version of *Scenes from a Marriage* is almost five hours long, split into six episodes. In the United States, a 167-minute version was released in cinemas. The film won BAFTA and Golden Globe nominations for Liv Ullmann (Best Actress—Motion Picture Drama) and a Best Foreign Language Film.

22. Gottman, John with Nan Silver (1999). *The Seven Principles for Making Marriage Work.* New York: Three Rivers Press; Gottman, John (2011). *The Science of Trust: Emotional Attunement for Couples.* New York: Norton; Gottman, John and Silver, Nan (2012). *What Makes Love Last: How to Build Trust and Avoid Betrayal.* New York: Simon & Schuster.

23. Charny, Israel W. (1992). *Existential/Dialectical Marital Therapy, ibid.*

24. Good marital fighting is described variously in many works: Bach, George R. and Wyden, Peter (1969). *The Intimate Enemy: How to Fight Fair in Love and Marriage.* New

York: Morrow; Charny, Israel W. (1972). *Marital Love and Hate: The Need for a Revised Marriage Contract and a More Honest Offer by the Marriage Counselor to Teach Couples to Love and Hate, Honor and Dishonor, Obey and Disobey.* New York: Macmillan. See also Charny, Israel W. (1992). *Existential/Dialectical Marital Therapy, ibid.*; Gordon, Lori H. (1990). *Love Knots: How to Untangle those Everyday Frustrations that Keep You from Being with the One You Love.* New York: Dell; Gordon, Lori with Frandsen, Jon (1999). *Passage to Intimacy: Key Concepts and Skills from the Pairs Program Which Has Helped Thousands of Couples Rekindle Their Love).* New York: Fireside Books; Wile, Daniel B. (1988). *After the Honeymoon: How Conflict Can Improve Your Relationship, ibid.*; and Blumberg, Susan L. (2010). *Fighting for Your Marriage: A Deluxe Revised Edition of the Classic Best-Seller for Enhancing Marriage and Preventing Divorce.* 3rd Edition. San Francisco, Jossey-Bass.

25. Two current conclusions taken from the Web about the necessity of marital fighting, both of which place a major emphasis on how the couples end their fights, are the following:

The famous TV psychologist (and I think professionally sound), Dr. Phil gives the *Dr. Phil's Rules for Fighting.* "Fighting is a part of any relationship. You are not ever going to merge or share your life with someone and not have conflict. It's not whether you fight that's going to determine the success or failure of your relationship; it's how you fight. More specifically, it's how you end a fight. We have found that if you know one thing about a couple you can predict with great accuracy whether they're going to get a divorce or whether they're not, and that one thing is how they end a fight."—Dr. Phil, http://www.drphil.com/articles/article/161.

The famous researcher of couples, John Gottman, doesn't exactly teach how to fight but does, importantly, teach how *not* to fight with insults and blaming. Moreover, he too offers the conclusion that some fighting is desirable: "Gottman has found in this research that fighting in and of itself is not the problem. In fact, couples who do not fight at all are more likely to end up divorced . . . The best bet is to teach [couples] how to recover after a fight." John Gottman's Couples Training Institute, http://couplestraininginstitute.com/gottman-couples-and-marital-therapy/. Gottman Couples and Marital Therapy. Retrieved October 10, 2014.

26. Bettelheim, Bruno (1967). *The Empty Fortress, ibid.* See also a fascinating book about the history of psychotherapeutic engagement of autism including a complex report of the so-complex Bettelheim who is alternately described by some people as having profound empathy, and by others as being a brutal hurting person—and by some simultaneously as both. Feinstein, Adam (2010). *A History of Autism: Conversations with the Pioneers.* New York: Wiley-Blackwell. Feinstein quotes Jacqueline Sanders "who took over from Bettelheim as director of the Orthogenic School in 1973 . . . What Bruno wrote and said wasn't actually what he believed. I sat with him when he talked to parents, and there was no one who could match his empathy. There were some parents who were terrified of him and others who were totally devoted to him" (quotation on p. 74).

27. Tustin, Frances (1992). *Autistic States in Children, ibid.* See also Gerhardt, Sue (2006). Why love matters: How affection shapes a baby's brain? *Infant Observation: International Journal of Infant Observation and Its Applications,* 9(3), 305–309; see also the Frances Tustin Memorial Trust, http://www.frances-tustin-autism.org/eng/main.php. On this site Tustin is quoted as saying (1986): "There is a saying that 'It is better to light one small candle than to go on cursing the darkness.' It has been my privilege to light one small candle to shed its light on the dark scene of psychogenic autism. With my advantages and opportunities, it would have been a professional dereliction not to attempt to do so."

28. The late Victor Sanua, a psychologist at the autism center at St. John's University, told me (personal communication) how time after time his publications, which also promoted a

psychological view of many cases of autism, were rejected a priori by professional publications. See Sanua, Victor D. (1983). Infantile autism and childhood schizophrenia: Review of the issues from the sociocultural point of view. *Social Science and Medicine*, 17, 1633–1651; Sanua, Victor D. (1984). Is infantile autism a universal phenomenon? An open question. *International Journal of Social Psychiatry*, 30(3), 163–177; Sanua, Victor D. (1989). Studies in infantile autism. *Child Psychiatry and Human Development*, 19(3), 207–227; Sanua, Victor D. (1986). The organic etiology of infantile autism: a critical review of the literature. *International Journal of Neuroscience*, 30(3), 195–225; and Sanua, Victor D. (1990). Leo Kanner (1894–1981): The man and the scientist. *Child Psychiatry and Human Development*, 21(1), 3–23.

29. Lyall, Sarah (2002). To more Europeans, love doesn't mean marriage. *New York Times*, March 25.

30. Quotation is widely attributed to Herman Hesse, but no source is found even on sites with sources of other Hesse quotations.

31. Quotation is widely attributed to Shakespeare, but no source is found. Any number of reviewers adamantly protest that this is not Shakespeare's writing, but do not know what is the source.

32. The Jefferson Monticello. University of Virginia. Extract from Thomas Jefferson to Francis Willis, April 18, 1790.

3

Neurosis, Depression, and Suicide Revisited

Traditional Disorders of Neurosis, Depression, and Suicide Revisited with a Democratic Mind Metaphor

THE NEUROTIC DISORDERS: UNDERSTANDABLE ASSUMPTIONS GONE AWRY AND EXTREME

Neurotic disorders refer to an intriguing variety of symptomatic conditions as well as to styles of life (see discussion of "neurotic styles" later) that intrude on a person's ability to enjoy and relax in a normal exercise of life.

These conditions are especially noteworthy when an individual is *not* suffering any objective major deprivation or stress such as in times of war, famine, or economic hardship, and is not suffering a major or personal loss, and *should* be able to enjoy a good quality of life yet cannot. In neurotic disorders the patient suffers, variously, nameless intrusions of anxiety or hypervigilance and emotional reactivity; or troubling interferences in normal body functions, despite the fact that no disease is present; or the mind is overtaken and held captive by repetitive ideas and/or compulsive behaviors that the patient feels helpless to fight; or the patient is paralyzed in a phobic inability to participate in one or another arena of life that feels so dangerous as to preclude the risk of participating in it.

Some years ago, the American Psychiatric Association's *Diagnostic and Statistical Manual of Mental Disorders (DSM)* dropped the word *neurosis* from its lexicon. *Poof*—the classic word was gone. The word does not even appear in the index to the book, and no explanation is given of the relationship of the newly named "disorders" (which have replaced "neurosis") to the so-rich literature about neuroses that was created by great psychiatric and psychotherapeutic pioneers in the twentieth century.[1]

However, notwithstanding the *DSM* injunctions against the "old-fashioned" concept of neurotic disorders, I am inclined—as are many other students of psychopathology and practicing therapists—to continue using this descriptively rich term, whose meanings are anchored in a precious literature of classical psychoanalytic-psychodynamic explorations of the mind over the span of a wonderful century of learning so much about our human minds. In general, I have the feeling that it makes more sense to look for treatments and solutions to most "neuroses" in the mind or in the ways that people organize their life experiences. In contrast to the "neuroses," the new "disorders" invite and support much more an approach of prescribing biochemical agents to change how a person feels and behaves physiologically, rather than how they are conducting themselves emotionally and thoughtfully as people.

A prime question about neuroses has always been how and why the patient brings such punishment on themselves. Dozens of answers have been advanced by different theorists: a flight from guilt-provoking libidinal-sexual or other pleasure impulses[2]; anxiety over lack of confidence in one's adequacy[3]; fears of loss of connection to significant others[4]; guilt over hostile impulses and uncharitably aggressive behaviors[5]; and succumbing to conditioning of fearful or avoidant responses to opportunity and challenge.[6] What these explanations have in common is that they all place the patient in the grips of *some rigid underlying paradigm of mind which they cannot shake off.*[7]

Psychologist Barry Wolfe gives examples of various "existential" dilemmas that can be the focus of what he calls the "self-wounds" that underlie anxiety disorders:

- Difficulty accepting one's mortality
- Difficulty accepting the inevitability of loss
- Difficulty accepting personal responsibility for one's thoughts, feelings, and actions
- Difficulty tolerating painful affects
- Difficulty facing the loss of a life plan that has been destroyed
- Fear of committing one's life to another human being

Wolfe described his model for treating anxiety disorders based on identifying the specific "self-wounds" that are feeding a given patient's disorder. Thus he describes how one patient suffering from panic disorder discovered that their self-wound was associated with their terror about growing old. Another patient suffering from obsessive-compulsive disorder discovered his terror was that "his intrusive violent thoughts would result in his causing harm to a loved one." A patient who was phobic about public speaking traced their symptom to an "inability to tolerate humiliation and failure."[8]

Failing the absolute test of conforming to their own self-imposed absolute ideas, the neurotic person then must suffer self-administered rituals of punishment such as they may be in their mind. While the suffering that is engendered is very unpleasant, and the patient may seek various ways to contain their suffering and overcome its quite real limitations on their life, it has been no small secret for many years that there are also secret pleasures that can accompany many such self-inflicted wounds.

In many of the theories that have been advanced, the focus is mainly on the *contents* of the paradigm (e.g., fears of separation and loss of relationships, or fears of excessively intense hostility toward others), which keeps the patient trapped, rather than on the *structure* or methods of experiencing (e.g., insisting on perfect success and adherence to one's idea and goal and vowing to destroy any opposition to one's truth). Our conception of Democratic Mind also relates to the fact that along with the contents of the mind, what is no less significant is the structural prison into which the patient is locked by their *total, unquestioning obedience to a guiding thought or model that dictates the way they must live, achieve, be, and appear.*

Renowned and ever-productive psychologist Albert Ellis[9] pioneered in identifying several basic mind fallacies—or wrong methods of organizing experience—that underlie the development of neurotic symptoms. Among these are the patient's absolute conviction that they must be loved by everybody in order to feel good; the belief that one must be adequate and successful in all of one's undertakings and not make mistakes or, perish the thought, fail; or the belief that one must always feel good and free of tension and anxiety. Ellis has shown how the irrational ideas that neurotic patients impose on themselves hold them in a locked grip from which there is no exit. So that even when one is actually doing everything up to royal snuff, there will be painful bursts of neurotic symptoms that make it impossible to enjoy one's good performance for fear that the next performance will indeed prove flawed. The person is in constant fear of the *possible* occurrence or reoccurrence of the fear they have placed at the center of their lives, such as experiencing being disliked or disapproved by someone, or doing badly in a particular task.

Another consideration is that while patients' conscious complaints are likely sincere and by no means should be disrespected, their unconscious pleasure and gratification at their own suffering may very well be the stronger force. In the language of our present model of a Democratic Mind, it can be said that much of the suffering may be celebrated in one's inner mind as a demonstration of loyalty to the nameless higher cause to whose absoluteness and certainty the patient is committed. I think this language really is not that different from what many classical psychiatrists and psychologists have noted brilliantly about the patient being enamored and even addicted to their suffering, but I am adding that the patient also gives themselves strokes for staying true-blue to a selected guiding personal ideology.

Each of the neurotic syndromes is its own sub-variant of the overall paradigmatic error of subscribing to a belief that some conditions of life *must* be fulfilled. Each human being who suffers a neurotic condition in effect has written their own software version of a basic paradigm, or an inner law, that is mandated by the highest authorities of one's mind, and that decrees that any violation or deflection from the absolute truth will be met with swift and powerful measures to bring the errant person back into place.

Thus, many people, including many of those who actually do become very successful, entertain strong ambitions for their work achievement. Medical psychology has identified a *Type-A personality*, where pressure to achieve work goals is expressed in nervousness, restlessness, agitation, and various psychosomatic symptoms of stress, and is known to heighten possibilities of heart attacks and strokes—a tough price to pay for what should be pleasurable additions to one's quality of life and not life-threatening hardships. Driven people demand of themselves that they must achieve whatever goal by whatever time and at whatever level of excellence. The possible experience of *enjoying* working well at a high level of quality is driven away by a burdensome and pressuring intensity of requirement and obligation. Lost are the grace and pleasure of expressing talent and skillfulness with a sense of satisfaction at one's good quality of work. Instead there is a driven obligation to perform and intimidating threats of reprisals if one fails to produce.

> ❖ He is beside himself with disquieting hyperemotional responses. He sits poised and tense as he speaks, and his bright rhetoric comes fast and sharp like a cutting knife. He reports that during the day at the university he needs to go to a bathroom to masturbate, and that he generally masturbates three separate times a day. He simply has to do so, he explains.
>
> He is a writer who is working on what he says must become the century's greatest novel. No, he cannot be satisfied with writing a good book and hoping it will be well received. It has to be recognized as the outstanding work of its time. I asked to read his manuscript when it was near completion and found that it was genuinely exciting (although I wouldn't have any idea if it could beat out every other novel in the century), but, intriguingly, it was fine writing only up to the last chapter. To my mind this last chapter, where the story of the novel has to be brought to its conclusion, was poorly developed and poorly written, even to a point of being "crazy" and not true to life. In contrast to all the preceding chapters in the book, which I found excellent, this final chapter was even aesthetically distasteful to me.

Had the writer been driven by his unconscious issues to destroy his very good novel, I wondered? I thought so. The writer's megalomanic insistence, "I have to be the best," was coming back at him in a boomerang that spoiled his strongly talented start.

NEUROTIC LIFESTYLES

The truth is that neuroses are really incorrect lifestyles, but what happens is that the dramatic symptoms that blossom forth from these ill-advised lifestyles are often so "medically" dramatic that attention is drawn to the syndrome of symptoms more than to the problematic lifestyle.

As long as there are florid symptoms of disquiet and suffering, the clinical picture "invests" practicing mental health professionals with the right to issue a clinical diagnosis of one of the neuroses or whatever "disorder" they are called in today's psychiatry. Nonetheless, the real and larger significance is in the underlying style of organizing life. The conditions creating the symptoms generally are an overall way of thinking and organizing oneself that can be characterized in the metaphoric language of this book as Fascist Mind paradigms, such as you must be outstandingly successful or you will be a dismal failure, or you must not be too happy or uninhibited especially when so-and-so in your life is suffering so much.

Some of the wonderful classicists in psychiatry suggested many years ago that authentic diagnosis of neuroses should not necessarily await the breaking out of actual symptoms, but should be applied as early as possible once it was clear that the patient was living according to what we call in today's language an *incorrect model*—driving too hard for success, feeling superior to others, being too fearful to be self-assertive, denying oneself various pleasures of body or experience—whatever the guiding distortion in the Mind template. Shapiro[10] and others have described how neurotic syndromes are often represented in *overall styles of life* that deserve to be defined as *neurotic lifestyles*. At any given point, these do not necessarily involve palpable symptoms that will qualify for a definition of disability in the conventional clinical-psychiatric sense, yet they already exert an overall inhibitory or even paralyzing impact on the day-to-day functioning, pleasure, and fulfillment of the individual:

- The hysterical personality wards off huge segments of information about life, making oneself so much a simpleton who dares not see, hear, or taste the forbidden apple of life and knowledge.
- The obsessional or compulsive personality diddle-daddles, obfuscates, complicates, and messes up. The possibilities of joy are pushed off beyond reach by deadening ambivalences and indecision. Affection and love are cut off by simmering thoughts of dissatisfaction, secret hates, and magical thoughts of deadly retaliation.
- The phobic personality creates a way of life of avoidance of feared places and events and forgoes major areas of being and doing.

Another way of defining the overall neurotic lifestyle is on the basis of identifying the key wrong idea or wrong approach to life, such as we saw earlier. Here is an additional formulation by the beloved psychoanalyst Karen Horney in her sensitive book, *Self-Analysis*:[11]

Horney outlines ten neurotic needs:

1. The neurotic need for affection and approval
2. The neurotic need for a partner who will take over one's life
3. The neurotic need to restrict one's life within narrow borders
4. The neurotic need for power
5. The neurotic need to exploit others
6. The neurotic need for prestige
7. The neurotic need for personal admiration
8. The neurotic need for personal achievement
9. The neurotic need for self-sufficiency and independence
10. The neurotic need for perfection and unassailability

The overall neurotic paradigm is all too clear: The mind-gods deny their subject a fullness of knowledge, love, and the power of the good life, and the gods generally are stipulating that one must achieve a defined goal—such as perfection or success—or suffer. In each case the neurosis rests on the patient's specific paradigmatic construction to which they remain devotedly loyal.

ANXIETY DISORDERS

The experience of anxiety states is well known: A person's motor, so to speak, speeds up to a point that feels like a frightening loss of control. The person feels pulled out of the ability to stay normally concentrated on life tasks and into a diffuse sense of tension, alertness to an impelling imminent danger, and an inner feeling of being terrified. An anxiety state is a state of obvious symptomatic malaise which clearly calls for help, and people flock in varying states or degrees of anxiety disorders to ask for relief from their physicians and mental health practitioners, as well as other sources of counseling or spiritual comfort.

The specific symptoms of anxiety disorders are dramatic and palpable, and include various configurations of an impressive variety of torturous experiences: palpitations, pounding heart or accelerated heartbeat, sweating, trembling or shaking, sensations of shortness of breath, choking, or a feeling of being smothered, a sense of loss of control of one's breathing, chest pain or discomfort, nausea or abdominal distress, dizziness, unsteadiness, lightheadedness, fainting, restlessness or feeling keyed up or on edge, being easily fatigued, difficulty concentrating or mind going blank, irritability, body muscle tensions, sleep disturbances (difficulty falling or staying asleep or having restless, unsatisfying sleep), derealization (feelings of unreality) or depersonalization (being detached from oneself), fear of losing control or going crazy, fear of dying, numbness or tingling sensations (paresthesias), chills, or hot flashes.

For some patients, anxiety attacks are enhanced by agoraphobia or anxiety about being in places or situations from which escape might be difficult or embarrassing, or in which help may not be available in the event of a panic attack. Agoraphobic fears typically involve characteristic situations for a given individual such as being outside the home alone, being in a crowd or standing in a line, being on a bridge, traveling in a bus, train, automobile, or plane, or being in a given social or social-professional situation.

❖ My personal reason for going for psychoanalysis beginning when I was in graduate school was severe anxiety attacks with uncontrollable sweating, which embarrassed me very much especially in professional meetings—and God forbid that I myself would have to be a speaker. It took two sequences of psychoanalysis, together over close to eight years, to get over my symptoms, but ever since then I have enjoyed fully participating in professional meetings and have had a wonderful time becoming a sought-after speaker in many places around the world.

A generalized anxiety disorder is defined in the *DSM* as excessive anxiety, worry, and apprehensive expectations about a number of events or activities such as work or school performance that has been occurring on more days than not for at least six months.

The suffering of the patient is indeed evident. Since there are generally any number of somatic expressions and experiences of suffering in several forms of the anxiety disorders, there is a natural tendency for many people to *think in medical terms* about the condition and its treatment. The medical orientation to anxiety disorders is clear: These are runaway physiological functions, and medication can be used to reduce, control, or contain them. The medical position is in its own way correct that even if the source of the runaway physiological functions is psychological, the panic and aggravation caused by the processes add enormously to the anxiety, and control of these symptoms in itself *will* reduce the person's anxiety and perhaps give one a better chance to overcome the personal sources of fright. On the other hand, it is also intuitively clear in most cases that these are disorders of the spirit and mind of the person, which are being expressed by the body in its continuation of and linkage to the mind, and are not basically produced by the body as its own illness, so to speak, and that if possible correcting the problem in the mind goes more to the core of the problem in its real origin.

Of course, when the patient's suffering of anxiety is too intense, *some* use of medication to reduce the immediate overwhelming quality of panic or anxiety is humane and wise. Insofar as a person is swamped by anxiety and suffering terribly, the treating professional needs to be sensitive to the pain and terror that the person is experiencing. Insofar as the patient needs help beyond their own immediately available ability to reorganize themselves, some external devices can be utilized, such as low doses of a tranquilizer, to cut the edges of overly distressful anxiety, but my recommendation is *not* heavy dosages aiming at suppressing the anxiety entirely. Certainly one should avoid the telltale doses one sees in the hollow-eyed people who have been left zombied out by massive doses of psychotropic medication, no longer able to be in contact with their real selves even if they wanted to. The reduction of panic should be to help patients organize themselves to begin the work of counseling or therapy in which, hopefully, they will relearn their guiding ideas and refill their hearts with greater love of life. This point of view is a far cry from relying on medications to do the job instead of helping the patient to do the job of reexamining their basic ideas and emotions. The main purpose of treatment is to put the person back into better contact with their own real self, desires, and potential.

Metaphorically, one can say that a Fascist Mind will tend to see anxiety not only as a discomforting symptom that needs to be suppressed so that people can be comfortable, but as representative of unrest, dissension, and a breakdown of the control and discipline that are required inside an individual. Since the purpose of fascist organization is to achieve perfect control and unquestioned organization of self toward a given goal, anxiety needs to be knocked out of existence. Over and over again, I have seen mental health institutions treat anxiety almost as a kind of insult and attack on mental health practitioners, and then the Establishment clinicians go to crazy lengths to stop the anxiety—for example, mega-medication, electric shock, and also recommendations to the patient to withdraw from life's challenges and experiences. Operating from this point of view, the preferred forms of treatment are going to be the interventions that suppress anxiety and end it. In the old *Cuckoo Nest* days, some anxious patients were sent for lobotomies! In truth their anxiety meant they were potentially closer to being helped in relationship therapies than patients who were not anxious, and the suppressive "therapy" of the lobotomy killed the possibility.

The further irony here is that, in the metaphor of this book, it is a fascist mindset to begin with that has "sentenced" the self to nervousness and agitation for failing to live in the one correct way that was prescribed or to produce what one was required to produce, and then the patient is subject to no less fascist-like controls to suppress his anxiety and real self. The various punishing anxiety symptoms befall the patient because they have violated certain absolute requirements. The anxiety is a panicked sense of catastrophe that a standard that has been commanded is not being achieved. But the treatments themselves continue the fascist point of view by seeking to suppress the anxiety so that the person is better able to fall into the ranks, suppress their real selves, and do what they are supposed to do.

On the other hand, an approach to treatment that is based on a democratic metaphor will seek symptom reduction through fulfillment and expansion of the personality. The psychological treatment of neurotic disorders to help the personality expand toward its real self includes cognitive-behavior management, or the reshaping of thinking and behavior, which states quite correctly that a person in a panic should slow down, attempt to identify the source of their panic, and revise their thinking to free themselves of misconceptions that may be forcing them into feeling so overwhelmed. Thus if we look once more at the concepts pioneered by cognitive psychologist Albert Ellis, in what he called "rational-emotive therapy," he explained much of anxiety as focusing on ideas such as I must always be loved; I must always succeed; I dare not fail; I cannot bear to be embarrassed; I must always appear well in the eyes of others; and so on.[12] Ellis' rational-emotive therapy teaches people how to give up these driving ideas of absolutes. His work showed that at any given point, proper application of a correction of the absolute idea will relieve major sources of anxiety for many people. The correction of anxiety disorders is therefore best done not simply by medical reduction of the symptoms of anxiety through medication, but by correcting the way of thinking. Correction of the incorrect totalistic and over-certain idea is generally expected to be effective treatment, and in many cases this is true to a significant extent.

❖ I remember as a young therapist when I learned to use effectively the intriguing cognitive techniques I learned from Ellis. A young man who came to see me was at home at the beginning of his summer vacation from college, and his plan was to return to college a little less than three months later. He was in terrible shape: depressed, suicidal, and confused, including some disorganized thinking that suggested the possibility of a developing psychotic condition.

> Obviously he was not at all in shape for the psychoanalytic type of therapy I was mostly trained to do in those days, and in any case obviously there was very little time available to help if he was to go back to college in the fall. The rational-emotive techniques seemed like a wise way to organize the therapy, and they indeed proved very helpful in quieting the young man down and helping him to go back to school.

Democratic Mind treats anxiety from a broad perspective of helping a person grow and become what they *really* want to become, especially in respect of fulfillment of one's unused potential for self-expansion, achievement, and creativity, and for growth in intimate relationships and the ability to love and be committed. If not debilitating, anxiety is viewed as an ever-welcome call of self-expressing dissatisfaction, questioning, and searching, processes that are to be honored and encouraged. If these processes are tolerated and developed respectfully, they will lead to new resolutions and choices through which the person will organize their behaviors differently, and the anxiety as a statement of not knowing how and what to do with oneself will be reduced accordingly.

This is a frame of reference that leads to more natural mind-based cures, both cognitive-behavioral and psychodynamic, not through suppression of anxiety but through working with the anxiety respectfully and even appreciatively. In designing treatment of anxiety states, suppressive behavioral regimes such as hospitalization, giving up a job, giving up a love relationship, or even the tried-and-true device of sending the patient on vacation are avoided as much as possible. Decisions need to be made not for purposes of blindly simplifying life, but on the basis of getting more closely in touch with what one really wants to do and how and what one really feels. For therapists who are of a persuasion that one needs to look more deeply at the inner spirit and "way of being in this world" from which a person's mindsets spring, the course of treatment is necessarily a longer one and involves getting to the inner wellsprings of self-love and self-confidence, emptying them of poisons—such as the accumulated hurts of being hated by a loved one such as a parent, as well as the poisons of hating others too much—and refilling the wells with fresh waters of self-love, love by others, and love of others.

The point of view that I use in treatment of excessive anxiety is based on a combination of several steps. The first step is to listen for immediate pain and loss in the patient's life—say the death of a loved one, being rejected by a lover, or a major failure and shame in one's life. However, often enough there is no such traumatic material awaiting catharsis, and the suffering patient has no immediate idea what to talk about.

Another important entry point into the patient's life is to go looking for the objects of their inner anger and hate. This probe is based on the consideration that anxiety often involves an overflow of hate and rage at sources of oppression in one's life, and that an overflow of anger may be causing much of the anxiety to begin with. In addition, the very suffering of the patient will naturally lead to further anger and rage over the very fact that they are suffering so much. Therefore, along with reassuring the patient that anxiety is generally very treatable and may even lead to very welcome changes in their lifestyle, I try to focus on teaching the patient not only to identify and accept but also to reduce the anger that is bursting in them.

The next issue to which I proceed in the therapy is to develop devices for reducing the anxiety over being anxious—for example, learning how the fear and shame of having anxiety causes more symptoms, and learning how to stop this fear. Paradoxical as it is, we need to teach ourselves not to be so anxious about being somewhat anxious, and then our anxiety lessens.

The patient and I then look at how they are organizing their everyday lives and seek to identify what absolute rules they have imposed on themselves—such as never to fail or never to be sexual or joyful—which have brought down on them punishment. In the process, I also seek to trace the trail of anxiety to its deeper psychodynamic roots, such as fears of incompetence or abandonment. In this connection there are generally "root stories" of hurt, rejection, overindulgence, or exploitation in one's childhood at the hands of one's parents: sometimes stories of major emotional complications with siblings such as rivalry or rejection, or guilt over having been cruel and uncaring to a brother or sister who may have been in special need of help, or sexual abuse.

Finally I attempt to guide the patient toward answering the core questions of what are the unused potentials they clearly want to fulfill in themselves. This search is based on the groundbreaking and marvelously thoughtful work on anxiety by psychologist Rollo May,[13] who pioneered a brilliant concept that anxiety is a statement of people's fears that they will not be able to achieve or realize their potential. Anxiety is thus treated as a call to being more of one's better self and fulfilling one's potential.[14]

Altogether, instead of being only scary symptoms, anxiety is the call of a freedom that fascism hates and democracy loves—to channel anxiety toward greater self-fulfillment.

HYSTERICAL NEUROSIS

Hysterical problems basically include a psychologically driven inability to utilize some basic body or mind functions, such as a degree of loss of sight or hearing with no physical basis, or a paralysis of the functioning of a limb, or disturbance or loss of sexual functioning. On the level of the mind, hysterical problems present as an inability to use one's mind effectively, such as an inability to think or concentrate in the stress of an examination situation, or an inability to concentrate sufficiently well in a critical business or professional meeting, or confusion to the point of disorientation in a tense emotional situation, or disorientation and discomfort when traveling to a strange location away from one's home such as overseas. Hysterical symptoms can also involve body functions that become hyper-excitable for no real physical reason, including dramatic medical symptoms such as hysterical vomiting, or even an epileptic-like seizure where there is no physiological disturbance in the brain, or amazingly even an actual hemorrhage. I learned the latter from a professor of medicine who urged me to treat our shared patient on the basis of this understanding.

On an emotional level, hysterical symptoms can involve doing things with poor judgment, without being aware either of what one is doing or of the emotions motivating the behavior, such as inappropriate sexual behavior—for example, a minister or priest who doesn't know he's getting caught up in sexually assaulting someone, or a girl who is so terrified of an out-of-wedlock baby that she doesn't let herself know when she is in fact actually pregnant.

Along with writing the concept of neurosis out of *DSM* psychiatry, hysterical neuroses too have disappeared. Today's lexicon has a series of dissociative disorders and somatoform disorders, including conversion disorders, pain disorders, and hypochondriases and body dysmorphic disorders, not unmeaningful word constructions in their own right. But in my opinion these are unnecessarily cut off from the rich literature and traditions of psychodynamic explorations of these very disorders in the context of a mega-concept of hysterical patterns of thought and emotion. Hysterical patterns of behavior and organization of experience refer to disconnection from and unawareness of what one is feeling and thinking, and a consequent and subsequent translation of these unowned emotions and thoughts into body experiences and/or behaviors that express the dissociated feelings and thoughts. In our model of a Democratic Mind, we see these "mental gymnastics" of disconnection and artful substitutions of "cover stories" through other symptoms as a suppression of undesirable information. The true information of one's real impulses and desires is censored, suppressed, and concealed. The range of hysterical symptoms that befuddle and complicate people's lives is enormous. Thus, in today's *DSM-5*[15] language, the roster of Dissociative Disorders and Somatic Symptom Disorders, each also with its convoluted "Talmudic subcategories" that we will not bring here, includes the following:[16]

Dissociative Disorders

- *Dissociative Amnesia*, or episodes of an inability to recall important personal information, usually of a traumatic or stressful nature, that is too extensive to be explained by ordinary forgetfulness.
- *Dissociative Fugue*, or sudden unexpected travel or wandering away from home or one's customary place of work, with inability to recall one's past, confusion about personal identity, or assumption of a new identity (partial or complete).
- *Dissociative Identity Disorder* (formerly *Multiple Personality Disorder* in earlier *DSM*), or the presence of two or more distinct identities or personality states, each with its own relatively enduring pattern of perceiving, relating to, and thinking about the environment and self.
- *Depersonalization/Derealization Disorder*, or persistent or recurrent experiences of feeling detached from and as if one is an outside observer of one's mental

Table 3.1. Dynamics of Fascist Mind in Selected Psychopathology: Anxiety Disorders

	01-02 **TOTALITY, OVER-CERTAINTY, ABSOLUTISM, AND MAGICAL THINKING**	*03-04* **CENSORSHIP OF INFORMATION, OBEDIENCE, CONFORMITY, AND INTOLERANCE OF DISSENT**
ANXIETY DISORDERS	Generally the patient is in the throes of powerful self-measuring demands on their self, which they judge themselves as failing (e.g., a demand of self not to fail in life task(s), and/or a demand not to be socially spurned or humiliated). Such concerns generally are covering up the desirable and healthy anxiety of the patient as to what and how they want better to fulfill their potential, and how they want to conduct their life more meaningfully. Secondary processes develop that within themselves can be powerfully upsetting. Patient fears anxiety as a further shame and sign of failure, and the fear of more anxiety only intensifies it. Many patients also have a great deal of trouble in accepting and managing their anxiety because they have been taught that anxiety is a sign of weakness and disturbance, and this frightens them more. There is generally deep anger at (1) sources of unloving, rejection, and hurt, which are in the background of one's difficulty in fulfilling oneself, and (2) primary people in one's	In the fearfulness of further anxiety attacks, the patient's field of experience and awareness are often restricted. Most striking, compliments and positive feedback as to being lovable or competent are often shaken off and even rejected as unacceptable. The patient is characteristically in a state of seeming obedience and conformity to their worst fears about themselves: fears of suffering more anxiety symptoms, fears of social failure and shame over the symptoms, fears of not fulfilling their basic demands of themselves, fears of failure, fears of the welling up and possible dangerousness of their angers, and fears of not fulfilling their real potential. The enslavement is to an inner system of restrictions of the personality. In some cases, these are also accompanied by undue social diffidence and conformity to social demands. However, in many cases the anxious patient retains a clear sense of self, does not succumb slavishly to societal demands for obedience and conformity, and

ANXIETY DISORDERS (*continued*)

	life, rightly or wrongly, for not being better protectors against the suffering the patient is enduring. *Role of anxiety: Generally, unless the anxiety is paralyzing, the more anxiety the better the prognosis, notwithstanding the upset and suffering of the patient. It also means the patient does not have to lock themselvesf up in worse defenses such as projecting onto others their fears or withdrawing from life. But if the patient is suffering too much, symptomatic help to reduce (not eliminate) the anxiety to a workable level is advised.*	has an excellent potential for becoming a competent and confident person.
05 **SUPERIORITY, EXCESSIVE POWER-SEEKING, AND PREJUDICE**	06 **VIOLENCE, RETALIATION AGAINST DISSENT, SACRIFICE, AND DESTRUCTION**	07 **DENIALS OF DOING HARM TO SELF AND OTHERS**
Superiority, excessive power-seeking, and prejudice generally are not strongly manifest in anxiety disorders. However, internally, in the patient's mind, there may very well be undue strivings to feel superior to others in compensation for, and often alternating with, strong feelings of inadequacy and inferiority in the qualities and areas of functioning in which the patient wants to succeed more.	**Doing Harm to Self** Emotional punishment and disturbances in functioning are turned against oneself, in a combination of retaliation for failing whatever absolute standard was demanded of oneself, and in direct expression of convictions in one's inadequacy and undesirability. There is a heightened struggle with anger, hate, and fantasies of revenge against primary sources of emotional hurt, and often also self-punishment for these angry feelings. **Doing Harm to Others** Violence and overt destruction of others are not generally present.	On the contrary, there is generally heightened awareness of the emotional harm being done to oneself, and also some concern about the negative impact of one's condition on one's loved ones and on one's relationship to one's loved ones.

Source: Created by the author.

processes or body (e.g., feeling like one is in a dream); during the depersonalization experience, reality testing remains intact but the depersonalization causes significant distress or impairment in social, occupational, or other important areas of functioning.

Somatic Symptom Disorders (previously Somatoform Disorders)

- *Somatization Disorder*, or physical complaints that result in treatment being sought or significant impairment in social, occupational, or other important areas of functioning, or excessive concern about health or symptoms.
- *Illness Anxiety Disorder*, or a preoccupation with having or acquiring a serious illness.
- *Conversion Disorder*, or symptoms or deficits that affect voluntary motor or sensory functions and can suggest a neurological or other general medical condition, but where it is judged that psychological factors are causing the symptom or deficit; for example, seizures or convulsions that are not involuntary physiological-neurological expressions but are "voluntary"—although unconsciously driven—motor or sensory behaviors.
- *Psychological Factors Affecting Other Medical Conditions* is the name given when psychological factors are judged to have an important role in the onset, severity, exacerbation, or maintenance of pain, although the pain is not intentionally produced or feigned or otherwise exerts an adverse effect on the patient's medical condition.

Note what is now a firm *DSM* tradition, that the "great" names of symptom clusters that most mental health practitioners "grew up" with, and that accumulated rich and important studies and reports in the literature, are gone, renamed, or swallowed up by some other category. Thus, as we saw, Multiple Personality Disorder is now only Dissociative Identity Disorder. I remember so clearly the overwhelming excitement in the field when the first and then an ever-increasing number of multiple personalities were "discovered." Even then I suggested the phenomenon was in no small part a reflection of the therapist's interest and reinforcement of the phenomenon, but there is no doubt the phenomenology existed and does to this day.

Hypochondriasis is another age-old word concept that has been swished out of existence—a condition also with a rich cultural history, such as in Moliere's play, *Le Malade Imaginaire. DSM-4* presented it as a preoccupation with fears of having a serious disease that is often built around a person's misinterpretation or exaggeration of present bodily symptoms. The preoccupation persists despite appropriate medical evaluation and reassurance, and the preoccupation causes clinically significant distress or impairment in social, occupational, or other important areas of functioning. Is there no one around today besides Woody Allen for whom we could have saved the classic word?

In all of the these variants of the old-fashioned "hysterical neuroses," punishment for the most part strikes soundlessly without the patient's direct awareness either of the forbidden experiences to which they had dared to come too close, or of the wrathful and ruthless response of their inner authorities punishing them. The hysterical patient is, after all, committed to various degrees of not-knowing, dissociation, and what had become known to the classicists of the last century as "le bel indifference" (unknowingness). The rule of life that is the hysteric's paradigm is to "see, hear, and feel no evil," where evil equals whatever wishes are forbidden. The classic hysterical symptoms of inability to see or hear or taste, whether in a literal or metaphoric sense, prescribe punishment even for daring to *wish* to see, hear, or taste some forbidden fruit of life, pleasure, or achievement. What happens is that the patient seemingly discovers almost coincidentally some defective machinery of sensation, experience, body, or mind functioning and is led by force of this outer manifestation of a paralysis of function to consult professional help.

The "simplest" explanations of hysterical phenomena in early psychoanalysis were that they are escapes from awareness of good old sexual desires. But the truth often also lies in other kinds of impulses or in an escape from a whole area or world of experiences, such as in an inner prohibition against attempting to succeed in learning (e.g., people who are psychologically compelled to fail to complete a course of study). There are classic cases of students who have finished all their requirements for a degree except a telltale one or two papers whose incompleteness ensures that they cannot succeed.

❖ The most dramatic case I ever treated involved a young woman who had completed successfully *all* her coursework and clinical practicums in a fine medical school. She had even completed a final research paper that required a full scientific study of an experimental group and a control group, and even had drawn statistically significant results in the study. But unbelievably, she never wrote up the research paper and therefore did not receive her M.D. degree!

In therapy she fought like a lioness against finishing the paper until one day I threatened to call her mother to join in her daughter's therapy sessions—and when the daughter refused to agree I threatened to do so against her will! Apparently having mother present was more frightening than getting her M.D. degree, and she now finally did submit her paper—and I never got to see mother! (Later, my doctor-patient sent me a fine bottle of wine with a handmade label simulating the degree.)

Hysteria is first and foremost a style of *not knowing*, which can refer to any number of broad patterns of feelings, such as not knowing one cares about someone or about some issue, not knowing one feels empathy for someone, or not knowing one's anger and rage—or one's sexual lust.

The inner mind and experiencing machinery of the hysteric is essentially a willing collaborator with an authoritarian regime that holds it in its grip. Often it is the

Table 3.2. Dynamics of Fascist Mind in Selected Psychopathology: Hysterical Neurosis

	01-02 **TOTALITY, OVER-CERTAINTY, ABSOLUTISM, AND MAGICAL THINKING**	*03-04* **CENSORSHIP OF INFORMATION, OBEDIENCE, CONFORMITY, AND INTOLERANCE OF DISSENT**
HYSTERICAL NEUROSIS *This is a classical concept that is no longer employed in* DSM. *In* DSM-5 *it appears in variations of "Somatic Symptom Disorders," including "Factitious Disorders" and "Dissociative Disorders"; or "Psychological Factors Affecting Medical Conditions"; also "Hystrionic Personality Disorder," "Avoidant Personality Disorder," and more.* *Here the description given is of the generic hysterical process of pushing away/repressing/denying/disssociating oneself from unallowable experiences.*	An unbearable impulse or reality is expunged from one's inner experience and accessible memory. A certainty of a romanticized nonthreatening world is reestablished in flights to postures of "all is well" and "no need to worry." Or the patient converts the original real concern into disguised somatizations or malfunctions—for example, hysterical visual problems up to and including blindness, hysterical hearing problems up to and including deafness, hysterical inability to concentrate or to learn, or even hysterical hemorrhage where the blood flow is all too real but the medical cause is from the mind and not in a diseased organ. Or the patient acts out the expunged part of self in a dissociated state, in which they do not experience their real self; for example, a girl who truly does not know she is pregnant until she gives birth to the baby. *Role of anxiety: Anxiety is pushed away if at all possible in happy-go-lucky denials of the stress, or in conversions of the stress to other disguised or dissociated behaviors that aim to protect the patient from feeling their real concerns.*	Prohibitions against unacceptable desires or memories in one's own mind are conformed to strongly. In addition, hysterical personalities often can be counted on to be cult members and "groupies" who do slavishly what is "called for" by leaders and society without question or personal decision.

HYSTERICAL NEUROSIS (*continued*)

05 **SUPERIORITY, EXCESSIVE POWER-SEEKING, AND PREJUDICE**	*06* **VIOLENCE, RETALIATION AGAINST DISSENT, SACRIFICE, AND DESTRUCTION**	*07* **DENIALS OF DOING HARM TO SELF AND OTHERS**
In being "good" and dissociated from impulses that have been defined as evil, some hysterical patients may make themselves superior to others who are defined as sinners, heathen, or low life. However, in many other cases, there is no strong association between disallowance of experience for self and superiority or power over others.	**Doing Harm to Self** Violence is against self for allowing a disallowed experience. The violence knows no limit, creating variously such serious dysfunctions as hysterical blindness, deafness, dumbness, impotence, and suicide. **Doing Harm to Others** On a societal level, hysterical phenomena can invite and trigger people to violence against others, such as the nonconformists (e.g., as in the history of dangerous hunts of "witches" and "heathens."). Hysterics are also prominent in groups of cult-believers and "groupies" who will do violence as if hypnotized in submission to the commands of their leaders. They may do serious violence to themselves (e.g., Jonestown mass suicides) or to others (e.g., again Jonestown—those who killed others, or the Manson cult killers). In terms of individual behavior, the hysteric themselves may "act out" violence to others in a dissociated state, such as a betrayed lover killing the betrayer, or a woman killing an undesired baby. However, for the most part hysteric states are not connected to doing harm to others.	Denial of a disallowed impulse as a part of oneself is the essence of hysteria. The impulse may be violence to begin with, which can then appear in dissociated forms. Or violence can appear in the effort to block out vestiges of another impulse—for example, self-abuse to one's own body in an effort to suppress sexual impulses, or persecutory accusations and witch hunts of others onto whom one's denied impulses have been projected. In most cases there is no acknowledgment of the punishment being done to self or others—real as the violence is, it can be more an artifact or consequence of the defense adopted than an expression of rage or violence in the usual sense.

Source: Created by the author.

therapist who is more interested and motivated to free the patient from the shackles of symptoms and certainly from the state of unknowingness than the patient themselves. Albert Ellis commented in the later years of his work that he has concluded that "most overly anxious, depressed, and hostile people . . . after a while only try moderately, if at all, to become really undisturbed. And even when they go for intensive psychotherapy, they only try half-heartedly to think, feel, and act differently."[17]

For the hysteric, paralyzing conditions of *malade imaginaire* are secretly celebrated as desirable alternatives to being free to be oneself. Even painful and really damaging psychosomatic consequences of self-induced bleeding, convulsions, and all manner of expulsions of body products can be understood to be one's just deserts for failing to heed the absolute dictates of a Fascist Mind rule that one has violated not to desire, or feel, or think, or do something or other quite human, which is not to be allowed.

OBSESSIVE-COMPULSIVE DISORDERS

Obsessive-compulsive neurotic conditions are even more obvious cases of the imposition of absolute binding demands in the mind of the patient. The recurrent and persistent thoughts, impulses, or images, which are experienced as intrusive and inappropriate in the patient's mind, can cause a hellish distress. Repetitive behaviors such as handwashing, putting things in order, checking something repeatedly (e.g., whether the gas has been left on), or mental acts such as praying, counting, and repeating words silently that the person feels obligated to perform in response to an obsession or according to rules that must be applied rigidly, can overcome much of a person's sense of being a normal human being to create a virtually driven or robotic person. If a person suffers repetitive thoughts obsessively, they may mistakenly take these thoughts to represent factual reality and invite actions based on a false certainty attributed to the repeated thoughts.

- ❖ One young man, who was having trouble separating emotionally from his possessive mother needed to find serious faults in his quite lovely wife and couldn't let go to loving her. His effort at therapy was unsuccessful and ended with a divorce that was driven by his incessant obsessive fault-finding, notwithstanding that he appreciated his wife in many ways and in part (not a large enough part) wanted to stay with her.

Psychodynamic understanding of obsessive-compulsive disorders has revealed clearly that the underlying inner paradigm dictates absolutely that no hostile thoughts at a given target will be allowed by the person's mind regime. Often there is also an accompanying rule that efforts at emotional separation and individuality, or intentions to be one's own authentic self, will also not be tolerated. In both cases disobedience is to be punished severely.

For some reason, the obsessive-compulsive disorders are frequently and passionately seized on by contemporary devotees of physiological approaches to psychiatry. It has seemed to me that there is a particular push to reclaim this disorder for the world of biology and to disclaim that any emotions or thoughts per se could possibly have created the disturbed living hell of an obsessive-compulsive disorder. Why this "love affair," I wonder? Perhaps there is a kind of association between the repetitiveness of the psychological activity and the repeated pulsing of nervous impulses. Or perhaps there is a flight from the web of unconscious hatred and murderous rage that is characteristically at the dynamic center of these symptoms—a subject that naturally invites massive psychological denials both by patients and also by the many psychological and psychiatric practitioners who haven't done their full homework of psychoanalyzing (meeting up with and owning) their own would-be "murderer" of members of their family that sits as part of their inner heart-minds. There is also the clinical reality that hardened or deteriorated obsessive-compulsives who are heavily and chronically into their symptoms are not very likely to be responsive to psychotherapy, and therefore really may need other interventions such as medication to try to break up or lighten the logjam these symptoms have on them.

In obsessive-compulsive disorders, mind-breaking repetitive thoughts and personality-imprisoning compulsions relentlessly invade and overpower the errant mind that dares to think, feel, or aspire to anti-regime thoughts and positions. Psychodynamically, we have learned that the obsessive-compulsive symptoms not only are efforts to censor, bar, and deflect the possible welling up of forbidden hostile thoughts, but also are fears that one's angry thoughts and wishes can have magical powers to really hurt the targeted person(s). Should the patient dare to deviate and attempt to break loose to try to find "a crack" that might let out angry thoughts that are forbidden by absolute rules (shades of the childhood ditty, "*Step on a crack, break your mother's back*"), the emotional consequences will be horrendous pain. Given the enormity of the offense, the "authorities" can be counted on to send in stormtroopers in the forms of mind-beating cruel obsessional thoughts and torturing compulsive rituals in retaliation.

My own experience in psychotherapy with a number of serious and long-standing cases has been surprisingly positive (though like the failed case noted above, definitely not all cases, and not with hardened or deteriorated cases). I tend to begin therapy with obsessive people with some efforts at teaching *thought-stopping*, or teaching the patient to order their mind to drop a given compulsive idea or to inhibit a given compulsive behavior (e.g., pulling one's hair) by virtue of one's creative willpower.

The results at first are generally limited, but even a small improvement helps, and can illustrate the fact that it is our minds that run the show. I also try various measures to help the patient generally calm down, such as helping them to sleep better. I then seek to evoke and free the waves of anger and hate, and the terror of unleashing these feelings from the mind, first by steady reflections and feedback of their inadvertent slippages, and then, as the patient becomes stronger, by directed work on their free associations.

Table 3.3. Dynamics of Fascist Mind in Selected Psychopathology: Obsessive-Compulsive Neurosis

	01-02 **TOTALITY, OVER-CERTAINTY, ABSOLUTISM, AND MAGICAL THINKING**	*03-04* **CENSORSHIP OF INFORMATION, OBEDIENCE, CONFORMITY, AND INTOLERANCE OF DISSENT**
OBSESSIVE-COMPULSIVE NEUROSIS	A highly certain world of repetitive thoughts, rituals, and compulsive actions is created. Patients are devoted to the perfection of their rituals. The rituals are defined virtually as imperatives, and unconsciously are endowed with magical powers to undo ominous threats. Psychodynamically, many o-c symptoms are revealed to be efforts to ward off deep anger, hatred, and magical fears of one's hatred actually doing harm to the other. *Role of anxiety: The experience of the obsessive-compulsive symptoms in themselves may create considerable tension and be severely upsetting to the patient. More free-floating anxiety generally is not seen, since the obsessive-compulsive symptoms bind the anxiety. Nonetheless, in some patients there is some "leakage" of anxiety. Insofar as anxiety is experienced more strongly, notwithstanding the patient's discomfort, it is a good prognostic sign.*	Information of deep anger and hatred is suppressed through the o-c symptoms. Obedience and conformity to others is not an issue. However, the essence of the o-c symptoms is that the patient is dominated by powerful needs to obey and conform slavishly to their own self-constructed rituals.

OBSERVSIVE-COMPULSIVE (*continued*)

05 **SUPERIORITY, EXCESSIVE POWER-SEEKING, AND PREJUDICE**	06 **VIOLENCE, RETALIATION AGAINST DISSENT, SACRIFICE AND, DESTRUCTION**	07 **DENIALS OF DOING HARM TO SELF AND OTHERS**
Superiority and power over others are not necessarily associated with the disorder, although there can be some linkage of perfectionism with superior disdain fcr others.	**Doing Harm to Self** Some o-c patients become so tired and demoralized that they become suicidally violent against themselves. **Doing Harm to Others** Overt violence is rare, but the psychodynamics of the condition center around enormous hatred and impulses to be violent to others that the patient fears may run out of control unless checked by o-c mechanisms.	Patients suffering o-c are generally so busy with their thoughts and rituals that they do not "see" the harm they are doing to themselves, nor are they sensitive to how they may be driving others around them "crazy" with new rituals. Patient does not characteristically do harm to others, and therefore there is no need to deny overt harm. Basic to o-c is that impulses of rage are denied and undone in the o-c symptoms. Patient is so busy denying the harm they want to do and feel on the verge of doing to whomever, that they are usually helplessly trapped from being able to acknowledge how much harm they are doing to their own self and imposing on the lives of others. Most often patients are unable on their own to make successful efforts to correct the situation.

Source: Created by the author.

❖ Therapist: You're concerned about what will happen to your mother as she gets older.

Patient: Yes. Don't misunderstand me, I don't like her, she's wicked, but I feel sorry for her as she gets older and weaker. I can't get out of my head the thought that something bad will hit her and I will find her in a pitiful state.

Therapist: This is another kind of thought that you can't get out of your head, just like the black thoughts about death and injury you told me are obsessively driving you crazy. It's possible that your thoughts and anger at your mother are pushing your own fears too.

The results of psychotherapy with patients suffering from obsessive-compulsive disorders who have shown motivation and an ability to engage in a sequence of sessions have been even heartwarming.

What has intrigued me the most perhaps, is that after patients have gained control over their obsessive-compulsive symptoms, there has characteristically followed another phase of treatment around basic existential questions of what meanings and purposes their life has. Freed from the demons that held them in their grip, the once ruminating and tortured patient can emerge as a fascinating and touching fellow human reexploring the basics of life.

Needless to say, the Democratic Mind gives free reign to angry and even bitter wishes to hurt someone. But it does not at all approve of any actual violent acts. The critical concepts that feelings are not the equivalent of actions, and in themselves cause no harm whatsoever to the object of hatred, are very much respected, but the Democratic Mind champions "free speech" in one's mind for experiencing one's anger.

PHOBIC NEUROSIS

A phobic neurosis may begin with a degree of tentativeness, namely that a person sometimes will feel fearful and withdraw from participating in some plane of activity—going to school, going to work, going into a crowd situation, going out socially such as on a date. There are some times that taking off from the responsibility or obligation to perform and giving oneself a break by resting up and not exposing oneself to a task that is anxiety provoking is exactly what the doctor ordered, and a person can then come back with renewed strength to perform subsequently in the feared situations. The danger is that in any number of cases a pattern of habitual withdrawal and avoidance of fearful situations can take hold.

Epidemiological surveys suggest that there is an amazing number of people everywhere "out there," in all societies, who live their lives for years limited by some strong phobic fears—for example, people who will never stay home alone, never go to the center of town or whatever other crowded places, never fly, or never drive a car—in some cases even after they have learned and received licenses. Some people even literally remain total prisoners for years inside their homes. Others have to give up truly wonderful job opportunities—sometimes even the dream opportunity of their work life—because they cannot bear to travel to a forbidden location or through a forbidden instrument of transportation (elevator, airplane), or they cannot undertake to separate from their familiar home, or leave somebody (a parent or a sibling) behind. The mind has ruled that to do one or another of these things is unsafe or treachery and will bring nothing less than total disaster, and one dare not violate the injunction of the mind-rulers. A certainty of not doing and not risking becomes the overriding security. All new experience is relegated to the intolerable and forbidden.

There are two major groups of phobias: *Specific phobia* refers to marked and excessive fear that is excessive or unreasonable in response to a specific object or situation; for example, fearing heights, animals, or undergoing a specific kind of medical procedure, or fear of going into town or to a shopping center or wherever. There is an immediate anxiety, and perhaps a panic attack, when the person is exposed to the fearful situation. In children, the responses are characteristically crying, temper tantrums, immobilization, or clinging.

Social phobia refers to a marked and persistent fear of one or more social performance situations such as meeting people, conducting a conversation in certain settings, participating in a group, dating, going to parties, dancing, whatever kind of sexually inviting situation, meeting with authority figures, or public speaking. The fearful person is generally preoccupied if not full of terror about how they will appear to others and/or how others will react to them. There is great fear of being embarrassed or humiliated. Inadvertent or coerced exposure to the fearful situation provokes intense anxiety and perhaps a panic attack.

In a full-blown phobic neurosis, a fearful paradigm builds up to its totality, and the person becomes imprisoned by a monstrous prohibition against being able to participate in one or another rudimentary area of life functioning. The person suffering the phobia often can acknowledge that their fear is excessive but nonetheless avoids the phobic situation lest they suffer intense distress. In time, the avoidance interferes significantly with academic, occupational, or social activities.

From the point of view of this book, the phobic neurosis is almost a literal replication of a Fascist Mind paradigm: The mind forbids the person to be present or perform in whatever situation, and it is also clear that there is a powerful sanction or punishment if the prohibition is violated. The surrender to a phobic pattern is a dedicated exercise of obedience and conformity to an order. It is understood that no dissent will be tolerated, for the punishment will be too great to bear. The courage it takes to break a phobia reminds me of the courage needed to oppose a terrifying totalitarian regime. Most of us can't do it all at once, but if we submit ourselves to steady tutoring in the art of desensitizing our fearfulness and embarking on small steps at a time to reclaim our power to be free, we often can recover. Intriguingly for me as a therapist, I am not sure that I know in advance who will go the full route of courage and recovery and who won't. And that reminds me of the facts that in collective situations of societal fascism and persecution, we don't really know in advance

Table 3.4. Dynamics of Fascist Mind in Selected Psychopathology: Phobic Neurosis

	01-02 **TOTALITY, OVER-CERTAINTY, ABSOLUTISM, AND MAGICAL THINKING**	*03-04* **CENSORSHIP OF INFORMATION, OBEDIENCE, CONFORMITY, AND INTOLERANCE OF DISSENT**
PHOBIC NEUROSIS	Phobic patient lives in a certain world "thanks to" absolute prohibition of the designated behavior. *Role of anxiety: Many phobias "seal off" anxiety effectively, which leaves the patient safe in the restriction of their behavior and less motivated to try to overcome the phobia. Whatever secondary anxiety or discomfort there is about the phobia is, of course, a welcome sign of a struggle of a more healthy potential in the patient. Insofar as the patient can proceed to experience and work on more fundamental anxieties about themselves, the grip of the phobia will be lessened all the more.*	There is obedience to one's own legislated phobia.

PHOBIC NEUROSIS (continued)

05 **SUPERIORITY, EXCESSIVE POWER-SEEKING, AND PREJUDICE**	06 **VIOLENCE, RETALIATION AGAINST DISSENT, SACRIFICE, AND DESTRUCTION**	07 **DENIALS OF DOING HARM TO SELF AND OTHERS**
Not generally expected to be associated with phobia.	**Doing Harm to Self** In many cases the phobia sets severe restrictions on the person's life. The phobia "does violence" to patient's own life, but is not generally associated with overt violence to oneself. **Doing Harm to Others** Violence to others is not associated with phobia.	Patients generally describe their being trapped in their phobia, and do not seem to have energy to face the harm they are doing to themselves, nor do they respond to knowledge of this harm with efforts to get better. The issue of doing harm to others is characteristically associated with the harm being done to one's family because of one's inability to function. It may be acknowledged, but even then without necessarily becoming a source of new energies to fight the phobia.

Source: Created by the author.

who will prove to be the courageous rescuers of lives against the background of a majority who will do as they are told—period.

❖ She was a young thirty-two-year-old mother who had been homebound for about a year, including being unable to go to work as a physical therapist. Now she had brought herself to leave her house to get to the therapist's office. She participated determinedly in the desensitization sessions, and within two and a half months was ready to go back to work half days.

❖ He did not come for help for himself, but because their teenage daughter had been hospitalized for a severe emotional disorder, and he and his wife wanted to know what they might do. He himself was a crabby forty-four-year-old lawyer and businessman who *hated* going to work but did so because "he had to." What had begun to frighten him symptomatically was not the workplace as such, but going on weekends to sail on yachts, which he had always loved. For him sailing signified a life of grace and camaraderie with other men that seemingly proved to him that he was not a loner and not a rejected personality, but now even approaching the marina flooded him with fears. He responded halfheartedly to efforts to desensitize the phobia of sailing, and then rejected them as useless. Efforts to talk about the meanings of his experiences at work, play, and in his relationships yielded only reluctant half statements amid a bitter blaming of the therapist that he was doing no good. Nor did he want to bring their daughter in for any family therapy. The impression was of a tormented man who needed to remain a very unhappy person and could not participate in the therapy of his phobia or even on behalf of his suffering daughter. Within a few weeks he stopped coming to sessions.

DEPRESSION AND SUICIDE

Depression

The contemporary literature of psychiatry—and in its wake also family medicine and popular magazine psychology—makes depression sound like the measles, or if it's really a bad case perhaps even like cancer, but the point is that the condition is treated as a disease that is visited upon the body from some endocrinological, metabolic, or other physiological cause, let alone is programmed by the fates of heredity.

Work your way through the standard psychiatric textbook with its endless permutations of depression and its concerns whether or not the depressed mood meets the detailed symptom criteria for being linked to "manic" or "hypomanic episodes" or is diagnosable with "catatonic features" or "melancholic features" or constituting a "dysthymic disorder," and it all certainly sounds like the soul has nothing at all to do with experiences of depression, and that it is all there somewhere in those powerful physiological forces running around in our bodies. But where have all the heartaches gone?

What has happened to all the "she loves me, she loves me not" experiences in this world? Who has put aside all the poetry of disappointment, hurt, loss, and despair over being rejected by someone or another? And what about being crushed by the discovery that the philosophy and political movements one believed in have betrayed one's most precious values, or whose leaders have been exposed as a gang of exploiters or even cutthroat killers of the very sort one prayed to rid the world of with the aid of the new philosophy? What about crushing discoveries that the company one works for has been marketing inferior products, say distributing dangerous medicines to hapless undeveloped peoples in the Third World, or that the super-duper barons of accounting in one's firm have conspired to report false business results for a company from which they have been milking personal profits in the hundreds of thousands or millions?

Aren't events like these enough to break one's heart and make a decent person feel depressed without any stray hormone having had a finger in causing that depression?

Once one gets depressed, various chemicals in our bodies indeed change reactively. This is the essence of a *psychosomatic* process. Various chemical hormonal-endocrinological changes then create processes that in themselves take off and spread the damages of depression even beyond the quantity of the original hurt. As stated earlier, some of these psychosomatic chain reactions of depression *can* be stopped and alleviated by medication of the physiological functions, but the medications don't contact the original hurt, loss, or insult. In fact, clinical experience teaches us to be careful not to medicate a grieving or raging soul prematurely! People need to hurt and grieve and hate as the case may be. If they don't have time to do so and legitimacy for their emotions, it can make them depressed!

Clinical experience also proves that administration of antidepressant medications like Prozac are associated with a very large toll of suicides, and a smaller but noteworthy number of aggressive outbursts up to and including homicide. There have been tens of thousands of cases of suicides, according to journalistic exposés, and a smaller but notable number of cases where murders have been implicated. Several reports have implicated Prozac in school shootings.[18]

The same issue takes on a greater poignancy when it involves youth. In the UK, the law has forbidden the use of Prozac-type medication (SSRIs) to minors. In the United States, the capitalist forces have succeeded in protecting their lucrative product, but at least a warning of potential side effects accompanies the medicine. There have been many (documented) acts of cover-up by pharmaceutical firms and/or psychiatric practitioners and institutions. Telltale evidence that something serious is afoot comes from the fact that several pharmaceutical companies that market somewhat different brands of a Prozac-type medication have been paying out tens of millions of dollars in settlements of lawsuits over suicide or homicide. A 2014 report says that Eli Lilly, manufacturer of Prozac, has paid "at least 10 million in settlements." Moreover, there have been lawsuits charging "deceptive marketing practices."

Another company, Forest Laboratories, which manufactures Lexapro, is reported to have paid over 300 million dollars in a federal criminal suit. Somebody is making an awful lot of money to afford such settlements. And something serious is awry if courts regularly award such settlements.[19] A not insignificant factor in any number of cases have been charges that drug companies in their own clinical trials have suppressed and concealed bad findings about these meds.

Conversely it is argued that there is also evidence that when medication is used, the rate of suicides decreases. Could be. And this would mean that selected use of the medication is still called for, but to date no one can offer a clue as to when to take this risk and when not. In general, a review in *Scientific American: Mind* concludes about antidepressants including Prozac-types that they are both "effective and ineffective . . . it depends on the definition of the word "work."[20]

My resolution of all the ambiguities is that one can use the meds when they are accompanied by psychotherapy. Antidepressant medication without therapy is dangerous. But this doesn't correct the fact that the industry has proven deeply corrupt with these "money trees." And that is no less than depressing.

In spring of 2015, the world was in shock over the deliberate crashing of a Germanwings (Lufthansa) airplane by its co-pilot, killing all 150 people aboard. Obviously we don't know any more than we read, but the preliminary reports seem to add up to a person who was depressed enough to seek psychiatric help (which he concealed from his employer), received medications, lived with his parents at age twenty-seven, told his girlfriend he would do something that would make everybody remember him for a long time, and, according to the girlfriend, would have crazy temper tantrums.[21]

Was he receiving real psychotherapy? Was he in sessions talking from his heart or largely reviewing symptoms with a doctor who prescribed medicine? Obviously we won't know until and if we are told. But this was certainly a man who needed to be working with a therapist on the meaning of the lives of other people beside his own.

My understanding of the phenomena of suicide and homicide while on Prozac is that the medication really *does* work to modify a critical chemical imbalance that is present in depression. The depressed patient then really feels better. The chemistry that anchors and exacerbates depressed feelings has been lifted. The patient has so much more available energy and power. But if the heartfelt causes of the depression are still present—the loss of a significant person, the shame and humiliation of failure, the treachery of betrayal of precious values, whatever—the depressed person now has the energy to *act*. Lousy as depression is in its own right, like many other symptoms it is also playing constructive roles of defending the person against worse. Depression depletes energies and thus protects people to some extent against acting out in suicide and homicide. The critical clinical implication is that medicine should not be prescribed without psychotherapy. Where the patient hurts inside is no less needing treatment than their brain chemistry.

The lists of disappointments in human life are endless. What of health and work issues—the above pilot is reported to have a worsening eye condition and may have been facing an end to his career as a pilot. Is serving in Vietnam a reason to be depressed? What about enduring the Holocaust? What about poverty? What shall we say of rotten marriages and the mounting sadness of coming home every day to an embittered joyless life? What about seeing our children growing up differently than everything we dreamed: a beloved child adopting an alternative sexual way of life (which we perhaps do not judge as wrong but which we may not at all want for one of our children); another beloved child divorcing and perhaps more than once; a son or daughter who leaves the faith of our forefathers and family; or plain and simple a youngster who moves so far away that there is no continuity in connection, celebration, and comfort as the seasons of life unfold?

Depression becomes a clinical psychiatric condition when a person is *stuck* with a depressed feeling and seems unable to work their way out to renewal of their optimism, hope, and ambition for life. I have no doubt whatsoever that depression is also directly caused any number of times by physical conditions of different sorts. It is, for example, an accompaniment of some serious diseases to a point where depression is almost a suggestive diagnostic indicator to the physicians for the possibility of some diseases even before they have been otherwise diagnosed medically. Depression is also certainly a response to the condition of being diseased or disabled, which is totally understandable as the sadness of a human being who is no longer able to function at whatever activities and skills they are used to exercising with a normal degree of ease. Obviously chemical configurations have in their power to depress a human being significantly, but it is bad medicine not to recognize seriously that so do all the human situations where, plain and simple, the human being is hurt, humiliated, brought to their knees, loses hope, does not see the way out of a bad situation, is left alone, loses someone dear, or a dear part of their lifestyle, or is otherwise seriously humbled by life.

The stuckness of depression can be physiological, but it also can be that the person is using a mind system for processing their natural feelings of sadness and loss that leads them to getting and remaining stuck with depressed feelings. Like other characteristics of Fascist Mind thinking, depression can be very easily the adoption of a total, fixed, and immutable negative position about life.

- After this failure, I can't believe in myself again.
- I can never lift my head up again after this great humiliation.
- I will never forgive myself for hurting my children in this way.
- There is nothing left for me to believe in this world.
- There is no way I can live with this loss.

Moreover, depression often has qualities of great rage at whomever and whatever are the focus of the loss and demoralization that one has experienced, but often the person does not know how to process such extensive rage, or cannot tolerate directing this rage at precisely the person toward whom it is directed—for example, a parent's rage at a beloved child who has disappointed them so deeply, or a child's

Table 3.5. Dynamics of Fascist Mind in Selected Psychopathology: Depression

	01-02 **TOTALITY, OVER-CERTAINTY, ABSOLUTISM, AND MAGICAL THINKING**	*03-04* **CENSORSHIP OF INFORMATION, OBEDIENCE, CONFORMITY, AND INTOLERANCE OF DISSENT**
DEPRESSION	The overriding feeling and conviction of the depressed person is that they are very much stuck as a failure and insignificant, and that the happiness in life that others enjoy is passing them by. There are bad moods and diminished interest and enjoyment of the activities and pleasures of life. The two major psychological components of depression are some form of loss and giving up, and a bottling up of a raging anger at one's bad fate, which is either so intense that it is too frightening to bear, or because one fears that the object of one's anger can't take it (e.g., to a parent who is a Holocaust survivor). While depression can very much be set off by altered chemical and physical states, including endocrinological and metabolic changes as well as by illness and infirmity, very often depression is a psychological anthem in an otherwise physically healthy person who is saying: *I cannot feel pleasurably alive*. *Role of anxiety: Anxiety does accompany some depressions that then qualify diagnostically as "agitated depression."*	Information of success, hope, and pleasure is avoided and suppressed to an extent commensurate with the need to be depressed. To the extent that the patient does accept compliments and affection and is able to generate some positive mood, accessibility to psychotherapy is more likely. The person who is trapped by and unconsciously committed to be depressed in a sense is in the grips of obedience and conformity to an injunction not to be pleasured and happy.

	Clinically, in severe cases these can be all the more difficult to manage—for example, intensely agitated feelings of worthlessness or intense intention to commit suicide. But in less severe cases, the old rule of thumb remains that some anxiety, however painful, is a sign of life and a better prognosis.	
05 **SUPERIORITY, EXCESSIVE POWER-SEEKING, AND PREJUDICE**	06 **VIOLENCE, RETALIATION AGAINST DISSENT, SACRIFICE, AND DESTRUCTION**	07 **DENIALS OF DOING HARM TO SELF AND OTHERS**
Superiority, power-seeking, and prejudice are not characteristically linked with depression. However, a person who has ruled in power and superiority over others and who then loses his control over others will often react with a strong depression over the loss of their power.	**Doing Harm to Self** Depression constitutes a considerable burden and harm to self. Depression often is violence against self that derives from turning against oneself the intense anger that one feels toward others, but is afraid or unable to experience and express. Some forms of depression of course predispose to the possibility of suicide, the ultimate violence against oneself. **Doing Harm to Others** The dysphoria and grayness of depression do impact harmfully on the others in the patient's life. Additionally, insofar as the depression is an immobilized fearfulness of expressing one's anger at the specific other (e.g., a spouse), the depression is symbolically also an attack on the other that is representative of the harm one wants to do the other.	Some people are depressed—gray, unhappy, restricted in their functioning—and don't know it until they get feedback, such as from a physician who suggests that their medical symptoms may be indicative of depression, or from someone else in their life. Most depressed people acknowledge their depression. Indeed, in some cases they are almost consciously only too happy to impose their depression on other(s) in their lives.

anger at a parent who is otherwise weak and ailing, at whom one feels too guilty to be enraged (e.g., the ubiquitous dilemmas of children of Holocaust survivors who cannot bear to feel angry at their victimized parents). The rage is then turned inwards at oneself and generally is aided and abetted by a magical twist also of blaming oneself unnecessarily for all that has gone wrong. So now depression is not only all the original sadness and loss of hope in the possibilities of a good life, but it is also a sad and angry *Account Rendered* to oneself for having failed in the requirement to produce a better life. Depression can result both from a guilt-ridden turning inwards of anger that is intended for someone else and a punishment of oneself for failure.

Psychologist Martin Seligman has given us the simple and brilliant concept of *learned helplessness* as lying at the core of much depression, and the sensible and optimistic implication of this concept is that the therapy of depression should include a good deal of strengthening and re-empowering a depressed person to generate new hopes and new plans for their lives.[22] Psychiatrist Aaron Beck pioneered in developing cognitive therapies for depressed and suicidal people designed to help them formulate new outlooks on their lives instead of remaining in the ruts of their black feelings.[23] The hurts, losses, and failures that really took place in a patient's life are not written out of existence, "forgotten," or suppressed, but an effort is made to re-sort the *meanings* attributed to them and to the possibilities of new life opportunities "after the flood." A Democratic Mind view of depression suggests that along with checking out possible physical causes, look for where your deepest disappointment and loss of faith in yourself and your life lie, and look for who and what it is in your life that have disappointed you so much that you are possibly very, very angry at them.

One veteran psychotherapist, Victor Raimy,[24] designed a scenario for treating depression where the patient is encouraged to imagine themselves in a darkened room in which they are to look about for an indication of a punishing presence that is present in that black empty space to torment them. Raimy would encourage the patient to speak to their Tormenter, to be angry at the Tormenter, and to attempt to build up the strength to chase it off.

Personally, given the choice, I would prefer to yell at the Tormenter I identify in my life than to be treated with medication. It is worth repeating that a serious paradox of pharmaceutical treatment of depression is that if the symptoms of depression are removed or reduced *before* the bitterness and hurt feelings that induced the depression are processed and lessened, all hell may break loose, including both suicide and homicide. These are explicitly noted as official potential side effects of Prozac, though as noted there have been charges that the manufacturer of Prozac has sought deliberately to conceal the data. However, we should not attribute these side effects *to* Prozac in the same way that one says aspirin can cause bleeding or an antibiotic can cause diarrhea. As proposed earlier, Prozac may work so well to reduce the depressing of emotions that a very upset person, who generally has a very real basis for their sadness and rage, may become emotionally stronger and free enough to act violently on their inner emotions. In general, we know in psychiatry that psychiatric symptoms also have homeostatic and balancing effects and shouldn't be removed too rapidly without real attention to their true causes. One might add that a great many studies of groups of various depressive disorders, including the rough-and-tumble bipolar disorders that in contemporary psychiatric thinking carry implications of having a high hereditary component, nonetheless respond best to combinations of medication *and* psychotherapy—better than to either mode of treatment alone.

Probably the most "popular" psychotherapy at this time for depression—at least as promoted in academic settings that campaign for "evidence-based therapy"—is cognitive-behavior therapy, which is generally credited to Aaron Beck.[25]

In my judgment, cognitive therapy gives us very wise and welcome tools for helping people turn off irrational (fascist) rules in their minds that obligate them to be depressed, but that joining such pragmatic cognitive tools with additional tools for accessing unconscious feelings gets deeper into the heart and soul of a person's depression. I think everyday heavy human reactions of loss, sadness, guilt, disappointment, regret, giving up, and so on are better helped by human understanding, inspiration, and corrective criticism, as well as recommendations for constructive rechanneling of oneself. Whenever possible, therapy should also address the restoration of intimate relationships in the patient's life, and, in conjunction with reviewing the patient's overall lifestyle, assist and motivate a resumption of belief in a purpose, cause, and participation along with other people in a community—including one's religious faith, local community, national or collective ethnic identity, professional cause, charitable causes such as volunteer assistance to the needy, commitments such as human rights advocacy, and so on. Medications can and should be used to reduce depression that is getting beyond the patient's ability to handle, to reduce intense suffering, and limit runaway disabling of everyday functioning. But drugs should rarely be used to censor, repress, deny, or otherwise get around human experiences and emotions. Even when painful they are precious. They are us—who we are and feel—for real.

What does the research show? Which psychotherapy is advisable for depression? Should medications be used alone or in conjunction with psychotherapy? There are so many studies about these issues with varying results that you can pretty much pick the conclusion you like the most from the beginning. Moreover, a number of researchers and thinkers have cautioned strongly that studies tend to show the results sought by the researcher. This bias is referred to as a "confirmation bias," where "preexisting notions anchor subsequent reasoning and can affect information gathering, analysis, and retrieval . . ."[26] The bias is evident also in psychotherapy outcome studies.[27] One study that I think is very important concludes that the combination of psychotherapy and antidepressants is slightly more effective than either alone. It also presents as its more important conclusion that the "type of treatment offered is less important than getting depressed patients involved in an active therapeutic program."[28] Again and again we see that it is people who matter the most, not meds, and not formulated techniques—however much they can add when chosen wisely.

Suicide and Suicidality

Most amazingly, suicide is nowhere to be found as a syndrome in the *DSM*! The question certainly needs to be asked how can it be that suicide doesn't even make it into the categories of mental illness in the *DSM*? Perhaps given that the person is dead, there is no longer a "patient" around to warrant a diagnosis, one might think cynically with a wan humor, but even that is not the case since there is also plenty of concern with postmortem diagnosis in medicine. Moreover, obviously in most cases the goal is to prevent the possible suicide. The often long process of being suicidal and moving toward a possible grim outcome of taking one's life certainly deserves a full treatment in the great book of psychiatric diagnosis as a crucially problematic mental state that needs expert treatment.

In what I would call the "epidemiological politics" of *DSM*, that is, the need of the psychiatric establishment to concretize and medicalize all disturbances of human experience and functioning, the omission of suicide from the *DSM* is an effort to relegate suicide to the role of a symptom of the "real" disorder—depression—and not a psychiatric disturbance in its own right.

But suicidality *is* a profound state of emotional-mental illness in its own right. A huge decision of whether to continue one's life or to terminate life is in progress! It is certainly a profound psychological process. This decision whether or not to take one's life is obviously a very human experience and psychological process that can't possibly be relegated to images of disease or to the constructs of a hereditary or physiological causation. Implicitly, suicidality contradicts the overriding metamessage of psychiatry that psychiatric conditions basically are medical and physiological, and perhaps this is a reason that out of the psychiatric book it has gone. But the fact is that the decision to commit suicide and the act of suicide are so much parts of the "book of life and death" that they can't be neglected or tossed out as a major subject in their own right and not just as a symptom.

There are several emotional pathways to suicide, so that one cannot reduce all suicidal behaviors to any one single pattern. However, posthumous reconstructions of suicides with the dead person's therapists or relatives and discussions with others who are alive after having made "unsuccessful" suicide attempts show that here, too, *getting stuck on the idea* is a vital aspect of many suicides. Once the idea of suicide takes hold, many a person proves unable to test or check the idea further against a possibility of letting go of the idea and rejecting it after all. Some patients who were in therapy following their suicide attempt report how a growing fascination developed in their minds with the idea of "going all the way," so that once the idea had been seeded and cultivated, it became almost inconceivable to turn back. There is even a kind of obligation that develops toward completion of the act as well as to the wholeness of the solution that has been conceived, and then a hypnotic fascination with the absoluteness and finality of the project.

This dynamic of being stuck with loyalty to an idea is, of course, superimposed on a base of other important dynamic issues such as deep feelings of deprivation of love and/or rage against family members, but the mechanism of totalistic thinking gives a final definition and impetus to the thoroughly irrational act that otherwise wouldn't have made sense.

I have found that working on this concept of going too far with the idea of suicide, getting stuck with it, taking it to an extreme, and getting excited at the totality of a plan have proven effective "handles," or points of entry, into the patient's mind in the psychotherapy of some survivors of suicide attempts. In each case I try to discover how the suicide plan was conceived and then how it developed. Many times when the suiciding person became stuck with their idea, no one who was involved in their lives applied themselves to break up their intention and plan.

Resnick described the great importance of confronting a potential suicider's plan for their suicide from the time that one discovers such an option is in the works.[29] This approach does not accept the understandable fear that asking a person about a potential plan for suicide might draw them *toward* acting on their thoughts more than they might have otherwise, or toward formulating such a plan that they really hadn't yet created. The point of view advanced by Resnick, which I have found very correct in my own clinical work, is that on the contrary one should press very hard to elicit from a potential suiciding person the full details of the plan they are in the process of organizing in their mind. Personally, I have never seen a case where this kind of inquiry has led to an exacerbation of the suicidal thinking or to spurring a person on to a suicidal act more immediately or energetically. What I have seen that fascinates me is that the sharing of the information of the suicide plan that has been developed seems to break a kind of spell of its unfolding further. If the plan was a secret beforehand, it now being known takes away some kind of magical power from it. Moreover, if the plan was a statement of the suicider's total emotional isolation, its revelation to another human being has moved the suicider into a degree of human connectedness that was not present before.

If the subject were not so grim and serious to begin with, an almost amusing aspect of the management of the suicide plan is that when I discover the suiciding person has already prepared their suicide note or letter, I demand that they deliver said decisive epistle to my hands, and in my experience, from the moment this is done the power of the suicide plan has been broken! I would certainly like to think that the humanistic meaning of what takes place is that because the therapist, as a representative of our human race, has broken into the isolation in the suicider's mind and cared enough to convey the wish that they not take their life, a change in attitude is facilitated. But I also can't help have the feeling that what is perhaps no less a major thrust or determinant of the breaking up of the suicide plan in this way is the simple fact that the *totality* of the secretly held and treasured plan has been broken by the sharing of the secret with another person.

Needless to say, management of the suicidal intention does not end with the revelation of the plan or any specific action of getting a suicide letter if it has been written. I now redouble my efforts as a therapist to address the core issues that have driven the potential suicider to consideration of taking their life.

In some cases, the suicide is an act of enormous fatigue and giving up the possibility of coping with an accumulation of burden and stress. In other cases, the suicider is driven by a powerful wish to take revenge on such and such person or persons in their life, almost literally by throwing their dead body accusingly at some very specific feet. In still other cases, the suicide is a plea for rest, a kind of swan dive into the welcoming arms of Earth where the unconscious archetypal fantasy is that a marvelous eternal rest and a kind of reunion with Mother Nature will take place. Sometimes suicide is a panicky flight from experiences of madness that are clawing away at the vital innards of a human being's experience, and there is a desperate need for release from the haunting persecution inside of their mind.

In terms of the conception that much of psychopathology is generated by succumbing to fascist thinking, there is a core idea or dynamic that is driving the suicidal plan in addition to what we learned of the stuckness of thinking about suicide once it begins. The core idea, such as one of the above dynamic themes, is held onto slavishly and turns into a kind of central belief or ideological fixation to which the patient becomes hypnotically obedient.[30] In each case, I consider it my responsibility to diagnose correctly the central or determining dynamic and then to advance psychotherapeutic interventions addressing that dynamic.

❖ Thus, a case where it was my judgment the girl planning to kill herself was out to leave her disfigured body as a revengeful accusation of her mother: "You are going to commit suicide so that your mother can see your body lying shattered in front of her," I said aggressively to the young woman whom I had begun to see following the referral of her church minister, who was very concerned that she had already made no less than three major suicide attempts in the course of seeing her previous therapist (who had worked with her forever kindly in an unending effort to be gently understanding of her).

"You're not going to have one bit of satisfaction from killing yourself," I continued, pretty much yelling at the young woman, "since you yourself are not going to be around to see your mother looking at your dead body! That's an illusion that you have cultivated, that somehow you'll be magically on the wall able to take in the pleasure of your great revenge. But nothing of that sort is going to happen. You're going to be plain dead, and your body will be shattered, ugly and disfigured by the leap you are planning to take from a high building."

She looked at me with hate, but also with a kind of clearing of some of the glaze from her eyes as she began to take in the reality that she would not be around to experience any satisfaction from punishing her mother with her death as she had magically believed. She also hated the idea of looking so ugly.

There also is a therapeutic strategy that I employ in addressing potential suicides that involves bringing in the patient's family—in other words, the people who are supposed to have the power to care that the patient not kill themselves. With good luck the family sessions that take place lead to members of the family conveying to the potential suicider that God forbid they should take their life, that they couldn't bear it, life would never be the same were they to die, and that they love and care for the person so much. But the truth is that in these therapy sessions following suicide attempts, there are scenarios where what *actually* happens is that the *lack of caring* of some members of the family, including the mother or father or even both, is revealed all too clearly, and in some cases even full-blown wishes of some in the family that the patient die are brought to the light of day. However, there is a strange paradoxical power to these revelations; somehow, seeing that it is so and who so want(s) them to die even helps many people to free themselves from being agents of the other person's horrible wishes toward them. Now they will be damned if they will give the other the satisfaction of killing themselves for them.

The great psychiatrist and family therapist Carl Whitaker[31] observed many times that when you see a suiciding person, go and look in their family and world of intimates to identify who it is among them that *wants* the suiciding person dead.

❖ A thirty-some-year-old woman colleague was in treatment with me for a severe depression. In the course of therapy I learned that a plan to take her life was crystalizing in her mind. She and I had known each other before she had sought treatment with me, and we had obviously liked one another; in fact, we had been attracted to each other as a man and woman and we had met a little socially, but we had never acted on our attraction and I felt free to take her into treatment when the time came that she requested it.

I was seeing her in individual sessions on the couch. There was little doubt that there was basically a good feeling between us of relatedness. She knew she was important to me and that I cared about her welfare. Nonetheless, the information she reported, including the contents of her dreams, suggested that depression was closing its grips around her, and that it was only a matter of time before she would act out a decisive plunge into a suicidal death.

I was very worried about her. I told her that I wanted to meet her with her parents who lived in the same city. She replied instantly and adamantly that she had no interest whatsoever in my meeting with her parents. I told her that I would call them myself, because I felt it was so important that we do something and not simply let the grim blackness overcome her. She replied angrily that she was totally against my or our meeting with them, and that she would not give me permission to call them.

"I don't give a damn whether you give me permission or not," I replied, "I'm so worried about you that I have to call them."

"But that's unethical," she screamed back at me, also as a knowing mental health professional. "You know you can't do something that I don't give you permission to do."

"I couldn't care less," I replied. "If you are headed down the chute so seriously, it doesn't bother me one bit to do something that is so to speak unethical if it could really help you."

> We fought, even deliciously, about whether or not I would call her parents, and my feeling was that the fight in its own right was very good medicine for this woman in her depression—since I believe that aggression is a prime antidote to depression. In any case, before I actually had to decide if I would contact her parents against her will (I believe I would have), she herself agreed after all to our meeting with them.
>
> We met in a series of four sessions, which indeed proved to be the basic and irrevocable turning point for the better in her therapy. In these sessions, I gave the parents the opportunity to tell their daughter how they would feel were she to take her life. What happened is that both mother and father seemingly said all the right things, but their affect and style in conveying the message of wanting their daughter to live were so shallow that it was obvious there wasn't that much real loving energy committed to her. Here, right before her eyes, and mine as a witness, was the clear-cut evocation of the original grayness of the emotional atmosphere in which she had grown up. She had been so much taken for granted as a pretty part of the scenery, but not as a real person whose life and welfare touched her parents' hearts and really mattered to them. The clarification that this was the background for the misery she had carried for so long in her heart was like a tonic for my young woman friend and patient, and she literally bolted forward in her therapy to a successful conclusion, and then on to a very healthy life including marrying for the first time after the therapy and having children.

The therapeutic philosophy that is generated from this point of view clearly views most states of suicide as derived from faulty ways of organizing one's ways of being in this world—including our emotional, cognitive, and spiritual ways of framing our experiences. What many modern-day non-psychiatrist therapists will do facing a suicidal patient is bring in a psychiatrist, if there is none on the case, who will introduce or increase medications or often will hospitalize the patient. The attention thus given the patient in the hospital, and the time and opportunity in the hospital (presumably including psychotherapy) for the patient to weigh what is going on in their life and to talk about the distress in their life may help.

However, there is also a percentage of such patients who commit suicide inside psychiatric hospitals, and certainly more who do so very soon after being discharged, and in some cases there is reason to suspect that the negative meaning of the hospitalization itself is what cements the patient's decision to go ahead and complete their killing themselves.

What is often missing in methods of managing suicidality is a conception of how the potential suiciding person is operating as a human being out of despair and loss of hope and a sense that there are no more options remaining in their life, and that the patient has now become a dispenser of death or what one therapist, Larry Gernsbacher, calls "an unconscious dictator." According to Gernsbacher, the common characteristics that are present in all suicides to some degree are narcissism, eccentricity, compulsivity, perfectionism, and irrationality, and the only way to interrupt the progression to suicide is to make the patient realize and give up the absolute qualities of their unconscious dictator.[32]

Obviously, suicide is an imposition of a truly violent solution onto a life situation. The patient has declared that having failed to achieve their goals in this world, they want out. While the simple interpretation of the suicidal act at face value is that the person has given up is not very hard to see, it is not always recognized that in treating themselves as deserving death, suiciding people often are also punishing themselves for not getting life right. They are ruling that they do not deserve better. In the name of the highest tribunal of their own mind, they are condemning themselves to deserve to die. There is a "kangaroo court" in the name of Fascist Mind principles that if you don't succeed the way you are supposed to, you are an abject failure and deserve to be eliminated. The favored and most beloved punishment of fascists, which is taking people's lives, is invoked against oneself.

In addition, and not only in the category of suicides where the driving dynamic to begin with is a wish to wreak revenge on a member of one's family, it is inevitable that a major meaning of virtually all suicides is the imposition on one's family and intimates of a huge burden of upset, guilt, and accusations of desertion. Virtually every case of suicide also has meanings as an act of interpersonal aggression against intimates. Fascist Mind thinking is inclined to punish errant persons; in suicide the punishment is both of oneself and of one's intimates.

Except under dire circumstances such as terminal illness or being tortured by an enemy who is going to kill us, most instances where a person takes a decisive decision to end their life in suicide are certainly acts of psychopathology. From the point of view of this book, it is also to be understood as a major example of Fascist Mind thinking. Yet many psychiatrically oriented writings—including the textbook in my first college course on abnormal psychology, whose instructor was the author of the text—insist that many people who commit suicide are not mentally ill in any way.

CONCLUSION

In this chapter we have reviewed some of the most "popular" psychiatric conditions of neurosis, depression, and suicide. In each case we have advanced an interpretation that a person's mind is dictating to them how they must act, and failing that—because the disallowed feelings are too strong to be stopped—the person punishes themselves and/or others in their life. It's a mind game that is just like dictatorial fascists like to play on the level of society. Therapy is a battle for freedom—of one's sexuality, anger, love, talent, will, or the dignity of one's identity against oppression.

Table 3.6. Dynamics of Fascist Mind in Selected Psychopathology: Suicide

	01-02 **TOTALITY, OVER-CERTAINTY, ABSOLUTISM, AND MAGICAL THINKING**	*03-04* **CENSORSHIP OF INFORMATION, OBEDIENCE, CONFORMITY, AND INTOLERANCE OF DISSENT**
SUICIDE	It is important to diagnose the motivations for suicide that tend to end up as a total and certain idea driving the suiciding person on. Characteristic motivations include the following: a) giving up, emotional exhaustion, lack of hope, a feeling one no longer has options; b) a strong desire for revenge, the suicide is planned virtually as thrusting one's dead body accusingly into the face(s) of an enemy; c) yearning for rest, regression, and reunion with "Mother Nature"; d) flight from inner torment and persecutory madness. Whichever idea underlies the suicidal impulse, treatment is needed to dislodge the idea from serving as a driving force for a suicidal plan. The suicide plan itself often becomes an obsessional conviction of a perfect "final solution." The patient may devote much time and thought savoring and working on the plan. Intriguingly, interrupting the planning sequence, such as taking away a suicide letter that has been prepared in	The triggering emotional reaction often holds the patient in its grip as a total idea to which they are obedient and which they confirm and reconfirm on the basis of all available information. Many times the need to obey or conform and complete the plan becomes the relentless driving force of the suicidal sequence, even more than the original sadness, despair, and rage that triggered the suicidal urge to begin with.

	advance, often will dramatically stop the suicidal behavior from progressing. *Role of anxiety: Anxiety is welcome. The worst picture is when the patient becomes so calm because the very plan to commit suicide spares them a continuing sense of struggle with life. In fact a serious sign of imminent suicide can be an unexpected calm or even happiness that signal a decision has been made to end one's misery.*	
05 **SUPERIORITY, EXCESSIVE POWER-SEEKING, AND PREJUDICE**	06 **VIOLENCE, RETALIATION AGAINST DISSENT, SACRIFICE AND, DESTRUCTION**	07 **DENIALS OF DOING HARM TO SELF AND OTHERS**
Superiority is occasionally the leitmotif of the suiciding person—"I am too good to allow myself to live so disgraced," or "I won't continue my life without enjoying the more privileged position that is due me." A motive of revenge against others is not infrequent, but superiority, power-seeking, and prejudice are not usually prominent as such in the drive to suicide. However, beyond psychophilosophical considerations of the superiority assumed "over God and nature" in taking one's own life, the suiciding person often does leave a terrible trail of imposed emotional wreckage on intimates.	**Doing Harm to Self** This is the ultimate possible punishment to oneself. Even when the predominant emotion is one of relief from unbearable stress, suicide involves murder of oneself. **Doing Harm to Others** The suiciding person also leaves a terrible trail of harm to others in their lives, such as their children, siblings, parents, even business associates and neighbors.	In the suicider's mind, there are often magical feelings of not going to die, and of surviving to harvest pleasure and the benefits of one's act, such as seeing the revenge wreaked on a given hated person, or "enjoying" an ultimate restfulness and reunion with "Mother Nature."

Note: Some of us accept the legitimacy and moral decency of a decision to commit suicide under certain unbearable conditions, such as in a concentration camp, although personally, were I in a camp, I pray first of all for the strength to keep looking for ways to escape and/or take revenge.
Source: Created by the author.

> Anxiety is the dizziness of freedom, which emerges when the spirit wants to posit the synthesis and freedom looks down into its own possibility, laying hold of finiteness to support itself.[33]
>
> —*Soren Kierkegaard*

> My depression is the most faithful mistress I have known—no wonder then, that I return the love.[34]
>
> —*Soren Kierkegaard*

> Man suffers most from the suffering he fears, but never appears, therefore he suffers more than god meant him to suffer.
>
> —*Dutch Proverb*

> The state of man: Inconstancy, boredom, anxiety [in the original French: "inquietude"]. Nothing is so insufferable to man as to be completely at rest, without passions, without business, without diversion, without study. He then feels his nothingness, his forlornness, his insufficiency, his dependence, his weakness, his emptiness. There will immediately arise from the depth of his heart weariness, gloom, sadness, fretfulness, vexation, despair.[35]
>
> —*Pascal*

NOTES

1. The word *neurosis* was dropped from *DSM-4* in 1994. The dropping of neurosis from the *DSM* was discussed in the previous book, *A Democratic Mind,* in a chapter titled "The *DSM* and the Human Condition." There are at least two separate issues involved in what from the point of view of intellectual history was a monumental change. The first issue is how the decision was made suddenly and arbitrarily by the powers that be who rule the *DSM.* While this may not be the most important issue, it is interesting in its right, and also brings up issues of totalitarian-type processes in the exercise of power on the part of professionals in mental health. The second and probably more important issue is the inherent correctness and incorrectness of this major change in the language and conceptualization of psychiatric problems. Does the dropping of "neuroses" advance or retard our real capacity to heal these conditions effectively? Does the slap in the face to a traditional conception of unconscious dynamics inspire or depress professional dedication and skill in treatment?

2. Freud, Sigmund (1952–1974). *The Complete Psychological Works of Sigmund Freud, op. cit.*

3. Ansbacher, Heinz, L. and Rowena, R. (Eds.) (1964). *The Individual Psychology of Alfred Adler: A Systematic Presentation in Selections from His Writings.* Paperback originally published in 1956. New York: Harper Perennial. See also earlier references to Adler's own writings.

4. Horney, Karen (1937). *The Neurotic Personality of Our Time. op cit.*; Horney, Karen (1942), *Self-Analysis.* New York: Norton. See also Horney, Karen (Ed.) (1946). *Are You Considering Psychoanalysis? op. cit.*

5. Saul, Leon (1956). *The Hostile Mind: The Sources and Consequences of Rage and Hate.* New York: Random House; Saul, Leon (1972). *Psychodynamically Based Psychotherapy.* New York: Science House.

6. Ullman, Leonard P. and Krasner, Leonard (Eds.) (1965). *Case Studies in Behavior Modification.* New York: Holt, Rinehart & Winston. (According to Leonard Ullman, this was "the first book to use the words 'behavior modification' in its title." Quotation from This Week's Classic Citation, CC/No.11, March 17, 1980.)

7. One needs to understand the considerable significance of the personality theory adopted for the treatment work of a clinician. It certainly makes a difference if one thinks that the patient is or is not capable of changing a wrong way of thinking or living, or needs to be quieted, tranquilized, or cleansed of crazy thoughts by medicines. It also makes a difference if one is looking for the patient's errors in thinking and living in one specific circumscribed area of life experience, such as sexuality or feelings of adequacy, power, or intimacy, or if one is looking at a wider range of functions. It also makes a difference whether or not one also examines the patient's *methods* of thinking and experiencing, and not only their contents—for example, whether the patient is open or closed to satisfying meaningful relationships or to new information, feedback and criticism, and more. There are many interesting books about personality theories, and any number of classic works that focused on the basic style of life of a patient. See, for example, the classic brilliant work of Reich, Wilhelm (1990). *Character Analysis.* New York: Farrar, Straus, and Giroux (original published in German 1933, and English translation 1945).

8. Wolfe, Barry E. (2011). The case of Rachel: An integrative psychotherapy for panic disorder. *Psychotherapy Bulletin,* 46(1), 8–13 (quotations from p. 8).

9. Ellis, Albert and Harper, Robert, A. (1961). *A Guide to Rational Living.* Upper Saddle River, NJ: Prentice-Hall; Ellis, Albert (1962). *Reason and Emotion in Psychotherapy.* Secaucus, NJ: Carol Publishing Group; Ellis, Albert and Harper, Robert A. (1968). *A Guide to Successful Marriage.* Hollywood, CA: Wilshire.

10. Shapiro, David (1974). *Neurotic Styles* (originally published 1965). New York: Basic Books; Shapiro, David (1989). *Psychotherapy of Neurotic Character.* New York: Basic Books; Shapiro, David (1996). Character and psychotherapy. *American Journal of Psychotherapy,* 50(1), 3–13.

11. Horney, Karen. (1942). *Self-Analysis, ibid.*

12. Ellis, Albert, *ibid.*

13. May, Rollo. (1996). *The Meaning of Anxiety* (originally published 1950). New York: W. W. Norton. The recognition and celebration of strong desires to be "more" can be integrated with exercises of techniques of quieting oneself *and* confirming one's heartfelt goals.

14. Here are examples of a therapist's possible instructions that are designed to address a patient's real and healthy desires for achievement and self-fulfillment along with relaxation techniques:

When you want very much to succeed at a task but it is frightening you, try breathing slowly and deeply a few times, and then see how your breath is being exhaled into a beautiful world around you and that you are part of a miracle of nature. Then think about what you really want to become.

When you are anxious, try to think of how or what it is you want to be more of your own true self. When you make contact with this real desire in yourself, see if you can organize more power for moving your life in this direction that you really want.

15. American Psychiatric Association (2013). *DSM-5 Desk Reference*. Washington, DC: American Psychiatric Association.

16. In the *DSM-5 Desk Reference*, the section "Dissociative Disorders" appears on pp. 155–159, "Somatic Symptom and Related Disorders" on pp. 161–167.

17. Ellis, Albert (1987). The impossibility of achieving consistently good mental health, *op. cit.* (quotation on p. 368).

18. The subject of Prozac-linked suicide, and less so but also murder, is discussed in *A Democratic Mind*. It has been fascinating but also frightening to watch the ins and outs of the struggle of some of the press with this issue. We reported in *A Democratic Mind* how Israel's leading (most respected) newspaper, *Haaretz*, went so far as to publish a *front-page story* translated from the *Boston Globe* about a huge toll of suicides of patients on Prozac. The number that was given in this article, as of that time many years ago, was 50,000 suicide deaths! Placing the story on the front page, and reprinting the incredible casualties and numbers was impressive, but so was what then followed in the newspaper . . . nothing at all! There was no follow-up story at the time. I didn't see any Letters to the Editor. The startling story was dead! And while I have no evidential knowledge, I certainly can wonder if pharmaceutical capitalism had anything to do with "killing" the story of Prozac being a killer for too many people—from my point of view, most probably when the medication is used incorrectly, without psychotherapy.

Over the years the grim results have exploded. There is an endless number of reports. As noted, there is also evidence that antidepressants including Prozac are implicated in homicidal thoughts and behaviors. Several reports have implicated Prozac in school shootings such as Columbine and others. See, for example, Davey, Monica and Harris, Gardiner (March 26, 2005). Family wonders if Prozac prompted school shootings. *New York Times*. http://www.nytimes.com/2005/03/26/national/26shoot.html?ref=topics&_r=0.

Documentary investigative journalist Michael Moore is reported to say "it's possible." In a 2012 review by *Forbes* magazine, the Establishment point of view is presented along with evidence that points to a meds-suicide connection, especially for children: Walton, Alice G. (February 2, 2012). New evidence on the antidepressant-suicide connection in kids. *Forbes*. Retrieved January 1, 2015.

19. *Injury Lawyer News* (August 19, 2014). Antidepressant lawsuits. http://injurylawyer-news.com/antidepressants/antidepressant-lawsuits/. Retrieved January 1, 2015.

20. Kelley, John (March 2, 2010). Antidepressants: Do they "work" or don't they? *Scientific American*. http://www.scientificamerican.com/article/antidepressants-do-they-work-or-dont-they/.

21. Gallagher, Ian and Hall, Allan (March 29, 2015). Is killer co-pilot's teacher ex-girlfriend pregnant with his child? Couple found out 'weeks before crash' as it emerges she left him because of "erratic" behavior. *Daily Mail Online*. http://www.dailymail.co.uk/news/article-3016420/Killer-pilot-Andreas-Lubitz-planned-marry-teacher-girlfriend-broke-relationship-just-weeks-Alps-crash-police-small-mountain-anti-depressants-flat.html.

22. Seligman, Martin, E.P. (1974). Depression and learned helplessness. In Raymond J. Friedman and Martin M. Katz (Eds.). *The Psychology of Depression: Contemporary Theory and Research*. Washington, DC: Winston-Wiley; Seligman, M. E. P. and Csikszentmahalyi, M. (2000). Positive psychology: An introduction. *American Psychologist, Special Issue on Happiness, Excellence, and Optimal Human Functioning*, 55(1), 5–14.

23. Beck, Aaron T. (1976). *Cognitive Therapy and the Emotional Disorders*. New York: International Universities Press.

24. Raimy, Victor (1975). *Misunderstandings of the Self.* San Francisco: Jossey-Bass.

25. Beck, Aaron T.; Rush, A. John; Shaw, Brian F.; and Emery, Gary (1979). *Cognitive Therapy of Depression.* New York: Guilford.

26. Rogerson, Mark D.; Gottlieb, Michael C.; Handlesman, Mitchell M.; Knapp, Samuel; and Younggren, Jeffrey (2011). Nonrational processes in ethical decision making. *American Psychologist,* 66(7), 614–523 (quotation on p. 615). The authors attribute this definition to Baron, Jonathan (2000). *Thinking and Deciding.* New York: Cambridge University Press.

27. Munder, Thomas; Brütsc, Oliver; Leonhart, Rainer; Gerger, Heike; and Barth, Jurgen (2013). Researcher allegiance in psychotherapy outcome research: an overview of reviews. *Clinical Psychology Review,* 33: 501–511.

28. Khan, Arif; Faucett, James; Lichtenberg, Pesach; Kirsch, Irving; and Brown, W. A. (2012). A Systematic Review of Comparative Efficacy of Treatments and Controls for Depression. http://www.ncbi.nlm.nih.gov/pmc/articles/PMC3408478/. Retrieved July 14, 2014.

29. Resnick, H.L.P. (Ed.) (1968). *Suicidal Behaviors: Diagnosis and Management by 48 Authors.* New York: Little Brown and Co., 73–81. As I noted earlier, I have found this book an excellent guide for many years. For contemporary sets of guidelines by the American Psychological Association and the American Psychiatric Association, see American Psychological Association Education Directorate (Web page), Suicide: What Therapists Need to Know, http://www.apa.org/education/ce/suicide.pdf. Retrieved September 21, 2014; American Psychiatric Association (Web page), Assessing and Treating Suicidal Behaviors: A Quick Reference Guide. (Based on Practice Guideline for the Assessment and Treatment of Patients with Suicidal Behaviors, originally published 2003).

30. Litman and Tabachnick summed up the key dynamics of suicide as follows: "Lethal 'committed' suicide nearly always involves a suicide plan which was developed gradually over a period of time and rehearsed in fantasy and preliminary action before finally being actualized as behavior. The final suicidal act is nearly always preceded by a period of increasing psychological crisis and emotional conflict during which the potential victim is consciously ambivalent, 'mixed up,' and confused as he tries to control and resist the largely unconscious fantasies and drives which push him toward self-destruction.

"Some of the more important unconscious fantasy systems which contribute to every suicide take the form of wishes as follows:

A tired wish to escape, surcease, sleep, 'death' . . .

A guilty wish for punishment, atonement, sacrifice, to make restitution . . .

A hostile wish for revenge, for power and control, to punish and to murder . . .

An erotic wish for passionate masochistic surrender, the greatest ecstasy, for reunion with the loved dead . . .

A hopeful wish for rescue, rebirth, rehabilitation, a new start, and a new life . . ."

Litman, Robert E. and Tabachnick, Norman D. (1968). *Psychoanalytic Theories of Suicide.* In H.L.P. Resnick (Ed.), *Suicidal Behaviors, op. cit.,* pp.73–81 (quotation on p. 74).

31. Whitaker, Carl and Bumberry, William M. (1988). *Dancing with the Family: A Symbolic-Experiential Approach.* New York: Brunner/Mazel; Napier, Augustus Y. and Whitaker, Carl A. (1978). *The Family Crucible: The Intense Experience of Family Therapy.* New York: Harper & Row; Whitaker, Carl A. and Keith, David V. (1981). Symbolic-experiential therapy. In Alan S. Gurman and David P. Kniskern (Eds.). *Handbook of Family Therapy.* New York: Brunner/Mazel, 187–225.

32. Gernsbacher, Larry Morton (1985). *The Suicide Syndrome: Origins, Manifestations and Alleviation of Human Self-Destructiveness.* New York: Human Sciences Press.

33. Kierkegaard, Soren (1844). *The Concept of Anxiety*. See Johann Karl Friedrich Rosenkranz, Rosenkranz's Philosophy of Education (February 18, 1887), *Science*, Vol. 9: 174–175.

34. *Bulletin: Comparative Literature Series* (1912). Texas University, No. 3, 43.

35. Pascal, Blaise (1662). *Pensées*, Section II (French). The Project Gutenberg of Pascal's Pensées, *Sections 127 and 131*. Introduction by T. S. Eliot. New York: E. P. Dutton. Reprinted with permission.

4

Personality and Character Disorders of Self-Entitlement and Power

PERSONALITY AND CHARACTER DISORDERS AS DISORDERS OF SELF-ENTITLEMENT AND POWER OVER OTHERS

Among the common, everyday emotional disorders in the lives of an amazing number of people is a range of problems that are considered neither neurotic or reactive manifestations of suffering and disturbances in everyday functions, nor manifestations of psychoses or major breaks with the rational and the realistic, but persistent personality disorders.

Once upon a time in mental health these were also called "character disorders." I think this is a good term that should not have been thrown out by the too frequently arbitrary decision-makers who re-create mental health nomenclature in each successive edition of the *DSM* as if there were a scientific or evidential basis (information from controlled scientific studies of various mental illnesses) for their decisions, which there isn't. In the case of "character disorders," I would guess that the implication of a moral defect, or a weakness in moral development, was too much for the American psychiatric culture that embraces a nostrum of not stigmatizing any person and trying to hide as much as possible any issues of moral disturbances in the person, as opposed to medicalized concepts of ills that somehow befall people. The personality/character disorders imply a mix of disorders of self-regulation and ethical faults that cannot be looked at for what they are because they violate the "rule" that nowhere are ethical values to be a consideration in "mental health"—only "illness" from ill-defined magic or chance, and most of all from biological (including genetic) sources. I continue to find the disorders of character a major aspect of many of the "personality disorders"—the current official name—for in most cases there is really something quite wrong with what we commonly call the character of many of these people.

THE ESSENCE OF PERSONALITY AND CHARACTER DISORDERS

Included in these disorders are self-restrictive personality disorders where a person lives in emotional poverty, shyness, a restricted range of living, and a life of retreating and failing to seek a full and fair share of "beingness"; narcissistic disorders where the person is overtly self-indulging and taking advantage of others for their own selfish interests; addictive personality disorders where the character problems are in undue self-gratification; aggressive ways of life as if with a license to be antisocial or excessively powerful; and paranoid personalities with their character defects of self-indulging suspiciousness and unreal accusation of others.

The common denominator of the personality disorders is an excess of self-serving or catering to oneself selfishly that dominates the personality and enslaves the person to their needs and desires. The child in a person predominates rather than being left behind in childhood.

There are various forms of retreats into one's self, self-indulgence, and self-entitlement. In some cases a person is genuinely unable to go beyond a very elementary concern with their own overly circumscribed world. In other personality disorders there is a much more clear choice of motive and purpose for grabbing all one can for oneself. In still others there are openly more malevolent aggressive intentions of using and abusing people. But there is a value in looking at a shared theme, in all of these disorders, of being so overinvolved with one's own needs and desires, whether unwillingly or willingly, that a well-rounded life becomes impossible to a great extent. Connections with other people are either shallow or full of unfairness, and other people are turned into tools for one's selfish pursuits.

I have divided personality and character disorders into the following three categories:[1]

- Group 1: Self-Defeating, Self-Damaging, Self-Restricting, and Borderline Personalities
- Group 2: Narcissistic, Self-Indulgent, and Addictive Personalities
- Group 3: Antisocial, Power-Seeking, and Paranoid Personalities

I think there is some value to highlighting a gradient of relative differentiation between the primarily self-restrictive personality disorders, the narcissistic personality disorders, and the more flagrantly abusive antisocial, power-seeking, and paranoid disorders in respect of the extent to which the person is taking their needs out on others. The self-restrictive personality disorders make for a person who often looks and acts the inadequate nebbish or ne'er-do-well and/or who is an unreliable pain in the neck to others because of their chronic weakness (from whatever inadvertent constitutional source or from an inner choice); the narcissistic, self-indulgent, and addictive are drains on others, and often seriously exploitative, because they are pandering endlessly to themselves; but the antisocial, power-seeking, and paranoid go major steps further in that many of them are out to overpower, use, abuse, and perhaps even destroy others—their lives are a hunting down of other people as their prey.

The self-restrictive personality disorders involve repeated self-defeating and self-damaging behaviors such as an inability to get a job or repeated failures to succeed in work and hold steady employment; a pattern of reduced social relationships or inability to perform simple social relationship skills such as making friends, maintaining a conversation, or spending friendship time with other persons; repeated failure to take care of oneself medically, such as avoiding going to a doctor even when there are signs of possible illness, and flagrant failure to maintain a routine of normal health prevention habits; lack of trust in other people; and eccentricity, inappropriate mood, and behavior that is odd or peculiar and can move into paranoid interpretations of benign events and unforgiving enmity. Therapy with these people is very difficult. Many never commit themselves to attempting real change, and there are more than a few hints of resistance to giving up one's "security in inadequacy," let alone those who are victims of constitutional limitations for which there may be no cure, although very often there are possible compensations available to those who make efforts to generate them.

The narcissistic, self-indulgent disorders are ways of being in the world that involve insistence on immediate gratification of one's overindulgences at the considerable expense and even direct exploitation of other people including one's closest family or intimates. There is strong resistance to learning from mistakes or taking corrections from others, be they therapists or members of one's family. In the long run, the person defeats themselves by adopting a position or way of being in the world that is designed to relieve anxiety and produce pleasure, and takes this position to its blind extremes where they themselves are consumed. Taking one's pleasure and satisfying one's desires and demands is the overriding dynamic of behavior in these cases.

The antisocial, power-seeking, and paranoid personalities are ways of being in the world by living at the expense of others and abusing others. Only rarely is there an availability to correction by one's family, therapists, or even representatives of a disciplinary legal system such as probation officers. There is rarely anxiety in the strongly power-driven person, at least so long as they are riding high on top of others. On the contrary, the posturing is often one of great certainty, and taking unquestioned command of other people and situations.

Insofar as anxiety does leak out, theoretically it would be a sign of the accessibility of some healthy conscience and an availability to humanistic influences, but there is also a danger that anxiety will bring on a compensatory rush of greater power-seeking, and perhaps cruelty as well, so as to cut off the human stirrings of upset and questioning. Sometimes tyrannical people do turn up in medical offices with hysterical somatization or psychosomatic illnesses, which are the pathway to which their denied anxieties are diverted, and occasionally they respond to their illnesses with a wave of good conscience and a resolve to be more humane or generous to others. However, we need to know very clearly that in general, power-driven people may cause huge destruction to others, whether on a smaller scale of hurting the lives of intimates, or by virtue of being agents of actual death to larger communities of people and nations. At the same time, in the long run many of them—but not all—tend to bring destruction on themselves as people, and society either abandons them or otherwise regroups to fight and overcome them.

Overall, all three types of personality disorders often involve people who are increasingly cut off from their community, and whose behaviors can lead to enduring impairments in social, occupational, or other areas of functioning. Unfortunately, however, and most important for us to know before we are carried away simply to a concept of an illness and the implication that people can't function well because they are ill, there are also too many exceptions: Narcissistic and certainly antisocial power-seeking and paranoid personalities may achieve major political power and leadership roles, and the period of their rule—whether as the head of a department of psychiatry, a head of a secret police service, or a head of state—becomes a period of bloody hell and grave suffering for many people. As leaders with power they can be high functioners who make the world around them sick, and thwart and destroy the natural life needs of countless people over whom they exert power.

The personality-and-character-disordered style becomes a total template for the person's life, which blocks out the reality requirements of other functions that are inconsistent with their safety-and-pleasure-seeking patterns. However effective the character disorder may be for a while in introducing temporary safety and pleasure in a person's life, the persons suffering a personality and character disorder do themselves in by becoming rigidly locked into a single way of experiencing and coping. The potential of the self to be a growing person is generally defeated by an inability to allow advice, learning, taking in new information, and especially knowledge of the consequences of one's behaviors, or any form of therapy. The belief system becomes a total commitment to a way of life that seriously limits and can even destroy the life of a person—for example, chronic distancing and withdrawal from people, self-defeating health habits or losses of employment, alcohol, drugs, obesity, gambling, suspiciousness, outbursts at people, and ways of manipulation, deceiving, lording it over, and plotting against other people that make life bitter and eventually bring on retaliation from others. On the bigger stages of life, many known actors who did rule their worlds cruelly for too long are, thank heaven, finally overthrown, expelled, brought to trial or imprisoned, or often killed by the people over whom they had ruled with an iron hand. But to avoid fairy tales of the good always winning over the bad, as noted, many of these go to their graves after having destroyed even millions of other people, and some of them even die in their own beds.

I think psychology and psychotherapy need objective ways to label these people—the more so if they are heads of states—as early as possible because so many lives are at stake.[2] I sometimes think that if we really knew how to look at the true emotional status of representative cross-sections of our human race, we might find that a *majority* of human beings are driven by selfish interests and are actively exploiting and/or hurting other people in their lives. It is a frightening thought about the stage of evolution of our species, which insults all that is lovely in human society but certainly fits the endless manifestations of excessive power-seeking and injustices, persecution, everyday violence, terrorism, genocide, and war making we encounter in human life.

I believe the personality disorders are so common, and so much sources of the unending problems in human affairs, that I am devoting to them much more attention and detail than even to some of the traditional mental illnesses.

AUTHENTICITY, COMMON SENSE, AND COMMON KNOWLEDGE IN PSYCHOLOGICAL DIAGNOSIS

In truth, once one understands the basic principle of personality disorders, one also can identify the role of this same principle in a further variety of conditions that ostensibly are separate illnesses with their own causes. Thus, many studies have revealed the profound rewards that patients unconsciously can draw from remaining ill or even making themselves more sick.

The basic issue is a battle—and choice—between striving for a high level of self-direction, potency, and capability versus turning to dependence and exploitation. The issue presents itself over and over again in many different aspects of our lives. There are clearly overriding patterns of organization of self that define a person as committed to a lifestyle of self-indulgence to an extent that leads to distortions of major aspects of reality. Self-indulgence includes actual physical acts like eating excessively and bizarrely and thus distorting reality in disregarding the quite likely future price of diabetes, heart disease, and loss of years of life. Obviously, it includes excessive drinking and drugs, but it also includes taking excessive power over others. Self-indulgence includes undue reliance on a defense mechanism like blaming another for one's weaknesses or making oneself superior by shaming and humiliating the other, or the distortions and disruptions of reality that follow from insulting deprecation of others.

There are too many possible paths to list all the basic ways that the paradigm of personality disorder can play out. Thus, every *DSM* generation will have to list all sorts of new substances that are being used abusively, as well as all sorts of behaviors that can become popular modes in any given culture and any given era. How about for our times, "Digital Instruments Abuse Disorders" or "Personality Disorders of Inability to Commit to Intimate Relationships"? And what about "Persecutions of Alleged Witches" for Salem back in America's colonial history, or "Persecutions of Designated Heretics" in Isabella's Spain, and "Dedicated Genocidal Persecution of Ethnic Minorities" in so many different venues and eras?

Obviously, the authentic diagnosis of personality disorders has to rise above the limiting dicta of the current political correctness in a culture—and that very much includes demands for political correctness within the psychiatric profession. Thus, in our time, I would also venture to create a diagnosis of a "Personality Disorder of Excessive Reliance on Psychiatric Medications" as an escape from anxiety, challenges, and coping, but there can't be anyone out there who will be foolish enough to think the *DSM* people will even hold a meeting to debate this proposal. Not dissimilarly, I would think of including a "Personality Disorder of Obesity" in the list of personality disorders that I chart here. As we've noted in alarm more than once, although the *DSM* has not ever listed such a disorder in its official list, 30-plus percent of Americans are obese, and the costs to their health, which include an actual shortening of life by years, are horrifying, but the long-standing political correctness of American culture regarding fat people still rules the *DSM* (with its floridly arbitrary and political judgments dressed up as if medical and scientific).

At least the *DSM* tells it honestly about itself when it says in the introduction to the section on personality disorders, "An enduring pattern of inner experience and behavior that deviates markedly from the *expectations of the individual's culture*"[3] (my italics). This means: Be like your society tells you to be, no matter how stupid, cruel, or totalitarian your current culture is! I think this formulation gives us a singularly truthful perception of how *DSM* is concerned with getting along and functioning well, almost no matter what the ethical meanings of your behavior.

My point of view is that the key or basic standard of mental health is not blind "good adjustment" to your surroundings, but a principled, forceful stand on behalf of protecting and fulfilling first your life and then, too, the lives of others. With this formulation we can say unambiguously that it is wrong for you to flagellate yourself even if your church or Jonestown leader tells you to do so, and it's wrong to harm and kill unarmed innocent others even if your government tells you to do so.

In my opinion, an authentic psychotherapist treats people according to accumulating knowledge as well as intuitive wisdom of whether given behaviors do harm to the person engaging in them or to others. The *DSM* list is near irrelevant. The power-seeking person Karen Horney described in *The Neurotic Personality of Our Time*[4]; the man or woman who enter into a marriage without revealing to their spouse that they are gay; and the parents who pay off Ponzi debts of a son who has been running a crooked business are nowhere to be seen in *DSM* lists, but they all have a bona fide disorder in their personalities.

So in truth I cannot possibly list all the forms of personality and character disorders. But we can understand and define the basic concept of a "too much" for oneself at the expense of (1) one's health, vitality, fulfillment of real talents, and capacity for meaningful human relationships, and/or (2) the physical or emotional safety and well-being of others.

PERSONALITY AND CHARACTER DISORDERS AND THE FUTURE OF OUR PLANETARY CIVILIZATION

To return to the opening frame of this chapter: Beyond the fact that a great many people earn for themselves diagnoses as personality and character disorders because they fit the *DSM*'s criterion that they are damaging their *own* capacities for everyday normative adjustment and functioning, if we adopt my proposal that all mental health diagnoses also involve the extent to which a person is doing significant harm either to themselves or to others, or both, we extend the concept to still huger populations. I would like to suggest a broad view:

1. Personality and character disorders are the most common, prevailing, and widespread psychiatric disorders of our time.
2. As disorders of self-indulgence and claiming excessive power over other people, personality and character disorders are in a sense the psychiatric face of the issue of our civilization's capacity to survive.

The sadness and nastiness of the upset and disasters that befall millions of individuals who are suffering personality and character disorders are awesome. Look at the tragedies of so, so many millions of people everywhere in their daily lives who are crippled by their inability to work, and/or feel and express love for other people, and/or experience a basic joy and gratitude for being alive. Each and every one of these conditions is painful in its own right, and from the point of view of human community, it means that at any given time an enormous number of our friends, neighbors, and fellow human beings are in poor psychological and/or physical and/or spiritual health. Consequences include:

- Criminality as a way of life with repeated periods of one's life spent jailed.
- Breakdown of the family unit, so that in the United States and some other Western countries more than half of the children do not grow up in homes with both parents.
- So many of us cannot live successfully in equitable and mutually fulfilling intimate relationships with others.
- Huge numbers of people everywhere who could be productive expect to be supported by one welfare system or another.
- People high and low who knowingly deceive, manipulate, and exploit others in their businesses and professions—for example, the manufacture of defective and even dangerous products such as medicines that are not licensed in certain Western countries being marketed elsewhere in undeveloped countries; or gargantuan swindles even with the complicity of seeming giants of integrity, like Bernard Madoff or the former U.S. accounting firm of Arthur Andersen, who were responsible for swindles that affected all of us.
- People who swagger openly or subtly while pushing around and lording over others in their families or over people who work for them or are otherwise dependent on them—including endless bureaucrats and service-providers who exploit people's needs for their services to be insulting and/or superior to them (most unfortunately including any number of medical and other health professionals!).

In a large sense, the personality and character disorders are an anthem of a pandemic human selfishness, readiness to grab from others, and readiness to hurt others. The diagnosable personality disorders are the psychiatric side of the moon, as it were, of the Zimbardo-proven readiness to lord over others,[5] the Milgram-proven readiness to hurt others,[6] and the Browning-readiness of "ordinary" people to go all the way and eliminate others entirely.[7]

I am not unaware of the fact that many people with personality and character disorders do not have much of a choice about being stuck in their self-centered lives. See for example the first group in this chapter of self-defeating, self-damaging, self-restricting, and borderline personalities. Characteristically, they were brought up in damaging ways that established their lifelong patterns—for example, a little girl who is encouraged unconsciously to become obese, or a little boy who is catered to and slobbered over. And while I am thrilled and deeply respect those people who grow up to see their faults in the mirror and themselves brilliantly change the course of their lives for the better, or those who seek psychological treatment and use it effectively, I cannot simply blame those who do not have this gift of self-correction. They are indeed casualties like many other medical casualties of forces outside and beyond them. Even so, I wonder if any of these weakened people would not have better chances of recovering if human society provided more clearly images and ways of life devoted to decent values of caring for oneself and others and for one's community. Even if there are millions of people suffering a "Black Plague of Personality Disorders," we cannot accept illness as "normal," and we need to be able to project in our cultural images, values, and goals how to be a healthy personality. Psychiatry in our time is so busy diagnosing and treating symptoms, it is no longer inspiring.

How sad that for the most part even in democracies we fail to generate an everyday community that values productivity both for oneself and one's community; encourages commitment, connection to others, and generosity; prohibits smoking and use of other known substances, bans hand guns and automatic weapons; fights violence including not allowing TV and other representations of violence for the *Clockwork Orange* gore of it all; and sets standards of appreciation of life, fairness, decency, pluralism, and democracy. *A life-loving culture in its own right can be a real treatment for personality and character disorders*—perhaps then there will also be more individuals with personality disorders who will then make good use of counseling and therapy on the basis of aspirations to live up to the culture valuing decency and caring for life. Certainly for the crazy, personality-disordered planetary civilization we currently live and are dying in, we need a changed paradigm of respect for life.

In my opinion, any student of our mental health professions who will violate the contemporary mode of focusing on concern for the dysfunctions of individuals by focusing on ethical goals for living is likely to be sanctioned and punished.[8] And yet the further absurdity is that a large number of writers in psychology already long ago came to the conclusions that the cultivation of goodness and decency make for better recovery from various psychiatric and relationship problems, and are the quintessence of mental health. Psychiatrist Silvano Arieti, who edited the *American Handbook of Psychiatry* in his era, was more than concerned with the complex symptom pictures of psychiatric syndromes, yet he concluded:

> Evil has a much larger role in human life than is generally realized. . . . We label as "evil" only the most terrible crimes, like those perpetrated by the Nazis. Actually human existence is pervaded by evil to a staggering degree . . . in the misunderstandings and resulting hostility between parents and children, in the disturbed relations between husband and wife, in the vindictive jealousy between brothers and sisters, business partners, or professional associates, in the heartless behavior between competitors, in academic intrigues. . . . What defines man is not only his nature but also his ability to transcend his nature . . . not only his origin but also his aims. The most important of them are the striving toward outcome, the assertion of individuality, and the practice of the common good. . . . The essential activity of man is the good deed. . . . Only when the individual is in full possession of his will and is fully conscious of it can his self flourish and grow.[9]

Why couldn't a student quote a distinguished psychiatrist like Arieti and be assured of receiving the approval of his teachers and supervisors? Yet, I don't think it will work if he wants to survive. In most programs that I know of, he better stay away from Arieti—an old-fashioned psychiatrist who saw people making choices more than biological conditions.

Is it possible that, in a sense, the large industry of Western psychology and psychiatry also is suffering from a kind of collective personality and character disorder of excessive self-involvement and self-entitlement? Psychologist George Kunz believes that "modern psychology only reinforces the cynicism that dominates American politics and society—a cynicism that leads to arrogant and contemptuous criticism of others, manipulation of the "system," and self-indulgent consumption or greed."[10]

The list of mental health thinkers who have discovered and affirmed the importance of integrity and responsibility is truly endless (although even assembling a list of them will not help the proverbial student that I refer to who is being examined and needs to reply according to a catechism that therapy is helping people who don't know how to help themselves get their needs expressed and fulfilled).

I once gave a talk on the ethical and anti-fascist basis of psychotherapy at a family therapy conference, and gave treatment illustrations of teaching patients to stop hurting others. A very politically powerful and deservedly charismatic European psychiatrist responded immediately in the discussion period that followed, with sweeping derision, "No, no, that is not therapy, that is morality, and we therapists heal people, we do not dispense morality." In the immediate politics of the conference he won, of course, because he articulated the known certainty of mental health—that we are just wonderful helpers who help everyone get their fair share of love and life, no matter that a person is disturbed and disturbing because he is going after an unfair share for himself. On the other hand, as noted, there are many therapists (and lots of ordinary people) who understand that being a fair and good person is mentally healthy.

William Doherty described psychotherapy as a "moral laboratory where dialogue makes moral reflection possible," and called for making character more fundamental than technique and acknowledging the need for psychotherapy to develop a social conscience.[11]

Social psychologist Elton McNeil addressed the deeper epistemological and value problem as well when he differentiated between psychological understanding that describes human behavior and psychological understanding that probes the essential sources of behavior. Writing many years ago about "cruelty and violence and that any age is capable of becoming the worst that mankind has ever known, once the veneer of self-control is removed," McNeil concluded in a way that remains true today:

> The comprehension of individual or group violence will continue to be a mystery if the form of development of human personality and the form to which human psychic structure can be modeled are treated as nothing more than an annoying gadfly pestering the concept of large-scale violence. The complexity of the human psyche has made it so forbidding an area of exploration that modern theorists have discounted human personality as an important influence in the affairs of mankind. . . . Yet, denying that the psychological nature of man has relevance in understanding human violence has produced only a bankrupt and barren vision of the future of humanity. Man's psychic nature cannot remain an unknown in the equation of violence or we will find ourselves presiding over the dissolution of the human race.[12]

A Czech psychotherapist and psychoanalyst, Michael Šebek, has observed that a democratic society must adopt a concept of morality that places high value on "respect for human rights, private property and the freedom of others," and that among the consequences of totalitarian values is the readiness to project one's own misery, failures, and badness onto external bad objects. Writing in a society that was emerging from several decades of communist rule, Šebek observed that the "new freedom . . . of a post-totalitarian society brings in a lack of clarity, differentiated power and control which actually stimulate antisocial manifestations which were suppressed by the external controls of the state."[13] Nonetheless he also posits that people have an "innate democratic factor" [or] an inner potential [which] urges an individual toward maturity and psychic health," and whether or not this potential is used determines much of one's psychiatric-emotional health.[14] We see that many thinkers in the mental health field have seen and articulated profound connections between being a good and decent person and being an emotionally and mentally healthy person. And the connections they posit are two-directional: being decent makes you emotionally healthier; being emotionally healthy predisposes you to be a person with greater integrity. Moreover, many thinkers have realized that integrity in human life is expressed both on personal and political levels.

I also believe that plain people know in their common sense that people who have genuine love-of-life heads on them are less likely to submit to or adopt totalitarian politics. When we are thrilled by wonderfully courageous people who take risks to rescue others, such as the "righteous gentiles" who rescued Jews during the Holocaust, and righteous Muslims who saved Armenians and Assyrians and others during the Armenian Genocide, I believe that instinctively we know that these people are models of a basic psychological and moral health that is to be envied by all of us even in our peacetime lives. The rescuers experience the meaningfulness of people, life, and choice. (I love the studies that show that some of the rescuers in the Holocaust acknowledged that they didn't like Jews, but that had nothing to do with their choices to rescue them—because they were fellow human beings and it was the only right thing to do.[15])

So what should the medical resident in psychiatry and the graduate student in clinical psychology or social work say when asked in an examination about treating a personality disorder? If they want to tell the truth, it's all there in the legitimate professional literature on being a better person both to oneself and to others. But if they want to pass examinations in most Establishment programs, they should talk diagnostic blah-blah, look for any signs of upset in the person to justify psychiatric medication, and vaguely propose psychotherapy to help the person fill their needs more successfully. A passing grade is then more likely.

SELF-DEFEATING, SELF-DAMAGING, SELF-RESTRICTING, AND BORDERLINE PERSONALITIES: SAD UNFULFILLED PEOPLE

Withdrawing, Avoidant, and Self-Damaging Personality Disorders

"I can't do many of the normal things other people do, and if I pretend to be able to function competently like others, I often play the fool's role."

The people suffering these personality disorders do not know how to fight or strive to give themselves better breaks and improve their lives. Their way of life is sparse, frugal, fearful, or clumsy, often enough with a chronic nebbish (weakling or ne'er-do-well) quality. Developing into a person who is emotionally stingy to oneself and who does bad things to oneself is often a response to original parental and family failures to love and respect a child genuinely for their own selves. Many people have been beaten into their self-defeating and self-restricting personalities, while others have been spoiled and seduced into not knowing how to really live for themselves—"spoiled rotten" is the familiar layman phrase—some were even both overindulged and beaten, still others have been taken captive of the parental demand that the children function for the parents' sakes. The child then grows up warped, unable to love themselves, and unconsciously continues to re-create and replay the original insult. Little wonder that life is too "big" for them.

"If I hurt myself or allow myself to be damaged or made ill or beaten or humiliated, then it is doubtful that something worse can happen to me."

In addition to plain not knowing how to be good to oneself and effective in life, the belief that the fates cannot possibly be so cruel as to beat a person who is already down and out seduces some people into beating themselves up in order not to be beaten up worse by life. In time, self-abusing people can lull themselves into experiencing actual pleasure at being hurt, humiliated, exploited, and abused. One often senses and even can see quite directly a kind of wry smile on the faces of many self-abusers as they describe their suffering.

Of course, if questioned, they will deny feeling pleasure, and many times they will also be outraged at the suggestion that they are pleasured or protected by their self-abuse. This is their big secret even to themselves, and they will not give it up so easily.

- ❖ A lovely young woman who was divorced from a man she really had known was unsuitable comes to a therapy hour feeling humiliated and worried about how she is going to tell the story of her starting up with another obviously unsuitable man. She works well in the session. She herself understands that inwardly she is saying, "If I know the relationship will not be good, then I can't get hurt."

- ❖ A bright young man in his mid-twenties who did not work was "dying" to make a connection with women but was unable to do so. He stopped coming to see me for therapy when I insisted that he get a job. "How can you say I am enjoying myself? I am not! I am suffering so much," he wrote me in a letter plaintively and angrily. Two pages later, he added, "Actually, you're basically right in what you say, and I am thinking of coming to you to talk about it, although I don't like the way you talk harshly to me."

Self-abusers can become so habituated to self-restriction and self-damage that even when they are suffering, their self-restrictive life has become their familiar and secure way of being in the world, and therefore their way of feeling safety and even pleasure in life whether they are aware of it or not. Often they hide behind reporting being more confused, but theirs is a kind of happiness nonetheless in protecting themselves against more fearful risks of normal life.

The young man just referred to was the darling of his mother's caring, sympathy, and infantilization. She loved having him continue to live at home, and saw no need for him to work. When I insisted he must get a job, she offered to employ him on salary to work for her around the house. She insisted she saw no difference between this arrangement and his being gainfully employed outside the family home.

Some withdrawing personality disorders can present themselves in quiet and contained ways as people who have cut themselves down to minimalistic living without necessarily damaging themselves in an obvious way. In older people who sit out their old age sadly and without activity, this may or may not be an appropriate response to physical limitations and/or to being worn out by life, but it is especially sad in younger people who live in their everyday modus operandi without purpose, drive, or meaning in many basic areas of life.

❖ He was in his young thirties. A fully trained lawyer, he had gravitated to the back rooms of a law firm where he was a devoted legal information specialist. He made no effort to handle cases himself. His relationships with his colleagues were superficially pleasant—he their dutiful researcher, period. No friendships or relationships grew outside of the work context.

Every day he came home to his rented room in a modest rooming house at exactly the same hour carrying a loaf of fresh bread and modest food supplies. He exchanged hellos with fellow tenants if they met on the way, but that was all. The door to his room would close behind him until the next morning. Whether in winter or summer, there were no visitors, there was no going out, there were no male friends and no female friends. Occasionally, on a weekend he would polish his car in the driveway, and when he finished he would return to his room, and the door would close again until the next workday morning.

Some self-damaging personalities bring upon themselves unnecessary and frequent surgeries and/or accidents and illnesses that are real medical conditions but could possibly be minimized or avoided had the person lived more sensibly and/or fought back against the condition. Any and all immolations of the body can secretly provide unconscious relief and a kind of self-love that people are unable to generate for themselves on the basis of genuine self-caring and loving or being loved by others in meaningful friendships and relationships. Health-delivery systems can identify these self-abusive patients relatively easily based on their inordinate use of services. They are happiest in their unhappiness. Misery, pain, and illness console them, for these are their more certain ways to "beat" life's risks.

In too many cases of being chronically abused by others, such as wives who submit to the beatings of husbands, the strange twists of the human mind also are able to transform the perception of the other person who is one's victimizer and torturer into being experienced as one's friend. A kind of union with one's victimizer can be experienced as making one safe from being alone and from an even more feared inner fate of seemingly being dissolved into nothingness. Being victimized by the other is unconsciously an act of being lulled into submission and incorporation into the other, which in the magic of the mind can be supremely comforting.

❖ He had beaten her regularly. When she was seven months pregnant with their first child, he kicked her in her stomach so hard that she lost the baby. After that beating she left him, sued, and won a divorce. Now he had come to her again asking that she take him back, and first of all he wanted her to give him back access to all of her monies. She felt good about his coming back. She had missed him so much and had been so lonely. When the therapist pointed out that taking him back would mean giving up whatever self-respect she had managed to regain, she said she wasn't sure she could refuse him no matter what he did to her. There was no continuation of therapy.

Borderline Personality Disorder

It is as if a lifelong curse has been cast on a person that says, Thou shalt not be able to achieve any enduring pleasures and satisfactions in your life, and thou shalt experience chronic feelings of emptiness especially in respect of love. Borderline Personality Disorder (BPD) is a particular form of self-defeating and self-restrictive personality disorder that has rightfully earned a considerable treatment literature of its own.[16]

These are cases where people cannot give themselves a full range of living experience, and their social lives and intimate relationships are limited and distorted. There is an *as if* quality to much of their lives, as if they are moving through a normal play of work, social connections, and whatever pleasures of experience, but in truth they are very stuck. Often they cannot marry, and if they do marry the marriages are often short-lived, for the couple is unable in some basic way to maintain a viable intimate unity, and the couple's experience is soon assaulted by explosions of one or both partners' selfish and nervous emotionalism.

There are borderline couples who do succeed in long-term living arrangements with one another, such as living in separate apartments and pretending to themselves that "soon, soon," they will marry—a "soon" that never comes to be. Others live together but without marrying and without emotional intimacy. For those who don't initially formally marry, if after their relative success together as an unmarried couple they nonetheless do marry formally, the outcome can be disastrous. The sheer symbolism of commitment to long-term intimacy and protection of one another that the marriage vows bring to the fore can set off uncontrollable nervousness and accusations that were not present previously—in some cases even after many years of living together without being married. Some do indeed marry and have children, but before too long life with them turns into a living hell of insults, rage, and physical aggression—toward the spouse or suicidally toward their own selves.

The borderline's inner software program further stipulates that should the person try to change their fate, unforgiving upset and failure will make them rue the day they tried.

The borderline pattern is one of markedly unstable relationships with people, with serious defects in one's self-image and a decided unsteadiness and impulsivity in conducting life. Most of the time, a chronic feeling of a gray, hollow emptiness is characteristic of borderlines. Their inner mind images tend to alternate between extremes of naive idealization and strong devaluation, and the use of emotions often swings to episodes of intensely dysphoric bad feelings and irritability. Borderlines are noted for displaying marked mood swings, and especially bursts of anger blaming others for the poverty of their lives.

Even in a well-executed traditional therapy, borderlines spend endless hours complaining, characteristically make little progress toward enriching their lives, and often develop a deeply angry system of complaints even against their long-term therapist who for a long time may have appeared to be for them a real friend. Therapists in turn are characteristically frustrated, disappointed, and drained by these patients who may end up becoming "the worst experiences" of some therapists' professional life (special training for therapists working with borderlines has long been highly advised).

❖ At age forty-two, she was a cracker-jack real-estate saleslady who worked for a major developer who was delighted to have her. She was an impressive expert on real-estate law and practice, and customers took comfortably to her voluble self-assurance. Yet the end of her working day meant her retreat to a sheltered, almost reclusive life. In her apartment, hours of self-indulgent eating (she was becoming increasingly obese) were accompanied by endless telephone conversations, especially with her mother, and also with a boyfriend who lived separately from her with whom she had a once-a-month dinner date in which, year after year, they even would review their "plans" for marriage someday. What was also pretty much assured is that she would regularly work herself into a breathless tirade of anger at someone or other and spend hours talking about the object of her anger in righteous indignation.

❖ At age thirty-four he was nowhere, even as seemingly he was meaningfully living an active life of a steadily employed engineer and was busy socially with folk dancing and dating. On the one hand, he was an obviously all-around nice guy, but in truth, inside of him he was deeply sad, empty, and chronically angry. His work was a humdrum routine for him with little meaning or ambition. Often he would come back to his emotionally empty home (in which he felt little pleasure) and lose himself in hours of computer games—sometimes he also played for hours when he had work that had to be done for the office, and then he would feel ashamed for his lack of willpower. His dating followed a characteristic path of initial social and sexual pleasure, then high hopes of a lasting relationship, followed by an inevitable souring and displeasure with him by the woman, to which he would react helplessly. As the years went by, a dog-worn sour look increasingly covered his face, for life was indeed basically lacking in meaning and connection.

I have come to a conclusion that many borderline patients have in common a childhood history of not being expected to grow up progressively and move on to next stages of greater maturity. Some are obviously overindulged and literally taught to continue seeking immediate and exaggerated gratifications—in effect in babyish ways. Others are left alone to be passive and continue to be children—going through the motion or appearance of movement from one age-stage to the next without a tension or excitement of becoming "bigger" and more grownup. Others are exploited to live—eat, play, experience, achieve—more for their parents than themselves.

In many cases there is also a deep concealed "well" of unconscious parental anger and even hatred at the child that is hidden even from the parent's consciousness let alone from the child, and can be ascertained only under the magnifying probe of psychoanalytic-psychodynamic scrutiny of what these parents really felt in their hearts or inner minds about their child. In any case it is clear even without deep observation that these children basically are not *loved*—meaning celebrated as growing, developing and maturing people for *themselves*. They are used for parent gratification or neglected.

I also believe that many people who grow up to be borderline personality disorders were allowed as children or unconsciously authorized to develop measures of unwarranted power in their families. These forever children control their parents and/or siblings through and on behalf of their exaggerated self-indulgence. They boss their world by being babies who must be and are over-babied. They are self-indulging "kings" and indulged "queens," and no one holds them to demand less and to grow up more healthy. Borderlines don't grow up. And people living with them are scared of them.

I believe the pattern I have described fits simply at "face value" the known facts of how adults with borderline personality disorders behave tragically all their lives: They are babies, unable to lead full adult lives. They are chronically addicted to one or more childish or fetishistic ways of pleasuring themselves. They demand too much instant gratification and they go c-r-a-z-y with a baby-like total rage when they feel thwarted or frustrated. In fact, they are unconsciously programmed to have to explode in this way periodically. Borderlines disappoint.

For those who do date and seek sexual and love partners, it is tragic to see how after a period of joy and optimistic excitement, they must destroy the relationship with such rage. For therapists who try with all their hearts and normally decent skills, it is sad to see the inevitable "murder" and dismissal of the therapist by the borderline patient. Over the years I have known many therapists who have vowed never to undertake therapy of borderlines after being badly burned by outbursts of intense rage of borderline patients and disappointed by their meager progress, if any, notwithstanding quite genuine efforts to help these tormented people. Therapists who dared—"stupidly"—to instruct a borderline to behave more maturely in some area of functioning could count on being "destroyed."

Until relatively recently, there were virtually no reports of successful therapies with borderlines, and even today one is hard-pressed to find reports of definitively successful or complete therapies. However, there are now reports of some degrees of success in well-conceptualized structured therapy approaches, based largely on cognitive-behavioral concepts, but also, however surprisingly, based on psychodynamic concepts of transference-based treatment.

ENCOURAGING REPORTS OF PROGRESS IN TREATING BORDERLINES: DIALECTICAL BEHAVIOR THERAPY AND TRANSFERENCE-BASED THERAPY

There have been some therapists who have learned/concluded that they can work toward limited goals with borderlines. They aim to improve rather than cure or heal, and they aim to reduce suffering or dysfunction in one or more specific zones or areas of functioning—for example, establish more independent living, leave the family home, begin or resume working, continue one's education, develop a minimal social life, or maintain relationships with one's children and/or spouse. Overall this has become my philosophy, and I console myself that there are medical conditions that cannot be cured at this time but where the physician can reduce suffering and improve quality of life, and it is not wrong to help people in their mental health in similar ways. I have also grown in my expectation that good therapy can be meaningfully helpful in many cases.

Dialectical Behavior Therapy (DBT) is a form of psychotherapy that was developed originally by Marsha M. Linehan at the University of Washington. It became the first therapy that has demonstrated scientifically some effectiveness in treating BPD.[17]

The dialectical concept at the core of this treatment combines a core acceptance of the patient and their feelings at any given time, together nonetheless with giving the patient feedback about how some of their feelings and behavior are troublesome, and offering them alternative behaviors. DBT draws on a wide array of skills for emotional self-regulation that are found in cognitive behavioral therapy, as well as assertiveness training and Buddhist mindfulness meditation. DBT seeks to teach the patient how to pay attention to the present moment and experience their emotions fully, but also with perspective and with capacities for tolerating distress and regulating emotions.

Additionally, Linehan seeks to counter the characteristically tense, biting relationship between borderlines and their therapists with an alliance that is based on "tough love." In 2000 Karen Scheel reviewed the empirical literature and concluded that the results are promising for the effectiveness of DBT, but she pointed out that the research base is still limited.[18]

In the same special section of the journal *Clinical Psychotherapy: Science and Practice*, Drew Westen also recognized that DBT is useful in producing "a promising initial improvement," but he too pointed out that its genuine effectiveness is still not known, especially in respect of producing changes that last.[19] Westen also pointed out that in some studies of DBT the patients were cared for to an unusual extent by the team committed to the new form of treatment, and as we observed in *A Democratic Mind*, it is characteristic of many early reports of new therapies that the results are unusually good precisely because of the genuine involvement of the professionals with the patients. Involvement and caring are the real cure that is helping them.

Table 4.1. Dynamics of the Fascist Mind in Selected Psychopathology: Personality Disorders—Self-Defeating and Borderline

	01-02 **TOTALITY, OVER-CERTAINTY, ABSOLUTISM, AND MAGICAL THINKING**	*03-04* **CENSORSHIP OF INFORMATION, OBEDIENCE, CONFORMITY, AND INTOLERANCE OF DISSENT**
PERSONALITY DISORDERS ***Group 1:*** **SELF-DEFEATING, SELF-DAMAGING, SELF-RESTRICTING, AND BORDERLINE PERSONALITIES** **including:** ***Withdrawing Personality Disorder*** ***Avoidant Personality Disorder*** ***Self-Damaging Disorder*** ***Borderline Personality Disorders*** **In *DSM-5* see:** **General Personality Disorder (p. 321)** **Schizoid Personality Disorder (p. 323)** **Borderline Personality Disorder (pp. 325–326)** **Avoidant Personality Disorder (p. 328)** **Dependent Personality Disorder (pp. 328–329)** **Obsessive Compulsive Personality Disorder (pp. 329–330)** **Other Specified Personality Disorder (p. 331)** **and Unspecified Personality Disorder (p. 333)** ***Page numbers refer to the Desk Reference to the Diagnostic Criteria from* DSM-5**	An over-certain world is maintained by restriction of self, avoidance of risk, and limiting of initiatives, thus clearly damaging the patient's quality of life. Withdrawing, avoidant, and self-damaging personality disorders create a way of life that is minimalistic, ascetic, self-abnegating, and/or self-hurting and self-torturing with chronic feelings of inadequacy, failure, depression, and lack of satisfaction. Borderline personality disorders live out lives of demanding overindulgence and rage at others for their feelings of deprivation. They also create a way of life that not only is seriously restricted, especially socially, but is built around a basic complaining and sense of outrage at others for spoiling their life. *Role of anxiety: Anxiety is suggested and is reflected in chronic disappointment and sadness, but is not usually experienced as a direct, energizing force. Strong free-floating anxiety, which is known to be a representation of accessible potential for growth, is not generally experienced. The larger qualities of the personality disorder*	Information about successes and experiences of happiness may be registered but for limited time periods, only to be replaced by rebound unhappiness and a return to recurrent states of morbid feelings. Conformity to an inner template of self-restriction, minimization, and self-damage is relentless. In some cases diffidence, self-abnegation, and deference to others are pronounced; in others there is a brutal demand to live one's impoverished life in one's own way. Borderlines create periodic uproars with their strong criticisms and outbursts of anger, and end up cut off from any number of people and settings. One can hardly see them as obeying and conforming to the dictates of the people and groups they insult and push away from them. But inside of them there is certainly strong conformity to their own inner guiding programs for ending up being angry loners. Protests to others are largely in the name of their demands for indulgence rather than for social values and common justice.

PERSONALITY DISORDERS–SELF-DEFEATING AND BORDERLINE (*continued*)

	style continue to work against growth—which at best will be slow in coming, uneven, and subject to strong setbacks.	
05 **SUPERIORITY, EXCESSIVE POWER-SEEKING, AND PREJUDICE**	*06* **VIOLENCE, RETALIATION AGAINST DISSENT, SACRIFICE, AND DESTRUCTION**	*07* **DENIALS OF DOING HARM TO SELF AND OTHERS**
Psychodynamically, it is not uncommon to discover fantasies and even very unreal convictions in one's specialness and superiority. In personal and family relationships there may be an exercise of demandingness and tyrannical power. But in the larger world, power generally is not sought.	**Doing Harm to Self** Person does much violence to self in restricting their life opportunities, and in frequent spoiling and damaging of opportunities for a better life. **Doing Harm to Others** Rare in a direct sense, but of course common as a result of disappointing others by one's poor or limited functioning, loner behaviors, and, in the case of borderlines, their rages. Borderline personality disorders have bursts of intense complaining and accusations of others including therapists. The attack leaves the object uncomfortable and feeling as if besmirched.	Violence done to self is accepted resignedly as inevitable. Overall there may be a quality of *as if everything is fine* in one's life, with gross denial of the restrictions and damages done to oneself. The blaming attacks of borderlines against others are treated by them sanctimoniously as objectively legitimate, with little question as to their own roles in bringing about the limitations in their lives.

Source: Created by the author.

A further complication is that there is a well-known "allegiance effect" in psychotherapy research that leads to the researcher's preferred therapy emerging as the most successful in comparison to others—according to one group of distinguished researchers, this allegiance effect accounts for no less than 69 percent of the outcome.[20]

Koerner and Dimeff reported a meta-analysis of a good number of additional studies not reported in Scheel's review, and also came to the conclusion that DBT was a promising form of treatment possibly for borderlines as well as for "other disorders in which dysfunctional behaviors served to regulate emotion such as substance abuse and binge eating disorder."[21] Marsha Linehan herself observed appropriately and modestly, "Given the high number of BPD patients combined with their poor outcomes in traditional treatment, low compliance rates, high hospitalization rates, serious suicide risk, and tendencies toward hostile behaviors that increase therapist stress, it is no surprise that any new treatment with even marginal data on empirical validity would be greeted with enthusiasm by the clinical community.[22]

A more recent meta-study of DBT for borderline personality disorder provides a more sober though still encouraging statement. The dropout rate from treatment was 27 percent. The results of treatment were moderate improvement with regard to suicidal and self-injurious behaviors. Follow-up after treatment showed "a small impairment."[23]

There is also another new, promising treatment—structured psychoanalytic transference-based therapy. In a remarkably rigorous comparative study, Clarkin, Levy, Lenzenweger, and Kernberg studied the outcomes of three yearlong outpatient courses of therapy for borderline personality disorder.[24] The three techniques that were evaluated are 1) dialectical behavior therapy, 2) transference-focused psychotherapy, and 3) dynamic supportive treatment. There were ninety patients, and overall the patients in all three treatment groups showed significant positive change in a number of qualities. The first two treatments were significantly effective also with improvement in suicidality—a significant issue for many borderlines. Transference-focused therapy and supportive treatment were associated significantly with improvement in anger and impulsivity. Only transference-focused therapy was seen as predicting change in irritability and verbal assaultiveness. Note that the transference-focused therapy involved a structured treatment rather than a free-flowing classical mode. The results overall are a stunning message of some hope at long last for being able to help some borderline patients more than most therapists thought possible.

Altogether, at this writing we appear to be at the entry to new terrain where therapists need to reorganize their sense of professional confidence and discipline rather than being vulnerable to the borderline's volatility, rage, and emotional turmoil. DBT and structured psychoanalytic transference-based therapies are long-overdue hopes for improvements in treatment of borderline personality disorder.

NARCISSISTIC, SELF-INDULGENT, AND ADDICTIVE PERSONALITIES: "NEVER SAY ENOUGH" DESTRUCTIVE LIFESTYLES

Narcissistic Personality Disorder

"I must have my pleasure and safety through getting my needs and cravings satisfied, and I cannot and will not take any frustration or bear any anxiety or pain."

Narcissistic personality disorder is characterized by a pervasive pattern of grandiosity and fantasy behavior, a need for admiration, and a lack of empathy in a pattern that has begun by early adulthood.[25]

According to the *DSM*, five or more of the following characteristics need to be identified for the diagnosis to obtain: grandiose sense of self-importance; preoccupation with fantasies of unlimited success, power, brilliance, beauty or ideal love; belief that one is special and unique and belongs in a category with other special and high status people or institutions; requirements of excessive admiration; a sense of unreasonable entitlement or expectations of especially favorable treatment or automatic compliance with one's expectations; interpersonal exploitativeness, i.e., taking advantage of others to achieve one's own ends; lack of empathy, envy of others or a belief that others are envious of one; arrogance, haughty attitudes or behaviors.

Some students of Western culture have concluded that, progressively, our Western culture has moved to and spawned an overall "age of narcissism." The motto of Western life has become a call to "do it for me," with progressively less attention to combining doing for others with doing for oneself. Ideally, neither being good to oneself and being good to others is to be at the expense of the other, although it is natural that the basic sequence begins with taking care of oneself and then broadens to include others. For good health, each dimension enhances the legitimacy and beauty of the other, but narcissistic people and societies go for the one half of the deal that is self-serving. [26] Narcissistic or self-serving and self-indulgent motifs are also at the core of many actual addictions. Many self-serving behaviors and escapes from managing conflicts and challenges responsibly also can be understood through the lens of narcissistic self-entitlement. Thus:

- What can be called a race to divorce in the Western world can be understood in many cases as a flight to one's safety and pleasure with little regard for the spouse and children.
- So too the gluttony and avarice of insanely crazy salaries of executives (along with reduced income and unemployment for so many workers).
- So too crazy, life-destroying obesity.
- So too other addictions.
- In our era there increasingly are descriptions of people who cut themselves off from real relating to others, and in a sense also from relating to themselves as living, experiencing people, by compulsive-addictive use of digital devices such

Table 4.2. Dynamics of the Fascist Mind in Selected Psychopathology: Personality Disorders: Narcissistic, Addictive

	01-02 **TOTALITY, OVER-CERTAINTY, ABSOLUTISM, AND MAGICAL THINKING**	*03-04* **CENSORSHIP OF INFORMATION, OBEDIENCE, CONFORMITY, AND INTOLERANCE OF DISSENT**
PERSONALITY DISORDERS ***Group 2:*** **NARCISSISTIC, SELF-INDULGENT, AND ADDICTIVE PERSONALITIES** **including:** ***Narcissistic Personality Disorder*** ***Alcoholism*** ***Substance Abuse Disorders*** ***Obesity*** **In *DSM-5* see:** **Narcissistic Personality Disorder (p. 327)** **Substance-Related and Addiction Disorders (pp. 227–283)** **Including:** **Alcohol-Related Disorders (pp. 233–237)** **Cannibis-Related Disorders (p. 239)** **Hallucinogen-Related Disorders (pp. 244–252)** **Inhalant-Related Disorders (pp. 252–256)** **Opiod-Related Disorders (pp. 256–260)** **Sedative, Hypnotic, or Anxiolytic Disorders (pp. 261–266)** **Stimulant-Related Disorders (pp. 267–273)** **Tobacco-Related Disorders (pp. 274–277)** **Other (or unknown) Substance (pp. 252–256)** **Non-Substance-Related Disorders (pp. 282–283)** **Gambling Disorder (pp. 282–283)** ***Page numbers refer to the Desk Reference to the Diagnostic Criteria from* DSM-5**	Healthy misgivings, self-criticism, and doubts are eliminated in the face of a driving need that one must satisfy one's cravings and eliminate any vestiges of discomfort, frustration, anxiety, or other emotional pain. The goal can be said to be tranquility über *alles*. In the process, other people can be used, exploited, and abused to serve one's own needs. Moreover, the addictive relief becomes habitual, and maintaining the habitual itself becomes conditioned as a way of life. *Role of anxiety: Anxiety is generally blocked by the personality style. A patina of an all-is-well good humor can be adopted in some of the self-indulgent disorders and further serves to keep away professionals as well as plain everyday people who want to help.*	There is little interest in conforming to the needs or demands of *others*, as the patient is occupied in serving their own needs and way of life for fulfilling their needs. It can be said that patient conforms slavishly to their own demands for self-indulgence. Information about the deleterious effects of self-indulgence is rejected.

PERSONALITY DISORDERS: NARCISSISTIC, ADDICTIVE (*continued*)

05 **SUPERIORITY, EXCESSIVE POWER-SEEKING, AND PREJUDICE**	*06* **VIOLENCE, RETALIATION AGAINST DISSENT, SACRIFICE AND, DESTRUCTION**	*07* **DENIALS OF DOING HARM TO SELF AND OTHERS**
In self-indulgent disorders, superiority is not necessarily a direct goal in its own right so much as an offshoot of a superior insistence on the right to self-indulgence. In the narcissistic personality disorders, there can be a high level of superior feelings to others, as well as the fact that the world is seen and made to revolve around the patient.	**Doing Harm to Self** The harm done to oneself is overwhelming. Any number of cases of self-indulgent personality disorders are life-shortening and life-threatening. Narcissistic personality disorders may succeed in creating a coterie of servants and groupies in their families or otherwise, but intrinsically their relationships are unloving emotionally and they often end up alone. **Doing Harm to Others** Self-indulgent people may sacrifice others who are seen as standing in their way. The involvement with self is not necessarily intended to hurt others, but the fact that others such as family members are very hurt generally does not impact on the patient and make them want to correct themselves.	Criticism, censure, and appeals to desist for the sake of the patient or for the welfare of others such as family members or the community may be agreed to verbally, but are typically short-lived.

Source: Created by the author.

as cellular phones, computers, and Internet, with little involvement in experiencing and feeling about themselves and other people.

- This has also become true of much medical care. Many people are complaining bitterly that their doctor doesn't speak to them. Not only doesn't he lift his head from the computer—a robotized smart but unfeeling source of information and advice—but he extends little comfort and hope.

What is commonly known as a fascist society is built around conformity to a godlike leader and/or ideology, and we have been rightly proud of democracies that they are far more by the people and for the people. But it has turned out that too much of Western democracies are built around slavish conformity to and overindulgence in personal gratification at the expense of mature integration of love and responsibility to oneself and to others.

Addictive Disorders: Including Alcoholism, Substance Abuse Disorders, and Obesity

"I cannot stop (drinking) (taking drugs) (eating). I can't help it."

The various addictive disorders such as alcoholism or obesity all have in common a basic paradigm that there is no such thing as "enough." For some this is particularly true when they are feeling bad and must have a "fix" or compensation.

Addictions can also be attached to overdoing and overinvestment in a given activity or space of life. Thus, there are sport addicts and sex addicts of all sorts; there are Internet/TV/Facebook/cellphone addicts; and there are certainly work addicts. Some of these sound trivial in comparison with killer-substance abusers, but over time these addictions too can wreck a person's marriage and family, body, and mind.

For most it becomes a habitual way of life, so that even the anticipation of bad experiences and inevitable bad feelings like tension, failure, and illnesses (that face all of us in life) justify taking a palliative to ward off in advance experiences of deprivation, frustration, weakness, and fear. The paradigmatic position in addictive conditions is that pain, deprivation, and dysphoric or unpleasant feelings of any sort are unwelcome, unbearable, and unjust; therefore they justify every possible means to squelch them and prevent their coming into being in the first place.[27]

How much of an antidote to pain is necessary? For the full-blown addict there is no boundary. Any degree of pain is treated as a failure. Any reminder of anxiety is a threat of floodgates opening up to total pain. The addict requires a dose of whatever will keep them perfectly anesthetized and/or on a high, propped-up feeling. By definition, the addict's way of being in the world or basic philosophical definition of the meaning of self is a priori: that existence can be tolerated only without pain. The addict becomes a hypnotized-narcotized organism who is no longer willing to feel pain or to suffer the possibility of unexpected bad feelings. The anesthetized experience and the pleasures of "floating" are reinforced, and a conditioned response sets in of needing to repeat and repeat the experience. The fact that progressively larger or more frequent doses are required to maintain the narcotic effect makes no difference. Nothing must stand in the way of the success of the paradigm—even if this means progressively and fatally damaging one's health, mind, or spirit for life and one's ability to function in the real world. Even when the addictive state hurts, it is, in its essence, pleasurable. In any case it's familiar and habitual, and the only way the person knows to live.

The obese/alcoholic/narcotic-addicted person is inured both to the good or even the desperate advice of caring family, friends, and physicians because the addicted are involved in destroying their prime enemy of dysphoric feelings. They operate with the conviction that the end justifies the means. In the multi-determination of human behavior, there also may be a personal hated object that is registered inwardly as the original historical source of one's discomfort and one's inability to bear stress, and the purpose of one's addiction can also be to destroy that hated personal object through the damage to oneself. Some of the time, addicts have histories of emotionally barren childhoods, and their addictions are ways of trying to stuff themselves. Other times there may be a history of having been overindulged, and the current addiction in effect is a continuation of the pattern of overindulgence. In some cases, the addiction in effect combines a pattern of learned overindulgence and hatred of the source of the same overindulgence in one's background that, after all, has lowered the addict's chances of a normal life. In any case, familiarity, conditioning, and habit set in. The addiction becomes the known way of life.

Unless a basic paradigmatic shift is induced where the person comes to revalue their own basic self to a point where they are willing to give up the "certainty" of their security, there can be no significant change.[28] There are much better treatment results with people who get help during incipient or early stages of addiction. (Personally I have found myself a reasonably effective therapist at the early stages, but unable to help much, if at all, people with chronic addictions—to the point that I do not accept most cases like this for treatment with me). Treatment results of addictive conditions are notoriously poor once the addiction is ingrained. Despite the fact that it would seem that the simplest rational analysis—namely that they are literally destroying their health and lives—would be convincing to these patients, the rewards of a "perfect solution" to life's anxieties and the security of repeating habitual patterns of behavior are more often the victor.[29]

The impulse to self-indulgence and self-protection becomes a paradigmatic attitude, and the template that one must always feel pleasured or comforted grows to become more powerful than the person. An idea and "a way" become the fascist conquerors of the individual. It is not surprising that there aren't too many pills for addiction in the psychiatric medicine bag.[30]

ANTISOCIAL, POWER-SEEKING, AND PARANOID PERSONALITIES: THE GOONS, TOUGHIES, AND DESTROYERS WHO HURT SO MANY PEOPLE

I introduce the third and last of my groupings of personality disorders with a heavy heart and a deep sigh, for I admit that I truly dislike (and worse) many (though not absolutely all) of the people who are the subject of this cluster of antisocial, power-seeking, and paranoid personalities.

With the exception of some basically nice people (I can call them overstuffed teddy bears or "Archie Bunkers") who vainly try to beat the rap of the existential anxieties that plague all humans by projection onto others and acting pseudo-tough and blustering their power over others, a large number of the antisocial, power-seekers, and paranoids are sources of an enormous amount of very real misery to others in human life.

They are basically people whose mind program grants them the right to take out everything on others. Many antisocials are, plain and simple, criminals. They have little to no conscience. They will take old peoples' pension monies in a scam without hesitation, they will sell a hospital fake medical technology that they pretend works, equip an army with weapons that backfire, and sell phony stocks in a nonexistent company named after their Aunt Tilly. They are crooks and scoundrels, and there are plenty of them everywhere in every community, including sometimes bona fide clergymen (of all faiths) who walk off with the church's assets, and professionals (including in mental health) who steal the proceeds of a professional conference (I've had the experience twice in two countries—and succeeded with legal pressure to recover the funds in one of the two).

The power-seekers are arrogant, mean, and exploitative. They are the colleagues at work who will step on you and over you for their own advancement and other interests; fellow professionals—yes, I again acknowledge including in mental health—who will lord over you and abuse you coldly and uncaringly; mentors and supervisors who will insult you, delay your progress, and drive you crazy—say when you need their assistance or approval of a thesis or graduation project and they delight in obstructing or stalling you; police and law officials who will beat you up and/or throw away the key to your rights to due process; neighbors who will drive you crazy about the garbage, shared plumbing line, parking places, or with the brashness of their excessive noisemaking; mates or other close intimates who blame and attack you angrily and menacingly for every shortcoming of theirs; drivers who will cut you off on the road, push you and pass you in crazy ways, and may well kill you; and an endless number of people who humiliate, enrage, and endanger us in any and every area of daily life.

The paranoids are crazy. But after you realize how terrified and driven many of them really are, you also see that most of them are pathetic and not really dangerous to others. Yet some of them are so very dangerous that they can even kill in complex schemes for thrills or revenge or conspiracy. And if they get elected to be commanders, generals, senators, or presidents, they can be the rottenest leaders, including the mass killers of their times. It is certainly a professional challenge to diagnose the majority who are not dangerous and those who are.

The full-fledged members of this cluster of personality disorders are largely unsavory characters. On a personal level, it is not worth spending time with them, but the more important problem is that there are too many of them that we cannot avoid dealing with them in our personal and collective lives. Unfortunately, we have no choice but to develop skills to cope with them without being naive or weak.

Beginning with parents who seriously hurt their children, people who misuse power over others are dangerous and can even be indirectly deadly. I believe, for example, that arrogant, insulting physicians contribute to actual patient illness and even death, for they literally insult the immune system and the hope that stimulates healing and recovery. The full-blown power-player paranoid personalities who are politicians or military leaders can translate their poisoned conceptions of a target group of people into policies of prejudice, or worse, into actual discrimination, persecution, torture, massacre, terrorism, and genocidal mass murder. They become responsible for the agonies and deaths of thousands and millions of people.[31] Unfortunately, even most of these are not obvious raving lunatics by current psychiatric standards, but I will be damned if, as a mental health professional or human person, I will call them *normal*. The least I expect of psychiatry is to identify them as *power-seeking* or *paranoid personality disorders*. The fact that there are so many power-driven personalities does not for a moment change my conviction that they are blatantly disturbed. I believe the mental health professions have fled and avoided these issues.

Consider the following specific situations:

- A practicing psychotherapist learns the following indirectly (from other sources) about a patient who is consulting him: In the patient's work life—be they a manager of a large group of engineers or head of a department of psychiatry—the patient conducts themselves arrogantly and imperiously, or in a way that, while outwardly refined, admits no intellectual differences or criticism by others and adamantly bars advancement and an appropriate equality to subordinates and colleagues.

  Will the psychotherapist consider these behaviors expressive of a disturbed personality? Will the therapist confront these behaviors in the course of treatment, even if the patient does not specifically identify this aspect of their lives as problematic for them?
- Consider a similar issue in the context of political behavior: In his role as a possible or incipient political leader of a movement or a political party, a patient, who has otherwise consulted the therapist because of some personal distress, is known to be prejudiced, dehumanizing, inciting people to hatred, and seeking to discriminate against and control a target group such as immigrants or an ethnic group, and perhaps even openly calls for and seeks to organize violence against this target population.

Will the psychotherapist characterize persons engaging in such behaviors by any of various designations of disturbance: megalomania, acting out, dangerously violent personality, or possibly a paranoiac or paranoid personality? Will the therapist thereby oppose the patient's behaviors, not only as statements of the therapists' personal political choices and philosophy, but from within the therapists' role and position as a mental health specialist who defines such behaviors as disordered and ill?

- What if a therapist learns the same information, not about a bona fide patient who has come to him or been referred to him, but about a person I shall call an "auxiliary patient," such as a first-level relative of a patient, or about another professional (in whatever field).
  Will the therapist apply to such "non-patients" the same kind of professional thinking they apply to their own formal patients even though the situation invites a way out for the therapist to claim they cannot diagnose a non-patient? Will the psychotherapist first of all characterize such behaviors as disturbed or pathological, and will the therapist seek to initiate whatever kind of containment may be possible?
  Thus, a therapist learns that another therapist in the community is having sexual relations with his patients. Will the therapist encourage the source of this information to take action? Will he himself forward a report for investigation by a professional society or the police, or remain comfortably passive?

Is there a sound basis in existing professional formulations for saying (what I believe professionals feel and know in their good common sense) that excessive power needs indicate a personality disturbance? If so, a tyrannical director of a mental health clinic will be understood to be both a nasty and a disturbed person by virtue of the fact that he suffers his staff to experience chronic humiliation, tension, and rage, and there will be no need to pretend that what everyone knows is happening in the department isn't so. Similarly, political leaders will be clearly identified as disturbed when they commit themselves to defining a target population as undeserving, inferior, and enemies of the people; or to forcing a murderous mass population transfer; or when they call on or coerce believers and followers to commit mass murder-suicide; or when they send people who oppose them into punishing psychiatric hospitals to break their spirits, or to killing work camps, concentration camps, and killing fields.

As I said earlier, I am devoting proportionally more writing to the array of personality disorders because they are responsible for so much of the misery in this world. In my opinion, these conditions are a critical problem for humane people and for humanity, and our mental health world has skirted the issue.

Antisocial Personality Disorder

"Give me my way at any cost. Other people's suffering means nothing to me."

Antisocial personality disorder is characterized by "a pervasive pattern of disregard for and violation of the rights of others," which begins in childhood or early adolescence and continues into adulthood."[32] The pattern has also been referred to as psychopathy, sociopathy, or asocial personality disorder.

According to the *DSM*, for the diagnosis to be given the individual must be at least eighteen years old, but the diagnosis also stipulates that there must be evidence prior to age fifteen of a bona fide conduct disorder, which is defined as a repetitive and persistent pattern of aggression to people and/or animals in which the rights of others or societal norms and rules are violated, and include bullying, physical fights, using weapons, being physically cruel to people or animals, stealing from an actual victim directly, aggressively forcing someone into sexual activity, destruction of property, deceitfulness or theft, or serious violations of rules.

Antisocial personality disorders involve repeatedly performing acts that are injurious to life: deceitfulness, repeated lying, and con jobs; aggressiveness in repeated physical fights or assaults; reckless disregard for one's own safety or the safety of others; consistent irresponsibility; repeated failure to maintain work obligations and/or financial obligations; and lack of remorse for causing harm, hurt, or mistreating others. The antisocial acts that count for this diagnosis are from age fifteen on.

I personally find the rules about age convoluted. My own working simplification is that *conduct disorders* refer to repeated physical aggression and violation of the rights of others, while *antisocial disorders* have an additional element of a kind of criminal, conscience-lacking mind that is set to steal the good things of life from others. Clinically, I have seen quite young children who are deserving of diagnosis as "psychopaths," or in the current nomenclature as antisocial personality disorders. As in so many of the unstable and unsatisfying word-constructions of psychiatry, the issue is much more the accurate diagnosis of the Mind program at work, and here I believe the real spirit of this category of antisocial personality is a person who not only behaves in violation of social and legal norms but is basically out to lie, manipulate, exploit, and abuse others. (Therefore, I would personally give "Mac" in *One Flew Over the Cuckoo's Nest* a spanking diagnosis of *conduct disorder* and not *antisocial personality disorder*. He was much too lovable and helpful to his fellow inmates for that.[33])

Personality Disorder of Excessive Power Strivings

"However young or old I am, and whatever my formal role, I am the one and only Captain of the Pinafore, and love lording it over you" (and it's not simply colorful or humorous as in Gershwin's opera).

Excessive power strivings poison the personality of the individual who is obsessed in his spirit and mind with power and is ready to do harm to other peoples' lives as an assertion or proof of his power, or in the process of gaining power. Because none of the existing formal diagnostic categories in psychiatry addressed adequately the issues of excessive power-seeking, I proposed in the formal psychiatric literature a new diagnostic category of a Personality Disorder of Excessive Power Strivings, which I first presented in the (English-language) *Israel Journal of Psychiatry*.[34] One of the reviewers who was asked to evaluate the article for possible publication wrote to the editor that he had a feeling the writer was "making fun of us"—probably in response to my referring to some arrogant heads of mental health departments (as I have in several of the illustrations in this book), but perhaps also in response to my basic conception that the mental health profession is devoted to promoting normal versus disturbed human behavior but has made no provision for defining the Hitlers, Stalins, and bin Ladens as disturbed, so that they were left to be designated as *normal*, God help us.

Because the proposed diagnosis of a personality disorder of excessive power strivings is quite new to the psychiatric literature, and certainly has not been accepted by the *DSM*, and even more because I believe the basic concept of excessive power strivings is relevant to a great deal of disturbed human behavior, I will present the details of this diagnosis more fully. The new diagnostic category is intended to fit into the current diagnostic schema of *DSM*. It also fits my earlier proposal (also in the literature of established psychiatry but never adopted) to examine in all psychopathology not only the burdens and damage people do and impose on their *own* selves and their own functioning, but also the harm they do to *other* peoples' lives and functioning.[35]

Excessive power strivings and the need to rule, humiliate, and dominate are phenomena that appear throughout the developmental cycle, beginning even with infants who take on (and obviously have been assigned or indulged) unduly powerful roles within their family, or virtual tyrants of any age who terrorize and dominate their parents or family groups. With the breakdown of family authority and tradition, there has been a dramatic increase of cases of children of all ages who are assigned or allowed to take over the power reins of a family to a grotesque extent, particularly adolescents, who have become insufferable controllers of their families. The fact that such a personality problem can be manifested at early stages of life and before an adult has gained actual work status and/or political power is a statement that excessive power strivings are not only visited upon lawyers, generals, and politicians, but are present in a wide variety of human beings, and occurs whenever internal and external checks and balances on the distribution of power and moral codes as to the value and inviolability of other people are not successfully promoted and internalized.

Alfred Adler argued that "our guiding ideal is concretized as power over others, and this problem is too much in the foreground for everybody, overshadows all other problems, and directs all movements of our psychological life into its path."[36] Annette Lee-Chai and John Bargh note, "The determining factor of whether an individual will abuse power is therefore not whether that person has a drive to gain and acquire power, because it would appear we all do, but rather the nature of the individual power holder's important, self-defining goals."[37] Plato observed, "The measure of a man is what he does with power."[38]

Personality disorders of excessive power strivings are manifested in schools, sports, and other group activities, adult work contexts and community life; in short in all areas of life, wherever people devote themselves relentlessly to capture control of the system, employ means to push others aside and down, or make charismatic efforts to capture and subordinate "public opinion" to their narcissistic power purposes. This phenomenon also shows up in temptations of power and over-certainty by mental health practitioners, including in psychotherapy.[39] The fact that excessive power strivings are widespread does not mean they should not be diagnosed. Early attention to manifestations of such personality disorder disturbance, if recognized by the mental health world as a bona fide form of significant emotional disturbance, would provide a new tool for addressing the destructive impacts of such personalities.[40]

The diagnosis of personality disorder of excessive power strivings is to be used when the individual displays prolonged and severe manifestations of the following criteria. The first criterion is the basic feature that is always present in this personality disorder. In addition, in order to establish the diagnosis, at least three other of the following characteristics should be present:

1. *Intense and extensive power strivings.* Power is the true goal, and even meritorious achievement goals are secondary to the real mission of achieving power. In the extreme, this characteristic manifests in various qualities of megalomania, at times including an actual goal of world control or world destruction fantasies.
2. *Lack of empathy for people and indifference to the suffering of others.* In the extreme, this characteristic is evidenced in disdain for and open joy in standing over victims, rituals of further abuse of victims and their memories, and sadism toward families of victims.
3. *"Street smart" alertness and remarkable cunning committed to seizing and expanding power.* In the extreme, this characteristic is expressed in gang terror, participation in terrorist groups, paramilitary, and secret killing squads and official government forces for the forced disappearance and execution of people.
4. *Ruthlessness in cultivation of power.* Stepping on other people regardless of the cost to them, including depressing and thwarting their talent and advancement in their work life, which can be manifested in disdain and disrespect of talent or in setting barriers to development and achievement. In the extreme, ruthlessness in cultivating power includes actual physical abusiveness and cruelty, including in the family violence or sexual abuse toward a spouse or child.
5. *Scapegoating and projection of blame onto targeted individuals or a group.* An insistent need to identify certain others as lowly, worthless, and intended victims. In the extreme, this characteristic includes an ideology and readiness to persecute, terrorize, torture, or kill members of a designated target group.
6. *Corruption by power and addiction to power.* Corruption—a person taking exaggerated liberties in their position of success and power; posturing of self-importance, highhandedness, narcissistic self-involvement and indifference to the needs of others; and addictive involvement with consolidating, expanding, and protecting one's power.

7. *Demands of other people to be dependent or to become obedient followers.* In the extreme, these demands culminate in insistence on blind conformity and obedience to orders to do harm either to oneself or to others or both, up to and including patterns of homicide-suicide.
8. *Emphasis on symbolism such as pure vs. impure, holy vs. infidel, chosen vs. condemned.* In the extreme, the seeking of power develops into a paranoid master plan for persecution of one or more groups of enemies who are defined as standing in the way of one's lofty and holy mission and purposes.
9. *A basic disrespect for the lives of others.* This is evidenced in callous or indifferent exposure of others to undue risks. Examples: Indifference to public health, such as in hazardous nuclear installations, and manufacturers and businessmen who subject people to major ecological and environmental hazards or dump on people products known to be dangerous or harmful; and inept or abusive military or political leadership sending soldiers on unnecessarily dangerous and probably fatal missions. The extreme of basic disrespect for the lives of others is what Erich Fromm[41] referred to as a necrophiliac fascination and love for inducing death.
10. *An absence of conscience in contexts of self-interest and opportunity.* In matters that do not pertain to personal power and advancement, the person may identify with ethical and liberal ideals. But in matters that are self-serving, there is indifference and blatant dismissal of recognized values of justice and fairness. In many cases, cynical lip service is paid to traditional values, but only as a disguise or even as an exploitative stratagem to garner more power. In the extreme, there is a readiness to step on and to destroy everyone in one's path toward one's goals of power.
11. *A homicide-suicide orientation.* Underneath a total passion with power and even readiness to destroy others, there is at times, surprisingly, also a movement toward self-destruction. In the extreme, the person plans or erupts impulsively into a sequence of murder of victims and then their own suicide. In our contemporary world, murder-suicide, of course, is an operation in the "thriving industry" of contemporary suicide bombers.[42] This paradigm can also be expanded beyond one's own self to a collective of which one is the leader. Often enough in addition to the obvious intention of victimizing one's designated enemies, there is no less an accompanying readiness to destroy and murder one's own people, a trend that followers of such leaders often fail to see until it is too late—for example, in "small" events such as with Reverend Jones in Jonestown and David Koresh in Waco, Texas; or in larger cases of national leaders like Hitler, Himmler, Stalin, Mao, and Pol Pot; or in the new faces of leaders of transnational genocidal terrorism such as Arafat and bin Laden, leading their nations into disastrous military expeditions and/or eliminating endless numbers of their own people as enemies of the regime. Ultimately, countless lives of the leaders' own countrymen are sacrificed on pyres of vicious self-adulation, self-serving ambition, and especially greed

for power and displays of contempt for others. Note that the leader himself may call for mass suicide or himself commit suicide, characteristically when megalomanic dreams of power prove to be thwarted.

The Problem of Diagnosing Successful People and Leaders as Suffering a Personality Disorder of Excessive Power Strivings

Understandably, the greatest obstacle to rational observation and diagnosis of personality disorders of excessive power strivings is the natural tendency to respect well-functioning people, and especially "successful" leaders and people who are powerful, because they are who they are and are winning and "succeeding" in their roles as leaders of their society.

In the evolutionary scheme, successful competition is natural and desirable. In societies where success, advancement, and leadership are honored, excessive power strivings may masquerade as capable functioning. In addition, many people believe that in order to protect their self-interest, such as to hold on to their jobs or to protect themselves against governmental power, they must accept and follow the authorities and leaders who are in charge. The result is that on every level of society one sees widespread readiness to conform and obey authority passively, blindly, and ritualistically—even when leaders call for acts of horror.[43] It takes unusually well-differentiated people, and healthy democratic groups and societies—which are also a minority in the world—to identify early on and stand up to the brokers of excessive power.[44] So in addition to identifying those who push for power over others, it is also necessary to identify those whose passivity, weakness, or lack of courage allow the demons to exercise their excessive and destructive power.

The present proposal is intended to provide a sound conceptual basis for identifying everyday phenomena of excessive use of power over others that are clear to people in their intuitive differentiation between responsible leadership and excessive power strivings. It is both amazing and also disheartening to see how many millions "fall" for grandiose, hate-trumping leaders.[45] Beyond the use of power in everyday relationships, we need a conceptual basis for authorizing all of us in democratic societies to be able to identify political or perverted power-maddened practices that should never be accepted and bowed to as prerogatives of leadership or authority. For a quite serious example at the time of this writing, two "legitimate" longtime rulers of non-Islamic countries who are reported to arrange systematically for the execution of influential opponents are Russia's Vladimir Putin and Rwanda's Paul Kagane.[46] As a world society we need to be able—and intellectually authorized—to identify as "disturbed" those leaders who imprison and torture their actual and potential competitors, genocidal leaders who persecute and murder their enemies, as well as the endless functionaries who slavishly and self-interestedly do the staffing and implementing of such leaders' persecutory policies. We also need to identify the huge numbers of people who are accomplices to the perpetrators and those who are bystanders.[47] These are all psychological and behavioral roles, and not only political behaviors. It behooves the science of human behavior to be able to describe and classify these behaviors; otherwise, our psychiatry and sciences of human behavior will have removed from our subject matter huge parcels of common everyday human behaviors that have enormous impact on most of us.[48]

The importance of strivings for power, superiority, and tyranny has not been lost on many mental health writers, including major figures such as Alfred Adler, Karen Horney, Erich Fromm, or Rollo May. Adler's[49] classic writings on strivings for superiority are the cornerstone of his individual psychology. Horney's contribution to neo-Freudian psychology included a strong emphasis on the excessive power strivings of neurotic personalities in whom she described needs for power, prestige, and possession, and a craving for domination over others for its own sake. "There is an essential disrespect for others, their individuality, their dignity, their feelings, the only concern being their subordination," and there is an "indiscriminate adoration of strength and contempt for weakness."[50] In his clarion confrontations of evil and destructiveness, Erich Fromm defined three major mechanisms of escape from true human freedom: "authoritarianism, destructiveness and automaton conformity."[51] Rollo May explored varieties of constructive and destructive power. He suggested that power be analyzed as exploitative, manipulative, competitive, nutrient, and integrative. Regarding exploitative power, he wrote:

> This is the . . . most destructive kind of power. It is subjecting persons to whatever use they may have to the one who holds the power. . . . Slavery is, of course, the obvious example—when one person has the power over the bodies and, indeed, over the whole organisms of many persons. . . . Exploitative power always presupposes violence or the threat of violence. In this kind of power there is strictly speaking, no choice or spontaneity at all on the part of the victims.[52]

In more recent years, there are ongoing developments in basic ego psychology and also in an applied area known as political psychology that aim to trace the follies, psychopathology, and tragedy-effecting behaviors of grandiose, narcissistic power-seeking behaviors.[53] Drawing on the works of Otto Kernberg[54] and Heinz Kohut,[55] Jerrold Post[56] has presented an extensive analysis of the narcissistic leader. Needing to be seen as all-wise and all-knowing, it is difficult for the narcissistic leader to acknowledge ignorance or error, or to seek or accept criticism, or even to take in information that is a priori unwelcome to him. "What is good for him is good for his country." Post also emphasizes how the narcissist is subject to self-righteous rage. Vamik Volkan[57] has emphasized the need of narcissistic personalities to have enemies; their internal concept of an enemy is vital for maintaining their inner psychic balance. Eric Brenman has described the psychological basis of cruelty as a "singular narrow-mindedness" where a person's mood squeezes out his humanity and maintains a "worship of omnipotence which is felt to be superior to human love and forgiveness."[58]

Michael Hogg and Scott Reid describe the characteristic descent of leaders to paranoid positions where they experience whoever in the world around them as their enemies and must take steps against them. They identify a "Stage 4," which they title "Abuse of Power."

> The leader gradually realizes that "he or she is effectively treated by followers as an out-group member . . . a deviant who cannot readily share in the life of the group. The leader may at this point try to veer away from the abyss by engaging in behaviors aimed at confirming his or her [belonging to the group]." If this is unsuccessful, a sense of rejection by, and distance and isolation from, the group may occur, which may embitter the leader and, since the empathic bond is severed, allow the leader to gain compliance through the exercise of power over others. This may involve coercive behavior and abuse of power.[59]

Robert Jay Lifton[60] has braved a very powerful path of research on totalitarian thinking, psychic numbing, splitting and doubling, use of a mechanism of healing/killing,[61] and unconscious pursuit of immortality in determining many destructive behaviors in human history. In a work with Eric Markusen,[62] the concept of a "genocidal mentality" is mapped (as well as its constructive antagonist of a "species mentality").

All these developments shed light and offer conceptual tools for encountering manifestations of abuse of power. In my judgment, they impel us to consider how to incorporate maps of manifest phenomena of excessive power-seeking on everyday levels of plain citizens, bureaucrats, and professionals, let alone of leaders.[63] There is no doubt that serious personality theorists and psychotherapeutic thought such as by the writers mentioned here have placed excessive power strivings squarely in the range of the disturbed, but formal psychiatric diagnosis has not. The implications of many writers are clear—*power corrupts the personality, and excessive power strivings are disturbed*, and not only when there is evidence of damage to one's own personality but because of the widespread damage such people also do to others and to society.[64]

To conclude, the manifestations of a personality disorder of excessive power strivings obviously fits the schema of disturbances of the Fascist Mind. The software program of the overly powerful states unambiguously something like this:"*Don't let anyone stand in your way; walk over anyone you need to in order to get where you have to go; crush those who are a threat to you, and in this way also prove to others who might have gotten in your way that you are ruthless and they shouldn't tangle with you. You will be a big success in this world because you aren't too soft.*"

Paranoid Personality Disorder

I accuse you! You can't be trusted! I have proof of your treachery!"

A paranoid personality disorder differs from paranoid psychotic states in that the person is not delusional. It is similar in that the person is living an oppressively suspicious life. The Mind paradigm that occupies the paranoid personality disorder is a repeated idea turned conviction that another or others are betraying one. This idea becomes the hidden solution to a whole range of existential anxieties that regularly concern all normal human beings, including fearfulness regarding one's competence for various tasks, concerns over loss of a love connection, concerns about one's status or position in the community, worries about world events, health issues, and so on—all of these can be "successfully" banished by a repetitive litany of accusativeness and a conviction that someone else is responsible for what is happening to me.

The results of paranoid personality disturbances can be bitter personal relationships. It also leads to unsettling disturbances in the chain of command of an organizational structure, with possibly disastrous consequences to the organization and the community it serves (see the brilliant portrayal of the paranoid commander in Herman Wouk's *The Caine Mutiny*[65]—although it is part of the author's fine writing that he leaves it not entirely clear whether the commander's disturbance reached the level of a paranoid psychotic process that went beyond a paranoid personality disorder). There is enormous havoc when paranoid suspicions and accusations are translated "successfully" into political platforms and the paranoid becomes a vested official leader of a society—the list of such leaders in the history even of democracies is tragically endless. There are, of course, fascinating tensions between the requirements of respecting and protecting the legal and political rights of people who are not paranoid and make accusations; protecting people's rights to bring charges that may still be quite true even if those bringing the charges are paranoid; protecting the emotional, political, and legal rights of the people who are accused by paranoid people; and protecting the integrity of organizations and communities that come under the poisonous control of paranoid political leaders. Altogether these issues cover some of the most interesting and problematic dramas of life.

Paranoid personality disordered people aren't exactly *crazy*, but one often wonders. They live a life of continuous distress and heightened suspiciousness of others. Some carry their distress on their furrowed brows and in suspicious narrowed eyes; others can look more worried and hurt rather than accusing; some are even smooth and, for a while at least, speak with a commanding aplomb and a seeming assurance of their being on the side of justice; while some others are more immediately obviously disturbed in their paranoid suspiciousness and are more likely to draw questioning thoughts of whether or not they are off their rockers. What all have in common is that they are preoccupied with persistent, basically *unjustified* doubts and accusations about disloyalty and untrustworthiness, such as the betrayal of a spouse, the treachery of a friend,the disloyalty of a colleague, or the plotting of a neighbor, spies, saboteurs, and terrorists in the community.

The life of the paranoid personality disorder is a lonely one. By definition the person cannot believe in confiding in others and asking for their help because of their suspicions. Worse than a worried lover, the paranoid often reads hidden meanings of humiliation and, worse, of threat into perfectly benign remarks and reactions of other people. Characteristically, the disordered paranoid personality is harboring a chronic grudge—obsessing about it, tracking it, and fantasizing retaliation and revenge. Many times, even the smoother paranoids break down from their seeming reasonable presentation of evidences and allegations of treacheries—which, after all, very much do take place in this world—and explode into a pique of intense angry suspiciousness. The breakdown of their control and the "frothing at the mouth" of revengefulness suggest (though do not prove, one should add very carefully) the likelihood of a disturbed way of thinking rather than a legitimate presentation of evidence. See the horrid one-man shows of the late Senator Joseph McCarthy![66]

Given their suspicions and accusations, paranoids make married life and family life very grim and heavy. Obviously, one prime playing field for expressions of suspiciousness is going to be accusations of sexual infidelity—for one has to be truly an infant not to know that sexual betrayal is alive and widely rampant in human affairs. Any married person with any sense in their head should know that a certain amount of energy needs to be devoted continuously to monitoring the possible unfaithfulness of the finest husband or wife (in fact, the monitoring itself becomes part of a language of caring enough to help influence one's mate not to stray in the first place).[67] Many times the major "evidence" that a married person has of infidelity is an amazing rush of intuitive knowledge that one's mate has been or is involved with someone else,[68] and it turns out to be quite accurate because there is powerful unconscious knowledge of such truths. So one shouldn't ever ignore or depreciate the rights of people to be suspicious about the sexual loyalty of their spouses. On the other hand, many times the suspicions are groundless or at the most are picking up impulses of a mate's flirting behaviors that are short of open betrayal. Moreover, the kinds of recurrent suspicions of infidelity that characterize the paranoid personality disorder are rooted in their basic suspiciousness more than in a flow of their natural self-protective security as mates who are legitimately watching out for their sexual and loyalty interests. When the paranoid accusations come out—grimly, grayly, and bitterly—it doesn't feel like there is very much sexuality in the air in the exciting libidinal sense of the word, or very much loving desire to be in a faithful union with one's mate, but rather an obsession with one's suspiciousness.

❖ They were both in their fifties, he a physician, she a high-ranking professional in the social welfare system. He was absolutely adamant that she was cheating on him.

"Why do you think so?" asked the therapist.

"I just know so," answered the physician. "She only gets back long after her office closes. I'm sure she goes from the office to be with someone else."

"But what makes you think she is with another man, and that she is his lover?" the therapist persisted.

The husband had nothing more substantial to say, only continuous and self-convincing angry restatements of his knowledge that she was going to another man. "I'm exhausted by him," said the wife. This has been going on for months. He keeps grilling me. I can't keep it up much longer, and I'm going to have to leave him if he doesn't stop."

In this case, the therapist was never able to ascertain in any convincing way whether or not the wife had been unfaithful at any time. It seemed that she had not,

Table 4.3. Dynamics of Fascist Mind in Selected Psychopathology: Antisocial, Power-Seeking, and Paranoid Personalities

	01-02 **TOTALITY, OVER-CERTAINTY, ABSOLUTISM, AND MAGICAL THINKING**	*03-04* **CENSORSHIP OF INFORMATION, OBEDIENCE, CONFORMITY, AND INTOLERANCE OF DISSENT**
PERSONALITY DISORDERS ***Group 3:*** **ANTISOCIAL, POWER-SEEKING, AND PARANOID PERSONALITIES** **including:** ***Antisocial Personality Disorder*** ***Personality Disorder of Excessive Power Strivings*** ***Paranoid Personality Disorder*** **In *DSM-5* see:** **Paranoid Personality Disorder (p. 327)** **Antisocial Personality Disorder (p. 324–325)** ***Page numbers refer to the Desk Reference to the Diagnostic Criteria from* DSM-5**	For antisocial persons, conscience and doubts are eliminated in the face of a total conviction in one's right to live out one's impulses and to do what one wants to do. An intense desire for and pursuit of power is the guiding end-all and be-all for excessive power-seekers. Paranoids move on to obsessive and suspicious accusations of others. In the process of all of the above, other people can be used, exploited, and abused to serve one's own needs. *Role of anxiety: Anxiety is generally blocked by the personality style. For antisocial personalities, it is most likely to appear in response to possible threats from agencies of control such as police, but rarely is anxiety bespeaking hopes or efforts for real personal growth. For power-seeking and paranoid personalities, anxiety is more likely apparent when there is a fear of losing control over others more than as a sign of really asking for help, even though intrinsically the anxiety is a window into a greater accessibility of humanistic experience by the patient, and there are times when such a door in fact does open to therapeutic dialogue.* *Paranoid personalities do show periodic leakages of anxiety, but typically will move as quickly as they can to bind their anxiety in more suspicious thoughts and behaviors.*	Antisocial personality disorders use information to further their own exploitative schemes. Power-driven people use information acquisitively to sharpen their control over others and consolidate power. Paranoids are masters of re-translation of information to fit their maps of life and distort information to make it fit their suspicions and accusations. All these personality types do *not* obey and conform to others so much as they are the commanders of the obedience and conformity of others to their wishes and dictates. Dissent toward them is hardly tolerated; it is resented, rejected, and invokes retaliation.

PERSONALITY DISORDERS: ANTISOCIAL, POWER-SEEKING, AND PARANOID PERSONLAITIES (*continued*)

05 **SUPERIORITY, EXCESSIVE POWER-SEEKING, AND PREJUDICE**	*06* **VIOLENCE, RETALIATION AGAINST DISSENT, SACRIFICE, AND DESTRUCTION**	*07* **DENIALS OF DOING HARM TO SELF AND OTHERS**
For antisocial disorders, superiority is implicit in brazenly taking a position of exploitation of others, and being "above" paying the price that other mortals have to pay for deviant and illegal behaviors. Superiority is certainly also the hub of power-seekers whose excessive power-seeking bespeaks unending superiority and prejudice toward other people. Paranoids may be involved more sickly in their own minds with their suspicions and accusations, but they are also very prone to seek to control and overpower others.	**Doing Harm to Self** Ultimately, the abuse and exploitation of others is likely to catch up with the patient, who becomes discredited and punished by people around them and by society. For the power-seekers, the pleasures of orgies of superiority and power over others are likely to protect the person who is riding high on the horse from doing many forms of harm to their own self. However, if and when opposition to their power mounts and their control is threatened, stress, disease, and breakdown become likely. **Doing Harm to Others** Much harm is obviously done to others by antisocial personality disorders in the course of exploiting others and imposing on them one's own needs. Doing harm to others is integral to the power-seeking personality, beginning with stepping on the opposition in competition and retaliation against dissenters to one's power, and culminating in crushing potential opponents and enemies. With paranoid personality disorders there are risks of explosive rage and revenge at whoever is seen as representing a threat to them. In domestic life, for example, many beaten wives need to escape their paranoid husbands who come after them (any number of actual murders do take place). On the level of society, paranoids can be the authors of grand plans of group persecution and genocide.	These patients consistently repeat whatever types of abuse, use, and exploitation of others. They routinely deny their actions and the considerable harm they are doing to others. They relabel their actions with whatever rationalizations, euphemisms, and, especially, justifications of one's entitlement to do what is "necessary" for the "welfare" of the child, family, organization, nation—whoever. Denial of doing harm continues even after there is firm evidence of harm being done to oneself and/or others. Regret, contrition, and disavowals of the harm and abuse one has done are rare.

Source: Created by the author.

and that she was no less involved than her husband was in the world of her work and busyness and in the long-since gray and practical kind of cooperative relationship that the couple had been living out without much affection or intimacy for many years. It seemed like the suspicions that the husband was now pouring out were coming as a kind of sad litany over too many years of lost opportunities for friendship and intimacy between them, and also the loss of meaningfulness in his life even as a physician, as he went about his work with a resolute military-like responsibility to do what he had to without much feeling for the wonderful significance of the medical profession in which he served.

They left the failed effort at therapy without any progress. It seemed to the therapist that although the wife was legitimately speaking of leaving her husband because of his suspicious accusations, she probably would not do so, and that the chronic suspiciousness was likely to become a permanent feature of the ways they filled their empty world with seeming content. Even paranoid fighting can be less boring than silence, emptiness, or aloneness.

CONCLUSION—THE DEVELOPMENT OF PERSONAL CHARACTER

Martha Crenshaw calls our attention to the truth that our field of modern psychology must also be wary of self-centeredness and self-serving when she writes, "Modern psychology only reinforces the cynicism that dominates American politics and society—a cynicism that leads to arrogant and contemptuous criticism of others, manipulation of the 'system' and self-indulgent consumption or greed."[69]

The effort to understand the unbearably common psychiatric disorders of personality and character disorders can lead us to a precious and meaningful conclusion: The task of developing ourselves as decent and capable people is a worthy lifelong task. It is obviously ethically the right way to live. It also is a true gift to our sense of meaningfulness in our lives—let alone to our actual mental health.

> Nearly all men can stand adversity, but if you want to test a man's character, give him power.[70]
>
> —*Unknown*

> According to Greek mythology, humans were originally created with four arms, four legs, and a head with two faces. Fearing their power, Zeus split them into two separate parts, condemning them to spend their lives in search of their other halves.[71]
>
> —*Plato*

O, it is excellent
To have a giant's strength, but it is tyrannous
To use it like a giant.[72]

—*William Shakespeare*

Most powerful is he who has himself in his own power.[73]

—*Seneca*

NOTES

1. In the official *DSM-5*, the personality disorders are organized into the following clusters: Cluster A: Personality Disorders: Paranoid Personality Disorder, Schizoid Personality Disorder, Schizotypal Personality Disorder.

Cluster B: Personality Disorders: Antisocial Personality Disorder, Borderline Personality Disorder, Histrionic Personality Disorder, Narcissistic Personality Disorder.

Cluster C: Personality Disorders: Avoidant Personality Disorder, Dependent Personality Disorder, Obsessive-Compulsive Personality Disorder.

There are also other personality disorders listed, including Personality Change Due to Another Medical Condition, Other Specified Personality Disorders, and Unspecified Personality Disorders.

The grouping I am using here obviously is different, but *not* because I am rewriting in any way the descriptions of the actual conditions, and I am certainly not rewriting any of the empirical observations of the course of any given symptom complex or disorder. Nor am I opposed to the specifications of personality disorders I have not included—which also can be fitted into my schema.

This book is not intended to provide an exhaustive list of any of the various types of psychopathology like a formal textbook does, but is intended to offer an overall conception of mental problems as doing harm to oneself or to others. Second, what I emphasize more is an idea-theme or paradigm in the inner character that can be seen at the heart of various psychiatric conditions more than the symptom picture as such. The person's basic Mind program for living is in some ways more important to me perhaps than the symptom picture that develops as a result of this Mind program. My hope is that the more we understand these "software" programs, the more we will be able to develop newly effective approaches to treatment.

In the case of the personality disorders, my first group includes conditions where the emphasis is on a person not being able to perform and win at life, who often takes advantages based on their inferiority. The conditions that make up the second group emphasize hedonistic overdoing and escape from responsibility. The conditions in the third group focus on nastiness, power over others, suspicion, and conspiracy.

2. See the controversy over whether psychologists and psychiatrists should refrain from "diagnosing" political leaders. William Doherty, who for years has championed attention to ethical disorders in therapy, led a campaign during the 2016 presidential election to allow diagnostic statements about Donald Trump. Doherty posted an online manifesto against "Trumpism" that has been signed by more than 2,200 mental health specialists. "Yes, for me this is an exception. What we have here is a threat to democracy itself," says Doherty. See Carey, Benedict (August 15, 2016). The Psychiatric Question: Is It Fair to Analyze Donald

Trump From Afar? *New York Times*. http://www.nytimes.com/2016/08/16/health/analyzing-donald-trump-psychology.html.

3. American Psychiatric Association (2013). *DSM-5, Desk Reference, op. cit.*, p. 324.

4. Horney, Karen (1937). *The Neurotic Personality of our Time, op. cit.*

5. Zimbardo, Philip G., Haney, Craig, Banks, Curtis W., and David Jaffe (ed. Zick Rubin) (1974). The psychology of imprisonment: Privation, power and pathology in *Doing unto Others: Joining, Melding, Conforming, Helping, Loving*. Englewood Cliffs, NJ: Prentice Hall, 61-73. *See also* Blass, Thomas (Ed.). *Obedience to Authority: Current Perspectives on the Milgram Paradigm*. Mahwah, NJ: Lawrence Erlbaum, 193–238.

6. Milgram, Stanley (1965). Some conditions of obedience and disobedience to authority, *Human Relations* 18: 57-76; Stanley Milgram, *Obedience* (film). University Park: Pennsylvania State Audio Visual Services. Milgram, Stanley (1974). *Obedience to Authority: An Experimental View.* New York: Harper & Row. *See also* Blass, Thomas (Ed.). *Obedience to Authority: Current Perspectives on the Milgram Paradigm*. Mahwah, NJ: Lawrence Erlbaum, 193–238.

7. Browning, Christopher (2013). *Ordinary Men: Reserve Police Battalion 101 and the Final Solution in Poland*. New York: Harper Collins (original publication 1992).

8. I pity the poor student—in departments and schools of psychology, social work, psychiatry, family therapy, and all the remaining counseling professions—who would dare speak or write on an examination about helping patients or clients to be more ethical people. Even the non-drug dispensing mental health business uses as its overriding metaphor concepts of helping people tell their narratives and stories, helping people cry out their pain, and empowering them to get what they really want and need for themselves, and similarly in respect of relationships such as marriages and families to tell one another one's real needs. But much more rarely are conceptions of responsibility, decency, nonviolence, or love held up as primary subjects and as the intended goals of mental health therapies—at best these good values may be expected to flow out of proper attention to expressing and pursuing one's needs and not the other way around.

9. Arieti, Silvano (1972). *The Will to Be Human, op. cit.*, 223, 252, 228.

10. Kunz, who calls for an alternative paradigm in psychology of "a psychology of responsibility," presents his critique in a study of the philosophical writings of Emmanuel Levinas. See Kunz, George (1998*). The Paradox of Power and Weakness: Levinas and an Alternative Paradigm for Psychology*. New York: State University of New York.

11. See Doherty, William J. (1996). *Soul Searching: Why Psychotherapy Must Promote Moral Responsibility.* New York: Basic Books.

12. McNeil, Elton B. (1966). Violence and human development. In Marvin E. Wolfgang (Ed.) (1966). *Patterns of Violence. Annals American Academy of Political and Social Science*, 364(1), 149–157.

13. Šebek, Michael. (1994). Psychopathology of everyday life in the post-totalitarian society. *Mind and Human Interaction*, 5(3), 104–109 (quotation on p. 105). Šebek also cites Winnicott's thinking on "ordinary good homes" as laying the groundwork for and fostering healthy democratic personalities. Winnicott, D.W. (1950). Some thoughts on the meaning of the word democracy. In *Home is Where We Start From: Essays by a Psychoanalyst.* New York: Norton, 239–259.

14. Šebek, Michael (1994), *ibid.*

15. Oliner, Samuel P. and Oliner, Pearl M. (1992). *The Altruistic Personality: Rescuers of Jews in Nazi Europe*. New York: Simon and Schuster.

16. Two classic works on borderline disorders are those of Masterson, James F. (1976). *Psychotherapy of the Borderline Adult: A Developmental Approach*. New York: Brunner/Mazel;

and Kernberg, Otto (1975). *Borderline Conditions and Pathological Narcissism.* New York: Jason Aronson.

17. Hayes, Steven C.; Follette, Victoria M.; and Linehan, Marsha M. (Eds.) (2011). *Mindfulness and Acceptance: Expanding the Cognitive-Behavioral Tradition.* New York: Guilford; Miller, Alec L.; Rathus, Jill H.; and Linehan, Marsha M. (2006). *Dialectical Behavior Therapy with Suicidal Adolescents.* New York: Guilford; Linehan, Marsha M. (2003). *Getting Through a Crisis Without Making It Worse: Crisis Survival Skills: Distracting and Self-Sooth.* New York: Guilford; Linehan, Marsha M. (2003). *From Suffering to Freedom: Practicing Reality Acceptance.* New York: Guilford; Linehan, Marsha M. (2000). The empirical basis of dialectical behavior therapy: Development of new treatments versus evaluation of existing treatments. *Clinical Psychology: Science and Practice,* 7(1), 113–119 (quotation on p. 114). See also Linehan, Marsha M. (1993). *Skills Training Manual for Treating Borderline Personality Disorder.* New York: Guilford Press; and Linehan, Marsha M. (1993). *Cognitive Behavioral Therapy of Borderline Personality Disorder.* New York: Guilford Press.

18. Scheel, Karen R. (2000). The empirical basis of dialectical behavior therapy: Summary, critique, and implications. *Clinical Psychology: Science and Practice,* 7(1), 68–86.

19. Westen, Drew (2000). The efficacy of dialectical behavior therapy for borderline personality disorder. *Clinical Psychology: Science and Practice,* 7(1), 92–94.

20. Luborsky, Lester; Diguer, Louis; Seligman, David A.; Rosenthal, Robert; Krause, Elizabeth D.; Johnson, Suzanne; Halperin, Gregory.; Bishop, Monica; Berman, Jeffrey S.; and Schweitzer, Edward (1999). The researcher's own therapy allegiance: A "wild card" in comparisons of treatment efficacy. *Clinical Psychology: Science and Practice,* 6(1), 95–106.

21. Koerner, Kelly and Dimeff, Linda A. (2000). Further data on dialectical behavior therapy. *Clinical Psychology: Science and Practice,* 7(1), 104–112 (quotation on p. 110).

22. Linehan, Marsha M. (2000). The empirical basis of dialectical behavior therapy. *ibid,* 10.

23. Kliem, Sören; Kröger, Christoph; and Kosfelder, Joachim (2010). Dialectical behavior therapy for borderline personality disorder. *Journal of Consulting and Clinical Psychology,* 78(6), 936–951.

24. Clarkin, John F.; Levy, Kenneth N.; Lenzenweger, Mark F.; and Kernberg, Otto F. (2007). Evaluating three treatments for borderline personality disorder: A multi-wave study. *American Journal of Psychiatry,* 164(6), 922–928.

The following are several books by Kernberg and his associates: Clarkin, John F.; Yeomans, Frank E.; and Kernberg, Otto F. (2006). *Psychotherapy for Borderline Personality: Focusing on Object Relations.* Washington, DC: American Psychiatric Association; Caligor, Eve; Kernberg, Otto F.; and Clarkin, John F. (2007). *Handbook of Dynamic Psychotherapy for Higher Level Personality Pathology.* Washington, DC: American Psychological Association; Clarkin, John F.; Fonagy, Peter; and Gabbard, Glen O. (2010). *Psychodynamic Psychotherapy for Personality Disorders: A Clinical Handbook.* Washington, DC: American Psychological Association.

25. Kernberg, Otto F. (1975). *Borderline Conditions and Pathological Narcissism, ibid.*

26. Lasch, Christopher (1991). *The Culture of Narcissism: American Life in an Age of Diminishing Expectations.* New York: Norton; Twenge, Jean M. and Campbell, W. Keith (2009). *The Narcissism Epidemic: Living in the Age of Entitlement.* New York: Simon and Schuster; Firestone, Lisa (2012). Is Social Media to Blame for the Rise in Narcissism? We're living in an increasingly narcissistic society. *Psychology Today.* http://www.psychologytoday.com/blog/compassion-matters/201211/is-social-media-blame-the-rise-in-narcissism.

We obviously all are living in a world that is colored—and seriously damaged—by a host of self-interests, whether by individuals like the all-time swindler Bernard Madoff; an endless number of rulers or heads of state who accumulate bizarre amounts of money for themselves;

or individuals, companies, organizations, or governments who greedily gather enormous power over others. But there is also widespread narcissism in the plain everyday life and personal relationships of all of us who have the bad fortune to have to live or work with unduly narcissistic people.

27. American Psychiatric Association (2013), *DSM-5, Desk Reference*, 324.

28. It is not surprising that therapy that shows some success, like the 12-step program for alcoholics, is more often rooted in a group experience in which the influence of the leaders and the influence of the group are joined with a guiding spiritual idea to loosen the dead-set addictive idea that is ruining a person's life.

29. The problem of addiction is widespread—I believe that all of us in effect are drawn toward some addictive process, and that it is one of our universal mental health tasks to put a halt to them and overcome them before they get us into deeper trouble. Just as the problem is widespread, so is there a voluminous literature on overcoming addiction, and I will only cite a couple of starters. I think it is only fair and responsible to note that many of the programs that are enthusiastically reported to be successful, such as 12-step programs, take as a center point an explicit traditional religious belief. Overall, my personal understanding is that any constructive reframing of the life-challenge a person faces may succeed in breaking the obsessive/tyrannical hold of the addictive sequence. The more constructive set breaks the hold of the obsessive addiction and reopens doors to inner tools for self-healing and for becoming inspired and dedicated to positive goals.

The *Dictionary of Psychology* of the American Psychological Association summarizes the 12-step program thus:

- admitting that one cannot control one's addiction or compulsion,
- recognizing a higher power that can give strength,
- examining past errors with the help of a sponsor (experienced member),
- making amends for these errors,
- learning to live a new life with a new code of behavior,
- helping others who suffer from the same addictions or compulsions.
- See VandenBos, Gary R. (2007). *APA Dictionary of Psychology* (1st edition). Washington, DC: American Psychological Association.

Originally developed as a process for treating alcoholics, the program has spawned many new groups that address other addictions with variations of the basic model. Thus there are programs including Adult Children of Alcoholics, Friends and Families of Alcoholism, Cocaine Anonymous, CoSex and Love Addicts Anonymous, Debtors Anonymous, Emotions Anonymous (for recovery from mental disorder), Food Addicts Anonymous, Gamblers Anonymous, Co-Anon (for friends and family of drug addiction), Co-Dependents Anonymous, and a great many more—for as we noted the addictive process can grab on to many, many paths. (In my hallucinatory moments, I would like to see an organization of Genociders Anonymous, but then again my wife says that I am addicted to romantic adolescent-like hopes for greater decency in this world.)

30. A very popular book that interprets addicts as being "on a spiritual quest even if they are not aware of it" is Chopra, Deepak and Simon, David (2007). *Freedom from Addiction: The Chopra Center Method for Overcoming Destructive Habits*. Deerfield, FL: Health Communications (HCI Books). The authors posit that addiction presents the challenge of finding nourishing substitutions to fulfill one's deep underlying needs for love, self-esteem, safety, and meaning. They present a method of treatment that includes an Ayurvedic diet, yoga, twice-daily meditation, and clearing of past emotional hurts.

Another approach is based on a person's ties to family and community. It has been called a daring approach in that it breaks up the tradition of protecting the privacy of a patient and creates an "encounter" with the world of people in his life. Galanter, Marc (1992). Overcoming Addiction: A daring approach to therapy puts substance abusers where they belong—among family and friends: Knowing the effect they have on their loved ones motivates many addicts to live a substance-free life. *Psychology Today*. http://www.psychologytoday.com/articles/200910/overcoming-addiction. Retrieved October 21, 2014.

31. Rummel, R.S. (1997). Power Kills: *Democracy as a Method of Nonviolence, op. cit.*
32. *DSM-5 Desk Reference* (2014): Antisocial Personality Disorder, 324–325.
33. Kesey, Ken (1962). *One Flew Over the Cuckoo's Nest, op. cit.*
34. Charny, Israel W. (1997). A personality disorder of excessive power strivings, *op cit.*
35. Charny, Israel W. (1986). Genocide and mass destruction, *op. cit.*
36. Quotation is from Adler in a chapter on "The Psychology of Power" written in 1928. Cited by Bargh, John A. and Alvarez, Jeannette. The road to hell: Good intentions in the face of nonconscious tendencies to misuse power. In Lee-Chai, Annette Y. and Bargh, John A. (Eds.) (2001). *The Use and Abuse of Power: Multiple Perspectives on the Causes of Corruption.* Philadelphia, PA: Psychology Press, 41–55 (quotation on pp. 44–45).
37. *Ibid.*, quotation on p. 45.
38. Plato (written 360 BCE) in *Symposium*. Jowett, Benjamin (1892). *The Dialogues of Plato Translated into English with Analyses and Introduction.* 3rd edition revised and corrected. Oxford: Oxord University Press.
39. Amundson, Jon; Stewart, Kenneth; and La Nae, Valentine (1993). Temptations of power and certainty. *Journal Marital and Family Therapy*, 19(2), 111–123.
40. Is the proposed diagnostic category of a personality disorder of excessive power strivings covered in existing personality disorders? See *A Democratic Mind, op. cit.*
41. Fromm, Erich (1941). *Escape from Freedom*, New York: Rhinehart; Fromm, Erich (1964); *The Heart of Man*, New York: Harper & Row.
42. Charny, Israel W. *Fighting Suicide Bombers, op cit.*
43. Milgram, Stanley (1974). *Obedience to Authority, op. cit.*; Kelman, Herbert C. and Hamilton, V. Lee (1989). *Crimes of Obedience, op. cit.*
44. In *Fascism and Democracy in the Human Mind*, I proposed that a degree of conformity and blending into others, whether on the level of primary family relationships or a person blindly following a leader (e.g., in a cult or on a larger scale of a Fürhur-led political party) also be considered aspects of emotional weakness and disturbance. Unthinking blind conformity to any power outside of oneself—versus independence and dignity in one's own identity—is another neglected dimension of desirable mental health diagnosis. The problem thickens immensely when we consider the millions of people who devote themselves punctiliously to the ritualism of a fundamentalist but recognized religious orientation—which we have no right to oppose no matter what our personal views. But I will suggest here that when the religious doctrine calls for violence and destruction, the mental health concept of doing no harm to one's life and to the lives of others has to supersede even a "religious" dictum.

See Specter, Michael (January 27, 2007). Letter from Moscow: Kremlin, Inc. Why are Vladimir Putin's opponents dying? *New Yorker*. http://www.newyorker.com/magazine/2007/01/29/kremlin-inc.

45. Looking at the 2016 presidential election, the pun is intended. See once again Carey, Benedict (August 15, 2016). The Psychiatric Question: Is It Fair to Analyze Donald Trump From Afar?, *ibid.*

Carey writes: "In 1973, the American Psychiatric Association adopted what became known as the Goldwater Rule, declaring it unethical for any psychiatrist to diagnose a public figure's condition 'unless he or she has conducted an examination and has been granted proper authorization for such a statement.'" Enter Donald J. Trump. The 2016 Republican nominee's incendiary, stream-of-consciousness pronouncements have strained that agreement to the breaking point, exposing divisions in the field over whether such restraint is appropriate today. Psychiatrists and psychologists have publicly flouted the Goldwater Rule, tagging Mr. Trump with an assortment of personality problems, including grandiosity, a lack of empathy, and "malignant narcissism."

46. French, Howard W. (April 19, 2014). How Rwanda's Paul Kagame Exploits U.S. Guilt: Washington's remorse over standing by during the genocide 20 years ago is enabling repression today. *International New York Times*. http://www.wsj.com/articles/SB10001424052702303603904579493440845328418.

47. Accomplices to evil are a worthy subject in their own right at every level of life. At a governmental level, accomplices include people such as the debonair Tarik Aziz, who was the sidekick of Saddam Hussein; or the Molotov of a Stalin or the Kissinger of Nixon, who are the showpiece advisers and lackeys (see Kissinger in respect of the highly questionable U.S. war in Vietnam, or in the double-crossing of the Kurds and other issues).

One is tempted to forget the accomplices and argue (questionably) that they have no blood directly on their hands, especially when they are themselves impressive or colorful personalities. In everyday life accomplices are everywhere, too, including in universities, where they are accomplice-members of dean's committees that deny tenure to a talented and responsible faculty member who dared to be an independent thinker. In family life they are the other or second parent who backs up their mate screaming ugly epithets at a problematic child. They are also the many engineers, technicians, laborers, secretaries, and businessmen who negotiate for and complete the contracts for gas furnaces at the Auschwitzes. Accomplices are evil. Accomplices need to be identified for who and what they are, stopped as early as possible, and held responsible for their actions.

As a teenager, I was a participant watching with overwhelming fascination a group orgy one night where we male counselors at a fine upper-middle-class summer camp circled round a would-be victim female counselor whom we had trapped in the oar house (note the auditory double entendre) on the lakeside and were preparing for her forced disrobing, if not more. Our charismatic leader was an older counselor who already had the awesome pedigree of being a law student at Harvard, and he was conducting the "trial" and announcing the punishments to our victim. Part of me definitely loved the possibility of seeing the girl naked, and my pulse quickened with the oncoming sexual adventure, but thank God I also was sickened at our abusiveness and had the presence to yell loudly at our leader and group to put a stop to the inquisition scene. It was a good lesson to me about myself that made me feel more confident of myself in tough political moments in the years to come, as well as taught me how some evil group behavior can be stopped by even a single strong protest, let alone if one mobilizes broader protests.

48. Charny, Israel W. (1982), *How Can We Commit the Unthinkable? Genocide: The Human Cancer*. Foreword by Elie Wiesel. Boulder, CO: Westview Press; Dicks, Henry V. (1972), *Licensed Mass Murder: Socio-Psychological Study of Some SS Killers*. London: Heinemann; Tamarin, George R. (1980). *Studies in Psychopathology*. Kennewick, WA:Turtledove Press.

49. Adler, Alfred (1917b). *Study of Organ Inferiority and Its Psychical Compensation, op. cit.*; Adler, Alfred (1932), *Individual Psychology and Its Results in the Practice and Theory of Individual Psychology, op cit.*

50. Horney, Karen (1937). *The Neurotic Personality of Our Time, op. cit.*; Horney, Karen (1942), *Self-Analysis, op cit.*, quotation on p. 56.

51. Fromm, Erich (1941). *Escape from Freedom, ibid.*; Fromm, Erich (1964). *The Heart of Man, ibid.*

52. May, Rollo (1998). *Power and Innocence.* Originally published in 1972. New York: Norton, 94–95.

53. So many world leaders have been described in press reports over the years as given to explosive outbursts. Thus—without any attribution of equivalence between them, and without any formulations of diagnosis: Adolf Hitler, Richard Nixon, and al Maliki. "Would you want to buy a used car from any of them?"

54. Kernberg, Otto (1975). *Borderline Conditions and Pathological Narcissism, ibid.*

55. Kohut, Heinz (1977). *The Restoration of the Self.* New York: International Universities Press; Kohut, Heinz (1984). *How Does Analysis Cure?* Edited by Arnold Goldberg. Chicago: Chicago University Press.

56. Post, Jerrold (1993). Current concepts of the narcissistic personality: Implications for political psychology. *Political Psychology*, 14(1), 99–121, quotation on p. 110.

57. Volkan, Vamik (1988). *The Need to Have Enemies and Allies: From Clinical Practice to International Relationships.* Dunmore, PA: Jason Aronson.

58. Brenman, Eric (1985). Cruelty and narrowmindedness. *International Journal of Psychoanalysis*, 66(3), 273–281.

59. Hogg, Michael A. and Reid, Scott A. (2001). Social identity, leadership and power. In Annette Y. Lee-Chai and John A. Bargh (Eds.). *The Use and Abuse of Power: Multiple Perspectives on the Causes of Corruption.* New York: Psychology Press, 159–180 (quotation on pp. 172–175).

60. Lifton, Robert Jay (1967). *Death in Life: Survivors of Hiroshima.* New York: Random House; Lifton, Robert Jay (1979). *The Broken Connection: On Death and the Continuity of Life.* New York: Simon and Schuster; Lifton, Robert Jay (1986). *The Nazi Doctors: Medical Killing and the Psychology of Genocide.* New York: Basic Books.

61. In his brilliant and memorable study of the physicians who staffed the Nazi concentration and death camps, Lifton arrived at a powerful formulation of a "healing-killing" dimension of human experience. He observed that in their powerful roles as healers, many physicians are drawn toward becoming actual killers of their patients and charges, generally in the name of an ideology of promoting health! Thus, in the Holocaust the Jews were compared by some to a diseased limb that must be amputated. Thus, too, in American and Australian histories, thousands of mentally retarded and other defective people—especially of minority racial/ethnic groups—were sterilized by physicians in the name of the betterment of the human race. Psychologically, the power invested in physicians to intervene in life or death situations triggers in some of them too easily a sense of omnipotence, and releases what is after all a universal tendency to overuse of power and abuse of others in the ostensible name of some good value—a chosen political system versus the rejected one, an espoused god versus the heathen and infidel, genetic health versus genetic decline, and so on of an endless web of lying doubletalk to cover the rotten use of power for hurting and killing other people.

62. Lifton, Robert Jay and Markusen, Eric (1990). *The Genocidal Mentality: Nazi Holocaust and Nuclear Threat.* New York: Basic Books.

63. One should also take note of the considerable damage done to many human beings in organizational structures and bureaucracies by power-seeking chiefs at various hierarchical levels. See Williams, Norma; Sjoberg, Gideon; and Sjoberg, Andree F. (1983). The bureau-

cratic personality: A second look. In W. Boyd Littrell, Gideon Sjoberg, and Louis A. Zurcher (Eds.), *Bureacracy as a Social Problem*. Greenwich, CT: JAI Press, 173–189. They refer to the regularity of human casualties in virtually every large organization in the face of bureaucratic personalities and their "studied friendliness, lack of affect . . . [and] posture of toughness" (p. 184). Williams also recalls R.J. Merton's classic observations of the rigidity of bureaucrats who come to view rules and regulations as ends in themselves. See Merton, Robert K. (1940). *Bureaucratic Structures and Personality*. Chapel Hill: North Carolina Press. *See* also Margolis, Diane R. (1979). *The Managers*. New York: William Morrow. Margolis similarly has described the faceless, emotionless affect of managers; Hummel, Ralph P. (2007). *The Bureacratic Experience: The Post-Modern Challenge*. Fifth edition. Armonke, NY: M.E. Sharpe.

Of course, the bureaucratic process is not at all the only source of incompetence in organizations. Thus, a particularly enjoyable but damningly real explanation of much incompetence in the higher ranks of organizations is the "Peter Principle." The underlying error here is the assumption by the organization, and most often the working person themself, that because one has been very successful in the past they doubtless will rise successfully to the challenge of promotion to a higher level. It takes a great deal of maturity and flexibility for persons to recognize, as early as possible, when they are over their heads. *See* Peter, Laurence J. (2011). *The Peter Principle: Why Things Always Go Wrong*. New York: Harper Reprint Edition (original publication 1969).

64. World-leading genocide scholar, R.J. Rummel of the University of Hawaii, has written powerfully about the quest for power lying at the heart of evil—including genocide. Rummel, R.S. (1997). *Power Kills: Democracy as a Method of Nonviolence, op. cit.*

65. Wouk, Herman (1952). *The Caine Mutiny*. New York: Doubleday.

66. McCarthy's closest colleague, who served as a kind of "executioner" during the persecutory McCarthy era, was an attorney named Roy Cohn. For many years after McCarthy was disposed, Cohn was the attorney and very close friend and "drinking buddy" of Donald Trump.

67. Charny, Israel W. (1992). "Catering and not catering affairs." In *Existential/Dialectical Marital Therapy, op cit.*, 220–244; Brown, Emily M. (2001). *Patterns of Infidelity and their Treatment. New* York: Routledge; Weeks, Gerald R. and Treat, Stephen R. (2001). Treating the extramarital affair. In *Couples in Treatment: Techniques and Approaches for Effective Practice*. New York: Routledge, 226–263.

68. Charny, Israel W. and Parnass, Sivan (1995). The impact of extramarital relationships in the continuation of marriages. *Journal of Sex and Marital Therapy*, 21(2), 100–115.

69. Crenshaw, Martha (2000). Review of Kunz, George (1998). The paradox of power and weakness: Levinas and an alternative paradigm for psychology. *Political Psychology*, 21(4), 860–861.

70. Attributed to Abraham Lincoln, but some researchers find no evidence that this statement was spoken or written by Abraham Lincoln. "Quote Investigator" conjectures that "something that was said about Lincoln was transformed into something that was said by Lincoln." http://quoteinvestigator.com/2016/04/14/adversity/.

71. English translation of Plato's *Symposium* by Benjamin Jowett [April 15, 1817–October 1, 1893, Oxford University]. Copy at http://classics.mit.edu/Plato/symposium.html _and another at http://etext.library.adelaide.edu.au/p/plato/p71sy/.

72. Shakespeare, William [1564–1616]. *Measure for Measure*, Act 2, Scene 2. In *The Complete Works of William Shakespeare Comprising His Plays and Poems*. London: Spring Books [no date given in book], 89–114.

73. Seneca [c. 4 BCE–65 CE, a Roman philosopher, statesman, dramatist, and writer]. Seneca, Lucius Annaeus. *Epistulae Morales (Letters)* [Seneca, Epistles, 2], Volume 2, No. 34. Trans. Richard M. Gummere. London: Harvard University Press, 1917. 3 Vols. Loeb.

5

Some Recognized and Unrecognized Psychiatric Disorders

SOME OLD-FASHIONED PLUS SOME NEWLY FASHIONABLE PSYCHIATRIC DISORDERS, INCLUDING DISORDERS OF EVIL IN OUR AGE OF EXTREMISMS

Mental illnesses come in endless forms, and the trick in recognizing them is to see their underlying totalitarian-like structure of imposing a given truth and controlling and terrorizing one's life and/or the lives of others. Once one gets the hang of defining the doing of serious harm—consciously or unconsciously—to one's life and/or serious harm to the lives of other people, one knows how to diagnose not only old standby conditions that have "earned" recognition in the official books of mental health, but also the new exotic, bizarre, and horribly destructive behaviors that humans, and different societies, are forever innovating.

This chapter is a "tour" of a small variety of psychiatric disorders, some recognized old-fashioned conditions, but also a bunch of newcomers, many of whom have not yet been formally "accepted" into the roster of official mental illnesses. We discuss briefly some traditional psychoses, including mania and depression, catatonic schizophrenia, and paranoid conditions—including paranoid thinking in a political context. We also look at a "hit" condition of our times, anorexia. What is most important in this tour is the picture that develops of mental disorders as an endless gallery of ways in which a person or also a culture choose to design their retreats from life, largely unconsciously but also with some conscious elements. They escape to Fascist Mind or totalitarian ways of controlling and stopping the world of natural experiencing in one's own mind and/or to imposing such domination on others (such as a spouse, children, employees, and so on). The fascist program also punishes "emotional heathen and infidels" for not obeying the rules and daring to oppose the control and supremacy of the fascist dictate.

We then move into terra incognita and meet up with a series of mental conditions that have not made it into the official rubric for diagnosing psychopathology. Underlying these conditions is a basic error in the way life experiences are organized—with denials and censorship of authentic emotions and total unyielding rules for life imposed on oneself and/or others. Many of these conditions also go unrecognized because they involve doing injury to others more than a dysfunctional state in the individual.

We look first at what I call the "Orphan Syndrome," which plagues many a self-made person who may have done wonders in "growing themselves" out of a rough beginning of their lives where, for whatever reason, they were alone and unloved. When they build their lives to provide themselves an opportunity to be loved by others, they often do not know how to receive love. Their very self-reliance and competence can make them unable to participate well in a give *and* take relationship, and in many cases they leave a spouse and/or children too alone and not warmly nurtured.

Next we look at a newly spreading condition in many countries of grown children who do not leave home! Some never try. Many do go out for a while but then turn tail and return home again. In any number of cases, these "grown kids" then become tyrants to their parents. These are tragic cases of arrested development. Both the young person and their parents and family lose so much but are unable to "break out of the jail" they mutually construct.

The next bedeviling conditions involve the rough stuff of violent destruction of life. Nowhere in the *DSM* does one find a category for any number of absolutely fascinating and baffling cases of perfectly normal people who go off on a wild caper, but they do happen in real life. Included here are bizarre, unusual stories of criminal behaviors that can even involve serious harm or a threat of harm to other people, such as when a "perfectly well-adjusted person" decides to be a criminal and go after a proverbial financial bonanza at the expense of the welfare of others. Some of these initially excite our laughter-incredulity at the craziness that the human mind can generate, and they may also touch off our admiration for a "Jesse James courage" we may wish for ourselves, but the fact that serious harm is or could have been done to others means these situations cannot be viewed simply humorously.

Several of the conditions we study involve terrifying expressions of the potential for violence that obviously awaits in the human psyche—or we wouldn't have so much of it over and over all through our lives. The arenas and examples of violence are endless in humanity and obviously can fill many books. We look, for example, at the heartrending and perplexing instances where "perfectly normal kids" commit a murder unexpectedly.

Continuing the subject of human violence, we look at a variant of our times, namely the terrorist. After all, suicide-killing can hardly be called normal, nor is it "simply" or "only" an instance of political choice. If we agree that protecting one's life is a supreme injunction of psychological normality for Western psychiatry and psychology, then suicide-killing can be seen as seriously disturbed or psychopathological behavior, beginning with the fact of taking one's own life. If we agree further that not doing serious harm to the lives of others is a cardinal requirement of good mental health, the suicide-killer qualifies as very disturbed a second time. Obviously suicide-killing is not good for living creatures. The conception of a Fascist Mind in this book will have no trouble accommodating a diagnosis of suicide killers not only on the descriptive level of their horrible destructive behaviors, but also in the context of our theory of Mind regarding how one can get seriously stuck on any idea—even at the expense of one's life and the lives of many others.

Suicide-killing is brazenly criminal and insane. Of course, the framing of suicide-killing as mentally disturbed behavior in no way should be allowed to give it a sympathetic cover of any sort or recourse to any of the defenses available for insanity. Nor should seeing the psychological aspects of the behavior be allowed to take away from our concentrating first of all on means of security to defend civilized people and communities against the dangers and horrors of these killers.

We move next to a new "American way" of going crazy—and being rotten—in eruptions of mass killing in "Columbines" (schools), shopping centers, and more. Kill—wildly, randomly, promiscuously—and be killed! It is an opera of death at the expense of so many innocent people along with the suicide of the contemptible killer.

These too are suicide killers like the terrorists. Sociologically, the ideological context in which most terrorists operate involves a commitment to a rabid killing ideology. These "Columbine killers" more often than not are loners, brooders, and warped people, but their misery triggers the same murder-suicide path of the terrorists. Both have in common a goal of destroying life—their own and others. Both also are representative of basic sociological patterns in the cultures that sponsor them of full-blown escape from the dignity and sacredness of life. In this respect, American culture, no less than terrorist cultures, has a good deal of reckoning to do about how it sponsors so much violence.

We then introduce a basically unknown syndrome in Western psychiatry that has been given the name of Sudden Unexpected Nocturnal Death Syndrome (SUNDS). In the process we shall also be seeing a sad example that without doubt is repeated frequently, where "one hand of the science of the healing professions does not know what the other hand is doing." We will have the pleasure of learning from an article in the *American Journal of Orthopsychiatry* in 1983 how open-minded, investigative, and culturally sensitive therapists, with assistance from the U.S. Centers for Disease Control in Atlanta, came to understand this profound and indeed deadly psychosomatic condition, and treated it creatively using culture-based rituals and an extended family-community approach to bring hope and peace to the tortured soul whose life was at risk. It is a wonderful detective-like story of scientific exploration and devoted professionalism. Yet years later, we see reports that the syndrome is still a total mystery to health authorities.

Finally, in this chapter we look at an "invisible condition" that is amazingly widespread but quite unrecognized in the formal psychiatric diagnostic system. The latter is busy with all sorts of mentally disturbed persons according to all the joyful symptoms of dysfunction, but if we look carefully we discover any number of cases where there is another identity playing a major role in the life of the disturbed person—someone who wants them to be disturbed and/or is "driving them crazy." Yes, often enough it is seemingly loving, devoted parents who do just that to their children, and of course, any number of dear life partners as in a husband and wife who spook one another. These are unconscious scenarios of "I hate you but won't show it openly," or "Be the carrier of the upset and shakiness in our lives while I make sure to look ever so composed and attractively put together." These are embodiments of the fabulous concept formulated by psychiatrist M. Scott Peck—the "People of the Lie."

OLD-FASHIONED PSYCHOTIC ABDICATIONS OF REALITY

The basic notion in a number of psychotic conditions is that interaction with human beings is too dangerous and coping with normal life tasks is too frightening, and the solution undertaken is to withdraw from normal social intercourse with people.[1]

Taken to its extreme, the solution of curtailing or avoiding social connections and coping with normal life tasks in order to reduce risks of being hurt, controlled, humiliated, and so on backfires on the person: The withdrawn person now is unnerved and frightened by the rigidly empty world they have created and can become increasingly demoralized and immobilized. Finally, the person loses their basic freedom to run their own life, takes on a public- and self-identity as a psychotic, is stigmatized, becomes habituated to the role, and can become fully locked into a chronic lifestyle as a psychotic.

The above is an old-fashioned down-to-earth explanation of giving up normal life for madness. Using a psychodynamic lens, we see most psychotic conditions as existential and interpersonal disorders that express feelings of deep inadequacy, a paranoid timidity, and/or anger that trigger a withdrawal from life and normal human interactions out of fear and terror rather than a biological condition. Using a "systemic lens" of understanding the huge meanings and power of relationships, we also seek to understand the soul of the individual who escapes normal life in relation to their network of relationships, and therefore what they are saying about and to others in their life through their madness. The first "psychodynamic" lens is for understanding the emotional heart of an individual person. The second systemic lens is for understanding how a person's madness speaks of and to others in their life.[2]

Biological conceptions of psychoses do not challenge or require much further understanding of the individual and his relationships—at least no more than what one wants to know about a patient in the course of treating him for any serious illness. With this approach to psychiatric disorders, you list the symptoms, consult the manual for names of the cluster of symptoms, check the menu of mind-altering drugs, and prescribe the best available relief. Forget Freud, Adler, Jung, Horney, Sullivan, Fromm-Reichmann, Rollo May, Whitaker, Minuchin, Haley, Satir, and Palazzoli. Let it be "Pills Away in a Brave World," where the meaning and meaningfulness of one's life are of little importance.

I believe that even if some psychiatric medications do cut back florid psychotic symptoms, and thereby do represent welcome advances for reducing human misery, at the core of the illness is a frightened human being who feels they lack the skills—and indeed often has not learned and developed these skills—for normal social interaction. There is much reason to argue that many psychoses in effect are psychosomatic conditions, with significant interactive changes in the patient's physiology as a result of psychologically induced processes; hence there are brilliant medications that can cut the chains of these symptoms. But at their core, many of the psychoses are what I believe human beings continue to know intuitively: a flight from life by people who feel inadequate for the tasks of life.[3]

A further psychodynamic and systemic conception is that a significant number of psychotic conditions also represent and express a secondary manipulative and exploitative personality that the patient chooses and/or allows to take over in their psyche. It is a "welfare personality," secretly (unconsciously) glad for all the attention that the psychiatric condition demands and gains, and secretly (unconsciously) glad and even triumphant to be spared the responsibilities of coping with life for oneself. In many cases, especially where the psychosis clearly conveys and emphasizes a message of "I can't cope with life," the secondary or replacement self takes over from early on in the process. In this inner conception of self, the psychotic person unconsciously celebrates and enjoys their specialness and their success in drawing, variously, attention, perhaps sympathy, being managed and organized by others, and the benefits one gains of being an object of concern and services from family and social and psychiatric services, as well as subtly being a kind of boss of others and commanding and commandeering the services received.

There have been some research that demonstrates aspects of this self-serving process, such as the work of Braginsky and Braginsky, who showed that hospitalized psychotic patients know enough to "prove" how sick they are if being too well will get them out of a hospital in which they want to stay; but if being too sick will get them removed from a more open ward on which they enjoy life to a more closed ward, they know enough to show how much better they are.[4] In other words, psychotic patients may display more or less severe symptoms depending on "what's in it for them."

There has been little professional consensus on this point of view—that psychosis often enough involves celebration and exploitation of disability—so that there has been too little buildup of clinical and research literature on this interpretation. I do not know how often this aspect of exploitativeness becomes so major a part of the psychotic illness that it needs to be addressed in psychotherapeutically oriented management of the patient. Personally, I have met a number of clinicians, in the United States, and in Australia in particular, who share this point of view and work with patients accordingly.[5] But this view is generally not accepted, and also is often viewed as politically incorrect. Again, we have a situation where a student who might dare bring up such a concept in Establishment courses and training could likely "lose his pants" (for the fun of it, a simile that plays on old-fashioned Freud). It is even more politically incorrect for me to add the comment that there were elements in Soviet psychiatry that spoke of an exploitative process in some psychotics, who in effect were seen as avoiding and escaping their responsibilities and challenges to be self-sufficient, productive people who contribute their share to the common well-being of society. Even if overall I found Soviet psychiatry deeply objectionable as an arm of totalitarian government, this conception seemed to me to address a side of truth that Western psychiatry, in its admirable greater respect for patient dignity and rights, was not seeing, and to this day seems afraid of investigating squarely. Here is a clinical example of the constructive application of this principle to treatment:

❖ This is a case referred to earlier of a young man of thirty living on a kibbutz in Israel who had been hospitalized, quite legitimately, with schizophrenia some four times. Finally, his family applied for private outpatient therapy. The therapist made it a basic condition that he go to work in his kibbutz every day in order for him to be admitted to therapy sessions that combined individual sessions for the man with family therapy and parental counseling.

The patient was so out of touch with an ability to feel safe in a work environment, and so out of touch with normal inner wishes to be and feel productive, that he was genuinely panicked. Moreover, he had so little work experience that in many ways he did not know how to work, and that in itself made him, like all new workers, nervous and frightened, except that in his case he also didn't have healthy habits for how to be normally nervous and afraid. At first he tried to get away with not working, and he was shocked to find that when he didn't go to work the therapist turned him away without conducting the scheduled session despite the fact that he and his parents traveled three hours each way to reach the therapist. When he then took to cheating and lying that he had gone to work, the therapist worked out with the kibbutz a reliable method for the kibbutz work manager to record and certify the man's work hours each day. Seeing there was no way out, and given his parents' insistence on therapy, he responded to the challenge placed on him and discovered that he was capable after all. Over many years after treatment was concluded, the man continued to do a normal day's work.

A combination of psychodynamic and systemic principles yields a conception of many psychoses as a pained, frightened withdrawal from normal social connections and life tasks, and a takeover by a secondary personality that unconsciously takes pleasure in arranging to be the object of family, social, and psychiatric ministrations and services, where the patient prefers to live this way over developing greater personal competence.

As we noted, this conception is not at all held in favor in contemporary psychiatry. This is a frame of reference in which one sees fixed ideas or totalities playing a major role in the patient's mind in creating and guiding the psychotic way of life. The implication of this frame of reference is that treatment needs to be addressed toward changing the rigid ideas, or what we are calling a fascist mindset more than anything else, though possibly also with the aid of medications to overcome florid symptoms more rapidly and to reduce the need for hospitalization so that psychotherapy can be pursued on an outpatient basis.

The various modal categories of psychoses contain their own specific paradigm of how to keep people at bay and oneself safe from threats of contact and closeness. For example, therapeutic experiences with catatonic patients have taught us that catatonics are terrified of letting go to a murderous, for them possibly world-destroying, rage that awaits inside their minds. The solution they come up with is to go to the extreme of paralyzing their functions as the alternative to their fears of going too far with their destructiveness. Immobilizing themselves is their solution to a possibility they really don't want of actually destroying people, or what they fear crazily will be the inadvertent destruction of a large part or even of the entire world. Again the clinical phenomenology in itself has been known for many years, but what we now want is to see how Fascist Mind thinking, or the extreme use of a single idea or position—*I am afraid that my murderous rage will get away from me, and I must stop myself from murdering the other(s)*—is at the base of the catatonic condition. The remarkable phenomenon of a stone-like paralysis that we used to see in catatonics before the use of psychotropic drugs, where a patient can maintain a distinctly uncomfortable position even for long periods of time, appearing to have been transformed into a statue, also gives us a glimpse into the tremendous power that can be available by virtue of the adoption of single-minded totalistic thinking.

Obviously the study of psychosis is a huge topic. We will continue looking briefly at some conditions including mania and depression, a bit more at catatonic schizophrenia, and at various paranoid psychoses through our lens of Fascist versus Democratic Mind.

AFFECTIVE PSYCHOSES—MANIA AND DEPRESSION

In these conditions emotion is experienced in extreme quantity and quality. Instead of experiencing normal hurts and disappointments and being able to ride out painful relationships and life events, the patient becomes captive to an extreme of despondency and is no longer capable of self-renewal following a period of hurt, mourning, and disappointment, or the patient is taken with an effusive, volatile hyper-emotionality or overdoing. Bitter anguished depression and/or a mania of pretending to be only and supremely happy convey the breakdown. In both cases the normal mechanisms for experiencing and overcoming hurt and loss are replaced by a "stuck record" of crazy extremes of emotionality as defenses against processing real emotions effectively.

The "stuck record" of responding with too much of the overdone affect can also be translated into the idiom of this book as an expression of a fascist model of totality and certainty. Both agitated depression, and the manic alternative that is chosen by a smaller number of patients suffering affective psychoses, are efforts to release oneself from real threats of deep mourning and despair, but again the patient ruins "a good thing" by turning their solution into an extreme. Psychotically depressed patients do not let go of being depressed. They turn their depression into a way of life to such an extent that they lose contact with whatever really was hurting them. Even their extreme symptomatic sadness is a smokescreen for their more real personal soul sadness. The manic patient, on the other hand, may have been on to a good idea of correcting their severe depression by going in the other direction of seeming joy, but their elation and euphoria are so exaggerated that the personality is flooded beyond its capacity to process the intense affects, and the person's capacity for judgment is impaired. Emotions and emotionality, which are intended psychologically to be tools of self-expression and to protect the organism by releasing accumulating emotions, become in their own right enemies of emotional stability. In both cases of depression and mania, the patient as a rational, coping person is overwhelmed not only by their original hurts and concerns, but also by the exaggeration of their emotional style of being in the world—whether depressed, manic, or both. Moreover, a suicidal solution to it all is a definite possibility.

Perhaps even more than other psychotic conditions, manic-depressive disorders, known in recent years as bipolar disorders, have been regarded for many years by most mental health professionals as a largely genetically transmitted illness. The fact that many manic-depressives do respond meaningfully well to medication with lithium has also reinforced suggestively the notion that the disease is intrinsically physiologically driven. In fact, the effect of the lithium, which is to slow down the rapidity and intensity of nervous system functioning, is a good example of how medication can impact very constructively on a psychosomatic process, but does not in itself prove that the illness is generated physiologically. Moreover, most research has concluded that a combination of medication and psychotherapy, especially family therapy, gives the best results in the difficult treatment of this condition.

A psychosomatic conception of the manic-depressive or bipolar condition is, as explained earlier about psychosomatic processes, that the condition can be triggered by psychological causes that then trigger enduring changes in physiological processes.

One intriguing psychodynamic proposition that has been offered about manic-depressives is that the patient often is a victim of a lifelong concern with being emotionally over-responsible for their family. Included in this group of manic-depressive patients are some very wonderful people who generously gave of themselves as children and literally carried the responsibility for the physical and/or emotional survival of their siblings and/or parents. Unbeknownst to them, the load of their heroic responsibility at too early an age also sapped their strength and set off a very high level of inner rage at being required to be so responsible for the welfare of others, and this unconscious rage wreaks havoc in their adult lives in their new relationships with their contemporary loved ones. In this respect, too, the totality of an idea becomes too burdensome to the patient who can never provide enough, and can never ask for sufficient help for their own self. Another hypothesis offered by some clinicians is that the basis of the condition may be in a history of being really loved and cared for in the early years, but then the bond was shattered by a traumatic loss. Manic-depressives are people who are bitterly alone with themselves, vainly trying to do it all on their own—without being in real connection and, heaven forbid, dependent on anyone.[6]

These patients often show a bitter resistance to allowing anyone—therapists very much included—to help modify their excessive emotion. "No way will you take away from me my depression/super-happiness or super-busyness as the case may be" is what the patient in effect often says, even ferociously, to anyone who wants to bring them (up) (down) from their (depression) (mania) to a more solid footing.

Treating manic-depressives is often a veritable battle to gain patient cooperation, beginning with taking medication and/or fulfilling medical requirements for regular checkups of possible problems caused by the medication, or reporting regularly for psychotherapy sessions, let alone taking any kind of behavioral instruction from a therapist and/or members of one's family.

There are many people who live chronically manic styles. Many of them are so brilliant and talented in their work and contributions to society that they carry on as recognized leaders in their fields, but for all their successes they are personally miserable and/or create unending misery for some of their loved ones and other close relationships in their lives. Their motto, "I can do it all by myself," makes them unable to be intimate with anyone.

❖ I knew a brilliant man who had been diagnosed correctly by the finest psychiatrists in the land with a bipolar condition and was cooperating with the lithium treatment they were giving him. But he was nonetheless deep down miserable. He applied himself outstandingly to his profession, and at the same time enjoyed an unending series of affairs with the best and brightest women (each of which would end, of course), but he was still deep down alone, agitated, and sulking.

He was a friend of mine and not formally a patient, but at one point he asked me if he could talk to me about his suffering and I agreed. I told him that he needed to develop a more respectful and empathetic relationship with his wife, to stop his flagrant daily insults and abuses of her and generally build a more positive family life. I suggested couple and family therapy in addition to the lithium he was taking.

He genuinely appreciated my advice but couldn't take it. "I can't stand that stupid cow," he said disparagingly, without any hesitation about possibly being nicer to his wife. I told him the minimum he needed was to stop his arrogant belittling and humiliating of her. "Out of the question," he ruled. I told him that without a network of committed personal connections, he would become increasingly sad, and that as he aged his manic-depressive symptoms were likely to get worse. He thanked me with true sincerity. "I've been to the best psychiatrists and I take their medicine, but you're the only one who has ever told me the truth." We continued to be friends.

Table 5.1. Dynamics of Fascist Mind in Selected Psychopathology: Affective Psychoses—Mania and Depression

	01-02 **TOTALITY, OVER-CERTAINTY, ABSOLUTISM, AND MAGICAL THINKING**	*03-04* **CENSORSHIP OF INFORMATION, OBEDIENCE, CONFORMITY, AND INTOLERANCE OF DISSENT**
AFFECTIVE PSYCHOSES—MANIA AND DEPRESSION	Exaggerated emotions are treated as statements of certainty. Emotions are no longer tools for self-expression and relationships with others, but themselves become the reality. Runaway emotions can create a total reality. The manic lifestyle is an assertion that one can do it all and handle it all by oneself—so that other people are excluded from genuine intimacy. The counterpart depression is a woeful statement that one is failing to do it all by oneself, or to live up to the high standard of providing for others one has set for oneself, and that no one can help. *Role of anxiety: Considerable anxiety may be present, but generally in a gross agitation that agonizes the patient. To a large extent anxiety is not easily accessible as an effective source of self-renewal and reorganization toward fulfilling one's potential.*	Patient shows conformity to their own exaggerated emotions and the map of reality they create—for example, manic plans for action, or extremes of renunciation of life opportunity as defined in depression.

AFFECTIVE PSYCHOSES— MANIA AND DEPRESSION (*continued*)

05 **SUPERIORITY, EXCESSIVE POWER-SEEKING, AND PREJUDICE**	*06* **VIOLENCE, RETALIATION AGAINST DISSENT, SACRIFICE, AND DESTRUCTION**	*07* **DENIALS OF DOING HARM TO SELF AND OTHERS**
Manic emotions characteristically bespeak assumptions of superiority and power over others—though not at all necessarily prejudices, but if the manic is a high leader and is prejudiced against target groups, watch out! (Some claim both Hitler and Stalin were such.) Depressive emotions are the opposite and involve losses of will and power. Clinically, the two often alternate. In psychodynamic terms, the two are often considered linked in an inner dialectical equivalence.	**Doing Harm to Self and Others** Manic conditions have a high risk of self-mutilation and suicide, and at times also flailing out at surrounding people violently, although most patients are not violent as such. Depression (including depression lurking as a counterpart of mania) by definition points toward *possible* suicide. Psychodynamically, it is understood that in many cases depression is based on the fact that the patient is unable to tolerate a buildup of deep rage at others; occasionally, a depressed person takes some other(s) along in murder-suicide. In both manic and depressive conditions, the patient backs up their exaggerated emotional "policy" with a readiness to harm their own and sometimes others' lives.	Patients characteristically deny they are extreme in their emotions. When asked, and even when confronted, both manics and depressives may lie about their intentions and plans to hurt themselves or others. The imminent violence in the making may be savored by the patient as the secret of a forthcoming climactic triumph over others, and as if over life itself.

Source: Created by the author.

Over time he came to a miserable end and died of cancer, wretchedly cut off from people, after "succeeding" even in estranging himself with his abusiveness from the hospital staff caring for him. Lithium does not replace family and people. It can help give a chance to make contact with people, but often the patient needs help and guidance to do so.

CATATONIC SCHIZOPHRENIA

As noted earlier, the most useful psychodynamic understanding of catatonic reactions is that the patient is murderously raging and fears the anger becoming transformed into a reality of actually murdering another person. An intense devotion to a murderous rage directed at someone is at the heart of the patient's quite well-meaning and very much nonviolent maneuver to paralyze themselves so that they will do no harm.

The solution of catatonic paralysis is obviously a statement of extremism. Before the advent of psychiatric medications, catatonics were known to put on exemplary performances of their capacity to put themselves into total states of inaction for amazingly long periods of time—days, weeks, months, even years. Instead of murdering whomever, they murdered themselves, which in this case means they paralyzed their own capacity to react in life.

The catatonic's rage can be and generally derives from a focus on a disappointing love object (what else is new in human affairs?)—for example, a man who was overwhelmed by his wife's unfaithfulness. However, in the raw, concentrated emotionality of the catatonic's rage against whoever is hurting them, the reaction can balloon into a consuming rage and develop into fantasies of destroying many other people, even a community or a city at large or more. The catatonic patients who feel like they want to kill off lots of people harbor what have been called world-destruction fantasies.

Years ago, before contemporary psychiatric medications were used to suppress such florid symptoms, I saw any number of both children and adults with this condition who had gotten it into their heads that if they so much as wiggled a finger, a whole city would go up in smoke! These were dramatic and heartrending scenes. The agonized state the catatonics worked themselves into was such that they had to stand guard against moving a finger. How hard they worked at keeping their control! The fascinating part was that notwithstanding their overwhelmingly destructive feelings, they really wanted *not* to be destructive.

PARANOID PSYCHOSES—PARANOID SCHIZOPHRENIA AND PARANOIA, INCLUDING PARANOID THINKING IN A POLITICAL CONTEXT

The resemblance between a florid paranoid state and the florid manifestations of political fascism is obvious. At the core of their organization, both share an obsession with persecution by others and a responsive desire to get back at the enemy.

However, what is less clear in the understanding of paranoid psychotic phenomena is that the extremism of the patient may not be simply or entirely craziness. It may also be the result of a basic structural error of going too far to an extreme of what, surprisingly enough, originally may not have been an altogether crazy idea at all. Many clinicians have observed over the years that one should look carefully for a core of truth in the accusative ideation of a paranoid patient—indeed, "even paranoids have enemies."[7]

Kaffman[8] has written significantly about the realism and coherence of the underlying theme of the paranoid person, and how the patient becomes committed to what he calls "monoideism," or a single-minded devotion to and total concern about the complaint. Kaffman, who otherwise also was a significant pioneer of family therapy,[9] called on clinicians to treat the paranoid patient by respecting the probable validity and underlying rational meaning of the patient's seemingly paranoid ravings.

❖ I remember only too well being called in to a private psychiatric hospital by the wife of a friend of mine who had suffered a psychotic breakdown. I found him no less than in a straightjacket, notwithstanding the fact that this was one of the better hospitals in its time, and I took advantage of my professional credentials to order the immediate removal of the straightjacket by the nurses so that I could visit with him and hopefully help him somewhat. My friend was raving wildly about his wife's infidelity and other manifestations of injustice in this world. Since not that long before I myself had kissed (though nothing more) his pretty lady in the basement of their home during a party, I knew for a fact that he was not entirely crazy!

What I did with my friend is hold him (without a straightjacket) in my arms, and tell him that he was obviously crazy with anger at his wife for having been unfaithful to him, and that he would be able to tell her how angry he is and have it out with her without his being crazy. Slowly but surely he quieted down to a state of non-craziness where we could be together for several hours quite rationally. (Needless to say, I turned over all my information to the therapist who went on to work with him. Professionally, this could not have been my case! And I was careful never to kiss this lovely lady again!)

Paranoid Thinking in a Political Context

A discussion of paranoid psychoses should not be restricted to everyday clinical paranoid disturbances of individuals who "get caught" and are identified by the mental health system. There are also paranoid conditions that are played out tragically on a larger scale in public political contexts. For a variety of mind-boggling reasons, many of these crazy paranoid ideas go undiagnosed and are treated as "politics." Even insane ideas of murdering whole groups of people because of their religious/national/racial/ethnic identity are often tolerated and even appreciated and honored as the utterances of a possibly great leader.

Table 5.2. Dynamics of Fascist Mind in Selected Psychopathology: Catatonic Schizophrenia

	01-02 **TOTALITY, OVER-CERTAINTY, ABSOLUTISM, AND MAGICAL THINKING**	*03-04* **CENSORSHIP OF INFORMATION, OBEDIENCE, CONFORMITY, AND INTOLERANCE OF DISSENT**
CATATONIC SCHIZOPHRENIA	Immobility of patient creates a world of super-controlled certainty. Psychodynamically, patient is saying, "I am on the verge of destroying so and so, and I fear letting my rage do that. I must maintain control over my body in order to protect others from my ominous power to destroy them." *Role of anxiety: Anxiety is tightly suppressed in catatonic non-expressiveness. When there is a "leakage" of anxiety, it is a positive sign of a possible move toward reentering life.*	Seemingly no information is accepted from the surrounding world, nor exchanged with others. Patient conforms severely to their own injunction against expression of natural energies and self-expression. Patient is seemingly without any mind-function participation in life—though in many cases it became clear that they were acutely aware of everything around them even during long periods of immobility.

CATATONIC SCHIZOPHRENIA (*continued*)

05 **SUPERIORITY, EXCESSIVE POWER-SEEKING, AND PREJUDICE**	*06* **VIOLENCE, RETALIATION AGAINST DISSENT, SACRIFICE, AND DESTRUCTION**	*07* **DENIALS OF DOING HARM TO SELF AND OTHERS**
A quest for superiority and power is not manifest in the patient's non-responsiveness, but psychodynamic exploration has shown many times that powerful fantasies of enormous power to destroy others, including world-destruction fantasies, are being held in check. Prejudice to others in the common sense of blind hatred of a group is not seen, but there is certainly a core of deep hatred against some other person(s).	**Doing Harm to Self** The wish to be violent to others is aborted in catatonic paralysis. In effect, the patient does harm to their own being—in order to forestall and prevent doing violence to others. **Doing Harm to Others** The patient is scrupulously inhibiting wishes to be violent to others, at enormous cost to their own selves.	The patient's paralysis is in service of denial of ominous rage. The patient denies rage to others, and then further denies the damage they are doing to themselves in paralyzing their own functioning.

Source: Created by the author.

Raphael Lemkin,[10] a Polish-Jewish attorney who is considered to have succeeded almost single-handedly in gaining the adoption of the *United Nations Convention on Genocide*, was aghast at the actual phenomenon of mass murder going unpunished on a political level. When Turkish war criminals who had been involved in the genocide of over one million Armenians were released by the British government, which had held them under arrest on Malta after the end of World War I, Lemkin wrote in outrage: "A nation was killed and the guilty persons set free. Why is a man punished when he kills another man? Why is the killing of a million a lesser crime than the killing of a single individual?"[11]

Similarly, on the level of ideas and public utterances, Israeli psychologist George Tamarin expressed indignation about the failure to identify public expressions of collective hate and incitement to murder as psychopathological so long as the people saying these things appeared otherwise to be functioning effectively in their everyday roles.

> Why is the same statement voiced in the first person singular diagnosed as a sign of delusion, but accepted as unquestioned truth when announced in the first person [of the in-group] plural? Why is an individual considered homicidal or suicidal forcibly committed to a mental hospital, while a high official representative of the nation and/or religious body enjoys full cooperation of psychiatrists and other scientists when he threatens with extermination of whole collectives?[12]

The historical record of real-life fascists who devoted themselves to persecute and destroy other human beings is the strongest condemnation of fascism and the characteristically heinous outcomes it produces. It is the same basic method of absolutist and totalistic thinking through which political fascism—whether Nazi, Communist, Pan-Turkism, Fundamentalist Islam, Agrarian Communist, Serbian Nationalist, also Ultra-Capitalist or any other Extremely-Faithful-to-Whatever—builds sweeping policies that often lead to terminating the lives of other people in the name of whatever single-minded thinking.[13]

George Perec, a French writer, wrote a striking novel in which he depicts savagely by way of fantasy a totalitarian insanity that is played out on an imaginary island at the southern tip of South America. Here "Sport Is King," and from the single-minded devotion to this theme the most obscene killing society is constructed. Athletes who lose are punished, such as by being stripped naked and made to jog past judges who beat them with sticks; if a spectator singles out an athlete with a thumbs-down gesture, the man is stoned to death. The life of an athlete is but "a single, endless furious striving, a pointless debilitating pursuit of . . . triumph."[14] This was Perec's brilliant rendition of the way the Holocaust was constructed. Perec himself was a Holocaust survivor.

Translated into the words of our current exercise, this is Perec's brilliant construction of how a Fascist Mind can transform any idea into its totality and unrelentingness, which can then become a basis for the destruction of life even on a grand scale. As noted, the concept of paranoia simply disappeared from the *DSM*.[15] Personally, as I have said, I believe that the concept of paranoia is very much needed, if only to describe the too successful and even excellent functioning of the worst monster-leaders mankind can produce, who seem to draw much of their sense of purpose, energy, and administrative genius from a coherent plan of persecution of defined victim groups. For me, that is truly nuts, and needs a name in psychiatry.

We also need a name for this kind of fascist mindset in the little people who don't make it to the very top of their nations and societies, but are there at smaller levels persecuting blacks or Jews or Chinese, or males or females or homosexuals, or farmers or shepherds or intellectuals, or members of whatever ethnicity or faith or group. Systematic persecution of others is their sick paranoiac way of life, and I am damned if I will agree to our mental health professions identifying these people for the most part as "normal" or "not psychiatrically disturbed," which is true under the current rules and definitions of psychiatry. The rules have to be changed.

A NEWER "HIT" DISORDER OF OUR TIME: ANOREXIA

A common and quite serious problem in our age is the insane self-starvation that constitutes anorexia nervosa. The patient, most often but not always a female teenager, becomes paralyzed with an overwhelming concern about being fat to a point where even objective evidence of weight loss, and ultimately even a threat to one's life, are insufficient to impact on the patient, who continues to associate virtually any ingestion of food with an experience of being engorged and becoming obese. Even today, with drastically improved methods of family therapy and confrontational interventions in hospital-based programs, anorexia leads to actual death in a statistically "small" but frighteningly real percentage of cases.[16]

There is, moreover, a large corps of young people whose anorexia is stable, so that from a medical point of view there is no danger to life, but from a larger psychomedical point of view the patient is "starving her/his life." On top of the skinniness, which perhaps can be accepted as a legitimate alternative way of maintaining one's body, there are obsessive fears of putting on weight, so that much of daily experience is pulled or driven by obsessive worry, which in its own right is a very unpleasant way to live. There is a drawn, pinched physical look (for females, often also a disturbance or cessation of the menstrual cycle) and, worse, a haggard quality to everyday experience of life. There is characteristically a deep sadness and a fulminating anger numbing one's joy of being, and to top it off there is a notable starvation of one's ability to be loved and to love. In short, anorexia is a rotten and dismal way of life even when it isn't dangerous to the point of being life threatening.

Moreover, beyond the crazy large number of young people whose lives and potentials for developing are seriously compromised and circumscribed by anorexia, there are a good number of "old anorexics" out there, meaning people over forty from whom the anorexia took its toll in their "failure to thrive" in love and life, and who continue into middle age and old age with what I shall call an "anorexic personality disorder" of chronic restriction of joy, pleasure, emotional nourishment,

Table 5.3. Dynamics of Fascist Mind in Selected Psychopathology: Paranoid Psychoses–Paranoid Schizophrenia and Paranoia

	01-02 **TOTALITY, OVER-CERTAINTY, ABSOLUTISM, AND MAGICAL THINKING**	*03-04* **CENSORSHIP OF INFORMATION, OBEDIENCE, CONFORMITY, AND INTOLERANCE OF DISSENT**
PARANOID PSYCHOSES— PARANOID SCHIZOPHRENIA AND PARANOIA, INCLUDING PARANOID THINKING IN A POLITICAL CONTEXT	A paranoid construction of reality creates a certainty of an enemy to whom magical powers are characteristically attributed. Paranoid suspicions of individuals are one level of disturbance. Paranoiac conceptions of large-scale conspiracies, such as projections on to an ethnic group or political group that they are out to destroy the world, are a more complex level of disturbance which can be packaged by better functioning people into real-life political platforms, and some of them are tragically "successful." Nonetheless, one needs to be careful to look for and respect the parts of paranoid constructions that are in fact accurate. This is true on the individual level, and is also true on a collective level. There are nations and groups that are committed to destruction of others! *Role of anxiety: A paranoidal construction of reality eliminates the need for and the possibility of anxiety, personal questioning or searching. The paranoid patient who is noticeably anxious, especially if the anxiety overrides the suspicious ideation, is very likely more treatable in psychotherapy.*	The paranoid conforms to his/her own distorted map of reality. Any evidence contrary to the paranoid construction is dismissed so that the image of the enemy is preserved at all costs. In addition, when the disorder takes on forms of paranoia and the patient joins (or leads!) an ideological or political movement, a systematic ideological definition of the enemy is created to which the patient demands of everyone to conform slavishly.

PARANOID PSYCHOSES— PARANOID SCHIZOPHRENIA AND PARANOIA (*continued*)

05 **SUPERIORITY, EXCESSIVE POWER-SEEKING, AND PREJUDICE**	06 **VIOLENCE, RETALIATION AGAINST DISSENT, SACRIFICE, AND DESTRUCTION**	07 **DENIALS OF DOING HARM TO SELF AND OTHERS**
Feelings of superiority are intrinsic to this condition, especially of the paranoiac states, and actual seeking of great power over others is common. The paranoid construction seethes with hostile prejudice towards designated targets. In paranoia, the prejudices against designated target groups are organized even more systematically and vitriolically.	**Doing Harm to Self** The paranoid's delusional hatred is a natural springboard for sulking revenge and retaliation. Patterns of homicide-suicide, combining murder of other(s) with suicide or setting oneself up to be killed, are also not uncommon. **Doing Harm to Others** Paranoids are at times dangerously violent and murderous, including episodic cases of mass killing, but there are also many paranoids who are more pathetic than dangerous. Paranoiacs committed to ideologies of mass murder of their enemies have been responsible for tens of millions of genocidal deaths (e.g., the Holocaust, Soviet mass killings of various ethnicities, and the genocide of Cambodians in "killing fields").* These are the ultimately dangerous madmen in our human civilization.	Paranoids deny the damages they are doing in the long term to themselves, and paranoids are not in touch with the destruction they seek to wreak on others. Characteristically they explain their positions as self-defense. Paranoiac political leaders traditionally justify even large-scale mass genocidal murders as serving the greater good of their people and society.

* *The personal paranoia of some of the central leaders of these regimes (e.g., Hitler and Stalin) is well established. In many cases other people—including the "ordinary people"—respond out of obedience to the leader, government, and the military, and the population as a whole conforms to the paranoiac blueprint to become willing killers, accomplices, and bystanders. Genocide in human history underscores the vicious contagion and availability to fascist thinking of perhaps even a majority of people at this state of human evolution. Although I referred earlier to some who suggest that Hitler and Stalin were manic-depressives, I personally subscribe more to the description of them as paranoids, and specifically as paranoiac. But if our basic conception of mental illness is to go beyond specific symptom patterns to identifying all extremist thinking and life-destroying actions as disturbed, it doesn't matter much which diagnostic category. Their attempts to destroy life are extreme, ergo they are bona fide mad.*

Source: Created by the author.

and affection in their lives. Altogether, there is an army of miserable anorexics who are certainly "not feasting," and in many cases are "barely enjoying a square meal" of happiness in their life journeys.

Another no less frightening way of thinking about this "popular" and what we referred to even as a "hit" disorder of our times (because it is so common) is that there is an army of robotized, joyless, and worried anorexic people in our midst. From the point of view of this book, this is an army of people who have given up their democratic rights to a pleasureful life in favor of being slavish, obedient conformists to crazy fascist rules about eating, which they allow their own minds to impose on them. They become slaves of their own Fascist Minds. The clinical description of anorexia is widely known, of course, but the point in our work is that anorexia is an excellent example of the way in which an otherwise "sane" mind—generally there is no other obvious thought disturbance or disconnection from orientation to reality seen in anorexia—can be taken over by the extremism of an idea, and the believer may even be willing to lay down their life for it!

Family therapy approaches have brought some new hope to the treatment of anorexia after it became clear that the results of individual therapy were notoriously poor. See especially the works of Salvador Munichin[17] and Mara Salvini Palazzoli.[18] Some hospitals have reported developing "tough love" confrontational feedback techniques for bringing home to serious anorectics the severity of their condition and "demanding" proof of weight gains. In both treatment approaches, one in effect is trying to break up a super-rigid plan of depriving oneself of food.

❖ It gives me pleasure to report that I had some success with a young male adult suffering from anorexia/bulimia by explaining to him this mechanism of going to the extreme with a rigid idea. He also could understand the idea of going too far with an idea from other evidence in his life history of taking a solution to a problem to the extreme. An important example for him was that already in his childhood, he had translated his criticism and anger at his father into an extreme "political" position of having nothing to do with his father. Now, as a young adult, he realized bitterly that he was without sufficient "maleness" because of his lack of identification with his father, and as a consequence was suffering a very hard time carrying on his life as a male adult.

Explaining to him in therapy how he imposed on his mind a demand for absolute and total consistency with an idea—in this case the idea that eating makes you fat, just as once he had committed his anger at his father to totally excluding him from his life—proved to be the effective step that freed him to stop the chain of anorexia/bulimia. His worst enemies were not food or father, but totalistic, all-or-none thinking backed up by violence against his body and self.

Anorexia can also be thought of as a member of a larger sad family of eating disturbances, which also include the opposite side of eating too much. Binge eating, or bulimia, also announces a person who feels so deeply unloved and who is desperately trying to handle life, in this case by stuffing themselves to a deprivation-assuaging fullness. There is also a sizable number who are then terrified of getting "caught" at whatever level of being too fat or too full, and they develop elaborate rituals of inducing vomiting to get rid of their overstuffing and to give back what they cannot own. There are also some patients who use self-induced vomiting without preceding it with an eating binge because they are afraid they will vomit nervously whatever is in their stomach when they are in a situation that is stressful to them.

❖ A capable young woman engineering student had fended off her mother's vitriolic attacks on her as a child by being a super-sweet girl who was always thoughtful, especially of her mother. Now as she faced her own adult life, she was terrified of any stress or confrontational situation, such as social occasions, family social life such as dinner with her boyfriend's family, oral examinations at the university, or job interviews. "I know it is wrong, but I tell myself that if I go and vomit beforehand, I'll be less nervous that it will happen to me against my will. I'm so afraid they will all see how terrified I am."

❖ Her rule evidently was: Beat yourself down before the other (originally mother) beats you down. She obviously had hoped that following her rule would spare her the worst pain, but she discovered that being so self-abusing was also exacting too much of a toll on her. In several cases of bulimia, I also have been able to help patients by describing their rituals as rules to which they had become enslaved, and to enlist their natural protests against being slaves to a self-dictatorial regime.

In all fairness, since I do not at all specialize and see a large number of cases of eating disorders in my practice, the few examples I am drawing on of patients successfully overcoming eating disorders after seeing their symptoms as a result of their being subjugated by an inner dictator are legitimate illustrations of the *possible* usefulness of the fascist paradigm, but are not in any way a scientific demonstration of a proven treatment approach. I have also been unsuccessful in treating several cases of anorexia, where the patients would not allow me to develop with them the concept of their fascist thinking. The metaphor was seemingly meaningless to them and was simply brushed away. Hopefully, there are other therapists who will be able to develop the use of this concept in the future, and perhaps more skillfully than I have. Nonetheless, anorexia-bulimia is such a vicious condition, with so many poor outcomes, that it is legitimate to report a method that produces even a few successful cases.

The larger point is not that I have found another cure for this or another mental problem, but rather that I think that this way of understanding many psychiatric disturbances as fascist thinking opens an intriguing perspective into how people try to "beat" their fears of life by laying down crazy, ritualistic rules for their behavior, and invites other possible ways of treating some of these disorders. Fortunately, somewhere deep inside, along with the enormous appeal of fascism for so many people, *a lot of people also hate the idea of being slaves to a fascist regime.*

Table 5.4. Dynamics of Fascist Mind in Selected Psychopathology: Anorexia

	01-02 **TOTALITY, OVER-CERTAINTY, ABSOLUTISM, AND MAGICAL THINKING**	*03-04* **CENSORSHIP OF INFORMATION, OBEDIENCE, CONFORMITY, AND INTOLERANCE OF DISSENT**
ANOREXIA	Patient is adamantly certain over the correctness of their adopted food regimen. The slightest infractions are treated as magically dangerous. Patient is totally committed to a rigid, perfectionist regimen to an extent that it becomes an ideology. *Role of anxiety: Patient is generally not in contact with experiences of anxiety. On occasions when patient does admit anxiety and one hopes that a more natural flow of normal human concerns is in the offing, almost invariably patient rushes back to obsessive involvement with the anorexic litany, and the window of hope closes once again.*	Patient conforms to a powerful system of rituals. No contradictory information is taken in, and no interference is allowed. The subject is closed off to question, inquiry, criticism, or rational feedback. Patients characteristically lie, cheat, and violate any seeming pledges they may have given. The routine of conforming to one's own routine becomes the end-all.

ANOREXIA (*continued*)

05 **SUPERIORITY, EXCESSIVE POWER-SEEKING, AND PREJUDICE**	*06* **VIOLENCE, RETALIATION AGAINST DISSENT, SACRIFICE, AND DESTRUCTION**	*07* **DENIALS OF DOING HARM TO SELF AND OTHERS**
In patient's own mind, there is an aura of self-defined superiority for having chosen the superior right way, but the prevailing mood is characteristically depressed and bitter rather than triumphant. Actual superiority over others in behavior as such is not seen, but patient characteristically creates a lock-hold power over the family, as well as over health professionals—although it is not clear that the pursuit of power in its own right is a motivating intention rather than a by-product of the vicious system of thinking. Prejudice to others is not emphasized, but there is little to no feeling for others, and there is perhaps disdain, including for those who may want to care for the patient.	**Doing Harm to Self** Patient adheres to ritual even at cost of terrible violence to their own body, and in any number of cases even in the face of possible death. Violation of food rituals is met with severe self-punishment in spirit and action. Although no conscious goal of self-sacrifice and manifest intention of death may be in evidence, violent abuses to one's health and many times even outright death are accepted without seeming regret, shock, or caring for self to fight off the dread outcome. **Doing Harm to Others** The harm is clearly to one's self, yet it also has a byproduct of exasperating and maddening others who want to care for the patient. Patient refuses to be helped by others, and makes few attempts to get better in response to others' efforts on their behalf. In worst-case outcomes there is a form of suicidal refusal to be helped, which leaves its mark on those who tried.	Patient characteristically denies any danger to health and to life. Patient also is characteristically unmoved by messages of hurting loved ones or others trying to help them.

Source: Created by the author.

SOME MISCELLANEOUS UNRECOGNIZED BEDEVILING SYNDROMES

Our point of departure is to understand the pattern of the fascist paradigm as a generic source or template of a whole variety of mental disorders, and to understand that most mental disorders derive from an incorrect use of one's mind and emotions much more than they are illnesses, or specific syndromes of symptoms. Once one understands the paradigm, it becomes more possible to spot and understand other, even unfamiliar, groupings of symptom pictures that have not yet been described in our established *DSM* literature. Instead of looking only at how people are suffering, one needs to look at how they are living their lives.

A beautiful statement about Samoan culture is that there are three perspectives:

> The perspective of the person at the top of the mountain, the perspective of the person at the top of the tree, and the perspective of the person in the canoe who is close to the school of fish. In any big problem the three perspectives are equally necessary.[19]

In this section, I will describe several syndromes not generally recognized or named in psychiatry, each fascinating in its own right, but in my opinion their larger significance once again lies in our seeing them as examples of ways of getting "stuck" on a single-minded program for life that denies uncertainty and refuses to admit consideration of alternatives.

THE "ORPHAN SYNDROME," OR SELF-MADE PERSON

As noted, this is a personality problem that will not be found in the *DSM*. In my experience it is not such an uncommon pattern of organization of one's self. It is a particularly interesting way of being in the world because it is, at one and the same time, an admirable and winning way of achieving for oneself great success, but also a way of falling into serious difficulties in one's intimate relationships.

I call this condition the "Orphan Syndrome." It applies to a kind of self-made person, often literally an orphan and other times a kind of psychological equivalent of an orphan in that for one reason or another the child did not have parents to rely on as genuine caretakers and at an early age had to strike out to parent themselves. The children I am referring to are ones who decide resolutely that they are going to succeed and achieve a good deal in this world. Given that they are gifted with sufficient talents, they push themselves into a pattern of work and seriousness about life—the same seriousness about winning is seen in the ways they play, assuming they even devote time to play in their drive to success, and over the years they achieve a good deal. As adults who are succeeding meritoriously, they enjoy many special satisfactions of the "self-made person." They often also get pleasure or honor from recounting the history of their humble beginnings and how with single-minded devotion they made it to their particular top. And yet, all their achievements and successes don't make up for the inner vacuum of the absence of a nurturing and containing parent. When the time comes that their inner emptiness can't hold them sufficiently to deal with life—these times often occur around the normal and natural crises that are expected in marriage and with children—their history of excellence may fade away into forms of a dread experience of "I'm no longer the success I was," which manifests itself in any of a variety of symptoms.

The problem for these self-made people begins with the fact that they are in some basic way funless. They can't laugh at themselves, and certainly they will not tolerate being laughed at. Their personal concepts of right and wrong are very clear cut. They entertain no doubts about their views. Insofar as they become involved in a collective philosophy or political ideology, they are likely to go all the way in their identification with their chosen idea system. Everything they undertake, they do with total, relentless seriousness and devotion. They cannot fail. By definition, they must win at everything they do, little realizing that this is their true failing.

The problems of the self-made "orphans" are then compounded by the fact that they impact badly, even disastrously, on those who are closest to them. For their intimates—wives or husbands and children—they set such an absolute standard that they leave little to no room for the other person to choose their own position. They are strict and adamant in their "scoring" of the other's behavior, and judicially grim in their dispensations of rewards and punishments. Understandably, a conflict pattern is likely to ensue with someone in their family, and then they are in real difficulty because they do not know how to cope with conflict as a process. They only understand that they must win out over all obstacles, and so they approach conflict with the same single-mindedness and lack of flexibility for understanding the other person and negotiating with them. Theirs is the one and only right way.

In my experience, the families of many "orphans" will drop out of therapy prematurely after seeing that even in a therapy context the orphan-personality once again is unable to draw on or mobilize any flexibility. Unless the relatives of the "orphan" want to go all out and break up the family there is little left for them to do, and they reorganize themselves in a resigned state of chronic disenchantment. Some of the spouses and children then turn away to some forms of alternative experiences that are kept secret from the "orphan," so that what can develop over the long term is a facade of family unity that sits above a cauldron of concealed disrespect and disavowal of intimacy. The stubbornness of the "orphan's" ideas and convictions, their dry, humorless devotion to their own version of total truth, and their intolerance and disdain for anybody who falls short of the standard they set—all combine to do in the "orphan." In my experience, "orphans" basically do not come in for therapy for themselves, but they do appear because they are nonplussed and genuinely upset at the wrong behavior of their family member(s) and/or by being rejected by them. They appear totally dismayed and to not comprehend why they have been rejected when a spouse wants to or actually walks out on them, or when a child betrays their most treasured values.

Table 5.5. Dynamics of Fascist Mind in Selected Psychopathology: The "Orphan Syndrome"

	01-02 **TOTALITY, OVER-CERTAINTY, ABSOLUTISM- AND MAGICAL THINKING**	*03-04* **CENSORSHIP OF INFORMATION, OBEDIENCE, CONFORMITY- AND INTOLERANCE OF DISSENT**
THE "ORPHAN SYNDROME"	There is a single correct way to live, which is to over-perform and achieve consistent success. *Role of anxiety: The "orphan" rarely experiences notable anxiety about his correct way of life, but does become upset and confused when their obviously correct way doesn't work, and especially when their family and intimates refuse to go along with their way of life.*	"Orphans" are characteristically extremely rigid in their adherence to their correct and superior ways of doing things, to which they demand of themselves unforgiving obedience and conformity. Their problems with family members and intimates are that they also demand of them to follow their absolute rules obediently.

THE "ORPHAN SYNDROME" (*continued*)

05 **SUPERIORITY, EXCESSIVE POWER-SEEKING, AND PREJUDICE**	*06* **VIOLENCE, RETALIATION AGAINST DISSENT, SACRIFICE, AND DESTRUCTION**	*07* **DENIALS OF DOING HARM TO SELF AND OTHERS**
The implicit assumption of a superior way of doing things and superiority through success is close to the surface.	**Doing Harm to Self** Violence to self is not common and would be a serious deviation from the success-oriented style of the "orphan." However, if the "orphan" believes all they have built up in life is lost, they can be at risk of suicide like other success-driven people when they lose "everything." **Doing Harm to Others** Violence to others as such is *not* intended and generally is objectionable to the successful "orphan." However, the "orphan's" policies toward dissenting family intimates can be emotionally tyrannical, and actual violence can be triggered in their family members who become exasperated and seek some way to protest the "orphan's" control of them—for example, a wife who becomes an alcoholic and acts out violently while her doing-it-right orphan husband is dismayed.	The "orphan" is unable to see that the polarity of absolute good-rightness versus bad-wrongness that they impose can impact on their families to drive them to the opposite or even failing and immoral behaviors.

Source: Created by the author.

A NEW SYNDROME OF GROWN KIDS WHO LIVE AT HOME FOREVER AND OFTEN RULE THEIR PARENTS ABSOLUTELY

The Italians call it *bamboccioni*, meaning "big babies," the Germans call it *hotel mama*, and the Japanese call it *parasite shinguru*, meaning "single parasite." The entry in *Wikipedia* says unambiguously that the syndrome "is a single person who lives with their parents beyond their late twenties in order to enjoy a carefree and comfortable life."

This is a new, spreading problem of young people who can't leave home to run their own lives. In my own clinical practice and personal life, I was surprised by the slow but clearly mounting number of cases I was encountering or hearing about of young people who either never made the move to leave home, or more often did leave but came back to be taken care of by their parents and settle in the safety of their family home. The reports now are of huge numbers of such situations in a large number of countries.

There is a further ugly side to many of these tragic abortions of personal development in that there are many cases where the adult child becomes the ruler—at times even a tyrannical ruler—of their parents, mocking and ordering them about, regularly demanding sums of money or other resources like a computer or a car, and sometimes backing these up with actual violence to their parents.

Some thirty years ago, I was on the sailboat of a very dear psychiatrist-psychoanalyst friend along with another psychiatrist-psychoanalyst friend that he invited. When we were out at sea the latter asked me, "What do you think of a situation where a son in his late twenties comes back home to live with his parents?" and proceeded to describe how said son "ruled his parents with an iron hand including extracting lots of money from them." We talked quite a lot, and I recommended very strongly that the family turn to family therapy, certainly with a goal of putting an end to the enslavement and humiliation of the parents, as well as obviously toward enabling the son—who was in no way objectively handicapped physically or otherwise—to get the heck out into the world and live his own life. Intuitively, I knew that my sailing companion was talking about his own family, but that he was too embarrassed to say so.

The syndrome of mature children staying at home or returning home to live with their parents has spread insidiously in the world. One survey by Eurofound of the European Union[20] in 2014 showed adult children between the ages of eighteen and twenty-nine who were currently living in their parents' household constituted a whopping total of 79 percent in Italy, 76 percent in Hungary, 64 percent in Poland, and so on across Europe down to a low of 23 percent—"only" a quarter—in Germany. The Japanese were reporting a growing number of cases a good number of years ago to the point where a *New York Times* article in 2006 wrote, "As the problem has become more widespread in Japan an industry has sprung up around it. There are support groups for parents, psychologists who specialize in it, including one who counsels shut-ins via the internet and several halfway programs . . . offering dorms and job training." The same article features an illustration of a nineteen-year-old who shut the door to his bedroom and "for the next four years did not come out. He didn't go to school, he didn't have a job. He didn't have friends. Month after month, he spent twenty-three hours a day in a room no bigger than a king size mattress."[21]

When you read the interpretations of these statistics, some emphasize the correlation between economic indicators in a given country and the rate of regressed adult children, but the no less real underlying issue of young adults living in their parents' home is that this is another new style of serious psychological disturbance of the ability to live life productively for oneself.

It is in fact an earthquake. In my own clinical practice in Israel, over the years I have become aware directly and indirectly of many more such cases, and many of them don't stop living at home at age twenty-nine (the upper age of the European Union statistic given earlier). There are adults well into their fifties who are moving toward their oncoming old age in the bosoms of their remaining parent or parents, who have been supported all their adult lives by these parents, and are going to live through to their own end of life from the inheritances of the parents' funds and real estate.[22]

As noted earlier, there is a further ugliness to many situations when an adult child openly becomes a tyrannical ruler of the parents, regularly extracting from them sums of money, insulting and mocking the parents openly, and sometimes also threatening and actually becoming violent to the parents. These are especially lewd instances of parents who are being pulled around by the nose by the children they brought into the world. Like any situation of submission to humiliation, domination, or enslavement by a person, the problematique belongs to both parties—the enslaver and the enslaved. The latter should be doing everything to fight back and fight off their enslaver.

Israeli psychologist Haim Omer says that there are two main types of such enslaving relations. "In one, the child is miserable, depressive, incapable and the parent says to himself, 'Well, what can I do? My child is unfortunate and can't help himself, so I will do it in his place.' A second type is vociferous and accusatory. The child says to his parents, 'You did this to me and you will pay for it. I am in this situation because of you.' Those parents live in constant fear. Some of the parents who come to us are the victims of incessant threats: 'You'll never see me again,' 'I will kill myself.'"[23]

Personally, I have had some success in treating such situations, but even more failures, and there is a still larger number of situations in families that I hear about from relatives, such as adult siblings, where no therapy is ever initiated. The syndrome is a new psychiatric form of "emotional obesity."[24]

Table 5.6. Dynamics of Fascist Mind in Selected Psychopathology: Grown Kids Who Live at Home Forever

	01-02 **TOTALITY, OVERCERTAINTY, ABSOLUTISM, AND MAGICAL THINKING**	*03-04* **CENSORSHIP OF INFORMATION, OBEDIENCE, CONFORMITY, AND INTOLERANCE OF DISSENT**
A NEW SYNDROME OF GROWN KIDS WHO LIVE AT HOME FOREVER	This writer's clinical experience is that little anxiety is manifested, and correspondingly I have not seen or heard such stay-at-homes asking for therapy. These kids who come home to stay do not develop or flow into a more normal push to greater independence and self-definition. Theirs is a certain and absolute way of life. *Role of anxiety: Living at home forever in itself is a full dose of tranquilizer. Although the child may show anxiety and indignation over demands that are not being made, a healthier anxiety for oneself and a wish to break out to make a life for oneself are rarely seen.*	Patient is set with a way of life that varies in its degree or restriction from locked-in and bed/room-ridden to a more mobile and even semi-social life with the family home as the guaranteed anchor. Whatever the plan of the restricted life, it is conformed to over and over again.

GROWN KIDS WHO LIVE AT HOME FOREVER (*continued*)

05 **SUPERIORITY, EXCESSIVE POWER-SEEKING, AND PREJUDICE**	*06* **VIOLENCE, RETALIATION AGAINST DISSENT, SACRIFICE, AND DESTRUCTION**	*07* **DENIALS OF DOING HARM TO SELF AND OTHERS**
The very imposition of a policy/way of life of staying home forever is an assumption of power over one's family. A not small number of these stay-at-homes also become tyrannical and at times violent in their demands for money, use of the car, or whatever. Claims of superiority over other people outside the family are unlikely.	**Doing Harm to Self and Others** The harm is in the way of life—so denying of pride in oneself and fulfillment of talent. This writer has not seen or heard of suicide of such stay-at-homes. As noted, some of these stay-at-homes become tyrannical to their family—sometimes viciously and violently—around their explicit and implicit demands to do as they want and receive all that they need and desire.	The writer has never seen such a patient acknowledge and express concern about what they are doing to their family.

Source: Created by the author.

STRANGE, CRAZY CRIMINAL BEHAVIORS INCLUDING "FOR THE THRILL OF IT ALL" (AS OPPOSED TO CRIME FOR CRIME'S PROFIT-MAKING SAKE): THE CASE OF AN EXTORTIONIST WHO THREATENED TO POISON A DAIRY

Here we bring an intriguing and almost amusing case that took place in Israel where a man threatened and actually did do a "sample" act of poisoning dairy products in a grocery chain.

What is noteworthy in this case, which we are taking as an example of a more widespread phenomenon, is that the extortionist was not a criminal in his life history in any way, nor to my knowledge did he have any history of bona fide psychiatric disturbance. He himself reported that what happened to him "shocked" him, for even after he had decided to pull back from his dastardly scheme, it was as if he couldn't bring himself to do so, and the reason for this was that once he had embarked on a path there was no way for him not to go the full course and take it to its climax.

The story unfolds like a real spy thriller. "Beware," he warned one of the country's major dairies in computer print-out lettering, "If you do not pay such and such ransom, I will plant poison in your dairy products."

A harrowing period of negotiations between the extortionist and the dairy followed, while simultaneously the police department worked hard to discover and trap the culprit. As a warning that he was serious about his threat, the extortionist ran a trial balloon of actually placing poison in a few dairy products at one supermarket. It was now clear to the authorities that the man was really dangerous to the public. Working with the police, the owner of the dairy company conveyed to the extortionist that they would pay the ransom. The extortionist now sent the owner instructions on how to make the payoff. The owner was to fly a helicopter along a specified air route, and somewhere along the way he would receive a signal to drop the bag of ransom monies from the air. Happily, the Police of the People of the Talmud nonetheless succeeded in outwitting the culprit, and he was caught with his hands in the cottage cheese and whisked off to face criminal proceedings. Said the culprit:

> When I prepared the germs that I put in the dairy products, I was myself shocked at the thought that a child might eat the product and be hurt. I decided to pull out, but what happened is that I found myself pushed by my tendency to finish things to the end. I was operating under the pressure of an uncontrollable urge. The need to go all the way and finish things has been with me all my life.[25]

So the old good detective advice, "Cherchez la femme," now needs to be modified to include an instruction to follow the trail of evidence to anyone who might have gotten into, what is from our point of view, a psychiatrically sick head of taking an idea to its ultimate totality and completeness.

CASES OF "PERFECT" AND "NORMAL" KIDS WHO MURDER SOMEONE—SOMETIMES THEIR PARENTS—UNEXPECTEDLY

Something similar seems to take place periodically in totally unexpected murders at the hands of otherwise "normal," "good," and even "perfect" teenage kids who, totally unexpectedly from the point of view of the family and school and the people who live with them and know them best, erupt in a tragic act of murder (or even a mass murder spree). This is one of several forms of violence in our crazy, violent world that we look at from our point of view that destroying life—one's own or others—is the *sine qua non* of mental disturbance. It may not be difficult to understand a case of a child who has been violently abused taking lethal vengeance on a parent, but it is a deeply perplexing stretch to come up with an understanding of the exemplary "good kid" electing to murder anyone (e.g., cases of murder for the thrill of it), let alone their parent(s). A Cain who is rivalrous with his brother is rotten but still "understandable," but were Cain to murder Adam and Eve who gave him life, who as far as we know had not abused him, we would have reason to be more perplexed.

Reconstructions of such tragic crimes, which occur once in a while in just about every community I know, characteristically reveal a history of suppression of normal aggression and a pattern of shallow obligatory goodness as dominant motifs in the pattern of the youngster's interpersonal relationships, rather than a natural and generous emotionalism. But what also comes through in the youngster's reconstruction of the horrible tragic act is that once they got an idea in their head they weren't able to drop it. For whatever reasons, be it a blinding experience of sexual infatuation that cannot be denied, or a moping plan of revenge against frustrating parents or siblings, the youngster gets it in their head that the way to clear the mounting tension is to go all the way. Then, although they have been an acceptably moral human being up until now, and certainly socialized with traditional values against murder, who has in fact never acted viciously before and really knows better, they have no machinery for banishing the terrible thoughts from their head. A lifelong pattern of training in certainty and compliance to one's own mind constructions, along with disavowal of aggression, takes its toll in a crime from which there is no return.

An example is a case in the United States of a quiet, bespectacled fourteen-year-old "Bible-carrying youth" from a genuinely good family, who one day was transformed into a murderer when he was carried away by his sexual arousal[26] while babysitting a young girl. These cases are shocking and tragic beyond words. The tragedy lies first in the harm done to another person, of course, but it is also in the fact that a good person who did not mean to do such harm cannot stop himself from going way too far.

There are perhaps added touches of evil and the tragedy in cases where "good kids" turn on their own families and murder their own parents and siblings. I have tracked newspaper reports of several of these cases over the years, and in some instances in communities where I have lived, I have been able to speak to the mental health clinicians who were charged with examining the youths after their gruesome

Table 5.7. Dynamics of Fascist Mind in Selected Psychopathology: Strange, Crazy Criminal Behaviors

	01-02 **TOTALITY, OVER-CERTAINTY, ABSOLUTISM, AND MAGICAL THINKING**	*03-04* **CENSORSHIP OF INFORMATION, OBEDIENCE, CONFORMITY, AND INTOLERANCE OF DISSENT**
• ***The Case of the Extortionist Who Threatened to Poison a Dairy's Milk Products*** • ***Cases of "Perfect" and "Normal" Kids who Murder Someone Unexpectedly***	A masterful crime rises up as a compelling emotional urge or perfect crime plan, or a compelling total solution develops to wipe out one's family or others and is accepted as making complete sense and worthwhile to be acted on. *Role of anxiety: As usual in the various psychopathologies, the more anxiety the better in that it is a statement of struggle and ambivalence that can help the person to stop their dastardly plan. For those who succumb, the problem generally is that the criminal plan becomes an all-consuming and all-relieving substitute for feeling anxious about oneself and what one really needs and even wants to be.*	The unexpected criminal may be trapped into "going all the way" with an idea that has gotten into his head which he can't drop. In a sense, the act may be consummated more out of conformity to the compelling thought than because of the original emotional urge or idea, including any expected tangible payoff.

STRANGE, CRAZY CRIMINAL BEHAVIORS AND PERFECT KIDS (*continued*)

05 **SUPERIORITY, EXCESSIVE POWER-SEEKING, AND PREJUDICE**	*06* **VIOLENCE, RETALIATION AGAINST DISSENT, SACRIFICE, AND DESTRUCTION**	*07* **DENIALS OF DOING HARM TO SELF AND OTHERS**
Superiority is inherent in the wish and readiness to impose one's will on others, certainly when it is also at the dire cost of others' lives.	**Doing Harm to Self** There is great harm to self as a result of exposing oneself to the punishment of society. **Doing Harm to Others** Doing harm to others is at the center of the criminal plan—to extort and hurt others.	A dissociated denial or splitting of awareness of doing harm to others makes the crime possible to begin with. When apprehended, the unlikely criminal is characteristically embarrassed, and claims not to have been aware of the ugliness and possibly devastating harm they were caught up in doing to others.

Source: Created by the author.

eruption. In all these cases, the reports were the same: youngsters who had no record whatsoever of violence or even known ill-temper, but who were unable to shake off the thought-impulse to destroy their family once it had occurred to them. In some cases they had been brooding with an inchoate image-plan of their dastardly act for some time. Their loyalty to their thinking was absolute and overrode any consideration of a moral obligation not to kill.

We assume millions of children at one time or another feel like killing their parents or siblings, and that a lesser but still large number even imagine-think about how they might do it, yet almost all of them know perfectly well they never would do anything of the sort. What happens with these exceptional cases of the dread killers is that they are beholden to their own minds controlling them, and are compelled to do what they have thought about doing. Can we say that the kids—like too many people—have become captives of their own Fascist Minds?

THE UNSAVORY SUICIDE-KILLERS OF OUR ERA, INCLUDING SOME CASES OF NICE AND QUIET "GOOD GUYS"—OR WOMEN—WHO BECOME SUICIDE-KILLER TERRORISTS

From the point of view of established Western Judeo-Christian values, the combination of mass killing of others followed by suicide of oneself constitutes an overwhelming violation of two basic values of our way of life and civilization. In the popular mind too, the behavior of the suicide bomber violates every code of lawful, rational, sane, and acceptable behavior and is intrinsically immoral and abnormal.

Suicide bombing is today a growing and spreading phenomenon in the world in which we live, and there are many who believe that a war of civilizations is in the making.[27] Suicide bombers are the proponents of a cult-religion that celebrates killing and martyrdom. Thus, in his time Osama bin Laden issued a *fatwa* in which he said,

> The ruling to kill the Americans and their allies—civilians and military—is an individual duty for every Muslim who can do it in any country in which it is possible to do it. . . . We—with God's help—call on every Muslim who believes in God and wishes to be rewarded to comply with God's order to kill the Americans.[28]

Are suicide bombings acts of mental disturbance? Not surprisingly, contemporary psychiatry has worked itself into a hole about the specific subject of suicide bombers, as well as terrorism in general, and also many other forms of violence. As we have seen earlier, even paranoia, which one would think would be picked up unambivalently by psychiatric thinkers as fitting the old-fashioned rules for defining craziness has been "excommunicated" from the *DSM*. At least three things have somehow happened to block contemporary psychiatry from being able to assert the obvious existential truth that people who go around killing others and themselves are not in good mental shape.

The first complication is that a person committing a terrorist act, just as the person committing violence in a family, is put on the mental examination table as if for an examination of all *other* aspects of their personality, and if in all other respects there are no signs of traditional mental disturbance, the absurd conclusion is reached that the behavior of destroying others was not done by an evidently disturbed person! The fact that a murder of normality is staring us right in the face in the very acts of totally hurting other people and oneself hasn't been allowed to enter into this silly system, which puts a stethoscope to the person to see if they are still breathing normally while ignoring the fact that they have been spilling blood all over the place.

The second problem that has developed in Western psychiatry and civilization is that if crazy thinking or behavior is defined as a *political* statement, then all considerations of the irrationality and madness of the thinking or behavior are deferred and even wiped out so as not to intrude on people's heavenly political rights to fight for their conceptions of what is right and just. Suicide bombing in many cases *is* very much a political statement, and much as I abhor suicide killings, I acknowledge that often enough they flow from a legitimate and understandable cry of personal and/or collective revenge and/or from legitimate political aspirations (whether or not I agree with them). Yet I believe that none of these motivations in themselves justify the suicide killings, certainly not of innocent civilians, and personally I think not even of most military foes.

The third thing that has gone wrong somewhere down the line is a derivative mistaken notion that the cardinal rule of free speech, which is at the core of the wondrous democratic way of life that we treasure, means that people can say *anything* they believe in without being responsible for the likely outcomes of their words leading to violence and death. Thus, the history of Islamic suicide bombers, including the infamous hijacker suicide murderers of 9/11, finds many of them praying at mosques in democratic countries like the UK and Germany, where imams regularly preached violent destruction of the infidel West.[29]

The Democratic Mind, intuitively and naturally, has to be opposed to the horrors of gruesome mass murder in the interests of *all* the victims, including the perpetrator who is committing suicide. A Christian-Arab, Habib Malik, speaking as president of the American-based Council for Christian Colleges and Universities, believes in a universality of moral values, by which he means—for me very touchingly and hopefully—that "the human mind and the human conscience will respond to the beckoning of moral universals and of natural laws at anytime and anywhere regardless of the context."[30]

Moreover, democracy is not only the rule of a majority. First of all, it is rallying behind a principle of freedom that is never to be abandoned, even if there is a majority vote that would allow totalitarians to gain power, if only because once a society is run by fascists and suicide bombers there is never again an opportunity to oppose the totalitarian way of life and return to peace-caring values. Are the suicide bombers cases of psychopathology? In conventional psychiatric terms, *no*. There is no psychopathology involved in political suicide bombings.

Table 5.8. Dynamics of Fascist Mind in Selected Psychopathology: "Good Guys" and Women Who Become Suicide Bombers

	01-02 **TOTALITY, OVER-CERTAINTY, ABSOLUTISM, AND MAGICAL THINKING**	03-04 **CENSORSHIP OF INFORMATION, OBEDIENCE, CONFORMITY, AND INTOLERANCE OF DISSENT**
"GOOD GUYS" AND WOMEN WHO BECOME SUICIDE BOMBERS	Participants in ideological terrorist movements buy thoughtlessly into a hypnotic goal of destroying the accursed enemy. They further override any possible consciousness of conscience by submerging themselves in an ecstasy of being part of their collective group and its goal, and/or in the satisfaction and conviction that they are exercising a real revenge for past collective losses. Many also have personal revenges on their mind. Ideological terrorists often represent a group ideology of loyalty, sacrifice, honor, and absolute obedience, and/or a culture that idolizes death over life. They are also characteristically promised great rewards for themselves and their families—on heaven and earth. Ideological terrorists vary dramatically, from fearless to mindless to bewildered and as if without will, including a few who are happy to be caught and stopped "against their will" in their tracks.	Ideological terrorists make themselves completely obedient and conform to the instructions of their movement, their superiors and the group context in which they operate. Ideological terrorist movements characteristically devote a good deal of effort to maintaining hypnotic influence on their messengers of terror, especially suicide killers, to the last minute. At times they have been known to revert to drugging their operative as well, but for the most part suicide bombers are not under the influence of drugs, and are carried by the power of their decision-making process and the influences of their handlers and group.

"GOOD GUYS" AND WOMEN WHO BECOME SUICIDE BOMBERS (*continued*)

	Role of anxiety: There are cases where anxiety over self-destruction and/or anxiety over the wrongness of killing others ("How can it be right to kill children eating ice cream?") does lead a terrorist to abort an attack. One wonders whether religious leaders and other leaders of culture could produce messages to encourage more resistance to consummating terrorist acts.	
05 **SUPERIORITY, EXCESSIVE POWER-SEEKING, AND PREJUDICE**	*06* **VIOLENCE, RETALIATION AGAINST DISSENT, SACRIFICE, AND DESTRUCTION**	*07* **DENIALS OF DOING HARM TO SELF AND OTHERS**
Superiority is inherent in the wish and readiness to take the lives of others. Suicide bombings have taken place everywhere—in medical centers, schools, churches, and mosques. No holds barred to kil ing everyone.	**Doing Harm to Self** Suicide is the murder weapon beginning with oneself. **Doing Harm to Others** Doing harm—in spades—is obviously the point of it all. Death to the victims and t-e-r-r-o-r to those who remain.	Apparently most suicide bombers have dissociated from their self-identity. In their minds, they are not doing harm, but are serving a greater good.

Source: Created by the author.

There are also sociological considerations such as data that suggest *some* clustering of suicide bombers among younger unmarrieds and unattached, also from among the poor and marginal, although these clusters, too, fade into a larger picture that suicide bombers come from all socioeconomic strata and all age groups, and often enough from the better educated.

The outstanding characteristic of suicide bombers is that they are ideologically committed. The suicide bombers embrace with their entire beings that they are shortly to submit to oblivion and nonexistence other people and themselves for theological and/or political goals. Psychologically, they also can be seen as submitting themselves to the thrills of being identified with and being parts of a huge group drama, but that too does not make for a psychiatric disturbance according to the prevailing norms in psychiatry. In some sense many of them are *happy* to do the "work" that they do. Amira Hass, an Israeli reporter for the respected *Haaretz*, described a female suicide bomber—a doctoral student in psychology, no less—as "a happy person who loves life."[31]

Have I myself now proven the very thesis to which I object, that there are suicide bombers who are not crazy or disturbed—beyond the fact that they are not disturbed according to the existing current *DSM* standards? Many academics and professionals in psychology believe the subject of terrorists is so much a political one that, although obviously aspects of human behavior are involved, the subject essentially is not a proper one for psychology or psychiatry. Further, in the liberal corridors of academic and professional psychology, the seemingly humanistic viewpoint is that terrorists have the right to their heartfelt political convictions and readiness to sacrifice for their causes.[32] There are also behavioral science thinkers who see terrorism "simply" as "another form of politically motivated violence that is perpetrated by *rational, lucid people who have valid motives*."[33] And there are mental health professionals who think suicide bombing is the greatest way to live (and die, of course, and who cares about the victims anyway). Adel Sadek, the recipient of the 1990 Egyptian State Prize, chairman of the Arab Psychiatrists Association and head of the Department of Psychiatry at Ein Shams University in Cairo, states unquestioningly that suicide bombing is a sublime peak moment of no less than superior mental health:

> The psychological structure [of the perpetrator of a suicide attack] is that of an individual who loves life. This may seem strange to people who are incapable of understanding [the suicide attack] because their cultural structure has no concepts such as self-sacrifice and honor. These concepts do not exist in a number of cultures, and therefore they offer stupid interpretations, attesting to ignorance. But we know this well, because our culture is one of sacrifice, loyalty, and honor. As a professional psychiatrist, I say that the height of bliss comes with the end of the countdown: ten, nine, eight, seven, six, five, four, three, two, one. And then, you press the button to blow yourself up. When the martyr reaches "one," and then "boom," he explodes, and senses himself flying, because he knows for certain that he is not dead. It is a transition to another, more beautiful world, because he knows very well that within seconds he will see the light of the Creator.[34]

Personally, I believe the Egyptian psychiatrist is off his rocker.

My readers know that my overall conceptual proposal is that all psychiatric diagnoses be based on an evaluation of the functioning of the person for their own self, *and* a person's impacts on the functioning of other persons. In this conceptual frame, the bare fact that a person is killing themselves and/or other people directly establishes a state of the most serious psychiatric disturbance. Further, I believe that from the point of view of an overall philosophy of the mental health professions, the subject of suicide bombers has to be faced! It would be a ridiculous absurdity if all the ideological killers in our world no longer also remain subjects of a discourse about what is desirable and healthy mental living and what is not.

Ultimately, not including killers in the world of psychopathology would mean that *abnormality* includes people who have breakdowns when they are supposed to be killers but become too disturbed and can't meet the requirements of their jobs, while *normality* includes all those who are exemplary and capable in fulfilling their jobs in the death squads.[35] It hardly sounds like a psychology of which Western thinking could be proud.

In my judgment, when all is said and done about conscious motivations and the power of cultures that promote and encourage suicide bombings, there is a crucial dynamic deep in the mind-spirit-soul of a person who elects to serve *D-E-A-T-H* on themselves and so many others.

SUDDEN UNEXPECTED NOCTURNAL DEATH SYNDROME (SUNDS)

This is a deadly psychosomatic syndrome that is common in some Southeast Asian countries. Since 1977 a good number of Southeast Asian immigrants in the United States have been reported as dying from this mysterious disorder. In the initial reports, this serious illness had an unusually high incidence among newly relocated Laotian Hmong refugees. All but one of the victims were men, the median age was thirty-three, all were apparently healthy, and all died during their sleep.

In 2001 the *Encyclopedia of Death and Dying* reported, "Since 1977 more than a hundred Southeast Asian immigrants in the United States have died from a mysterious disorder known as Sudden Unexpected Nocturnal Death Syndrome (SUNDS). The encyclopedia noted further that there have been "numerous studies of SUNDS, from many vantage points including toxicology, heart disease, sleep apnea and other sleep disorders, genetics, metabolism, and nutrition," but that "medical scientists have not been able to determine its exact cause." The entry then adds, "Medical opinion appears to favor an impairment of the electrical pathways and specialized muscle fibers that contract the heart. It is widely held, however, that some type of intense stressor is likely an additional risk factor."[36]

The fascinating description of this very serious syndrome is that the person suffers crushing pressure on the chest that interferes with breathing to the point of actual death. This is a culture-derived form of expression of mental-psychosomatic distress that does indeed lead to actual death when not treated or treated incorrectly through useless standard Western psychiatric methods.[37]

The above encyclopedia also cited an earlier medical folklorist, Shelley Adler, who postulated that SUNDS is a "supernormal nocturnal experience that is part of traditional Hmong beliefs" that can trigger the fatal syndrome. The experience is referred to as a "night-mare," not in the modern sense of a bad dream, but rather in its original denotation as the nocturnal visit of an evil being that threatens to press the very life out of its terrified victim.

The Hmong nightmare is known as *dab tsog*. It causes cataclysmic psychological stress that can trigger sudden death. Hmong refugees experience a culture-specific manifestation of the universal nightmare phenomenon. The *dab tsog* attack in Laos is related to the larger nightmare tradition of several peoples, and has taken on danger of a fatal outcome in response to the peculiar stresses of the Hmong refugee experience in the context of the trauma of war, migration, rapid acculturation, and inability to practice traditional healing and ritual. The power of traditional belief in the nightmare can cause cataclysmic psychological stress to male Hmong refugees. As more nationals from Asian countries have appeared in the West in recent years, either as immigrants or as migrant workers, cases of sudden unexpected death have mounted in these populations in Western parts of the world.

Understanding the syndrome has been—and for many still is—like a "whodunit" detective story. But it appears the answer was found and ignored. In 1988 a touching and exciting report was published in the *American Journal of Orthopsychiatry* in which mental health clinicians figured it out correctly and initiated a genuinely effective treatment.[38] Nonetheless, to this day there are many instances where the above understanding is not recognized or known, Southeast Asians are believed to die without cause, and medical professionals keep looking for exotic organic causes without any understanding of the psychosomatic issue.

It makes a lot of sense that the traumatic war experiences plus the trauma of migration were incorporated into the nightmare syndrome, but it is important to note that the same syndrome has also appeared in migrant workers from Southeast Asian countries such as Thailand who do not have a war background—the upheaval and aloneness of the migrant laborer experience plus whatever awaits in a given person's soul from their life background and susceptibility to the nightmare will do the trick.

The fact that information on this psychosomatic syndrome has been in the literature for years and should have received greater recognition by professionals but has been ignored and unknown is, to say the least, disturbing. Is it primarily because psychiatry can't stop bypassing the soul and keeps looking for organic causes? The brilliant report of correct diagnosis and effective treatment was published by Joseph Tobin and Joan Friedman, who describe the case of a Hmong refugee in Chicago who was suffering deeply the frightening symptoms of crushing pressure on his chest, and how a Western practitioner was smart enough to consult the Centers for Disease Control (CDC) in Atlanta. The therapist learned of the rising prevalence of the syndrome among Laotian refugees and was sufficiently clearheaded and honest to recognize that standard Western psychiatric treatment that had been attempted first was totally worthless and inappropriate. The report describes how the therapist then brought in an indigenous healer who centered around time-honored folk rituals for getting rid of the dangerous spirits that were threatening the patient's life, including bringing together the extended family group in the exorcising of the evil spirits, and then the family group festively celebrated the success of overcoming the spirits. Patient, family, and extended community gave thanks for the rescue. To sum up, the successful therapy included a) enlisting the assistance of an indigenous healer from the Hmong community; b) crafting a series of wise "treatments" that involved folk rituals for exorcizing the demons plaguing the poor patient; and c) using "family and extended community therapy" in the festive dinner.

THE NEW "AMERICAN WAY" OF MASS KILLING AT COLUMBINES, SHOPPING CENTERS, AND OTHER PUBLIC PLACES

A "Made in USA" specialty is to go to a public place and murder people randomly. Sometimes the victims include a specific person against whom the killer has a grudge, but that "understandable" killing is expanded more disgustingly and frighteningly to any and all other people who are in the range of the murderer.

In Columbine, two senior students used a firebomb to divert firemen, propane tanks that were turned into bombs and placed in the cafeteria, and ninety-nine explosive devices in the school and bombs set in cars. The total dead was twelve students and one teacher, and an additional twenty-seven students and others were injured.

One summary of the findings of the FBI and its team of psychiatrists and psychologists came to the conclusion that the terrible evil was committed in a quest for "fame . . . they were gunning for devastating infamy on the historical scale of Attila the Hun. Their vision was to create a nightmare so devastating and apocalyptic that the entire world would shudder at their power." For whatever its worth, the mental health experts also came to the conclusion that one of the students was "hurting inside," and that the other was an "out and out psychopath."[39]

In December 2012, there was a terrible shooting in the lower grades, including the kindergarten, at Sandy Hook Elementary School in Newtown, Connecticut, where twenty children and six adults were killed. The country was in an uproar, and yet, unbelievably, in the fourteen-month period following the shooting mass deaths in Newtown, there were "at least 44 school shootings." These shootings took place in twenty-four states across the United States; one-third of the events were on college or university campuses, and two-thirds were in K-12 schools.[40]

Not surprisingly, the phenomenon of mass shooting also turns up outside the United States. One can say bitterly that this is "another successful export" of American culture to the rest of the world. On July 22, 2001, a gunman first exploded a car bomb downtown in Oslo, Norway, killing eight people. From there he drove to the island of Utoya and killed sixty-five youth attending a camp. The event was called "the worst massacre in Norway's history since the Second World War."[41] Other countries in which "Columbines" have been reported include Germany, UK, Japan, and China. In some of the incidents, the child perpetrator reports that he "just felt like it"—an act of revenge, bravado, or what the child may call "fun" for the excitement.

One study in 1999 of thirty mass killings in the United States and Canada concluded that two-thirds of the perpetrators had definite or probable psychosis.[42] A survey in March 2014 that reviewed four previous summaries including the 1999 study came to two important conclusions: 1) "individuals with severe mental illness are probably responsible for approximately half of such killings," and 2) "mass killings are increasing in incidence."[43]

In my book on suicide bombing I concluded, "Murder-suicide thinking is also likely to reflect a serious psychological problem in a given child; but more often than not it also reflects—perhaps more importantly than personal problems—a larger cultural setting in our West that has failed grievously to teach the children a basic respect for life." I suggest that what in the West may be excitement-seeking events of an aimless violence reflects a larger cultural failure to hold life sacred."[44]

"PEOPLE OF THE LIE"—INVISIBLE DESTROYERS OF OTHERS' LIVES

Finally, we look at the most difficult phenomenon to diagnose because, for all intents and purposes, it is *invisible*. These are situations where A drives B—and sometimes more people—in their lives to mental despair and abandon, but you can't *see* them doing it without special equipment such as a family therapy or psychoanalytic lens. Once one knows about the syndrome, one needs to question whether such a pattern is operating each time one sees a chronic psychiatric disability in a family member and sees no evidence of forceful, genuine attempts at interventions by an ostensibly healthy spouse or parent.

M. Scott Peck, an American psychiatrist, aptly called such destructive persons "People of the Lie."[45] Because Peck wrote from a popular and even extreme Christian view, it may be that the monumental publishing success he enjoyed derived to a great extent from readers who identified with his religiosity or who were charmed by the combination of psychiatry with Christianity. But I have always harbored the thought that it was Peck's so-correct identification of "People of the Lie" that brought in many of his readers, because there is a hunger for this knowledge—there are so many well-dressed normal-looking people out there who are making the lives of others deranged or miserable, and observers outside the family often do not see clearly what is happening.

In Peck's case, along with the fact previously noted that he may have attracted many readers because of his intense Christian religious orientation, professionally he repelled many readers and in effect lost much of what would have been his place in the history of mental health research because he pursued adamantly a method of exorcism as the major and perhaps even sole treatment he proposed, and this religious-folklore concept is far from acceptable in contemporary psychological science, certainly not for the majority of people who have not grown up in a culture that honors exorcism.

Nonetheless, the concept of "People of the Lie" is in itself very sound, and I think that many people resonate to the concept on the basis of their own life experience. Plain and simple, even as the phenomenon is hidden and perplexing, there are people in our lives who drive people around them absolutely nuts, but they do so in ways that are disguised (though no less powerful) and don't produce an obvious picture of someone beating another down emotionally.

In sports, even the apparently competent and knowledgeable coach gets fired if and when his team loses a lot. In our everyday lives there are any number of likable people, even jolly souls, who are presiding over monstrous emotional damage in the people around them. Thus, one case I reported earlier involved an otherwise very delightful man whose brother committed suicide and hung himself in the surviving brother's office (I wonder what he meant by that), who brought up two highly disturbed and disturbing children, and who saw several of his employees become basically weak personalities if not also borderline alcoholics.

Here are further details of a case to which I referred earlier of a father who took no action to get his housebound daughter out into the world to work or school or any other normal activities with others:

❖ The daughter is basically homebound. Father and daughter had a regular "routine" where they would talk regularly about her organizing herself to go to some activity. For quite some time she expressed a wish to join a health club in which she would exercise regularly, and at long last she managed to get to a shopping center to outfit herself with sparkling new gym clothing. But when push came to shove she couldn't make it out of the house—and father plain didn't push, not even with the help of the therapist with whom the father ostensibly had a very respectful and even friendly relationship.

The mother of the girl is a shadow of a person—including the fact that she doesn't drive and therefore doesn't do the family shopping, all of which the father does. The mother lives out an even more bizarre over-connected (symbiotic) relationship with their young adult daughter. Mother and daughter have the longest talks virtually every night for several hours and seem to be engaged in a relationship process that is working toward the young woman's development, but mother, too, takes zero steps toward getting the daughter out.

The daughter has been frozen now for some four years! There have been a number of attempts at therapies, and there was one period in which family therapy led the parents to intimate to their daughter that they would force her out of the house, to which the daughter responded quite admirably by going out and getting a job as a cashier in a supermarket for about three months. She was terrific at her job, but couldn't develop even minimal social interaction with other staff at the market, and when the family therapist went on an extended vacation she quit her job and ran home to safety. There is also another child in the family who is a serious underachiever and another child who has erupted into acts of violence.

Both parents are highly intelligent people and both are working professionals. The father even stands out impressively in his high-level professional work, and he is also a delightful conversationalist who makes himself appear like he has profound insights into life and people. The father had enjoyed an earlier period of meaningful therapy for himself with a gentle and wise lady therapist who helped him to gain some peace of mind regarding his own history of having been, in his words, an object of his mother's hatred and her wishes for his death. Clearly, both parents are "People of the Lie."

CONCLUDING NOTES

We mental health professionals will live much more sanely if we have a commonsense approach to diagnosing mental conditions than cumbersome lists of symptoms. A great deal of discomfort and pain and even overall destabilization are characteristic parts of life for all people, but if these "downs" are processed constructively toward recovery and growth, the symptom-suffering person does *not* have a mental condition. Similarly, doing some harm to others is inevitable for all of us, but again simple good sense can generally differentiate between those who are organized—consciously or unconsciously—to doing major or long-lasting damages to the other in contrast to the everyday insults and pains we human beings cause others all the time.

We advance the proposition that a definitive test of an abnormal mental condition is not whether a person feels bad at any time—we all do—but whether a person *basically* is doing significant harm to himself and/or to other human beings. Protecting, promoting, and saving life is mentally healthy. Hurting people, taking away from their ability to fulfill themselves, or destroying them is mental illness—and the sooner we get our definitions straight, the more we will be able to do more to further life. Meaningful psychotherapy is a devotion to life.

> A sick thought can devour the body's flesh more than fever or consumption.[46]
>
> —*Guy de Maupassant*

> The mind is like an iceberg, it floats with one-seventh of its bulk above water.[47]
>
> —*Sigmund Freud*

At the center of your being you have the answer; you know who you are and you know what you want.[48]

—*Lao Tzu*

Let us consider that we are all partially insane. It will explain us to each other; it will unriddle many riddles; it will make clear and simple many things which are involved in haunting and harassing difficulties and obscurities now.[49]

—*Mark Twain*

NOTES

1. I still love many of the old masters of psychiatry, wise and caring people that they were, and I think they were basically right that many psychotic people are, in their essence, running away from a life they hate and/or fear so much it is worth their while to give it up. Thus, see the classic workmanship of the editor of yesteryear's guiding handbook in American psychiatry: Arieti, Silvano (1955). *Interpretation of Schizophrenia.* New York: Basic Books; and Arieti, Silvano (Ed.) (1959). *American Handbook of Psychiatry,* 3rd edition. New York: Basic Books, 419–454. See also the classic contribution that psychosis is an escape from people in Sullivan, Harry Stack (1947). *Conceptions of Modern Psychiatry.* Washington, DC: William Alanson White Foundation; and Sullivan, Harry Stack (1953). *The Interpersonal Theory of Psychiatry.* New York: Norton.

In respect of the treatment of psychosis, there are many, many more reports from the old days of psychotherapy of touching the aching souls of psychotics. How well I remember my very first treatment case in a mental hospital where I was thrown into the scary, murky waters of doing therapy with a catatonic patient in a serious (though not extreme) state of sculptured-like stiffness and mutism. What on earth should I do? I solved the problem by holding in my left hand a copy of an extraordinarily touching book by Marguerite Sechehaye, a Swiss psychoanalyst, on how she treated a schizophrenic patient who got well, and doing what she described! My patient also got well—and those were the days without medication! *See* Sechehaye, Marguerite (1951). *Symbolic Realization: A New Model of Psychotherapy Applied to a Case of Schizophrenia.* New York: International Universities Press. See also earlier citations of her work.

See similarly the classic heartrending story of a famous patient who got well: Green, Hannah (1964). *I Never Promised You a Rose Garden, op. cit.*; as well as the professional writings of Hannah's beloved therapist, Frieda: Fromm-Reichmann, Frieda (1959), *Psychoanalysis and Psychotherapy: Selected Papers,* edited by Dexter M. Bulard, foreword by Edith V. Weigert, Chicago: University of Chicago Press.

2. In every generation there arise courageous, sensitive therapists who approach the disturbed person genuinely, even and perhaps more so when the patient is in a state of psychosis, and do not rely on the tried and true techniques of psychiatry for suppressing symptoms rather than engaging the person.

Among the great therapists—most of them psychiatrists—who courageously went toward psychotic patients to woo them out of their hiding places, see the beginnings of a new genre both of enlisting the families of psychotics and of organizing strategies to beat patients out of their strategies of controlling the people in their worlds by Italian family therapist Palazzoli, Mara Selvini et al. (1978). *Paradox and Counterparadox: A New Model in the Therapy of the Family in Schizophrenic*. New Brunswick, NJ: Transaction. See also the trailblazing work in the United States of Karon, Bertram P. and Vandenbos, Gary R. (1981). *Psychotherapy of Schizophrenia: The Treatment of Choice*. Lanham, MD: Rowman & Littlefield. Karon and Vandenbos demonstrated experimentally the greater effectiveness of psychotherapy over medications for schizophrenics. See also the descriptions of heartfelt and wise treatments with several disturbed patients by Honig, Albert (2001), *Hard Boiled Eggs and Other Psychiatric Tales, op. cit.;* and Honig, Albert (1972). *The Awakening Nightmare: A Breakthrough in Treating the Mentally Ill, op. cit.*

3. There are also exciting reports from several different countries around the world of those who have dared to set up therapeutic communities or to transform a psychiatric hospital into a therapeutic community. Thus, see among others the works of famous British psychiatrist Laing, R.D.: Esterson, A; Cooper, D.G.; Laing, R.D. (1965). Results of family-orientated therapy with hospitalized schizophrenics. *British Medical Journal*, 2(5476), 1462–1465. Laing's famous basic works include Laing, R.D. (1967). *The Politics of Experience and the Bird of Paradise, op. cit.*; Laing, R. D. (1970). *Knots, op cit.*; and Laing, R.D. (1971). *The Politics of the Family and Other Essays, op. cit.*

See also the innovative work of American psychiatrist Loren H. Mosher and the Soteria approach, which resulted in Mosher being "forced to leave his key position in American psychiatry" (www.moshersoteria.com); he had been no less chief of the Center for the Studies of Schizophrenia at the National Institute for Mental Health; and see "The Open Dialogue Approach" in Finland: Seikkula, Jaako and Olson, Mary E (2003). The open dialogue approach to acute psychosis: Its poetics and micropolitics. *Family Process*, 42(3), 403–418.

There have also been conclusive reports that "plain" laymen who volunteered to put in time steadily building a human relationship with a chronic psychotic patient could succeed in inspiring some patients to reorganize themselves to return to a modicum of normal life in the community. See, among others, a report from several countries in the European Union (2011). *Long-Term Mental Health Care for People with Severe Mental Disorders*. Written by Jose Miguel Caldas de Almeida and Helen Killaspy, with contributions from Angelo Fioritti (Italy), Filipe Costa (Sweden), Jean Luc Roelandt (France), Marcelino Lopez (Spain), and Jan Pfeiffer (Czech Republic). http://ec.europa.eu/health/mental_health/docs/healthcare_mental_disorders_en.pdf. Retrieved October 6, 2014.

Granted, all of these "people-touching" techniques of treatment of psychotics require so many people and so many days and months of caring and devotion. There is a blessing in medications that abort the cruel symptom-chains of many psychoses. But the medications do not solve the problems of loneliness, fearfulness, and ineptness, nor the patient's adoption of a strategy of controlling people in their environment and milking them to be their perpetual supporters, nor the patient's anger. These are issues for corrective relationships with people such as (but not only) in good psychotherapy.

4. Braginsky, Benjamin M.; Braginsky, Dorothea D.; and Ring, Kenneth (1969). *Methods of Madness: The Mental Hospital as a Last Resort*. New York: Holt, Rhinehart and Winston. Braginsky, Benjamin M. and Braginsky, Dorothy D. (1967). Schizophrenic patients in the psychiatric interview: An experimental study of their effectiveness at manipulation. *Journal of Consulting Psychology*, 31(6), 543–547; Reprinted in Robin M. Kowalski and Mark R. Leary

(Eds.). *The Interface of Social and Clinical Psychology: Key Readings.* Lanham, MD: Rowman & Littlefield, 78–84.

5. See in this connection the above-cited book by Honig, Albert (2001). *Hardboiled Eggs and Other Psychiatric Tales, ibid.* There are several references in this book to using work assignments for patients where the assignment is intended as a real part of treatment and not simply as a routine for life in the hospital.

6. On the psychological meanings of manic-depressive states, see once again the works of early masters such as Arieti and Fromm-Reichman: Arieti, Silvano (1959), Manic-depressive psychosis. In Arieti, Silvano (Ed.) (1961). *American Handbook of Psychiatry*, 3rd edition. New York: Basic Books, 419–454; and see Fromm-Reichmann, Frieda (1959), *Psychoanalysis and Psychotherapy, ibid.*

7. Berke, Joseph H.; Pierides, Stella; Sabbadim, Andrea; and Schneider Stanley (Eds.) (1998). *Even Paranoids Have Enemies: New Perspectives on Paranoia and Persecution.* New York: Taylor & Francis.

8. Kaffman, Mordecai (1981). Monoideism in psychiatry: Theoretical and clinical implications. *American Journal of Psychotherapy*, 35(2), 235–243; Kaffman, Mordecai (1981), Paranoid disorders: The core of truth behind the delusional system. *International Journal of Family Therapy*, 3(1), 29–41; Kaffman, Mordecai (1981). Paranoid disorders: The interpersonal perspective. *Journal of Family Therapy*, 3, 21–30; Kaffman, Mordecai (1983). Paranoid disorders: Family sources of the delusional system. *Journal of Family Therapy*, 5(2), 107–116.

9. Kaffman, Mordecai (1963). Short term family therapy; Kaffman, Mordecai (1985). Twenty years of family therapy in Israel. *Family Process*, 24(2), 113–27.

10. Raphael Lemkin's seminal work in which he also coined the very word *genocide* was Lemkin, Raphael (1944), *Axis Rule in Occupied Europe.* Washington, DC: Carnegie Foundation for International Peace. Several of his important and touching works remained unpublished for many years (several publishers to whom he turned in his time decided there would not be enough of a commercial market for books on genocide). Steven Jacobs is a scholar who has been reconstructing several of Lemkin's unpublished writings. See Jacobs, Steven L. (1992). *Raphael Lemkin's Thoughts on Nazi Genocide: Not Guilty.* Lewistown, NY: Mellen; and Jacobs, Steven L. (2012). *Lemkin on Genocide: Written by Raphael Lemkin.* Lanham, MD: Lexington Books. Some excerpts from Lemkin's writings were published posthumously in a chapter in a book co-edited by Samuel Totten and the above Steven Jacobs, which is otherwise devoted to the autobiographies of scholars who have contributed to the development of the new field of genocide studies. The title of the chapter is based on a *New York Times* editorial on October 20, 1953, that celebrated Lemkin's tireless battle to have the *U.N. Genocide Convention* adopted and ratified, which referred to Lemkin as "that exceedingly patient and totally unofficial man." See Lemkin, Raphael (2002). Totally unofficial man. In Totten, Samuel and Jacobs, Steven Leonard (2003). *Pioneers of Genocide Studies.* New Brunswick, NJ: Transaction, 365–399. A further contribution to publication of Lemkin's work is Frieze, Donna Lee (Ed.) (2013). *Totally Unofficial: The Autobiography of Raphael Lemkin.* New Haven: Yale University Press.

11. The original source is: Lemkin, Raphael (date unknown). Unpublished papers. With permission of the Rare Books and Manuscripts Division, the New York Public Library Astor, Lenox and Tilden Foundations. Cited in *Internet on the Holocaust and Genocide*, Issue Eight, January 1987, 3; and Jacobs, Steven L. (Ed.) (2012). *Lemkin on Genocide: Written by Raphael Lemkin.* Lanham, MD: Lexington Books.

12. Tamarin, George R. (1980). *Studies in Psychopathology, op. cit.*

13. See the publication of the first encyclopedia on the subject. Charny, Israel W. (Ed.) (1999). *Encyclopedia of Genocide*, Associate editors: Rouben Adalian, Steven L. Jacobs, Eric Markusen, Marc I. Sherman, Samuel Totten. Foreword by Bishop Desmond Tutu and Simon Wiesenthal. Santa Barbara, CA: ABC-Clio.

14. Perec, George (1988). *W or the Memory of Childhood*. Boston: David R. Godine (quotation on p. 159).

15. The removal of paranoia from the *DSM* was discussed at some length in *A Democratic Mind* in a section titled "Paranoia—A Category that Might Have Helped Develop a Psychiatry for the Hitlers and bin Ladens—that Has Been Made to Disappear." As I have described, like other time-honored concepts and names, it was dropped summarily and unceremoniously by the officiating authorities who make these decisions in institutional psychiatry. No rationale was given for the change, and the change itself was not discussed—it was simply executed. When I requested clarification of the change from the American Psychiatric Association, I received a reply that the dropping of paranoia would be "explained" on pages 409–430 of *DSM-III-R*. I panicked initially (though not to the point of needing medication, of course). How could I have missed such an extensive explanation over twenty-one pages? But the explanation turned out to be a misnomer, for there was no explanation whatsoever in *DSM-III-R*, just a categorical ruling given in a couple of lines on one of the pages of the twenty-one-page section.

16. Sullivan, Patrick F. (1995). Mortality and anorexia nervosa. *American Journal of Psychiatry*, 152(7), 1073–1074.

17. Minuchin, Salvador (1974). *Families and Family Therapy, op cit.*; Minuchin, Salvador; Rosman, Bernice L.; and Baker, Lester. (1978). *Psychosomatic Families: Anorexia Nervosa in Context, op. cit.*

18. Palazzoli, Mara Selvini (1977). *Self-Starvation: From Individual to Family Therapy in the Treatment of Anorexia Nervosa*. New York: Jason Aronson; Palazzoli, Mara Selvini, et al. (1978). *Paradox and Counterparadox: A New Model in the Therapy of the Family in Schizophrenic Transaction*. New Brunswick, NJ: Transaction.

19. Tamasese, K.; Peteru, C.; and Waldegrave, C. (1997). *Ole Taeao Afua*: a qualitative investigation into Samoan perspectives on mental health and culturally appropriate services. Report for the Health Research Council of New Zealand. Wellington: The Family Centre.

20. European Foundation for the Improvement of Living and Working Conditions (2014). Social Situation of young people in Europe. 3rd EQLS Policy Brief. http://www.eurofound.europa.eu/publications/htmlfiles/ef1404.htm?utm_source=socialmedia&utm_medium=posts&utm_campaign=youthsocialsituation20140325.

21. Joans, Maggie (January 15, 2006). Shutting themselves in. *New York Times Magazine*.

22. Malick, Sib (March 26, 2014). This is their second childhood: Close to half the young people up to age 29 in Europe are living with their parents. *Guardian*. Reprinted in *Haaretz* (Hebrew).

23. Shani, Ayelett (March 21, 2014). A room with a view of entitlement: Talking to Prof. Haim Omer, sixty-four, psychologist, teaches at Tel Aviv University. Wants to promote his book 'World of Temptations: Keeping Children Safe in an Age of Abundance' (Hebrew). *Haaretz English Edition*. http://www.theguardian.com/society/2014/mar/24/dependent-generation-half-young-european-adults-live-parents.

24. See also Shriver, Lionel (2014). *Big Brother*. New York: Harper Collins. This finely written novel is the story of an adult older brother who, after becoming obese, moves in with his sister and her family. After the brother overstays his welcome, the sister's husband delivers an ultimatum: It's either him or me.

25. See the news story: The blackmailer at Strauss Dairy Co. *Yediot Achronot*, October 7, 1987. (Hebrew) for one of the newspaper accounts of the incident. After being captured, the criminal also said, "Somewhere inside of me I wanted to be caught. I wanted someone to stop me from completing this task. I myself couldn't stop myself."

26. See Charny, Israel W. (1982). *How Can We Commit the Unthinkable?*, 371, for excerpts from a letter by the heartbroken father whose three-and-a-half-year-old girl was killed by a "Bible-carrying youth" babysitter. The letter was published in a front-page story in the *Philadelphia Bulletin*, June 5, 1959.

27. The best-known statement of a forthcoming clash between Islamic and non-Islamic civilizations is that of Huntington, Samuel P. (1996). *The Clash of Civilizations and the Remaking of World Order*. New York: Simon and Schuster. Of course, suicide bombings are also employed by Muslims in their own wars among themselves, such as in the Iran-Iraq war, or in various attacks by competing Sunni and Shi'ite groups, so that the analysis of suicide bombings developed here is intended to pertain to all such acts and not only to Islamic suicide bombers against the Western world.

28. Osama bin Laden, World Islamic Front, February 23, 1998, cited by Federation of American Scientists (2001). *Jihad against Jews and Crusaders: World Islamic Front Statement*. Available from http://www.fas.org/irp/world/para/docs/980223-fatwa.htm [original Arabic text version available at http://www.library.cornell.edu/colldev/mideast/fatwa2.htm].

29. In February 2003, Sheik Aba Hamza al-Masri was fired from his post at the infamous Finsbury Park mosque, one of London's largest mosques, by the British Charity Commission, which has the authority to oversee places of worship in the UK that receive charitable funds. The mosque, which was seen as linked with al-Qaeda, had been raided by British antiterrorist police who found false passports and credit cards. Among other sermons, Hamza had called America's spaceship, Columbia, "a trinity of evil against Islam" because the astronauts included Americans, an Israeli, and a Hindu, and called the loss of the Columbia spaceship "a punishment from God." (*BBC News* [on the web] (2002). Mosque in the spotlight. January 23; *BBC News* [on the web] (2003). Imam fired from London mosque post, February 4.

30. Malik, Habib (2003). Can Christians and Muslims relate in peace? Address to the Presidents Conference of the Council for Christian Colleges and Universities, February 2–4. Text retrieved from the Internet September 16, 2003, at the site of the Council for Christian Colleges and Universities, www.cccu.org/conferences/eventID.189/past_conferences_details.asp.

31. Hass, Amira (2002). The suicide-bomber, says the doctoral student, is a happy person who loves life. *Haaretz*, July 16, B4 (Hebrew). A paragraph-long sub-headline to this story says at greater length, "In the Palestinian community, the opinion generally held is that the suicide bombers operate out of despair, poverty and a loss of life; but in the Hamas they insist that the motivation is patriotic and even a love of life. Under the surface there is controversy in the Gaza Strip about suicide bombings, but the opponents are afraid to come out publicly. 'No one will convince me that religion allows a person to kill a child who is eating ice cream,' says one Islamic activist who now has doubts about suicide bombings, but he won't be quoted."

32. Habib Malik has this to say about the naiveté of so many liberal thinkers who want to preserve a picture of man as good and human society as more decent than not: "The generally sorry state in which Islamic moderation finds itself renders it for all practical purposes an elusive mirage in the quest for international dialogue between the West and the Islamic world. . . . Lone liberal Muslims here and there, especially at dialogue conferences, or among exile emigre communities in the West will speak of the need to reinterpret doctrines . . . The Islamic

establishment on the whole, however, remains conservative and unyielding, unmoved by such overtures and refusing to entertain seriously these reformist outlooks." Malik, Habib, *ibid.*

33. Ruby, Charles L. (2002). Are terrorists mentally deranged? *Analyses of Social Issues and Public Policy*, 2(1), 15–26 (quotation on p. 15) (italics in author's abstract).

34. An article titled, "Class Isn't Over Yet Stupid!" appeared in the Egyptian newspaper *Hadith Al-Madina* in the form of an open letter to President Bush. Excerpted from interviews in *Hadith Al-Madina* (Egypt), April 23, 2002. Cited in *Al-Quds Al-Arabi* (London), April 23, 2002, and *Iqraa TV* (Saudi Arabia/Egypt), April 24, 2002. Published by the Middle East Research Institute (MEMRI), an independent, nonprofit organization that translates and analyzes the media of the Middle East [4/30/02, No. 373]. www.memri.org. The statement of the Egyptian psychiatrist is, of course, diametrically opposed to everything we say about the mental health meaning of suicide bombing, but it does confirm that there are mental health meanings and not just political meanings. The statement is further striking in that an identity of a professor of psychiatry is used to create a rhetoric of glorification and legitimization of the combination of murder and suicide.

35. In a report of a suicide bomber who turns back, a woman terrorist changes her mind in a moment of inspiration. "'I look at the sky,' Ms. Ahmed recalled . . . speaking English as she described a kind of awakening. 'I look at the people.' She said she remembered a childhood belief 'that nobody has the right to stop anybody's life.'" In our professional language the woman is a psychological heroine as well. She overcame a powerful push of psychopathology in herself and reclaimed her normality. See Bennet, James (2002). Rash of new suicide bombers showing no pattern or ties. *New York Times*, June 21, A1, 10.

36. In Howarth, Glennys and Leaman, Oliver (Eds.) (2001). *Encyclopedia of Death and Dying.* Vol. 2. Sudden Unexpected Nocturnal Death Syndrome. New York: Taylor & Francis. See also the same author's separate report. Adler, Shelley R. (1994). Ethnomedical pathogenesis and Hmong immigrants' sudden nocturnal deaths. *Culture, Medicine and Psychiatry*, 18(1), 23–59.

37. Hufford, David J. (1982). *The Terror that Comes in the Night.* Philadelphia: University of Pennsylvania Press; Gibson, Parrish, R.; Tucker, Myra; Ing, Roy; Encarnacion, Carol; and Eberhardt, Mark (1987). Sudden unexplained death syndrome in Southeast Asian refugees: A review of CDC surveillance. *Morbidity and Mortality Weekly Review*, 36(1), 43–53.

38. Tobin, Joseph Jay and Friedman, Joan (1983). Spirits, shamans, and nightmare death: Survivor stress in a Hmong refugee. *American Journal of Orthopsychiatry*, 53(3), 439–448.

39. Cullen, Dave (2004). The Depressive and the Psychopath: At last we know why the Columbine did it. *Slate.* http://www.slate.com/articles/news_and_politics/assessment/2004/04/the_depressive_and_the_psychopath.html. Retrieved April 20, 2014.

40. Strauss, Valerie (2014). At least 44 school shootings since Newtown—New Analysis. *Washington Post.* http://www.washingtonpost.com/blogs/answer-sheet/wp/2014/02/13/at-least-44-school-shootings-since-newtown-new-analysis/. Retrieved February 13.

41. *Huffington Post*, Canada (2014). Norway's planned memorial to Utoya mass shooting is powerful. Posted March 5 and updated March 10, 2014. http://www.huffingtonpost.ca/2014/03/05/norway-mass-shooting-memorial_n_4907109.html.

42. Hempel, Anthony G.; Meloy, J. Reid; and Richards, Thomas C. (1999). Offenders and offense characteristics of a nonrandom sample of mass murders. *Journal of the American Academy of Psychiatry and the Law*, 27(2), 213–225.

43. Treatment Advocacy Center (2014). Backgrounder: Are Mass Killings Associated with Untreated Mental Illness Increasing? www.treatmentadvocacycenter.org. Retrieved February 5, 2015.

44. Charny, Israel W. (2007). *Fighting Suicide Bombing: A Worldwide Campaign for Life.* Westport, CT: Prager Security International (quotation on pp. 24–25).

45. Peck, Scott M. (1983). *People of the Lie: The Hope for Healing Human Evil. op. cit.*

46. Guy de Maupassant [French writer, August 5, 1850–July 6, 1893] (1887). Le Horla et autres contes fantastiques. *The Project Gutenberg E Book of Le Horla and Others*, by Guy de Maupassant.

47. Freud, Sigmund (1915). *The Unconscious.* In *The Standard Edition of the Complete Works of Sigmund Freud.*Volume XIV, 1914–1916. London: Hogarth Press, 159–204.

48. Attributed to Lao Tzu [604 BC–53 BC in Henan, philosopher and writer, known as founder of philosophical Taoism]. However, some scholars dispute the attribution and believe it is from an inspirational work on Taoism.

49. Twain, Mark (Samuel Clemens). August 19, 2006. *Christian Science.* Chapter V. *Project Gutenberg's Christian Science*, E Book #3187.

II

DEVELOPING NEW PSYCHOTHERAPY FOR A DEMOCRATIC MIND: INCLUDING OVERCOMING AND TREATING SOME CONDITIONS OF VIOLENCE AND EVIL

6

Ultimate Choices: To Be For Life or Not To Be

THE ULTIMATE CHOICES OF PROTECTING OR DESTROYING THE GIFT OF LIFE IN SMALL AND LARGE WAYS

The Tragic Readiness of "Ordinary People" to be Perpetrators of Destruction, Terrorism, and Genocide

The most basic choices we need to make in life are between advancing life and its opportunity, for ourselves and/or others, *versus* increasing the probability of premature death, for ourselves and/or others. Life confronts us all continually with such choices in respect of our health, work, social relationships, values—*everything*.

The greatest miracle of life is life itself. One's right to fulfill one's life opportunity begins first with a wholesome selfish right to do everything possible to protect oneself. This legitimate selfish concern then expands naturally to caring for increasing circles of people who are connected with us, first quite naturally our loved ones in our families, then more broadly our "tribes," and in time these "selfish" aspects of caring can extend further to a conviction in the deservability of *all* human beings to live their lives as fully and safely as possible.

Those who love life, its miracle of an opportunity to exist, the joy of being in this world, and the warmth of human interconnection and love will oppose doing harm to human beings on whatever pretext. Those who do not experience the miracle but live for some kind of gluttonous pleasure, especially to gain power over others, will necessarily regard life as another tradable commodity that they are prepared to destroy when it serves the purposes of their power.

Regrettably, too, when those who are too weak to know how to fight for their lives come under attack, they will enable perpetrators to do their destruction more easily.

This does not necessarily mean the victims in any way *wanted* to be victims, but it does mean they can play a role in making their tragic outcome more likely.

- *A Democratic Mind treasures and honors life.*
- *A Fascist Mind is prepared to sacrifice life to its purposes—and thrives on destruction.*

A Democratic Mind reacts in life-respecting ways to the many problems of everyday life, such as taking care of one's health and enhancing relationships with one's loved ones, as well as to larger choices about how to live life in one's society. A Democratic Mind will reject a totalitarian politician who calls for overextending police procedures that grievously limit peoples' basic freedoms and rights to choose how to live and function. A Democratic Mind will reject a dictator who calls for the destruction of another ethnic group who speak a different language or practice a different religious way of life. A real conviction in the sacredness of life intrinsically provides protection against adopting goals of destruction of others *as if* in the name of life. Thus, in respect of history, a truly Democratic Mind cannot celebrate the French Revolution's replacement of an authoritarian king with the avaricious guillotines that destroyed those who were perceived as opposing progress toward liberty. In contemporary life, an honest opposition to abortion—which in its own right is a point of view deserving of respect—will not be taken to justify denying other people their right to choose abortions, and certainly will not be accepted as a legitimization of murdering proponents of the right to abortion. Except in true self-defense, the taking away of life ostensibly on behalf of supporting life will be understood most times to be the work of fascist thinking.

In many cases, we have to admit that even among the perpetrators, actions taken against life, or the failure to take actions on behalf of life, may be determined to a large extent not by willfulness and malice aforethought, but by passivity, accommodation, and obedience to prevailing authorities. Amazingly, an enormous amount of destruction of life results from a lack of consciousness or awareness of what one is doing rather than willful murder. There is no doubt that tens of thousands of executioners in the most despicable events of genocide are what Christopher Browning has called "ordinary men."[1] They do what they are told to do by their superiors, and are unable to generate sufficient awareness and thought—and certainly are unable to think from a moral perspective—to decide that they will not follow orders to destroy others. Many people who are *not* out for a "kick" through destroying others are not made of a psychological or moral fiber to be capable of recognizing and admitting the evil of their behavior. They dance first of all to culture values of obedience, conformity, and going along with others in whatever the prevailing activity mandated by their group, elders or wise men, church, government, or other authority—even if the activity is immoral and abominable.

PSYCHOTHERAPISTS DON'T LIKE TO SEE AND DEFINE EVIL IN ORDINARY HUMAN BEINGS

It is very "romantic" and cheerful to see just about everything in life essentially as an opportunity to affirm life with good emotions and thoughts. Psychotherapists love doing that—their profession couldn't be a nicer one, seeing how it is pitched to such a noble cause. But the other side of the same coin is that many psychologists really don't like to see, hear, or know that they are also being called to work with *evil*—which we are defining as harming and destroying the life opportunity of oneself or others. Ernesto Spinelli makes the point:

> Psychological theories . . . tend to shy away from using the term *evil* in their explanation of behavior that may be viewed as evil. It is rare to find in the psychotherapeutic literature any in-depth analysis of the notion of evil. . . . The moral and existential dimensions of evil are avoided in psychotherapy by transforming possible evil behavior into psychopathological language.[2]

In the history of human thought the concern about evil is endless. One Amazon reader made an important point about the study of evil, noting that it is a subject that "both fascinates and repels."[3] Through the centuries, the subjects of evil and man's capacity and obligation to choose between good and evil run eternally through human thought. Already in the Bible the prophet Isaiah calls out: "Woe to those who call evil good and good evil, who put darkness for light and light for darkness, who put bitter for sweet and sweet for bitter!"[4]

> A Native American elder once described his own inner struggles in this manner: "Inside of me there are two dogs. One of the dogs is mean and evil. The other dog is good. The mean dog fights the good dog all the time. When asked which dog wins, he reflected for a moment and replied, the one I feed the most."[5]

Endless cultural greats have remarked on the choice between good and evil. Philosophers have lined up on all sides of the subject. Philosopher Immanuel Kant was a forceful defender of the inherent dignity of all persons. He insisted on the illegitimacy of political revolution. He felt that the violent overthrow even of an authoritarian and despotic regime would unleash lawlessness, and therefore rejected revolutions in favor of a process of slow and gradual reform toward a just state. His dictum was, "There shall be no war." Any number of philosophers have argued that Kant went too far in outlawing violent revolt—and I personally am inclined to agree with them in the cases of brutal genocidal regimes, which I believe should be opposed with all means possible. Other philosophers feel Kant did leave the door open to some uses of violence for achieving justice and order on an international scale.[6]

On the other hand, Friedrich Niezsche correctly exposed the falsehoods of Christian piety, but his "solution" was to lionize the will to power. Among others the Nazis loved him.[7] For many of us the concepts of good and evil are basically simple and clear, and in fact are sometimes referred to even in law as constituting a "natural ethic." This ethic is consistent with the guiding concept of this book where we define *good* as what advances life and *bad* as what destroys life. But like everything else in human life, the concepts of good and bad have been twisted and warped and subjugated to the gods of power. Thus, in totalitarian regimes and in fundamentalist religions, *good* is whatever advances the cause and *bad* is whatever opposes it.

Let's turn back to psychotherapy, and also even to criminology. A criminologist, Melissa Dearey, argued recently that the concept of evil has to be taken far more seriously in the development of criminological theory.[8] As we noted, many—I believe a majority—of therapists run away from the concept of evil in their work. A *New York Times* article states that "most psychiatrists assiduously avoid the word evil, contending that its use would precipitate a dangerous slide from clinical to moral judgment. One psychiatrist, Michael Stone of Columbia University, who has examined several hundred killers, concludes otherwise: "We know from experience who these people are, and how they behave," and it is time, he said, to give their behavior "the proper appellation." Another psychiatrist, Robert Simon of Georgetown Medical School, points out that "evil is endemic, it's constant, it is a potential in all of us. Just about everyone has committed evil acts." And yet Simon retreats to the party line of excluding the subject of evil from psychiatry. "When you start talking about evil, psychiatrists don't know anything more about it than anyone else."[9]

In matter of fact, in psychology and mental health there are a large number of very significant thinkers who have emphasized the profound importance of encountering the choice between good and evil, and yet at the same time the field of mental health as a whole has almost scrupulously avoided adopting the subject as a key aspect of psychotherapy. Au contraire, a mere reference to good and evil many times is enough to disqualify a professional from acceptance in the high society of the field.

The issue is a critical one for everyday mental health practice because there really are a lot of people around who are doing destructive things to life. But it also raises a much broader issue for the role of the psychological professions in society. Do we students of the human mind have anything to contribute to reducing the terrible toll of larger violence on our planet? I don't think that our professions have a moral right to avoid these issues, even if it means no more than acknowledging that we haven't learned enough as yet and have not been creative enough to come up with useful ideas (which, happily, I don't think is the case).

Ernesto Spinelli puts his finger on the issue according to the blurb on the book jacket of his *The Mirror and the Hammer*. "Spinelli challenges psychotherapy by asking if it has retreated from its early promise of being a pivotal agent in our attempts to discover what it means to be 'human,' in exchange for its current role as a pacifier of personal and social unease."[10]

How is it that a human being who, in the biblical metaphor, is "born in the image of God," who is born of a mother and father and in many cases enjoys a childhood with a reasonable degree of sensitivity and caring, and who grows up to construct intimate relationships with a mate and children of his own can lend themselves so readily to the hellish evil of destroying other human beings? The knowledge that plain "normal," "everyday" people were the perpetrators of the Holocaust was advanced fairly early after the Holocaust by a variety of observers.

First came evidence that the known perpetrators were not "insane" or "abnormal," whether psychologically or sociologically. Psychologist Gustave M. Gilbert studied major Nazi war criminals at the Nuremberg Trial and concluded that one could *not* see the principal Nazi personalities as abnormal. He added that "without the support of 'normal and respectable' leaders in that society, without a considerable following among the masses of the people . . . it would hardly have been possible for the Nazi leaders to precipitate as great a social catastrophe as they did."[11]

Psychiatrist and famed Rorschach specialist, Douglas M. Kelley, also studied the Nazis on trial at Nuremberg and concluded: "They simply had three quite unremarkable characteristics in common—and the opportunity to seize power. These three characteristics were: overweening ambition, low ethical standards, [and] a strongly developed nationalism which justified anything."[12] Another famous Rorschach specialist, Molly Harrower, examined the psychological tests of the Nazi criminals who were on trial in Nuremberg and concluded that even well-integrated, productive personalities are no protection against "being sucked into" processes of deceptive myths and ideology of committing evil on a grand scale.[13] Adding a bitter note for those of us who are mental health clinicians and physicians, psychiatrist Frederic Wertham presented blistering indictments of well-known psychiatrists and pediatricians in Germany who were responsible for the so-called "euthanasia program" ("T4") or the mass killings of mental patients.[14]

One specific chapter that is of special interest is that of the master killer-organizer of the Nazis, Adolf Eichmann.[15] An Israeli psychiatrist-psychologist team (a married couple), Shlomo and Shoshanna Kulcsar, examined Eichmann when he was awaiting trial and came up with a picture of an emotionally pale bore who was slavishly committed to order and organization.[16] According to Kulcsar, Eichmann was "an alienated personality," "a bureaucrat par excellence," "had no empathy," "was inhuman, more correctly *ahuman* in the strict sense of the word," and "hid behind conformism."[17] Earlier, in an entirely different context, psychologist George Bach had studied spouses who were in jail for having murdered their mate, and in the reconstruction formulated the concept of "*thinging*," which means that these people had not at all seen their spouses as human beings but as *things* who were out of place and needed to be reordered even at the expense of their deaths.[18] Returning to Eichmann, the late Father Thomas Merton commented powerfully, "One of the most disturbing facts that came out in the Eichmann trial was that a psychiatrist examined him and pronounced him *perfectly sane*. I do not doubt it at all, and that is precisely why I find it disturbing." Already at this early date, the beloved Trappist monk presciently assessed the staggering implication of these findings as a warning that the perpetrators of the future who will push the buttons of nuclear or other massive destruction will be, in many cases, "the perfectly normal ones."[19]

Continuing the accumulation of evidence for the same troubling conclusion that the Nazis were psychiatrically much the same as others, at least *in the accepted terms of normality-abnormality*, English psychiatrist Henry Dicks of the famed Tavistock Clinic went back to Europe to examine Nazi mass killers who were still in jails serving their sentences for war crimes and found that they were mostly examples of weak-egoed, emotionally deprived individuals whose secret resentments were covered under normal social and group pressures by conformity and unquestioning obedience, and whose resentments broke to the surface under the enabling conditions of the Nazi culture. Overall, they were *not* different from millions of other people, said Dicks.[20] Psychologist Hans Askenasy translated the emergent findings that the Nazis were not abnormal in a standard psychiatric sense into a cry of a serious question about all human beings by titling his book, *Are We All Nazis?*[21] Robert Jay Lifton wrote in his study of the doctors who served in the death camps of the Holocaust: "The disturbing psychological truth is that participation in mass murder need not require emotions as extreme or demonic as would seem appropriate for such a malignant project. Or to put the matter another way, ordinary people can commit demonic acts."[22]

We have to face the facts that it is an endless number of plain, everyday, non-prejudiced people who carry out the orders of killers. In many situations it is the civilians who shoot, burn, and drown the victims without being commanded. Thus, following the end of the Holocaust and World War II, a sizable number of Jews who returned to their homeland in Poland were murdered by their neighbors and fellow citizens who liked the Germans' idea of having a world without Jews.[23]

Another source of information that converges on all the observations of actual killers in the Holocaust is, of course, the sterling research of Stanley Milgram, who proved in his famous experiments that the potential for being a destructive human being is latent in a *majority of everyday human beings*. In Milgram's brilliant series of experiments, in which he instructed people to give what seemed like very damaging and even possibly lethal electric shocks to subjects in simple psychological learning experiments, the overall rate of people who complied with the instructions of the experimenter was 65 percent! Milgram concluded that given the instructions of an authority, a majority of people from all socioeconomic levels are capable of doing serious and perhaps even lethal harm to fellow human beings.[24]

Returning to the Holocaust, over the years, additional study has developed not only of the well-known leaders of the killing in the Holocaust but also of the rank-and-file participants in the executions, and it is here that the concept of "ordinary men" has come to the fore. This is the title that Christopher Browning gave his outstanding work in which he showed that the typical participants, hence the majority, in a German army police battalion that executed many Jews were everyday people who went about completing the tasks assigned them with considerable indifference.[25]

Some time after Browning's work, another scholar, Daniel Goldhagen, authored a book, *Hitler's Willing Executioners: Ordinary Germans and the Holocaust*, which not only presented the same findings as Browning but transformed them into a biting accusation of the German people's long-standing commitment to "eliminationist antisemitism."[26] Goldhagen's not-unjustified accusation of the deep culpability of the German people so catalyzed emotional responses to the book that it became a best seller. At the same time, paradoxically, by his intense accusation essentially *only* of the Germans as murderers on the basis of their committed antisemitism, the book obscured the very critical information that it also reported, namely that there were many other victims of the Nazis in addition to Jews, and that the perpetrators were *everyday* ordinary men from many peoples along with the Germans themselves.[27]

In an exhibition of the history of the Wehrmacht that was created by the Institute for Social Research in Hamburg, Germany, which enjoyed prominent display in a variety of cities in Germany and Austria over some years, there are many photographs of victims of atrocities and of the atrocities as they are being committed that were taken as *souvenirs* by the German soldiers with their personal amateur cameras—often to show off to their friends and families. It is impossible not to understand that the killers included *everyday German soldiers* and not only specialists from the death squads of the German SS, a myth that prevailed in respect of the Holocaust for many years. The creator of the exhibition, Hans Herr, said:

> The Wehrmacht was a huge body that included 20 million soldiers, of whom 12 million fought in the Eastern front. This was not a small select group of SS, or physicians who executed experiments on prisoners. This means that in every family in Germany of today there was a grandfather, father or husband soldier, and therefore confronting the Holocaust becomes a personal matter for every one of us. This is very difficult.[28]

Of course, the fact that many ordinary people can be and are co-opted into being mass killers does not mean there aren't people with a special devotion to the role, who are moreover committed to a totalitarian ideology and devoted to violence as a way of life. Michael Mann studied the biographies of 1,581 men and women involved in the Nazi genocide and concluded that "they resemble 'Real Nazis' more than they do 'Ordinary Germans'"; many were "long-term Nazis," "prewar extremists," and for whom "'careers' in violence were common."[29]

From the point of view of a theory of personality, James Waller concluded that although there may be initially some splitting or dividing of the self so that people who wouldn't ordinarily commit genocidal murder do so—

> [o]ver time . . . fundamental internal alterations in the psychological constellation of the perpetrators will increasingly diminish the need to compartmentalize. Harming victims can become "normal" behavior. The human psyche [is] driven by integration towards a unitary self [which] is fundamentally altered as a result of the power of the social forces in a given situation or organization. . . . A unitary self-conception offers the clearest explanatory principle of how ordinary people become capable of committing extraordinary evil.[30]

In my own early publications in journals,[31] and then in my book, *How Can We Commit the Unthinkable? Genocide: The Human Cancer*,[32] I summarized the data reported earlier of studies of major killers in the Holocaust and concluded that we need a basic theory of psychology in which all of us "normal human beings" must confront a universal potential for genocidal destructiveness on one or another level of perpetrator, accomplice, or bystander, and that it is incumbent on all of us to confront this potential.

Daphna Fromer and I conducted a series of empirical studies of the potential for doing harm to others of Israeli students in the helping professions—psychology, medicine, and social work. In the studies of the Israeli student health professionals, we created a series of scenarios. One scenario involved situations where health authorities in a developing country considered it advisable first to limit and then to curtail the treatment of the severely handicapped who could least benefit from treatment, and then as their situations were described as becoming more severe, the health professionals proposed a policy of involuntary mass "euthanasia." The results of the study were that 39 percent of the students saw themselves as curtailing treatment when instructed to do so, 17 percent agreed to participate in planning the so-called "euthanasia," and 11 percent even agreed *themselves* to undertake to end the patients' lives. On the assumption that the callousness and cruelty might have been the stronger when directed at another people in a far-off developing country, the same experimental scenarios were rerun describing Israeli patients in Israeli hospitals, and the resulting figures of 38 percent, 12 percent, and 9 percent were not significantly different.[33]

In a second scenario, the same Israeli student health professionals were asked to examine Arabs in Israel in connection with a developing government plan to expel the Arabs from the country in a forced migration. The scenarios we created were also purposely given several descriptive turns and colorings reminiscent of Holocaust events. Thirty-four percent of the students saw themselves accepting the order to examine the Arabs in their roles as health professionals when ordered to do so by the government in this context. The health professionals were also asked to undertake examinations in order to determine who would be given exemptions and allowed to stay on in Israel either as a workforce or because they were too ill or infirm to tolerate the expulsion. Now the student-professionals were ostensibly helping people to be exempt, but of course in the process they were fulfilling the overall program of expulsion. Twenty-three percent of the students agreed to follow orders to conduct examinations when a partial forced migration was ordered; and 21 percent, essentially the same number, agreed to follow orders when a full-force migration was planned.[34]

In another study we approached people who came to view Claude Lanzmann's epic nine-hour film on the Holocaust, *Shoah*, at the Tel Aviv Museum, and were asked to give their opinion of the brutal murders of forty-nine unarmed civilian Arabs who had innocently violated a curfew. It was the first day of the Suez Campaign in 1956.[35] The unarmed Arabs were men, women, and children who were innocently returning from a day's work in the fields when an early curfew was set by the Israel Defense Forces on that very first day of the war. In this study we were quite obviously studying a group of subjects who cared very deeply about the wanton murders of the Jews in the Holocaust, and the question was would they care—however less or differently—about the evil murder of another people by our own Jewish people. Sixty-two percent opposed the massacre of the unarmed Arabs, but 38 percent either accepted or "explained" the necessity of the murders.[36]

In sum, the results in all of these studies showed that a regrettably large number of subjects identified themselves as ready to participate in doing harm to, or approving, or even facilitating the deaths of unarmed civilians. An inner psychocognitive decision whether or not to commit oneself to preserving and protecting human life is a major developmental task in the minds of all human beings.[37]

In another study, which in a sense serves also as a cross-cultural comparison because the study takes place in a different historical context and a different country, *after* American Lieutenant Calley was put on trial for the massacre of civilians at My Lai in Vietnam, Kelman and Hamilton asked a large number of Americans whether they would have followed orders and participated in the murders of the villagers had they been serving with the U.S. troops in My Lai. Sixty-seven percent of the respondents said, first of all, that most people will follow orders and do what Calley and his troops had done, and 51 percent said of *themselves* that they would have followed orders and killed.[38] These results are more severe than the previous Israeli studies and are more comparable to those of Milgram's original studies.

Anthropologist Alexander Laban Hinton examined the readiness of the Cambodian people to torture and murder one another in a land whose folk-characterization used to be that it was a "gentle land" inhabited by nonviolent Buddhists who were always courteous, friendly, and ready with a smile. The Khmer Rouge, wrote Hinton, were "agents of death" who, like reactionary forces anywhere, systematically reduced the cognitive dissonance between those forces in society supporting life and those supporting destruction of life—"the gentle ethic" and "the violent ethic." Thus Hinton described the dehumanizing process in Khmer Rouge ideology:

> People were instructed to be like oxen: "Comrade Ox never refused to work. Comrade Ox was obedient. Comrade Ox did not complain. Comrade Ox did not object when his family was killed." A soldier told one "new" person that it was better that her mother had died rather "than a cow . . . [cows] help us a lot and do not eat rice. They are much better than you pigs." Part of this extreme devaluation stemmed from the fact that "new" people were often regarded as "war slaves." Many times we heard soldiers shout, "Prisoners of war, you are pigs. We have suffered much. Now you are our prisoners and you must suffer." While sometimes tolerated, such "enemies" were expected to work hard and be obedient. If they committed offenses, their execution would be no loss.[39]

The descriptions are always the same. Thus I ask the reader about whom is the following description: "While I was lying on my back, I looked down the ravine and saw a lot of women coming up and crying. When I saw these women, girls and little boys coming up, I saw soldiers on both sides of the ravine shoot at them until they had killed every one of them." A report of a Holocaust survivor?

Intrinsically, yes, but in fact it is of another holocaust, told by a witness to the massacre by the United States Army of Sioux Indians at Wounded Knee. Historian David Stannard added, "By 1890 . . . 80 percent of the natives of California who had been alive when California became a state, had been wiped out by an official policy of genocide."[40]

In how many cultures does one find descriptions of how heads were cut off to the glee of the mob, how bodies were fed to dogs, how soldiers took pride and competed in their abilities to split a man in two, open his bowels, tear babes from their mother's breast, or cut out fetuses from their wombs?[41] In how many cultures do you not find glee at mass murder of whomever? A document in Arabic was found distributed to the terrorists who attacked the World Trade Center in New York and the Pentagon in Washington, D.C., on 9/11.

According to famed reporter Bob Woodward of the *Washington Post*, the document was "a cross between a chilling spiritual exhortation and an operational mission checklist" and "may turn out to provide the most vivid and penetrating glimpse into their mental states": "Purify your heart and clean it from all earthy matters," the terrorist killers are told. "The hours left you in your life are very few. From there you will begin to live the happy life, the infinite paradise. Be optimistic. The Prophet was always optimistic."

Regarding the night before, they are advised: "You must pray, you must fast. You must ask counsel from Allah, pray all night, continue to learn the Koran. Cleanse your hearts. . . . Later you will begin the live the happiest life in the eternal Garden of Eden. . . . The Garden of Eden has already been beautified for you and the beautiful angels who have dressed themselves in their most beautiful dresses are calling you."

When you enter the plane, pray: "Oh God, you who open all doors, please open all doors for me, open all venues for me, open all avenues for me. Remove from me the burden I carry."[42]

THE EVIDENCE IS OVERWHELMING ABOUT PROBABLY EVERY SOCIETY

The evidence is simply overwhelming:

- In every society, bar none, there are significant numbers and clusters of people who seek and/or are available to lead or to participate in the persecution, expulsion, or outright murder of whichever target groups.
- In every society, bar none, including democracies—though thank God infinitely less so in democracies where structures of checks and balances give a great deal of, though not absolute, protection against the potential for genocide than in totalitarian societies[43]—there are distinct possibilities of a takeover of power by would-be perpetrators of genocide.

- In every society, bar none, an even larger number of people and clusters of organizations, including vaunted groups of professionals such as in law and medicine, and including our mental health professionals,[44] are more than likely available to be silent bystanders, if not benefiting bystanders, if not active collaborators and accomplices, if not full-blown perpetrators, when the full force of the making of a holocaust swings into powerful momentum.
- In every society, bar none, everywhere we go in the world we find the same readiness to devalue, dehumanize, and persecute others to create ideologies of superiority and chosen status; justify enslavement, expulsion, and ethnic cleansing; and generate a euphemistic language justifying destruction of human life en masse.[45 46]
- Of course, at any given point in history, *some* societies are more inclined to foster prejudice, dehumanization, and violence than others. In creating a proposal for a Genocide Early Warning System, Chanan Rapaport and I developed a conceptualization of how in each society there are *societal forces supporting human life* versus *societal forces moving toward destruction of human life*, and that these can be analyzed and measured in every society as indicators of the probability or readiness of a society to engage in genocide and thus be used in an early warning system for genocide.[47]
- The overall conclusion is inescapable: We human beings and our societies are seriously inclined to evil[48]; projection—holding others at fault for our failings including our evil[49]; dehumanization—or "killing" the humanity of the other[50]; cruel violence; and endless mass murder and genocide of tens and hundreds of millions of human beings.[51]

Does all of this belong in a book on psychology and psychotherapy? It feels strange and certainly not something to which we are accustomed. Yet obviously we are talking about a topic we have been too scared and naive to handle well in our books on the basic psychology of humans. I believe we need very much to revise our basic textbooks on the nature of man.

A basic psychological theory of man needs to postulate that both doing harm to oneself and doing harm to others are "sick" or disturbed or abnormal, as described earlier in my proposal in the mainstream journal *Psychiatry*. I also suggested in this article that psychiatric disorders be divided into two groups: Disorders of Incompetence, Vulnerability, and Personal Weakness and Disorders of Pseudocompetence, Invulnerability, and Doing Harm to Others. I postulated that these are often interchangeable types of disturbances, that they can shift into one another, and that clinical diagnosis needs to rest on assessment of *both* dimensions of disturbing one's own functioning or doing harm to the function of others.[52]

Samuel Totten, William Parsons, and I created a compilation of many events of genocide in the twentieth century, or the "Century of Genocide,"[53] including genocide of the Hereros in southern Africa; the Armenian Genocide by the Turks; genocide by famine of the Ukrainians by the Soviets; genocide by mass deportation by the Soviets of whole nations to locales where the conditions could not support life; the Holocaust—of the Jews, also of Gypsies and other peoples and the destruction of disabled peoples; and more cases of genocide in Indonesia, East Timor, Bangladesh, Burundi, Cambodia, various indigenous peoples, Rwanda, and Bosnia-Herzegovina.

The above book was originally published *before* the threat of genocide in Kosovo mobilized the world community to respond through NATO to abort the beginning slaughter. Even after all that had been learned from the Holocaust, when Kosovo erupted in the last year of the twentieth century, one after the other of the news reporters and commentators were seemingly astonished at the discoveries of mass graves. Everybody knew they existed, but somehow it was still unbelievable when they were finally unearthed. One after another columnist wrote with horror how they could not believe or understand the cruel events that had taken place. Thus too, the journalists were aghast at scenes they saw of abject cruelty, such as Serbian youths taunting a seventy-year-old grandmother that they would burn her, as if the journalists representing our civilization did not remember anything from earlier events of genocide. A similar incredulity accompanied the discovery of mass graves from Saddam's era after Iraq was crushed by the United States. Since the beginning of the twenty-first century, how many more cases have there been! How many new cases will there be in the next thirty years, would you say?

Genocide is a cancer of human experience, and full-blown "cures" are not yet in sight. Our brains seem to be wired to believe that the human(istic) qualities of decency, caring for others, and integrity, which many of us indeed feel as givens of our human nature, make it unlikely to impossible for (most) human beings, certainly human-looking beings with good smiles and maybe frolicky moustaches, to commit mass murder. But this is not so. There are many individuals who are committed to life and will not aid and abet a genocide, but there are many—perhaps even most—who will be drawn into enabling or committing genocide. The inescapable conclusion is this: Human beings as a species and our societies are seriously inclined to genocide, but to this day, notwithstanding overwhelming evidence and information flooding our mass media, we still do not believe and accept this truth about our species. *Our civilization continues to be in denial—and the mental health professions join in the denial.*[54]

WHERE ARE WE IN FORMULATING A PSYCHOLOGY OF GENOCIDAL DESTRUCTIVENESS?

I am convinced that our discipline of psychology has not worked out a comprehensive make-sense theory of the ubiquitousness of violence at every level of human life. I do think that a great many pieces of the puzzle have been identified—in some cases, brilliantly, like Stanley Milgram and Philip Zimbardo, and I do think some individual scholars like Ernest Becker and Robert Jay Lifton have really gotten it that much violence is basically a kind of effort at immortality. But you will rarely open a basic psychology text that teaches how deeply violent man is and the core reasons. And you will rarely open a psychotherapy text that instructs therapists how to deal with violence. Simon Baron-Cohen has written:

> The standard explanation is that the Holocaust echoed in many cultures historically across the globe as an example of the "evil" that humans are capable of inflicting on one another. Evil is treated as incomprehensible . . . and indeed the concept of evil is routinely used as an explanation for awful behaviors.
>
> Why did the murderer kill an innocent child? Because he was evil. Why did the terrorist become a suicide bomber? Because she was evil. But when we hold up the concept of evil to examine it, it is not explanation at all. For a scientist this is, of course, wholly inadequate.[55]

According to a United Nations report in 2014, since 2000 *6 million* people have been murdered around the world in plain old interpersonal violence.[56]

At this point in the history of human thought and science, for the most part we have only a very beginning sense of the possibilities of translating psychological understanding of the sources of human destructiveness into meaningful new applications and tools for the *actual* prevention of genocidal killing. Nonetheless, based on our faith in the process of scholarship and science, one can expect that models of the sources of man's destructiveness in time will point the way to possible new structures, interventions, and "treatments" that can be expected to reduce human violence to some extent.

Note that many years ago social scientists seemed to offer nothing more than two highly simplistic, extreme, and *basically unusable* models for the explication of man's proclivity to destroy so readily. On the one hand, there was the seminal contribution of the Freudian psychoanalytic paradigm that stated that in man's true self, at the level of his basic nature in the underlying or unconscious realm of the very structure of the personality, there raged diabolical forces that sought to create death, essentially in fulfillment of a primordial drive toward reconciliation with completion of the inevitable process of death that awaits each living creature. *Freud was basically right, but so what?* What can be done with this understanding? There were some pious hopes that psychoanalysis would enable people, and especially national leaders, who would of course submit themselves to psychoanalysis (*joke*), to develop a usable insight into our human struggle with death and our potential for violence, but in truth, even in the earlier heydays of psychoanalysis, no one really believed it was realistic to expect civilization to be changed. The instinctual position on the face of it implied a near-absolute hopelessness about man, that for all our pseudo-civilization we would never be able to restrain the destructive forces that were ultimately in the essence of our beings. *And damn it, so far that's more true than not, and our world is seething.*

The alternative and seemingly progressive interpretation offered by social scientists focusing on the interactional processes between man and his environment was that destructiveness is the ultimate of aggressive responses that develop in response to frustration: Given economic privation, sociological pressures such as discrimination, ecological limitations such as overcrowding, and psychological deprivations and aggravations such as an absence of love or a lack of support for one's dignity and self-confidence, man responds with the machinery available to him in nature: to attack and fight. This interpretation became known as the *frustration-aggression hypothesis.* This *social interpretation* that men could live in peace given non-frustrating conditions and structures was welcomed as seemingly more hopeful, but nonetheless it also failed in the face of evidence of the reality that there is no possibility whatsoever that human beings and societies can be spared all serious frustrations. Moreover, the evidence is overwhelming that much destruction comes about also from people who are not deprived (e.g., the educated and family-rich backgrounds of some 9/11 killers). Violence in our world seems to grow plentifully both on "hunger" of all sorts and being "well fed"—that's the human way.

Still, either and both theories gave off a kind of charm and sense of hope that here is the best of human thought struggling to cope with man's age-old readiness for violence, and surely a day was coming when psychological theory would unlock the riddle. The years immediately following the gargantuan evil of World War II were an especially positive period of naive hope—surely man was on the march toward solutions. Today, the post–World War II naivete of hope has given way to an overwhelming clarity that mass violence against innocent, unarmed, noncombatant civilians, let alone soldiers in combat, simply abound in era after era of human civilization. For Americans the climax so far seems to have come in 2001 on 9/11. For all the information on the Holocaust, Stalin's Soviet gulags, Mao's starvation of the Chinese people, and Pol Pot's Cambodian killing fields, it seems that (to paraphrase Sinclair Lewis's classic book in the 1930s) many Americans still dreamt somehow that "it can't happen here" in America.[57] However, following the ingeniously destructive attacks by al-Qaeda on 9/11 on the Pentagon in Washington and especially on the World Trade Center in New York, with the surrealistic collapse of the Twin Towers symbolizing the possibility of a collapse of civilization itself, much of the innocence and state of denial is over for Americans and all others who held onto the naïve, wish-fulfilling belief that although there are cruel human beings, the problem is not so widespread as to be a threat *everywhere.*

What does develop authentically from the original or classical psychoanalytic paradigm is the truth that a dark side of potential for violence is present in *all* human beings. A powerful implication for the individual who seeks to be normal, stable, and able to cope effectively with life is that unless one makes contact with and maintains an inner dialogue with the dark side of one's nature, there is a greater danger of this side of one's humanness erupting in terrifying and even unintentional catastrophic violence.

This understanding is crucial on the larger level of group and society in the endless procession in history of evil exercises of power over countless groups of human beings, witch hunts, enslavement, persecution, torture, and genocide. Democratic society and government must make provisions for defending the pursuit of life in freedom against the many variations of tyranny, not only from without, in the person of well-marked enemies, but also from within one's own society, when people and groups seek to win power through a clever use of the democratic process to control and then destroy the structure of the democracy.

Another not entirely convincing theory "in nature" is that man is perhaps an aberrant species. Ethologist Konrad Lorenz argued that virtually all species in the animal world restricted their killings and destroying to *extraspecific aggression* (that is, wars against other species) and almost universally refrained from *intraspecific aggression* (that is, destructive wars against their own species) except in cases of territorial overcrowding, but that man as a species represents an aberrant mutation in nature.[58] What Lorenz did not take into account was the fact that humans utilize their powerful capacities to conceptualize and symbolize in order to achieve a redefinition of a victim species as not being of their own kind. The target people are characteristically the objects of long-term processes of *dehumanization*—though sometimes the "othering" of the victims is completed amazingly rapidly. By the time the policy of destruction is set in motion, perceptions of the victim people are polarized to a point where the "kikes" or "gooks" or "vermin" are essentially not human. The victims are defined as subhuman, *as if not of our species*, therefore not deserving of the protections that presumably are owed to people of our own kind. When the dehumanization is cast in a political language of the invincibility of a given religion (e.g., the Crusades by Christians or a jihad by Moslems), the despised designated victims are defined as nonbelievers, antigod, heathen, and infidel.

When the dehumanization is accompanied further by demonization or attributing to the very same people who are being dehumanized a serious and even total potential for destroying us, the gates of hell are opened.

- They are not human.
- They are out to destroy us.
- We must destroy them first.

This is the most important conclusion that Chanan Rappaport and I reached in our studies that were devoted to building the Genocide Early Warning System (GEWS).[59]

There is a paradoxically hopeful implication to this understanding that because the killing, even if instinctual, is made possible by certain kinds of symbolization, there is therefore still reason to hope that human society can find ways to counter and inhibit such dehumanizing concepts and/or projections or attributions of evil onto others. For example, if the leaders of many of the world's religions would join forces to announce convincingly that they opposed derogation or discrimination against any other people, over time they could contribute to a major cultural shift. Certainly this would be a counterforce to the preaching in so many houses of religion that honor, inspire, and authorize killing the accursed other.[60]

The psychology of dehumanization seems closely linked to two natural mechanisms for the perception of danger. The first is the seemingly endless need (a need that is so strong that often the "differences" are constructed from trivialities) to differentiate ourselves as a group from other groups. The second is a need to perceive any number of other groups as dangerous and enemies. In many cases, of course, there are real differences. Human beings differentiate themselves from others because they are strangers, look different, speak a different language, act differently, live on the north or south of the border, engage in a different way of being in the world, pray to different gods and icons, and so on. We are so afraid of differences, often blindly so, that we tend to hate those who are different from us, and assign them dehumanized identities.

There are, of course, real threats of being attacked by others. There is realistic reason for fear and hatred in that we know for a fact that many people are living out "programs" to hunt, kill, and destroy others. Moreover, it is not easy to be objective in assessing the dangerousness of others, and people generally exaggerate considerably their judgment that the other is out to attack them and thereby trigger their basic instinct for self-defense prematurely.[61] Perhaps this is so in evolution because so much is at stake: A wrong perception can mean being caught totally unprepared. On the other hand, the very fact that one people perceives the other as intending to destroy it sets off interactions with the other people that increase the likelihood of destructive acts. Each people's perceptions feed the other, and these result in processes of escalation and self-fulfilling prophecies that move the probabilities of violence toward ever-increasing certainty. These perceptions of danger then fuse with the blind processes of dehumanization of others. The spinning vortex of positioning oneself as superior to the stranger and then protecting oneself from the dangers of these strangers who are perceived as serious dangers, and in the reality of nature often *are* potentially real threats of our destruction, carries people through the ages blindly in ever-repeated historical dramas of mistrust, war, and genocide. Tragically, civilization has not yet been able to put a stop to these processes.

One must also acknowledge that going beyond an animal-legacy competition for survival in human life there are any number of people in our species, as we have seen, who clearly delight in destroying other people with unrestrained passion. Ambitiousness, self-serving, primitive competitiveness over the resources of life, untroubled acceptance of a right to execute those who stand in one's way or who arouse a sense of threat, as well as insatiable exercises of power over others are sources in our human nature of human destruction. In fact, there is now considerable evidence that a failure to accept to some degree these natural forces of aggression and power and self-serving in all of us in itself can trigger an even greater readiness to be cruel and uncontrollably destructive. Rubinoff wrote of the "Devil's deception" and "evil as a promise of good." He concluded: "It is only through the imaginative reliving of temptation [to express evil] that we develop the strength of character to resist it when it appears like the devil disguised as reason—for the Devil, if you remember, is the master of disguise."[62]

The proper and desirable psychology of these various dark and potentially destructive sides of our normal human personality seems to be, first of all, an acceptance of our natural human drives to ambition, competition, power, aggression, and even some measure of destructiveness. But then there must follow restraint of the excesses of these qualities, an outlawing both by oneself and by society of doing actual harm to human life, and a streaming of the vital energies that are obviously inherent in these characteristics to other choices and commitments to protect, build, and enhance the safety and quality of our own lives and others' lives.

The reality is that for sensitive, thinking individuals this pattern of insight and acceptance of responsibility can work very well, but we are still far from solutions for larger populations and for runaway collective processes. So we not only have the many people in this world who do not commit themselves to nonviolence, but we also have a majority of human institutions—including nations and religious and political-sociological movements—that have not made commitments to peace. *Millions of people and many societies have not made commitments to protecting and enhancing life.*

INNOCENT AND "BANAL" CAUSES OF VIOLENCE

A remarkable thesis that has entered into serious candidacy as a further explicatory tool for understanding the sources of much human destruction is that there are a variety of other characteristics of human nature that *innocently* lead human beings into more and more extreme positions without their having *intended* at all to engage in the violent behaviors that are a consequence of that position.[63] Philosopher of science Anatol Rapoport proposed, "The "psychology" of the system may be entirely independent of the psychology of its human components. If this conclusion is correct, we need not search the human psyche for attributes that explain the murderous tendencies of certain forms of human organizations."[64]

We know how everywhere in the world bureaucratic structures systematically shape people to fit into the existing scheme of things, and about people's needs to *order* things about them, even to turn human beings into *objects* to be ordered at any cost. Bureaucratic-defined-and-driven behaviors are the major emphasis in what Hannah Arendt brilliantly called the "banality of evil,"[65] which, among others, the award-winning film *One Flew Over the Cuckoo's Nest* portrayed so vividly in the evils rampant in a psychiatric bureaucracy.[66] It is a bureaucratization of life, so that people are the *things* that bureaucracy orders, and the conformists do the bidding of the bureaucracy.

Banal causes of aggression also include a wide variety of everyday psychological processes, which in their own right are not directed toward creating aggression, but which lead human beings into being aggressive as they blindly fulfill the imperatives of these processes. Among the everyday banal processes that underlie murderous aggression are conformity to what others do, and the stupidity of doing what one is told to do especially if mandated by an authority. People follow the immoral instructions of authorities such as in the Milgram experiments in which a professor tells experimental subjects to administer potentially lethal electric shocks to other subjects who have done nothing more than give the wrong answer to a routine learning experiment; most people are ready to abandon and blend themselves into whatever mass movement is the popular form of belief in their era; human beings can be duped easily into saying that the shorter of two lines is longer (the famous Asch experiments); they can be hypnotized into giving their approval to quacks and strong men with charismatic powers and go off on murderous safaris against whomever the leader designates (as in the bizarre cases of the Manson group and the murder-suicide deaths of several hundred in Jonestown). In short, most people follow orders and adopt the prevailing norms of their immediate society no matter how totalitarian and destructive it is. Given these qualities, we understand even more fully the considerable significance of leaders, and especially powerful leaders of a totalitarian government. The powers assigned to the leader not only are inherent in the structures of government and military and secret-police powers, but derive from the qualities in people and societies of conformity, obedience, suggestibility, and surrender of self to collective experiences.[67]

There is, moreover, the tremendous impact of the group on individuals. It has long been known that the experience of being part of a crowd or group can loosen many inhibitions in individuals by creating a state of excitation and exultation. We now know a great deal about the contagion of violence and genocide in groups and collectives, and how the forces of madness can inflame a group and society and seemingly demand their release in great collective orgies. Holocaust survivor and recounter Elie Wiesel has depicted the buildup of a collective program in his allegorical book, *The Oath*, the story of a twentieth-century blood-libel pogrom in a small town.[68] The group also creates a model for copying the behaviors of the others and "doing what everyone else is doing." It takes a rare strength of individuality and principle to stand up to and differentiate oneself from the approved or consensual group process.

Another banal process that supports the possibilities of leaders, governments, and societal momentum toward mass destruction is the fact that most people will stand by inactively in many situations where their neighbors, let alone a stranger group that has been the object of a broad propaganda of dehumanization, are subject to torture, forced migration, incarceration in concentration camps, or execution. Not only is there a perhaps understandable practical decision not to endanger oneself, but a considerable body of social research of the "bystander phenomenon" has shown that even when there are no direct costs or risk, many people tend to slough off responsibility for the victim to others.[69] To be a bystander is to walk past a victim who needs help as if he were not there; it is also to stand and gape and perhaps celebrate the victim's plight; it is also to take advantage of the victim's misfortune, such as to take his job or possessions when he loses them. In the context of governmental persecution of victims, to be a bystander is also to avoid helping the announced enemies of one's government in the face of a government's awesome power and the likelihood of retribution against those who would help the victims. It takes a rare courage of individuality and integrity to oppose one's government, let alone a totalitarian government, to help a potential victim.

In a magical scene, Elie Wiesel picks up the horror of a moment of connection between a bystander and a victim on the way to being destroyed. In a never-to-be-forgotten passage in *The Town Beyond the Wall*, Wiesel describes how a bystander standing discreetly behind the curtain in his upstairs apartment sees the Jews below being led off to the concentration camp, and how one victim's eye as if photographs the bystander's face in a moment of poignant knowledge of one another. Wiesel deftly portrays the truth about how a bystander can choose to play his role as the seemingly unknowing one after he has, in fact, seen the hell taking place.

> Not even anger or interest. Impassive, cold, impersonal. The face was indifferent to the spectacle. What? Men are going to die? That's not my fault is it now? He, standing behind the curtains, watched. The police beat women and children, he did not stir. It was no concern of his. He was neither victim nor executioner; a spectator, that's what he was. He wanted to live in peace and quiet.[70]

Not to be forgotten are various structural laws of dynamics of behavior, such as the tendency of people to test going "all the way" with their energy, and the needs for power and intoxication with power to which people succumb so easily. There are primordial pulls to which many people respond atavistically: to let one's power out to its maximum point; to be drawn to seek the complete wholeness or maximum of a process or structure of power; to taste the "thrills" of risk, excitement, and horror; and also as if to defy life and the gods by exploding the hugest explosions possible no matter what the cost to life.

We know furthermore how the structuring of situations and institutions can bring out the power-crazed need of otherwise sane and sincere human beings by entrusting them with too much power over one another. Stanford University social psychologist Philip Zimbardo effectively demonstrated this process in his famous jail simulation experiment in which some students assumed the roles of jailers and others the roles of prisoners. Within a few days the experiment had to be halted because the student jailers had taken to their roles with an unexpected vengeance and cruelty.[71] Moreover, there are some—all too many—individuals who devote themselves assiduously to the cultivation of power and brutal exercise of their power over others.[72]

Once having turned to torturing and taking the lives of other human beings, the executing human beings or organizations are driven by an equally banal series of laws of human nature such as perverse, intoxicating pleasure with their triumphant power in their status as dispensers of life and death; self-identification with their own behavior; and an inherent rigidity against being able to be self-critical and correct the actions with which they have become identified. Granted, even the fervor and passion that many of the executioners now display as they stay committed to their evil tasks of destroying others (such as the examples of the guillotining French Revolution becoming devoted to the pageantry of its executions, and how the Nazi death machinery continued resolutely even after Hitler's fall was ensured and the end of the war was in sight), the key to the continuing activity of some perpetrators still may not be so much their motivation and passion to destroy, as it is that they are carried along blindly by the lawfulness of the chains or sequences of human behavior. Incredible as it sounds, in a sense, the continuation of the killing becomes beyond their control. But this in no way means they should be seen as less responsible for their actions. They see with their own eyes that they are torturing and killing.

The banality of natural psychological processes explains much of how people and societies delude themselves into not being aware that they are killing fellow human beings. It offers some explanation of much (though not all) of man's disgusting record of murder on a basis other than an inherent availability to cruelty, sadism, or even an indifferent competitiveness that simply wipes out creatures that stand in one's way in the competition for life and its resources. A great deal of even the most serious violence may not be intended motivationally to destroy, but represents the culmination of blind, automatic processes and chains of behavior that, up until now in human evolution, human beings did not know or care to know how to control despite their consequences in the deaths of so many other people. Nonetheless, again I emphasize unambiguously that one has to remember that it is human beings who are allowing and agreeing to let these dynamics operate on them and must be held responsible for their behaviors.[73]

SACRIFICING OTHERS TO ACHIEVE ONE'S OWN IMMORTALITY: THE INNER EXPERIENTIAL GATEWAY TO MASS MURDERING

Notwithstanding all of the above, there remain powerful questions as to how human beings can bear to experience being mass killers. There must be emotional rewards to destroying many other people, and it should be the task of psychiatry and psychology to identify the satisfactions engendered by being genocidal terrorists and killers. Probing the inner psychology of genocidal killing more deeply leads to an important dimension of psychological thought—that a major key to the readiness to destroy human life may be human beings' bitter fears and flight from their own mortality. The conclusion is an appealing one intellectually because it attaches so logically to the phenomenology of the actual behavior we are trying to understand psychiatrically, namely, that the perpetrator *is taking away the lives of his victims for his own use or benefit in order to spare his own life.*

Psychiatrist Robert Jay Lifton, who has blazed a brilliant trail of exploration that began with studies of the survivors of Hiroshima[74] and continued with studies of Vietnam veterans[75] and physicians in the Nazi concentration camps,[76] and with Eric Markusen of the "genocidal mentality,"[77] has conceptualized a series of paradigms or models through which people seek to overcome mortality and achieve the illusion of immortality.[78]

A closely related conceptualization is that a clinging to a sense of omnipotence underlies human cruelty. Writing in a work devoted to Kleinian psychoanalytic theory, Brenman proposes that the "worship of omnipotence, which is felt to be superior to human love and forgiveness," serves as "a defence against depression," and together with a "sanctification of grievance and revenge" is channeled through "a singular narrow-mindedness of purpose . . . [into] squeezing out humanity and preventing human understanding from modifying the cruelty."[79]

In my writings, I have extended the themes of seeking immortality and omnipotence to a concept of *sacrificing the other*: The essence of sacrificing is that the genocider assigns other people the fate of death that he fears for himself. I have proposed that "[t]he guiding motif of the genocider is a proclamation to his victims: '*Better you should die than I!*'"[80] Just as in the many-centuried history of sacrifices, including infants, by sacrificing the other the killer seeks to be spared that outcome for himself. Murdering others, certainly repeated mass murders, might be thought of as a renewal of the ancient archetype of sacrifice as an effort to escape one's own death. A target people who have been dehumanized as not really of our species, and at the same time who are perceived as overwhelmingly dangerous to the continuation of our species, is sacrificed so that we may live on. Philosopher Ernest Becker wrote, "No one explained this dynamic more elegantly than [psychoanalyst Otto] Rank. 'The death fear of the ego is lessened by the killing, the sacrifice of the other through the death of the other one buys oneself free from the penalty of dying, of being killed.'"[81]

I propose additionally that the fear may be not only of actual death, but also of possible inner lifelessness and emptiness, which may drive a person to project onto the other that the other poses a threat to one's life and therefore must be destroyed first; let alone that becoming a persecutor in its own right is, typically, a compelling commitment and experience that makes one feel more alive.[82] All of these processes take place not only in individuals as such, but also in the unfolding experiences of individuals within family groups where a great deal of projection, scapegoating, and emotional destruction of one another takes place; in group life where people lose themselves in what was characterized by the sociologist Le Bon as the stupidity of crowd and mass behavior[83]; and especially in never-ending prejudices and persecutions between all conceivable ethnic/racial/religious/political identities.

THE ULTIMATE CHOICES OF OUR HUMAN IDENTITY: TO PRESERVE OR DESTROY

Whatever the dynamic forces to which we are responding, there come points of truth in our lives in which each of us as human beings must decide in actuality what to do and what not to do. The ultimate crucial level for determining human behavior is defined by the *choices* of goals that people make and the means they will use to reach their goals. It is very important for psychiatry to address scientifically the considerable extent to which people are unconsciously drawn to doing all manner of harmful things that they would oppose in calmer moments of conscious choice (e.g., joining the majority in following illegal and inhuman orders of one's military commanders).

It is no less important for us also to achieve a comprehensive psychology of the conscious choices people ultimately make. Even some people who are predisposed by their inner dynamics toward committing genocide may be ones who conscientiously resist orders to kill because of a genuine religious or other moral commitment not to slaughter civilians. Moreover, the knowledge of how to correlate choices of means and ends with one another further defines the ways in which people use their energies for or against life. A morally wrong belief that the ends justify the means leads over and over again in history to situations where, in the declared pursuit of life, liberty, justice, or religious values, human beings kill—in the name of their values and gods—anyone and everyone who stands in their way. Note also the other side of the coin, that an overemphasis on spiritual values in one's choices of the means one uses in life may lead decent people to be unnecessarily helpless in the face of the brutality of those who are committed to evil and are not swayed by considerations of decency.

The choices of goals people make are both personal and within contexts of collective processes. Many people in our various societies are exposed to powerful institutional processes that adopt violence and genocide as their explicit purposes—as this book is being written, ISIS is the latest prominent member of this rotten club. Once persons succumb to such indoctrination, it no longer matters what would have been the outcome of their own inner personal psychology of use of their aggression-energy; they are corrupted by joining the ideologies and machineries of destruction.

Genocide brings to the fore the fullest crystallization of our human choices as to what kind of persons we will be. In the face of a potential genocide to another people, each of us faces the choice whether or not to agree to be a perpetrator (or persecutor), accomplice, or bystander, or to do everything possible to oppose the genocide in whatever ways might be available to us, such as to be a rescuer or to join in an underground resistance.

IDENTIFICATION WITH VICTIMS OF GENOCIDE

When a possible genocide looms over one's own people, the range of choices can be very limited by the brutal realities of history and the overwhelming power of the genocidal agent. But even here there are times when we have some degree of choice as to whether or not and to what degree we will make ourselves available, as individuals and collectives, to be victims, including times when we can fight back in resistance to the genocidal power.

After the genocide has befallen one's people, and before the next genocide to we-know-not-which people(s), we also have basic choices to make as to how to incorporate our relationship to a genocide in our collective memory and identity. For many of us, certainly those of us who are fellow ethnics of a victim people, our natural identification with the victims seems totally automatic. Thus, how can one not weep or rave when learning of the telegraphed instructions of the arch administrator of the Armenian Genocide, Turkish Minister of the Interior Talaat: "This is not a moment to waste time in feeding ["the children of a certain people"]. Send them back (i.e., to the desert), and advise us when this has been done."[84]

Yet, even in our seemingly automatic identification with the victims, we also are making choices of how we construct our identification. There are several possibilities as to who we become in our memorial: identification and protest—or refusals to remember. Here are a number of the many possibilities of reactions to victims of genocide:

1. We can be broken by our identification and succumb to irrevocable traumatic damage.
2. We can be damaged in our own moral and spiritual self so that we need to strike out to hurt others in retaliation for our pain and outrage—
   a. on a personal level, such as in family abuse (e.g., sad cases of survivors who are abusive to their children);
   b. on a collective level, such as jingoists who are blindly committed to revenge against perpetrator people or to other peoples in militant nationalism or terrorism. Thus, "Kill all the Arabs" is a passionate slogan that appears in Israel periodically, especially after a terrorist incident such as the explosion of a bus in which innocent people of all ages are killed. It is as if an attempt to remedy the vulnerability of being victims, but in truth it is a contribution to perpetuating a cycle of violence.
3. We can be truly reverent and empathic in our identification with the victims of a genocide. We can commit ourselves to sincere memorials of the victims and contributions to the welfare of survivors and their families, and we can help victims of other genocides or participate in anti-genocide activities.
4. "Exclusivist victims": We can take a position that *our genocide is the only one*, no other genocide matters—certainly our genocide is the "most genocidal event" there has ever been. Thus, there is a prominent Jewish scholar who has created a definition of genocide that so fits the specific aspects of the Holocaust it in effect rules out the possibility of any other genocide being defined as genocide, which in the judgment of many of us is not only bad scholarship but conveys an unwarranted superiority of the Jewish people and condescension and humiliation of others.[85]
5. We can extend our identification to be with *all* victims. Here one combines caring about the victims of one's own people with caring for the victims of all other peoples, moreover not only the victims of the past, but also the victims of present-day genocides, and also in anticipation of the victims who are to be in future genocides.
6. We can reach not only a reverent but also an activist commitment to a *pro-life* position for *all* human beings. This is the fuller extension of a sincere identification with victims, which moves us forward from reverent memorials of past

events to an active commitment to the sacredness of the lives of all human beings, and includes committing meaningful aspects of our own lives and resources to the protection of the inherent right to life of all peoples.

7. Some readers may note that the above options are laid out in a "Kohlberg-type scale" of ethical development. Kohlberg gave us such a scale for understanding people's resolutions not to commit murder by identifying the level of self-protection versus more genuine caring for life.[86]

IDENTIFICATION WITH THE PERPETRATORS (PERSECUTORS)

The awesome power and triumphant bestiality of the perpetrators from time immemorial cannot be put aside as an irrelevant aspect of human experience, and in this respect, too, each human being needs to choose how they will incorporate this aspect of humanness into their identity.

I have come to the sad conclusion that killers for the most part do not regret what they have done. Years ago I attempted a survey of physicians in Europe to see what happened to post-Holocaust killers at the time of their late-life illnesses, and we were able to find very, very few instances of natural "confessions" and bouts of "conscience" even at these potential confessional moments in a person's life. This survey of several hundreds of European physicians was attempted in 1981 in the course of our extensive mailings around the world to announce the forthcoming First International Conference on the Holocaust and Genocide, which took place in Tel Aviv in June 1982.[87] Dan Bar-On studied the children of persecutors in the Holocaust, and not only found that the majority (but not all) of them are unable to achieve true regret for the deeds of their parents, but through them also assembled important evidence of the almost total failure of the parents themselves ever to have shown any kind of regret for what they did.[88] That killers protect themselves to avoid legal difficulties is understood. Psychologically we also understand that in order to avoid driving themselves crazy, killers need to protect themselves from the powerful "cognitive dissonance" that would result were they to acknowledge what they had done. The result could be a split in their experience of themselves, if they believe themselves to be "good people." I would add to this a concept of "spiritual dissonance" as well, that the unbearable experience can be one of heartfelt shame and guilt in response to the unbelievable tragedy caused to others, and not many people are prepared to accept such a spiritual experience.

I have also come to a worse conclusion that the crime of killing is for many, for long periods of time, actually deeply satisfying. There are apparently many genociders who survive, are proud, feel good, and thrive. In an interview with a Russian who served as an executioner in Stalin's camps, he described his work as follows:

> Nothing special, 24 hour a day duty, day after day. In the morning you went with a vehicle to the station, awaited the train, received the victims, transported them, distributed

> them to their cells . . . Regular work. . . . Early in the morning we went to the guard room, took arms, received a glass of vodka, took the lists and went through the cells, took the people out and put them on the trucks.[89]
>
> Interviewer: Did you sleep well? After all you killed people? Did it bother you?
>
> Answer: No, I can't say that it bothered me. I didn't think about it very much. Sleep? I slept well. During the day it was possible to go out for trips in the area. It was a beautiful area. Of course, it was boring without women.

Similarly, an Israeli commando killer, who was charged with special missions for executing Arabs in their villages who had been identified as terrorists, reported in an interview[90]:

> I remember I felt very good. I was actually elated. I went up to the roof of our base with the other guys and we knocked off some beers. In the debriefing I earned a lot of praises . . . As time passed I felt better and better. I fell in love with the idea. I felt like a king. Strong. The best. This was the phase in which a covert competition began in our unit of "who kills more." Then there also began the period of people idolizing me, especially the younger soldiers.

In this particular case, after discharge this commando was upset and emotionally unstable, just as we saw in many Vietnam veterans in the United States, and this too is an important aspect of the fate of some persecutors, but at the moment I want to emphasize how for a long time it was good for him to be a killer.

THE ISSUE FOR EVERY ONE OF US IS TO RESPECT LIFE, INCLUDING INSIDE OUR OWN MINDS TO OURSELVES

There is a frightening common denominator shared by the rotten perpetrators of destruction in this world, their sidekick collaborators who we know as accomplices, their more reticent and ostensibly innocent bystanders, and, however surprisingly, also those victims—individuals and collective groups—who don't do enough of what they realistically might have been able to do to prevent or reduce the probability of their being victims (but definitely are in no way responsible for the horrible actions of the perpetrators, and certainly not for all the aspects of being victims over which one has absolutely little if any control). *What perpetrators, accomplices, bystanders, and the too-available victims have in common is a lack of respect or dedication to life.*

In the case of the perpetrators and their associate henchmen, there is obviously an active disrespect for life and a readiness to destroy lives or to let them be destroyed by others. In the case of victims who might have fought back, there is a tragic failure to act sufficiently vigorously to defend life against the risks of destruction.[91] Although it has become politically incorrect to say anything critical about victims, I also want to look at them truthfully, though always respectfully and sensitively, even as again I want to make it absolutely clear that I only hold those who themselves do and allow the destruction responsible for their evil, and not the victims.

The role designations of perpetrator, accomplice, bystander, and victim become more strained and metaphoric when we move this model to how an individual functions *within* their own mind *toward their own self*, and yet there is little question that inside of our minds, too, there are constructions of these inner roles in our psychology, and unconsciously they do play influential roles in our life. The perpetrator is a part of us that is ready to do us serious harm; the accomplice or bystander are parts of our mind that agree to another part of ourselves doing us harm; and the victim is a part of our mind that elects or agrees to our role of being the loser or sufferer.

We know one of the greatest triumphs of human emotional development is that we develop a *self-observing ego* through which each of us in effect is constantly monitoring our own self. The self-observing ego has a considerable strength in our personality structure for enabling us to make adjustments, corrections, and also major changes in our lifestyles when we see that we are off the track. On a moral level, the self-observing ego can be called a conscience, and although for a long time the mental health field treated all conscience as an unduly oppressive force, it has become clear to many psychotherapists that conscience is, in fact, a very healthy and desirable function so long as it is not allowed to become extreme and punitive. Thus, in relation to matters of health, the self-observing ego is our capacity to monitor what is happening in our bodies and the ways we are treating ourselves (it is amazing how often we know we are getting sick long before our doctors diagnose us); and it includes our ability to receive feedback from others, including from our health practitioners, so that we can take the steps that are possible and necessary to protect and restore our health. There is, after all, so much we can do. We can correct our teeth and gum maintenance, reduce our cholesterol, gain control over our runaway blood pressure, rest regularly, adopt regimens of exercise, and so much more. Insofar as we do not exercise the various corrective options that are available to us, we become accomplices within our own selves to those behaviors that in fact will harm us and even do us in.

Using the not-trivial issue of smoking as an example, I would suggest the following construction of a series of metaphors for seeing an individual's own role in their own possible health or self-destruction:

- If smoking is now without doubt known to be a killer that leads to so many grave (pun intended) diseases, the act of smoking justifiably qualifies a person as a perpetrator toward one's own self, along with being a victim, of course.
- Active denial or belittling of the information that is easily available about smoking in today's society ("I know plenty of people who smoke and don't get sick") qualifies a person as being an accomplice to one's own destruction.
- To remain indifferent to the information on the subject of smoking defines a person as a bystander to one's own self-destruction.

Similar metaphors can be applied to a wide variety of behaviors in respect of one's management of aspects of one's health, interpersonal relationships, and emotions and attitudes. Fascist mindsets lock into a given way of operating, whatever its rewards (i.e., the thrills of driving too fast, or being the "top dog" or person in charge in a social system or business situation, or dominating and possessing one's lover). The Fascist Mind does not let go despite feedback information and signals that suggest that the chosen way of operating can lead to disaster. On the other hand, a more democratic mindset means observing and taking in information and modifying one's relationships, emotions, and behaviors rationally according to the feedback information that comes back to us. Thus, if one finds oneself driven to all-consuming ambitiousness and overwhelmingly tiring efforts to achieve fame and competitive success, and the feedback is that the strain will wear us out and maybe even bring on an illness like heart disease, a Fascist Mind does not stop, and a Democratic Mind does.

GENOCIDE CHALLENGES US ALL TO LEARN TO CARE ABOUT ALL HUMANS

My perhaps sad but also inspiring conclusion is that our knowledge of the choices we make throughout our lives—whether to protect or harm life—challenge us all as human beings who are participating in the present and future of human evolution, and not only those of us who are members of ethnic groups that have memories of the past genocides of our peoples. We need to look for new ways to achieve for ourselves, and to teach and promote in others, the ability to refuse to participate in killing acts, so that we can develop a new culture-wide resistance to the very concept of killing.

The battle against becoming a killer is a developmental ethical and spiritual challenge that individuals and collective groups must undertake if human life is to be protected. It is not a given. It requires the power and authority of the State to threaten and follow through with punishment of perpetrators. It benefits from the injunctions and teachings of religion of the precept *Thou Shalt Not Kill*. But the most powerful deterrent to violence is an inner spiritual decision not to harm others.[92]

In the course of the Israel War of Independence, the beloved poet and columnist, Natan Alterman, published a poem in the newspaper *Davar*, about a young lad:

> He cut through the captured city in a jeep
> A stalwart young lad . . . a lion of a youth!
> And in the desert street
> An old man and a woman
> Pressed against the wall in fear.
> And the lad grinned with his milk teeth:
> I'll try the machine gun . . . and he tried!
> The old man barely caught his face in his hands . . .
> And his blood splattered over the wall.[93]

Alterman went on in the poem to say explicitly that one should never attempt to call such events "minor details in a larger heroic chapter," and that the Jewish people in Israel need to recognize that we (Jews/Israelis) were also "pushed under the guise of 'necessity' and 'revenge' into the arena of perpetrating crimes against humanity." David Ben Gurion, the first prime minister of Israel, was so deeply moved by Alterman's powerful call to moral purpose that he wrote to congratulate him for being "a pure and true voice for human conscience—if this conscience does not beat in our hearts these days, we will not be deserving of greatness," and then ordered a mass printing of Alterman's poem as a pamphlet published by the Ministry of Defense and distributed to every Israeli soldier.[94]

In recent years, after one of the suicide killings in Israel by an Arab, another Israeli Arab wrote a column in *Haaretz* in which he decried the ugly criminal killings[95]:

> The criminal suicide killings in the heart of Jerusalem and Tel Aviv are deserving of the fullest condemnation of every Arab who is concerned with the image of his people in human society. Palestinian Arab people, the majority of whom have chosen the path of peace, will not forgive the small and insane fundamentalist groups who turn a small number of their children into live bombs and send them to blow up under the illusion that in this way they will go to Heaven . . . I do not protest and condemn these attacks and the transformation of a human being into a live bomb in order to appear as a good Arab in the eyes of the Israeli society. I do this for my own Palestinian Arab people and for my own humanity.

It takes a rare courage of individualism and integrity to oppose totalitarianism and to help a potential victim, especially when this puts one at risk. In the Holocaust, Pastor Martin Niemoeller—who was to die in a Nazi concentration camp (Sachsenhausen near Berlin)—reminded us powerfully of how we must all speak out for every one of us, for otherwise there is no one left to speak out for us when the time comes that *we* are the victims.[96]

The single most urgent task facing us as a civilization is to cultivate new levels of abhorrence, resistance, and antibodies to the joys of killing other people. The joys of killing and harming are built into our human nature as a possibility, but they are only one possibility, while another possibility in nature is to be guardians and celebrants of all human lives.

Anthropologist Alexander Hinton suggested (like Rappaport and myself in our Genocide Early Warning System[97]) that genocide in the making can be recognized by monitoring a society's and a state's cultural patterns that foster violence, promote or enjoin violence against devalued groups through ideology, and do or do not produce "a euphemistic discourse of destruction." Hinton writes, "Once genocidal violence is taking place, we can attempt to interfere with or counteract the individual-level response that converts a person into an agent of death."[98]

I often wonder if our various professions around the world, which by definition are to serve peoples' better living, have not been notably dishonorable and cowardly in the face of the authorities and societal systems that impose on people demands for blind obedience and conformity. I very much include our mental health professions in my question. Have we as individual professionals and in our professional societies been sufficient models of creative anxiety and courage in fighting tyranny—for example, opposing more bravely the persecutory witch hunts in the period of McCarthyism in the United States; standing up against identifiable cults, and even more so against powerful established religious groups that impose mass conformity rituals and behaviors on adherents, such as those that deny people elementary rights to medical care or education, or deny sectors of people such as women the right to vote or to education; or battling the acquiescence of authorities to pressures by fundamentalist groups or political majorities to censor certain historical information (e.g., in the curricula of Israeli schools where several massacres of Arabs by Jews in the course of Israeli history and the genocide of the Armenians are excluded from the curricula of most schools)? However well or poorly, psychiatry addresses the *victims* of human dysfunctions,[99] as it avoids the frontier of addressing the choices people make whether to be victimizers (perpetrators or persecutors) of others.

As the twenty-first century develops, dare we dream that psychotherapists can contribute to the evolutionary emergence of a new "ordinary man" who does not harm and kill his fellow man at the drop of an ordinary fight over one's farmlands, personal insults, nationalistic threats, bad collective historical memories, or what have you of human experiences and conflicts that have driven too many of the best and the finest of people into "ordinary violences?"

If you like humor of the absurd, try this one: Yuval Harari writes that if we don't hurry up to face the real truth of what our species is, we may miss the opportunity altogether before an entirely new species come in and takes our world. Harari is decidedly pessimistic in his diagnosis of our current human situation.[100]

Whether we like it or not, we have to acknowledge that a proclivity for cruelty and tyranny is endemic and springs naturally in our species. We have to see cruelty and destructiveness as aspects of our basic humanness and revise the fairy tale presentations of "normality" and goodness in our basic psychology texts. They are lies. True, they speak to other intrinsic instinctual sides of our humanness that further life, but they are only parts of the true picture of Mind.

Today, many Americans are waking up to the truth. 9/11 on American soil "helped" a lot, and the brutal displays of cruel murder by the Islamic State are elevating Americans' awareness of evil. But the myth of human goodness nonetheless holds on stubbornly, let alone that even today so many Americans make themselves ignorant of events outside their local lives.

CONCLUSION

If our mental health professions do not address the victimization/doing of evil to others, will not the field of mental health be revealed as trivial? For we will have failed to contribute to what appears to be the grandest challenge of evolution: to be more human.

> The only thing necessary for the triumph of evil is for good men to do nothing.[10]
>
> —*Edmund Burke*

> Let not any one pacify his conscience by the delusion that he can do no harm if he takes no part, and forms no opinion. Bad men need nothing more to compass their ends, than that good men should look on and do nothing.[102]
>
> —*John Stuart Mill*

> He drew from under the table a sheet of strangely scented yellow-Chinese paper, the brushes, and slab of India ink. In cleanest, severest outline he had traced the Great Wheel with its six spokes, whose centre is the conjoined Hog, Snake, and Dove (Ignorance, Anger, and Lust), and whose compartments are all the heavens and hells, and all the chances of human life.[103]
>
> —*Rudyard Kipling*

NOTES

1. Browning, Christopher (2013). *Ordinary Men, op. cit.*
2. Spinelli, Ernesto (2000). *Interpreted World: An Introduction to Phenomenological Psychology*. London: Sage (quotation on pp. 564–566).
3. Amazon customer review of Hart, William (2004). *Evil: A Primer: A History of a Bad Idea from Beelzebub to Bin Laden*. New York: Thomas Dunne Books. Retrieved April 4, 2014.
4. *Bible: Isaiah*, 5:20.
5. This wise legend is quoted prominently in the excellent book by Baum, Steven K. (2008). *The Psychology of Genocide: Perpetrators, Bystanders and Rescuers*. Cambridge: Cambridge University Press, 237.
6. Kant, Immanuel (1797). *The Metaphysics of Morals*. Cambridge: Cambridge University Press, 1991. Abbreviated and translated by Mary Gregor and included in *Practical Philosophy* (Cambridge Edition of the works of Immanuel Kant, 1996).
7. Nietzsche, Friedrich (2003). *Beyond Good and Evil: Prelude to a Philosophy of the Future*. London: Penguin. Note there are others who do not see Nietzsche as the prophet of power but as a perspicacious psychologist. See Wernick, Uri (2016). *Nietzschean Psychology and Psychotherapy: The New Doctors of the Soul*. Lanham, MD: Lexington Books.
8. Dearey, Melissa (2014). The Banality of Evil: Genocide, Slavery, Holocaust, War. In *Making Sense of Evil: An Interdisciplinary Approach*. London: Palgrave Macmillan, 186–204.
9. Carey, Benedict (February 9, 2005). For the worst of us, the diagnosis may be 'evil.' *New York Times*.
10. Spinelli, Ernesto (2001). *The Mirror and the Hammer: Challenging Orthodoxies in Psychotherapeutic Thought*. Thousand Oaks, CA: Sage.
11. Gilbert, Gustave M. (1979). *The Psychology of Dictatorship: Based on an Examination of the Leaders of Nazi Germany*. Westport, CT: Greenwood (original publication New York: Ronald Press, 1950).
12. Kelley, Douglas M. (1961). *22 Cells in Nuremberg: A Psychiatrist Examines the Nazi Criminals*. New York: Greenberg (original publication in 1947).

13. Zillmer, Eric A; Harrower, Molly; Ritzler, Barry A; and Archer, Robert P. (1995). *The Quest for the Nazi Personality: A Psychological Investigation of Nazi War Criminals.* New York: Lawrence Erlbaum/Routledge. Other studies of the roles of mental health clinicians in the Third Reich have added to the same frightening picture. See Cocks, Geoffrey (1985). *Psychotherapy in the Third Reich: The Göring Institute.* New York: Oxford University Press.

14. Wertham, Fredric. (1966). *A Sign for Cain: An Exploration of Human Violence.* New York: Macmillan; See also Strous, Rael D. (2006). Hitler's psychiatrists: healers and researchers turned executioners and its relevance today. *Harvard Review of Psychiatry*, 14(1), 30–37; Strous, Rael D. (2006). Nazi euthanasia of the mentally ill at Hadamar. *American Journal of Psychiatry*, 163(1), 27; Strous, Rael D. (2007). Psychiatry during the Nazi era: Ethical lessons for the modern professional. *Annals of General Psychiatry*, 6(1), 8–14.

15. Recent historical work has proposed that Eichmann was much more passionately committed to the Nazi anti-Semitic ideological ideal of ridding the world of Jews. See Schwartz, Jack (September 6, 2014). Eichmann, anything but an ordinary man: In her magnum opus on the career of the 'architect of the Holocaust,' German scholar Bettina Stangneth provides a revealing portrait of a man who was far from being a dutiful clerk. Stangneth, Bettina (2014). Review: *Eichmann Before Jerusalem: The Unexamined Life of a Mass Murderer* (translated from the German by Ruth Martin). New York: Alfred A. Knopf. In *Haaretz English Edition*, www.haaretz.com/life/books/1.614147. Says Schwartz: "Far from the abject creature who claimed he was no more than a dutiful clerk carrying out the wishes of his masters in the Nazi genocide, Eichmann was an unreconstructed Nazi, unregenerate, unrepentant, who reveled in his deeds and only regretted not carrying them to their conclusion. Moreover, he was a brilliant actor who could play a variety of parts with a chameleon's gift for becoming whatever his audience wanted to see."

The above information has been interpreted to mean that Hannah Arendt was completely off in her formulation of what I believe is a brilliant concept of the "banality of evil." See Arendt, Hannah (1969). *Eichmann in Jerusalem: A Report on the Banality of Evil.* New York: Viking (original work published in1963). Christopher Browning, whose outstanding work we cite a good deal, is quoted as saying, "She had the right type but the wrong guy. There were all sorts of people like Eichmann pretended to be, which is why his strategy worked." Cited by Schuessler, Jennifer (September 2, 2014). Book portrays Eichmann as evil, but not banal. *International New York Times.*

Personally, I am not so sure. I do accept that Eichmann was only too glad to kill Jews, and I accept also that he was an artful fake, but I accept that he was both a prototype of obedience and a totally ambitious man, too.

16. The team of psychiatrist and psychologist who examined him while in jail in Israel, Shlomo and Shoshanna Kulcsar, found that emotionally Eichmann was unable to experience aggression and that he was a completely dutiful, colorless and, believe it or not, aggression-avoiding personality who was doing what he was assigned to do. See Kulcsar, I. Shlomo; Kulcsar, Shoshanna; and Szondi, Lipot (1966). *Adolf Eichmann and the Third Reich.* Springfield, IL: Charles Thomas; Kulcsar, I. Shlomo (1968). The Psychopathology of Adolf Eichmann. In Juan J. Lopez Ibur (Ed.). *Proceedings: Fourth World Congress of Psychiatry, Madrid 5–11, September 1966.* New York. Excerpta Medica Foundation, 1687–1689; Kulcsar, I. Shlomo (1976). De Sade and Eichmann. *Mental Health and Society*, 3(1–2), 102–113; Kulcsar, I. Shlomo (1978). De Sade and Eichmann. In Israel W. Charny (Ed.). *Strategies against Violence: Design for Nonviolent Change.* Boulder, CO: Westview, 19–33.

17. Kulcsar, I. Shlomo (1978). De Sade and Eichmann, *ibid.* (quotations on pp. 25–27). Kulcsar's thesis is that the executed Nazi mass murderer could not tolerate aggression in his conscious experiencing, but acted out the worst possible actual destruction of people. Kulcsar compares and contrasts Eichmann to de Sade, who, in Kulcsar's view (along with some literary critics), indulged in *fantasies* of sadism in the service of discharging these impulses without raising a hand to do any actual violence.

18. Bach, George and Wyden, Peter (1969). *The Intimate Enemy, op. cit.*

19. Merton, Thomas N. (1967). A devout meditation in memory of Adolf Eichmann. Reprinted in *Reflections*. Merck, Sharp, & Dohme, 1(3), 21–23.

20. Dicks, Henry V. (1972). *Licensed Mass Murder, op cit.*

21. Askenasy, Hans (1978). *Are We All Nazis?* Secaucus, NJ: Lyle Stuart.

22. Lifton, Robert Jay (1986), *The Nazi Doctors, op. cit.* (quotation on p. 5).

23. Fulbrook, Mary (2012). *A Small Town Near Auschwitz: Ordinary Nazis and the Holocaust.* Oxford: Oxford University Press; Gross, Jan Tomasz with Gross, Irena Grudzinska (2012). *Golden Harvest: Events at the Periphery of the Holocaust.* New York: Oxford University Press; Browning, Christopher (2013). Review of *Golden Harvest: Events at the Periphery of the Holocaust, ibid.* In *Holocaust and Genocide Studies*, 27(3), 498–500.

24. Milgram, Stanley (1974). *Obedience to Authority, op. cit.* Says Milgram: "[The results] raise the possibility that human nature, or—more specifically—the kind of character produced in American democratic society, cannot be counted on to insulate its citizens from brutality and inhumane treatment at the direction of malevolent authority. A substantial proportion of people do what they are told to do, irrespective of the contents of the act and without limitations of conscience, so long as they perceive that the command comes from a legitimate authority" (quotation on p. 189).

25. Browning, Christopher (2013), *ibid.*

26. Goldhagen, Daniel Jonah (1996). *Hitler's Willing Executioners: Ordinary Germans and the Holocaust.* New York: Knopf.

27. A great majority of scholars of the Holocaust and genocide who reviewed Goldhagen's book were critical of its monocausal emphasis—without questioning the truth of antisemitism as a powerful cultural force in Germany. Herbert Hirsch called the thesis "an over-simplification," and also charged that Goldhagen reconstructed others' works and "created his own version of what previous scholars attempted to say." Richard Tidyman also criticized the "monocausal answer" to the Holocaust and Goldhagen's claim that his thesis was totally new. However, he did credit Goldhagen for going beyond Browning's original findings about "Police Battalion 101" by studying a number of battalions—and that again it was clear that many men did have the opportunity not to kill Jews but *chose yes to murder*; also that Goldhagen has drawn a fuller picture of the lives of the men—how "they went to bars, drank, sang, had sex, and talked . . . enjoyed themselves knowing full well that they had and would commit further massacres." At the same time, Tidyman added another definitive criticism, "If antisemitism is the motivating force, then how do we account for the other victims of the National Socialists such as Gypsies, Russian POW's, Jehovah's Witnesses . . . mentally ill people in Germany in the so-called 'euthanasia' (T4) campaign . . . and countless others." See Hirsch, Herbert (1997). Review: Daniel Goldhagen and the 'Straw Man': A contemporary tale of selective interpretation. *International Network on Holocaust and Genocide* [Macquarie University], 12 (1–2), 20–24 (quotation on p. 20); and Tidyman, Richard (1996). Review: Goldhagen, Daniel Jonah (1996), *Hitler's Willing Executioners: Ordinary Germans and the Holocaust. International Network on Holocaust and Genocide*, 11(3) (quotations on pp. 18, 17).

28. Shapiro, Inah (1997). An accusing exhibition explodes the 50-year-old myth of the Wehrmacht's integrity and non-participation in SS murders. *Haaretz*, May 5 (Hebrew).

29. Mann, Michael (2000). Were the perpetrators of genocide "ordinary men" or "real Nazis"? Results from fifteen hundred biographics. *Holocaust and Genocide Studies*, 14(3), 331–366 (quotation on p. 331).

30. Waller, James E. (1996). Perpetrators of the Holocaust: Divided and unitary self-conceptions of evildoing." *Holocaust and Genocide Studies*, 10 (1), 11–33. See also Waller, James (2007). *Becoming Evil: How Ordinary People Commit Genocide and Mass Killing*. 2nd edition. New York: Oxford University Press.

31. Charny,Israel W. (1971). Psychology of genocide. *International Problems* (Israel), 10(1–2), xxxxi–xxxxvii. (Hebrew); Charny, Israel W. (1971). Normal man as genocider: We need a psychology of normal man as genocider, accomplice or indifferent bystander to mass killing of man. *Voices: The Art and Science of Psychotherapy*, 7(2), 68–79.

32. Charny, Israel W. (1982). *How Can We Commit the Unthinkable? Genocide: The Human Cancer, op cit.*

33. Charny, Israel W. and Fromer, Daphna (1990). A study of the readiness of Jewish/Israeli students in the health professions to authorize and execute involuntary mass euthanasia of "severely handicapped" patients. *Holocaust and Genocide Studies*, 5(3), 313–335.

34. Charny, Israel W. and Fromer, Daphna (1990). The readiness of health profession students to comply with a hypothetical program of "forced migration" of a minority population. *American Journal Orthopsychiatry*, 1990, 60(4), 486–495.

35. Rosenthal, Rovik (Ed.) (2000). *Kfar Kassem: Myth and History*. Tel Aviv: Hakibbutz Hameuchad Publishing House (Hebrew).

36. Charny, Israel W. and Fromer, Daphna (1992). A study of attitudes of viewers of the film "Shoah" towards an incident of mass murder by Israeli soldiers (Kfar Kassem, 1956). *Journal of Traumatic Stress*, 5(2), 303–318.

37. Charny, Israel W. (1990). To commit or not commit to human life: Children of victims and victimizers—all. *Contemporary Family Therapy*, 12(5), 407–426.

38. Kelman, Herbert C. and Hamilton, V. Lee (1989). *Crimes of Obedience: Towards a Social Psychology of Authority and Responsibility*. New Haven: Yale University Press.

39. Hinton, Alexander Laban (1996). Explaining the Cambodian genocide in terms of psychological dissonance. *American Anthropologist*, 98(4), 818–831 (quotation on p. 825); see also Hinton, Alexander Laban (1999). Comrade Ox did not object when his family was killed. *In Encyclopedia of Genocide, op.cit.*, 135.

40. Stannard, David E. (1992). *American Holocaust: Columbus and the Conquest of the New World*. New York: Oxford University Press. Cited in Suhl, Jacob (1997). Goldhagen and "ordinary Germans." *Macquarie University Genocide Studies Newsletter*, 3(4), 6–10 (quotation on p. 9).

41. See American Indian scholar, Ward Churchill's descriptions of the treatments of indigenous peoples by white colonizers in the Americas: Churchill, Ward (1997). *A Little Matter of Genocide: Holocaust and Denial in the Americas 1492 to the Present*. San Francisco: City Light Books. See review by Charny, Israel W. in *Readings: A Journal of Reviews and Commentary in Mental Health* (American Orthopsychiatric Association), 2000, 15(1), 18–22. Reprinted in *Journal Genocide Research*, 2000, 2(2), 302–310.

42. Woodward, Bob (2001). In hijacker's bag, a call for death: FBI agents find prayers and a checklist of practical terrorism. *International Herald Tribune*, September 29–39, 1, 4.

43. Rummel, R.J. (1997). *Power Kills: Democracy as a Method of Nonviolence.* New Brunswick, NJ: Transaction Publishers.

44. Cocks, Geoffrey (1985), *ibid.*

45. It is striking how in the worlds of victims, too, we find periodic efforts to categorize a given victim as the *most* suffering of all victims and/or as far more betrayed, trapped, or dealt with cruelly than others, and thus a new series of hierarchies is launched—now of chosen victims who are seemingly superior to other victims. Obviously there is room for *objective* comparisons of differences in the extent and nature of suffering of victims under different circumstances, but only up to a certain point, and certainly not when the comparisons are used as a basis for endorsing any elite status to some victims and an undervalued status to others. Thus, in respect of cases of genocide, the emotional or experiential claim of all victim peoples that they endured incomparable suffering is understandable and acceptable. From the point of view of their experience, they really did endure unique suffering, and they deserve our unqualified respect and sympathy. But these personal emotional responses are different from attempts to attribute to some terrible events, such as the Holocaust, superior and untouchable meanings, sometimes even with mystical theological overtones, in comparison with the genocides of other peoples.

For an important yet sensitive refutation of this position (which in no way detracts from the awesomeness and historical significance of the Holocaust), see Charny, Israel W., with Adalian, Rouben Paul and Jacobs, Steven L. (1999). "Holocaust": The word and its usage. In the *Encyclopedia of Genocide, op. cit.*, 40–43. This critical entry in the encyclopedia shows that the word *holocaust* belongs to all peoples.

Writing even more boldly, former Israeli Minister of Education, Yossi Sarid, dared to go all the way in a major article published in the influential *Haaretz*, first in English in the Special Supplement of the English-language edition on the eve of Passover April 16, 2003, and then in Hebrew in the Special Supplement on the eve of Israel's Independence Day, May 6, 2003—each on a symbolism-rich day in the Israeli calendar. In each language edition of the newspaper, it received a different headline: Sarid, Yossi (2003). No monopoly on absolute evil: The Germans are not the only nation on earth capable of being its victims—and Israeli children must be taught this. *Haaretz English Edition*, Passover Eve, April 16, B8); Sarid, Yossi (2003). Remember what was done to you by Amalek—but not only to you. *Haaretz Hebrew Edition*, Eve of Israel's Day of Independence, May 6,Heh4. Says Sarid, "There is no difference between *genocide* and *holocaust*: 'Genocide' and 'holocaust' are synonymous terms. . . . Every genocide—if it is truly genocide and not merely a propagandistic counterfeit of genocide—is a holocaust, . . . The lesson is . . . universal."

46. The subject is also related to how victim peoples legitimately focus on the memorials of their people, but too often at the expense of denying other co-victim peoples who were murdered at the same time. Thus many times Jews have denied/ignored the fates of Roma (Gypsies) alongside them, and also the murders of gay people, Russian POWs, and Jehovah's Witnesses. See a fine work by Berenbaum, Michael (Ed.) (1990). *A Mosaic of Victims: Non-Jews Persecuted and Murdered by the Nazis.* New York: New York University Press; Berenbaum, Michael (1999). The Holocaust, non-Jewish victims in. In *Encyclopedia of Genocide, op. cit.*, 324–327.

Similarly, many Armenians have censored away the genocides of the Assyrians and Yzedis and Greeks that were committed by the Turks alongside the Armenian Genocide. A special issue of the Web magazine *GPN Genocide Prevention Now* was published on the subject: *Special Issue: Armenian Genocide and Co-Victims*, Special Issue 5, Winter 2011. The table of contents for this issue and the individual articles can be found on the website of the Institute on the Holocaust and Genocide in Jerusalem at http://www.ihgjlm.com. As of 2015, the year of the centennial of the Armenian Genocide, there are more references in Armenia to the co-victims, and the Armenian Parliament has voted to designate a day of remembrance of the victims of all genocides (in addition to the day devoted to the Armenian Genocide), and the United Nations has designated December 9 as the International Day of Commemoration and Dignity of the Victims.

47. Charny, Israel W. (1982). In collaboration with Chanan Rapaport. Toward a Genocide Early Warning System. In *How Can We Commit the Unthinkable?, op. cit.*, 263–331. (This chapter and additional writings about this chapter have appeared in many different publications over the years.)

48. Neumann, Erich (1969). *Depth Psychology and a New Ethic, op. cit.*; Rubinoff, Lionel (1978). In nomine diaboli: The voices of evil. In Charny, Israel W. (Ed.), *Strategies Against Violence, op. cit.*, 34–67.

49. See Berke, Joseph H. et al. (Eds.) (1998). *Even Paranoids Have Enemies, op. cit.*, 189–202.

50. Charny, Israel W. (1999). Dehumanization—"Killing" the humanity of another. In *Encyclopedia of Genocide, op. cit.*, 155–157.

51. Rummel, R.J. (1994). *Death by Government, op cit.*; Rummel, R.J. (1999). *Statistics of Democide: Genocide and Mass Murder since 1900.* New Brunswick, NJ: Transaction.

52. Charny, Israel W. (1986), Genocide and mass destruction, *op. cit.* See also Charny, Israel W. (1996), Evil in human personality, *op. cit.*; Charny, Israel W. (1997). A personality disorder of excessive power strivings, *op. cit.*

53. See Totten, Samuel and Parsons, William S. (Eds.) (2012). *Centuries of Genocide: Critical Essays and Eyewitness Testimony.* 4th edition. New York: Routledge. Both the original publication of this book in 1997 under the title *Century of Genocide* and a later second edition included Charny, Israel W. as a third co-editor. For all the excellence of this best-selling book, like all compilations on genocide that I know of, it too fails to include any number of genocidal events, for example, the Japanese in Manchuria, including the infamous Nazi-like experiments they conducted on victims of many non-Japanese nationalities (like with Mengele later, again led by a physician!), Tibet, Mozambique, and more. Sometimes the reason for the exclusion can be that emerging definitions of *genocide* are not sufficiently settled about given events—for example, the nuclear bombings of Hiroshima and Nagasaki are considered genocide by some highly reputable scholars such as Leo Kuper but not by many others, but more times the exclusions are a result of the fact that the machinery of world awareness, recording, and collective memory for the god-awful events of mass destruction of human lives on our planet is just beginning to take form, and there have been so incredibly many events of mass murder that no one to date has put together a "full" list.

54. See the forthcoming section in this chapter on "Innocent and 'Banal' Causes of Violence."

55. Baron-Cohen, Simon (June 6, 2011). Explaining "evil" and human cruelty. Excerpted from book by Baron-Cohen, Simon (2012). *The Science of Evil.* New York: Basic Books. In *International New York Times.*

56. World Health Organization Geneva (2014). World Report on Violence and Health. http://apps.who.int/iris/bitstream/10665/67403/1/a77019.pdf?ua=1.

57. Lewis, Sinclair (1935). *It Can't Happen Here.* New York: Doubleday Doran. There are at least two different levels on which to see the illusion that *it can't happen here (in America).*

The one, which 9/11 permanently erases, is that America is so strong and geographically so separate and majestic, that no one can attack and get away with committing mass murder in the United States. *Forget it.* The second is that democratic America itself could never suffer its own transformation into a fascist killing society. *Pray this be so forever, but guaranteed it is not.*

58. Lorenz, Konrad (1966). *On Aggression.* New York: Harcourt, Brace & World.

59. Charny, Israel W. with Rapaport, Chanan (1982). Towards a Genocide Early Warning System, *ibid.*

60. See Charny, Israel W. (2007). A proposal for a "Worldwide Campaign for Life" by the leaders of many religions and other world leaders and heroes. In *Fighting Suicide Bombing, op cit.*, 166–189.

61. Charny, Israel W. (1982). The tragic illusion of self-defense. In *How Can We Commit the Unthinkable, ibid.*

62. Rubinoff, Lionel (1978). In nomine diaboli, *ibid.*, 42, 59.

63. Charny, Israel W. (1982). Destruction in the quest for life. In *How Can We Commit the Unthinkable? Genocide the Human Cancer, ibid.*, 91–126.

64. Rapoport, Anatol (1974). *Conflict in Man-Made Environment.* Baltimore: Penguin Books (quotation on p. 73).

65. Arendt, Hannah (1969). *Eichmann in Jerusalem, ibid.* (original edition 1963.)

66. Kesey, Ken (1962). *One Flew Over the Cuckoo's Nest, op. cit.*

67. I have been trying to understand these "banal" everyday aspects of our human psychology for a long time. See Charny, Israel W. (1982). Destruction in the quest for life; and more recently, Charny, Israel W. (2015). I did nothing wrong! Denial and the improper management of emotions. In *The Genocide Contagion: How We Commit and Confront Holocaust and Genocide.* Lanham, MD: Rowman & Littlefield, 2016, 135–160.

68. Wiesel, Elie (1986). *The Oath.* New York: Schoken (original publication 1973).

69. Latane, Bibb and Darley, John M. (1970). *The Unresponsive Bystander.* New York: Appleton-Crofts; Sheleff, Leon Shasholsky (1978). *The Bystander: Behavior, Law, Ethics.* Lexington, MA: Lexington Books; Staub, Ervin (1999). Bystanders to genocide, in *Encyclopedia of Genocide, ibid.*, 127–128.

70. Wiesel, Elie (1964). *The Town Beyond the Wall.* New York: Atheneum (quotation on p. 150).

71. Zimbardo, Philip G., *op. cit.* (several references were given earlier). A wonderful story is told by Christine Maslach, Zimbardo's wife. When the famous experiment was underway, she was Zimbardo's fiancée, and she came to the university to see with her own eyes the awesome study of the simulated jail that had been built in the Psychology Department at Stanford University. While she was "outside," she met one of the "jailers" and liked him a lot as a nice person, but then later she saw him in action and was shocked to see how especially cruel and sadistic he was. It was her shock and outrage and then her courage to tell Zimbardo that he must stop the ongoing evil that led to him ending the experiment. See Zimbardo, Philip G.; Maslach, Christina; and Haney, Craig (2000). Reflections on the Stanford Prison Experiment: Genesis, transformations, consequences. In Blass, Thomas (Ed.). *Obedience to Authority: Current Perspectives on the Milgram Paradigm.* Mahwah, NJ: Lawrence Erlbaum, 193–238. I love using the above illustration when I teach classes in marital therapy, explaining how genuine love relationships and marriages are opportunities for telling *and being told* critical truths that can help both parties become better people.

72. Charny, Israel W. (1997). A personality disorder of excessive power strivings, *op. cit.*

73. I have always been impressed that even bona fide crazy people and people with neurological illnesses, are making inner *value choices* whether or not to hurt other people.

74. Lifton, Robert Jay (1967). *Death in Life: Survivors of Hiroshima, op. cit.*

75. Lifton, Robert Jay (1973). *Home from the War: Vietnam Veterans—Neither Victims nor Executioners*. New York: Simon & Schuster.

76. Lifton, Robert Jay (1986). *The Nazi Doctors, op. cit.*

77. Lifton, Robert Jay and Markusen, Eric (1990). *The Genocidal Mentality, op. cit.*

78. Lifton, Robert Jay (1979). *The Broken Connection, op cit.*; Markusen, Eric (1999). Psychology of Immortality: Robert Jay Lifton's perspective on the psychology of immortality and its relevance for genocidal killing. In *Encyclopedia of Genocide, op. cit.*, 484–485.

79. Brenman, Eric (1988). Cruelty and narrow-mindedness. In Spillius, Elizabeth Bott (Ed.). *Melanie Klein Today: Developments in Theory and Practice. Vol. 1: Mainly Theory.*

80. Charny, Israel W. (1982). Sacrificing others to the death we fear ourselves. In *How Can We Commit the Unthinkable? ibid.*, 185–211 (quotation on p. 192, italics added).

81. Becker, Ernest (1973). *The Denial of Death*, op. cit. (quotation on p. 130); Rank, Otto (1946), *Will Therapy and Truth and Reality*. New York: Knopf. Cited by Becker, *ibid.*

82. Charny, Israel W. (1999), Psychology of sacrificing. In *Encyclopedia of Genocide, op. cit.*, 485–487.

83. Le Bon, G. (1903). *The Crowd: A Study of the Popular Mind.* London: F. Unwin. (Translated from the French.)

84. This is the text of a Talaat telegram, September 21, 1915, reprinted from the *Daily Telegraph*, May 1922. I am, of course, only too aware of the claims of the deniers of the Armenian Genocide that this and other telegrams are fakes, let alone their larger sweeping denial that there simply was no Armenian Genocide (just as other deniers tell us there was no Holocaust of the Jews some years later or no gas chambers). For an authoritative rebuttal of the telegrams being fakes, see the memorable scholarly work of Professor Vahakn Dadrian authenticating the telegrams: Dadrian, Vahakn (1986). The Naim-Andonian Documents on the World War I destruction of Ottoman Armenians: The anatomy of a genocide. *International Journal of Middle East Studies*,18(3), 311–360.

85. Katz, Steven D. (1994). *The Holocaust in Historical Context.* New York: Oxford University Press. This volume was identified as the first of three, but no further volumes have appeared. Note that such claims for the super-uniqueness of the Holocaust are not the only ones claiming "specialness." There has been, for example, a prominent Armenian scholar who attempted to make comparisons, as if the suffering in the Holocaust should be defined as *less* than the suffering in the Armenian Genocide because the Germans utilized such highly efficient machinery as the gas chambers for killing the Jews—a ridiculous comparison that is insulting to the tragedy and suffering of the victims, let alone that millions of Jews endured persecution of many years and months similar to the persecution endured by many Armenians in their long, forced, murderous trek through the desert. (I am purposely refraining from giving a source note here in order to avoid shaming a valued colleague who has not made exclusivity a central concept of his work.) There is another side to this issue too. There are also instances of scholars who fight back against the over-claims of the uniqueness of the Holocaust by speaking about the Holocaust in ways that are abrasive and insulting of memory and compassion. In this writer's judgment, those who oppose the exclusivist position must also be very careful in doing so not to lose reverence and respect for the tragedy and the always unique aspects of any given genocide such as the Holocaust.

86. Kohlberg, Lawrence (1973). The claim to moral adequacy of a highest stage of moral judgment. *Journal of Philosophy*, 70(18), 630–646. See also Focus on Lawrence Kohlberg. Whole issue of *World Psychology*, 1996, 2, 3–4.

87. Charny, Israel W. and Davidson, Shamai (Eds.) (1983). *The Book of the International Conference on the Holocaust and Genocide.* Tel Aviv: Institute on the Holocaust and Genocide.

88. Bar-On, Dan (1981). *Legacy of Silence* (1991). Cambridge, MA: Harvard University Press; Bar-On, Dan and Charny, Israel W. (1988). Children of Holocaust perpetrators—how do they form their own "moral self"? *Psichologia* (Journal of the Israel Psychological Association), 1(1), 29–38 (Hebrew); Bar-On, Dan and Charny, Israel W. (1992). The logic of moral argumentation of children of the Nazi era in Germany. *International Journal of Group Tensions*, 22(1), 3–20.

89. "Ordinary people will do the job—we shot them: Gregory Niasov didn't have troubles sleeping. A guard in a concentration camp in Siberia, after he shot innocent men and women. After he would check in his weapon, he would go to have a drink of vodka, eat and sleep. Forty years later, still without pangs of conscience, he tells the story to the Soviet writer, Razagon." Article in *Haaretz*, January 18, 1989 (Hebrew, translated from *Der Spiegel*).

90. "Commando killers all their lives: What happens to the commando killers after they are discharged from the Israeli army? An investigative report: 'Nigger serves his master but can't free himself. Five commando killers tell about murdering Palestinians and about the emotional crisis in their lives after being discharged.'" *Anashim* [*People*] (Weekly News Magazine, Tel Aviv), January 14–20, 1997, cover plus pages 6–11 (Hebrew).

91. Lenin warned, "People always have been and they always will be stupid victims of deceit and self-deception." Lenin, Nicholai (1913). *The Three Sources and Three Constituent Parts of Marxism* [cited in *Bartlett's Familiar Quotations*].

92. Livingstone, David (2011). *Less Than Human: Why We Demean, Enslave, and Exterminate Others.* New York: St. Martins.

93. Alterman, Natan (1977). *Hatur Hashvii* [The Seventh Column]. Tel Aviv: HaKibbutz Hameuchad, Book 1, 149–151 (excerpt from longer poem in Hebrew (translation from the Hebrew by this author). Published with permission of Acum and the Open University of Israel.

94. Ben-Gurion, David (November 21, 1948). *Ibid.* [with the poem by Alterman]. Published originally by the Israel Ministry of Defense. Tel Aviv: Achdut Printing Co. (translation of the excerpt from the Hebrew by this author).

95. Mohammed Ali Taha. For my humanity. *Haaretz*, March 18, 1996 (Hebrew).

96. Pastor Martin Niemoeller was a Protestant minister who bravely opposed the Nazis. The stirring poetic statement by Pastor Niemoeller has been reproduced many times and is a true inspiration to all of us everywhere on our planet:

> First they came for the Jews
> and I did not speak out—
> because I was not a Jew.
>
> Then they came for the communists
> and I did not speak out—
> because I was not a communist.

Then they came for the trade unionists
and I did not speak out—
because I was not a trade unionist.

Then they came for me—
and there was no one left
to speak out for me.

Reproduced from the *Encyclopedia of Genocide, ibid.*, 399.

97. Charny, Israel W. (1982). Toward a Genocide Early Warning System, *ibid.*

98. Hinton, Alexander Laban (1996), *ibid.* (quotation on p. 829).

99. For a review of the literature fifty years after Auschwitz on the medical and psychological effects of the Holocaust on its victims, including a powerful review of psychiatry's failures to confront the subject of the victims' suffering authentically and fully, see Krell, Robert and Sherman, Marc I. (Eds.) (1997). *Medical and Psychological Effects of Concentration Camps on Holocaust Survivors.* Volume 4 in Series: *Genocide, A Critical Bibliographic Review.* New Brunswick, NJ: Transaction.

100. Chamovitz, Daniel (November 28, 2014). Homo Sapiens May Have Won the Human Race, But Are We Happy?: Review of Harari, Yuval Noah (2011). *Sapiens: A Brief History of Humankind.* London: Harvill Secker. *Haaretz English Edition.*

101. Edmund Burke [(January 12, 1729–July 9, 1797), born in Dublin, was an Irish political philosopher and member of the House of Commons in London, and is regarded as the father of modern conservatism.] Quotation is widely attributed to him, including by President John Kennedy, but there is considerable doubt and controversy whether Burke is the source.

102. *Inaugural Address delivered to the University of St. Andrews, Feb. 1st 1867, by John Stuart Mill, Rector of the University.* People's Edition. London: Longmans, Green, Reader, and Dyer.

103. Kipling, Rudyard [1865–1936] (1902). *Kim.* London: Macmillan.

7

Treating Emotional Violence and Evil

PSYCHOTHERAPY OF DISORDERS OF DOING HARM TO OTHERS

Overview of the Five Parts of This Chapter

This chapter is an effort to write systematically a series of advisories for therapists about how to treat situations where human beings are harming others. There are very few places in the professional literature where a psychotherapist can find advice and instructions on how to handle the many kinds of disorders of people doing harm to others, including the outright violence that is so common even in family relationships, as it is in all of human life.

On the one hand, this is an innovative effort to address forthrightly a critical subject about which our field is lagging. On the other hand, it is entirely clear that this presentation will be an incomplete treatment of a vastly difficult and truly complex subject, let alone that one of the conclusions we must advance is that there are any number of aspects of evil where the profession of psychotherapy really has little to offer beyond recognizing the evil that is taking place for what it is—although that in itself can help to save some people.

The chapter is constructed in five parts as follows:

- *Part One*—Upgrading Psychiatric Diagnosis by Combining Diagnosis of Personal Functioning with One's Impact on Others
- *Part Two*—Perpetrators, Accomplices, Bystanders, and Victims, and Trying to be None of Them
- *Part Three*—(The Biblical) *Job* Fights Back against Tragedy and Total Disaster
- *Part Four*—Psychotherapy of Emotional Violence
- *Part Five*—Psychotherapeutic Engagement of Evil

We also begin by looking again at the traditional disorders of doing harm to oneself and expanding on the connecting bridge we are building to disorders of doing harm to others. In the process we will distinguish between and identify the common denominator in the different roles of perpetrators, accomplices, bystanders, and victims—those who are too available to be victimized—namely a notable degree of a readiness to hurt life or to allow life to be harmful.

We begin with reiterating a basic theme of this book—that *all* psychiatric and psychological diagnosis should combine an evaluation of how a person is doing harm to their own self and how a person is doing harm to other human beings. Such diagnosis embodies and supports the basic principle of psychotherapy, which we believe should also be a central underpinning of all our human culture, that there is nothing more important and beneficial to mental health than teaching human beings sympathy, respect, and responsibility for protecting human life—their own life and the lives of others.

No doubt it is shocking for some that we identify a commonality not only between the first three role groups who enable violence but also with *some* of the victims insofar as they have not protected themselves sufficiently against possible evil and in that way have facilitated its execution—though without in any way blaming them for the evil that is being done to them. In all cases the psychotherapist should be committed to advancing the key principle of respect and protection of human life.

We continue with engaging the psychology of totally tragic and disastrous conditions, which we name *Job* conditions following the figure in the biblical book *Job*. Here we try to carve out a pathway from tragedy to renewed life—much of it with the help of the angry emotions even though they tend almost automatically to be labeled as bad and pathological in our normative Western culture. Of course, psychotherapy of *Job*-like victims of disasters begins with helping people to acknowledge and mourn their great losses, but then there follows a coupling of sympathy and comfort with encouragement to experience anger and fight back with a healthy toughness to cope and move forward from their loss and tragedy. Although for some religious people the concept of anger over loss being directed against one's gods is heretical, the notion of fighting *for* our lives is also consistent with some of the best religious thinking—and obviously we have to leave it to individual people to work out their theological position.

We go on to a model for treating psychologically generated violence (not ideological), such as in families. The key to treatment of actual violence is reinforcing the inviolability of life ("you know that doing harm to another person is wrong"), *along with* promising the patient that we respect their anger and will help them to direct it effectively to pursue their goals ("but I promise to help you with expressing your anger in ways that can really help your life").

We also address a topic that is rarely honored in the psychological literature of how to cultivate healthy mental violence in one's own head as a procedure for catharsis or release of oneself from the tension of hate and a strengthening of one's boundaries against committing actual violence.

Finally, we go on to explore, at least in beginning ways, the psychotherapy of evil including "hidden evil," both so rampant in human life. In our conclusions, we emphasize facing and identifying evil that is being directed against us, helping victims to know when and how they are being abused and that they are not at fault, and how they may make efforts to meet evil squarely and respond to it with firmness and power. Regrettably, most evil people do not seek therapy, nor are they responsive for the most part to requests by family to go for emotional help. "Treatment" is often limited to helping impose limits and sanctions on the evil person either by the people in their lives (e.g., family or work contacts, or by police, lawyers, and courts). Nonetheless, most evil people will try adroitly to continue their styles as they are.

We also touch briefly on a concept of, yes, inviting evil people with whom we have an ongoing relationship, such as difficult members of our families, to adopt alternative and more positive ways in response to our making it clear to them that we will not put up with their harming us. Finally we have to look at how to limit and contain as much as possible evils that basically cannot be fought and confronted successfully. Unfortunately, there are a good number of evil forces in the lives of all of us that cannot be routed to a fully "happy ending," but we need to learn to protect ourselves as best we can.

The Democratic Mind understands that psychological health is based on a basic respect and wholesomeness in managing the brilliant opportunity of life—both for ourselves and in relationship to other human beings. Psychological health is loving life, supporting life, and not doing harm to life.

PART ONE: UPGRADING PSYCHIATRIC DIAGNOSIS BY COMBINING DIAGNOSIS OF PERSONAL FUNCTIONING WITH ONE'S IMPACT ON OTHERS

This book emphasizes that in *every* mental health case the clinician needs to think *both* about what kinds of harm a person is doing to thenselves *and* what harm they are doing to others in their family and personal network and community.

The treatment that follows this way of diagnosing differs from conventional psychiatric and psychological treatment today, where even people who are hurting others often are understood to be suffering from some form of emotional hurt such as feelings of inadequacy, and much of the therapy is focused on helping them with their inner unhappiness in the hopes that they will then also stop being nasty to others.

A common example is marital therapy that does not address a husband's or wife's rejection of their spouse straightforwardly, but only seeks to help them with their hurt feelings based on the assumption that these are generating their rejection of their spouse. In such cases therapists stay far away from statements like, "You've not shown much warmth to your husband," and "Do you understand that you are repeatedly humiliating your wife calling her names?"

The present suggestion is that therapy often is better served by focusing directly *both* on the difficulties one is having personally *and* no less on the truths about what harm one is doing to others. This perspective avoids treating harm and insults to others as if they are "only" derived from people's unhappiness within themselves.

Integrity in Relationships and Mental Health

Combining objective diagnosis of the difficulties being experienced inside a person and the harm they are doing to others lays down a basis for calling on people to take responsibility both for what they are doing to themselves and to others. This approach aims at helping people with their own inadequacies, personal fears, and tensions, but not at the expense of avoiding the truth of their impact on others. The approach is more true to a broader range of commonsense facts and realities that are taking place in peoples' lives, including the guilt that decent people feel, even if unconsciously, when they are doing wrong to others. Legitimate guilt feelings are not neurotic, and they can be tapped in order to generate desirable behavior changes.

A psychiatrist, Deane Shore Berson, has observed:

> The idea that only perception matters is one of the more subtle and dangerous values that many mental health professionals impart. . . . Something else matters: the survival of humanity. For this, we must agree to perceive certain things (lying, stealing, murder) as bad. . . . In a training program for psychiatrists, a doctor presents the case of a man wanting help for impotence with his mistress. Though the doctors discuss treatment techniques, none mentions that this man's conscience might be what is making it difficult for him to have sex during an affair. This silence on ethical concerns may be teaching these students that faithfulness and marital vows are irrelevant considerations for both doctor and patient. . . . Therapists who claim 'It's all a matter of perception' help create a society where wrong is no different from right. . . . Might we then be partially responsible for a society where more and more people are acting as though there were no difference between right and wrong?[1]

In a framework that calls for diagnosing both how people feel toward themselves and how they impact on and affect other peoples' functioning and well-being, *the integrity of relationships becomes no less important than the capacity to function.* Psychological health is defined to include the maintenance of a basic wholesomeness and integrity in relationships, especially with one's intimates. In this extended schema of diagnosis, it is not only the ability to remain functional or avoid dysfunction that is the basis for a psychiatric diagnosis of normality or health, but also the ability to support and enhance the functioning of one's intimates.

This concept of diagnosis calls for a paradigmatic shift from a kind of self-centered or narcissistic involvement only with a given human being's ability to function without being disturbed, crazy, and dysfunctional to looking at relationships with other human beings and the extent to which a person is facilitating, supporting, standing up for, and assisting in the creation and protection of the lives of others. Disturbance is seen when one cultivates despair, sorrow, and incompetence either in oneself *or* in one's partner in marriage, partner in parenting, one's children, one's extended family, or also in colleagues/employees at work, neighbors, and others.

Earlier I presented a formulation of psychological and psychiatric diagnoses as combining what I called *Disorders of Incompetence, Vulnerability, and Personal Weakness* with *Disorders of Pseudocompetence, Invulnerability, and Doing Harm to Others.* Pnina Blitz and I then extended this schema for understanding and diagnosing the two classes of disturbances as they manifest themselves in marital, family, and parental relationships.[2] In each case, counterpart styles of disturbances that are based on doing harm to oneself and doing harm to others are examined carefully. The diagnosis of the degree of disorder is based on an objective appraisal of the degree of damage to oneself and/or to others in the family that has been done, is being done, or is implied or unfolding for the future. The classification of disorders is arranged along the familiar and traditional continuum of degrees of disturbances in neurotic disorders, personality disorders, and psychotic disorders. Throughout the entire continuum, one judges the extent to which a person is taking away the self-esteem, joy of life, well-being, power, security, and ultimately perhaps life itself either from oneself or from one's spouse, children, or other family members.

The neurotic range of disturbance refers to generating an overall level of malaise, vulnerability, and restriction of competence in oneself and/or others. On the personal level, the level of disturbance is one of disabling anxiety, attrition of spirit, or disturbed mood and loss of well-being. A person suffering a neurotic level of personality disturbance in marital relationships is unable to enjoy thenselves as a member of the couple, or systematically intrudes on and disturbs the spouse's enjoyment of their self in the relationship such as by being insensitive to the other's needs, blaming the partner for tensions, denying their own personal limitations or faults, or demanding that the spouse be the servant of their demands. In family relationships, neurotic disorders similarly involve an inability to enjoy oneself as a member of a family, or disturbing others' enjoyment of family relationships. Neurotic parenting involves an inability to enjoy oneself as a parent, a lack of capacity to enjoy the children and/or the other parent, disturbing the child's enjoyment of being a child in the family, or disturbing the other parent's parenting.

Personality disorders refer to more severe and chronic damaging of the spirit and life opportunities. In traditional diagnosis of disturbances of personal incompetence, the personality-disordered person is unable to be stable and productive in their life. Generally excessive demands for immediate self-gratification are evident. In diagnosis of the additional personality disorders of doing harm to others that we propose, we see the person hurting, frustrating, and driving other family members crazy with their unreliability, irresponsibility, unkept promises, squandering of resources, and imposing the burden and shame of their failures and malfeasance on the dignity of the family. These cases include exploitation of family financial resources and physical abuse—including the cases of incest that are being discovered with increasing frequency in virtually all cultures,[3] very much including religious communities.

The definition of the psychotic range of disturbances will be the most unfamiliar and strange to the reader who is accustomed to traditional definitions. But it continues from the same logic of defining the degree of interference with one's own rights or the rights of others to the gift of their lives. We are accustomed to the word "psychotic" as describing a person who is *crazy*, which means a person doing such severe damage to their own self that they are seriously incapable of functioning in the reality of life. Our definition here adds to the traditional flagrant and colorful mental breakdowns where people act crazy (such as hallucinations and delusions) any form of doing severe harm to oneself that incapacitates basic functioning, and then also adding any severe harm that people do to others that results in one or more other persons becoming seriously incapacitated and unable to live life safely and enjoyably.

Thus, in this unfamiliar way of organizing the mental disorders, a choice to commit suicide is defined as a "crazy," or technically a psychotic, act (other than in rational situations such as severe torture, certain death at the hands of totalitarians, or other terminal situations that cannot be overcome). Suicide is a severe and extreme act. If the suicide is by someone who could have gone on living with hopes for solutions to their despair, the act is nuts. There is nothing that can be crazier. Earlier we discussed the strange fact that suicides in themselves are not even included in the *DSM* and hence not even defined as psychopathological. The further absurdity is that if a person who takes their own life has not shown traditional symptoms of disturbance such as depression or delusions, the suicide itself may not be treated as a sign of emotional or mental disturbance. But if the suicide is to the best of our judgment an unnecessary giving up on the search for more constructive solutions to one's problems, there is hardly a more disturbed way than taking one's life. The schema proposed here is that we call the unnecessary taking of one's life as *crazy*. Note that this is the way plain everyday people talk about most suicides, and our untraditional proposal brings professional psychiatry into line with people's commonsense knowledge that killing oneself is an ultimate nuttiness.

Continuing with our emphasis on disturbing and harming *either* oneself or others, we add also all situations where a person takes away from others their right to life and the capacity to enjoy the quality of their lives with the result that human beings who might have enjoyed rewarding lives in dignity are forced or relegated to non-personhood or nonexistence. In our proposed schema, the "psychotic" range of disturbances includes any and all forms of behavior that destroy the possibility of others' normal lives, such as murder, driving another person to suicide, or driving the other person crazy.

It is especially noteworthy—and special fun to note—that at last we have a theoretical schema that also provides a basis for diagnosing people who drive others nuts! Thus, a "psychotic" level of doing harm to one's spouse is defined as damaging the spouse's ability to function normally, driving the spouse crazy or to suicide, driving them to crime, or so demoralizing the spouse that they succumb to major illness, let alone actually murdering one's spouse. A psychotic way of doing harm to one's family is defined as causing severe damage to the functioning of one or more members of one's family, driving them crazy, making people in the family so terribly miserable that the family home feels like a nuthouse and everyone is out of their minds, driving family members to suicide, driving them to crime, or murdering them. A psychotic level of doing harm in one's parenting is defined as destroying one or more children's ability to function, driving them to become mad or to suicide, delegating or encouraging them to be criminals, murdering a child, and also incapacitating the other parent's ability to function or murdering them.

These terrible phenomena are not abstractions. They are all familiar and frequent enough occurrences in life that we all see. We shake our heads in disbelief at these phenomena knowing that we have witnessed something truly crazy, but because in many cases there is no available conceptual framework in psychology or psychiatry we tend to shrug off the unbelievable as some kind of exception, and then we go on with our available traditional professional language in mental health, even though it is not covering a huge spectrum of very disturbed human behavior. In contemporary mental health diagnosis, there is no such thing as driving someone else nuts or to death, yet we know we see these things in real life.

Of course, such changes in existing concepts are necessarily disruptive and challenging to the professional establishment, and invariably raise serious problems that previously have been kept on the sidelines in the existing politically correct professional discourse. They also generate enormous resistance. The conceptions laid out here are so unfamiliar that it will be hard for mental health professionals to work with them. They feel at first like violations of ingrained, almost religious-like definitions since yesteryear. But there is a simple, straightforward logic to what we are proposing: Mental disturbance is first and foremost doing harm to life. What is basically different and unfamiliar in the new schema presented here is that craziness is not defined as it usually is in psychiatry only by one's own strangeness and being bizarre, but by a degree of disruptive serious harm to the pursuit of *life*—either and both one's own and others' lives.

An important reminder. It has to be entirely clear that insofar as a criminal act of physical abuse or murder has been committed, the psychological definition of madness that I propose is *not* intended in any way to mitigate against the criminal responsibility of the perpetrator—and no mercy at all is intended because the killer is "crazy" in the new sense that I propose use of the word. Legitimate humanitarian understanding and allowances for those people who truly cannot control themselves mentally can still be provided for in the law, but in all cases "crazy" destructive behaviors to other people must remain fully subject to legal judgment and punishment as mandated by the law. We are talking about a broader view of craziness, but not of any loosening of the legal consequences of hurting and killing others. Our schema is intended to make a psychological and ethical point that gets lost when we think of madness only in traditional terms as the person's own mental confusion and disorientation. In its essence, madness is much more the craziness of ruining the most precious gift of all, namely the priceless opportunity of life, either for oneself or for others. Again, I think this usage of the concept of craziness is truer to the ways ordinary people speak naturally. When people hear of a terrorist suicide bomber who blows up a building full of people, let alone blows himself up too, they say spontaneously, "That's crazy!" and I think they are right.

Granted, everything we are saying here is from the point of view of *our* Western culture, including its profound Judeo-Christian imprints, and notwithstanding the fact that we too know that there are other cultures that do *not* value life as we do and some (too, too many!) that even deify death. Do we have a right to allow ourselves to believe in the rightness of *our* conception that life is sacred, and to regard our way of thinking as essential to the advance of civilization? Do we have the right to impose our conception of the sacredness of life on other cultures (such as Nazism, Japanese kamikaze, or contemporary Jihadic Islamic suicide bombers) in our international legal tribunals and governmental bodies? *I believe strongly the answer is yes.*

Again, if one listens to the plain, everyday, natural language of people in the Western world, events such as 9/11 are spontaneously thought of by many people as the work of "madmen" because the warped idea of taking one's own life and others' lives deserves to be condemned as insane. Common sense says that the devotion of oneself to making death for whomever is no less than madness, and I don't believe that it should be any less the case in our Western psychology and psychiatry. We should not be ashamed of mental health professions that are grounded firmly in valuing life for all.

If the guiding value-principle in medicine as a whole is that human life should be saved, protected, and made as healthy as possible, then I think it is no less correct that the central value in mental health should be that sustaining human life is mentally healthy and that wantonly destroying human life is mentally ill (always with the exception of genuine self-defense).

In our current era of rampaging worldwide terrorism, this way of thinking also restores the dignity and meaningfulness of the mental health professions. We now have a conceptual basis for publicly stating that the rotten, crazy behaviors of killing civilians all over the globe are undesirable mentally ill acts.

The following is an oath that was found in a house in Kabul used by a Pakistani Islamist group fighting along with bin Laden's al-Qaeda: "I, Amir Maawia Sididiqi, son of Abdul Siddiqi, state in the presence of God that I will slaughter infidels my entire life. . . . May God give me strength in fulfilling this oath."[4]

Again I ask whether the obvious terrorist political goals of the speaker justify accepting his attack on life as a mentally healthy (at least as not a mentally unhealthy) though lousy political statement—the only problem for us Westerners being that he represents a competing ideological power bloc that we have to fight for our own survival in the jungle? *I don't think so.* I think any totalitarian conception that infidels and whatever enemies should be killed en masse and that the world should be conquered for the glory and power of any ideology is psychologically sick because it is anti-life and spiritually evil. It is, of course, also politically dangerous and needs to be fought against with all our power because it is truly dangerous to life.

Our mental health professions have largely refrained from making any defining statements about "political events," and I think this is both cowardly and unsound scientifically. Ours are the sciences of human behavior, and terrorism is human behavior! So what do we have to say about it?

A fiery anti-American preacher in a mosque in London told his congregants following the September 11 attacks on the Pentagon and World Trade Center that the attacks were organized by the United States itself as "a dirty plot against mankind in general and Muslims in particular."[5]

Obviously this bizarre claim is warping the facts and is a corrupt use of language in defense of a fascist ideology. Again, as I think of my training in mental health, such rotten distortion of known reality in its essence is crazy. In fact, I can't help wonder if this degree of distortion is any different from the violations of reality by traditional psychotics. *Does the use of such nutty thinking for a political purpose make it any less nuts?*

Conclusion: The Sacredness of Life

The Western value of the sacredness of life needs to be the core value of civilization (always remembering that we in the West also have brutal fascists like the Nazis and Communists).

Jonathan Glover is a British philosopher-ethicist. In his book, *Humanity: A Moral History of the Twentieth Century*, Glover searches for the psychological tools that await in our moral traditions that can be cultivated in our moral imagination to restrain us from being so destructive. He observes that the bulwark that religion was supposed to provide by now is significantly eroded, but he identifies three possible bulwarks:

1. Sympathy for human life
2. Respect for human dignity
3. Moral identity—adoption of the belief that "I am the kind of person who would not do that sort of thing" (but he cautions that moral identity can be defined otherwise and quite warped, as the Nazis did)[6]

Murders of people are the prime mental health (and medical) problem in our human existence. They are the number one cause of unnatural death. The following is how I believe mental health professionals should be trained and instructed for everyday management of serious threats of murder, and I think these are also the correct instructions for human society at large.

1. Threats of murder are dangerous: call out the police and someday perhaps an international police army as urgently as possible.
2. Threats of murder are nuts, crazy, mentally ill, psychotic; remember the dangerous person(s) cannot be released into civilized society until it is demonstrated that they are no longer dangerous or violent. You don't just let Ebola run around.

Table 7.1. Treating Emotional Violence and Evil

DISORDERS OF INCOMPETENCE AND PSEUDOCOMPETENCE IN MARITAL, FAMILY & PARENTING—DISORDERS OF DOING HARM TO *S E L F*

Top Left of Chart

DISORDERS OF *INCOMPETENCE, VULNERABILITY AND PERSONAL WEAKNESS*	**MARITAL DISORDERS OF *INCOMPETENCE, VULNERABILITY AND PERSONAL WEAKNESS***	**FAMILY DISORDERS OF *INCOMPETENCE, VULNERABILITY AND PERSONAL WEAKNESS***	**PARENTING DISORDERS OF *INCOMPETENCE, VULNERABILITY AND PERSONAL WEAKNESS***
Reactions to anxiety through exaggerated disavowals of competence, mastery and strength	Reactions to anxiety through exaggerated disavowals of competence as a spouse, pronounced vulnerability in interactions with spouse, and a position of weakness in marital relationship	Reactions to anxiety through exaggerated disavowals of competence and executing family tasks, pronounced vulnerability, and position of weakness in family relationships	Reactions to anxiety through exaggerated disavowals of competence and pronounced vulnerability, position of weakness in parent/child relationships and/or with other parent
NEUROSIS: INABILITY TO ENJOY ONESELF AND LIFE	***Inability to enjoy oneself as a member of a couple and to enjoy the spouse relationship***	***Inability to enjoy oneself as a member of a family and to enjoy family relationships***	***Inability to enjoy oneself as a parent and to enjoy the child(ren) and the other parent***
Renunciation of power in self	Renunciation of power or the right to assert self and make demands of spouse	Renunciation of power or the right to assert one's self and make demands of family members	Renunciation of power or the right to assert one's self and inability to make demands of child(ren) and/or the other parent
Excessive demands of self	Excessive demands of self in spousal relationship, position of a sufferer in the marital relationship, low self-esteem as a spouse, and neurotic worry and concern about the reactions of spouse	Excessive demands of self in family relationships, position of a sufferer in family relationships, low self-esteem as a family member, neurotic worry and concern about the reactions of family members	Excessive demands of self in parental relationships, position of a sufferer in parenting relationships, low self-esteem as a parent, neurotic worry and concern about the reactions of child(ren) and/or the other parent

DISORDERS OF INCOMPETENCE AND PSEUDOCOMPETENCE IN MARITAL, FAMILY & PARENTING—DISORDERS OF DOING HARM TO *O T H E R S*

Top Right of Chart

DISORDERS OF PSEUDOCOMPETENCE, INVULNERABILITY AND DOING HARM TO OTHERS	**MARITAL DISORDERS OF PSEUDOCOMPETENCE, INVULNERABILITY AND DOING HARM TO OTHERS**	**FAMILY DISORDERS OF PSEUDOCOMPETENCE, VULNERABILITY AND DOING HARM TO OTHERS**	**PARENTING DISORDERS OF PSEUDOCOMPETENCE, INVULNERABILITY AND DOING HARM TO OTHERS**
Reactions to anxiety through exaggerated disavowals of incompetence, vulnerability and weakness (or avowals of exaggerated strength, invulnerability, or superiority)	Reactions to anxiety through exaggerated avowals of pseudo- competence as a spouse, pronounced pseudo invulnerability in interactions with spouse, position of pseudostrength and control in marital relationship	Reactions to anxiety through exaggerated avowals of pseudo- competence, pseudo-invulnerability, position of pseudostrength and control in family relationships	Reactions to anxiety through exaggerated avowals of pseudo-competence and pseudo-invulnerability, position of pseudostrength and control in parent/child relationships and/or with other parent
NEUROSIS: DISTURBING OTHERS' ENJOYMENT OF THEMSELVES AND THEIR LIVES	***Disturbing other's enjoyment of the marriage and of the spouse relationship***	***Disturbing others' enjoyment of the family and of family relationships***	***Disturbing child(ren)'s enjoyment of being a child in a family and/or the other spouse in parenting***
Denial of weakness and vulnerability	Denial of weakness and vulnerability as a spouse in the marital relationship; excessive demands made of spouse	Denial of weakness and vulnerability as a family member in family relationships; excessive demands made of family members	Denial of weakness and vulnerability as a parent in relationships to child(ren) and/or other parent; excessive demands made of child(ren) and/or the other parent
Claiming power over others	Claiming power over spouse; perpetrator, accomplice or bystander to emotional suffering of spouse; excessively high self-esteem as a spouse; lack of worry and concern about spouse	Claiming power over family members; perpetrator, accomplice or bystander to emotional suffering of family members; excessively high self-esteem as a family member; lack of worry and concern about family members	Claiming power over child(ren) and/or other parent; perpetrator, accomplice or bystander to emotional suffering of child(ren) and/or other parent; excessively high self-esteem as a parent; lack of worry and concern about child(ren) and/or the other parent

(continued)

Table 7.1. ***(continued)***

DISORDERS OF DOING HARM TO *S E L F*

Middle Left of Chart

	MARITAL DISORDERS	FAMILY DISORDERS	PARENTING DISORDERS
PERSONALITY AND CHARACTER DISORDERS: RESTRICTION OR EXAGGERATION OF SELF IN STYLE OF EXPERIENCING, DISTURBANCE IN ABILITY TO DELAY NEEDS, AND REPEATED SELF-DESTRUCTIVE BEHAVIOR	***Disordered regulation of one's needs in the marital relationship, especially oversensitivity and childish demands for gratification from one's spouse***	***Disordered regulation of one's needs in family relationships, especially oversensitivity and childish demands for gratification from one's family***	***Disordered regulation of one's needs in parenting relationships, especially oversensitivity and childish demands for gratification from one's child(ren) and/or other parent***
Repeatedly upset and hurt, excessive demands for comfort	Repeatedly upset and hurt by spouse, excessive demands for comfort from spouse	Repeatedly upset and hurt by family members and family life, excessive demands for comfort from family	Repeatedly upset and hurt by child(ren) and/or other parent, excessive demands for comfort from one's child(ren) and/or the other parent
Demeaning of self	Repeatedly humiliated and blamed by spouse	Repeatedly humiliated and blamed by family members for own needs	Repeatedly humiliated and blamed by child(ren) and/or the other parent
Narcissistic overconcern with self	Repeatedly overdemanding and pressuring of spouse for own needs	Repeatedly overdemanding and pressuring of family members for own needs	Repeatedly overdemanding and pressuring of child(ren) and/or the other parent, for own needs
Abuses of oneself and self-punishment	Abuses of oneself as a spouse – emotionally or physically	Abuses of oneself as a family member – emotionally or physically	Abuses of oneself as a parent – emotionally or physically
Damaging one's life opportunity seriously	Chronic inability to achieve intimacy with marital partner	Chronic inability to achieve intimacy with family members	Chronic inability to achieve intimacy with child(ren) and/or the other parent

DISORDERS OF DOING HARM TO *OTHERS*
Middle Right of Chart

PERSONALITY AND CHARACTER DISORDERS: REPEATEDLY DISAPPOINTING, INTRUDING ON OR UPSETTING OTHERS, AND EXPLOITATION OR HURTING OF OTHERS	MARITAL DISORDERS ***Disturbing other's ability to achieve and maintain effective regulation of needs in the marital relationship***	FAMILY DISORDERS ***Disturbing others' ability to achieve and maintain effective regulation of needs in family relationships***	PARENTING DISORDERS ***Disturbing ability of one's children and/or the other parent to achieve and maintain effective regulation of their needs in family life***
Disappointing and upsetting	Repeatedly disappoints, upsets, hurts spouse	Repeatedly disappoints, upsets, hurts other family members	Repeatedly disappoints, upsets, hurts child(ren) and/or the other parent
Demeaning and dehumanization of other	Repeatedly humiliates, blames or relates to spouse with contempt and devaluation	Repeatedly humiliates, blames or relates to family members with contempt and devaluation	Repeatedly humiliates, blames or relates to child(ren) and/or other parent with contempt and devaluation
Narcissistic overconcern with self at expense of others	Repeatedly overdemands and pressures spouse for own needs at expense of other	Repeatedly overdemands and pressures other family members at expense of their needs	Repeatedly overdemands and pressures child(ren) and/or other parent at expense of their needs
Exploitation of others, abuse and cruelty	Abuses spouse emotionally, sexually, or physically	Abuses other family members emotionally, sexually, or physically	Abuses child(ren) and/or other parent emotional, sexually or physically
Damaging seriously other's life opportunity	Potential growth and development of spouse seriously blocked	Potential growth and development of family members seriously blocked	Potential growth and development of child(ren) and/or other parent seriously blocked

(continued)

Table 7.1. *(continued)*

DISORDERS OF DOING HARM TO *S E L F*

Bottom Left of Chart

PSYCHOSIS: BREAKDOWN OF ABILITY TO FUNCTION IN THE ORDINARY WORLD	**MARITAL DISORDERS**	**FAMILY DISORDERS**	**PARENTING DISORDERS**
	Breakdown of ability to function as a spouse in the ordinary everyday world	***Breakdown of ability to function as a family member in the ordinary everyday world***	***Breakdown of ability to function as a parent in the ordinary everyday world***
Extreme inability to function	Extreme inability to function in the marital relationship	Extreme inability to function in family relationships	Extreme inability to function as a parent with child(ren) and/or with the other parent
Irreversible self-destruction, e.g., suicidal	Irreversible self-destruction, e.g., being driven crazy in response to one's spouse, or being driven to suicide	Irreversible self-destruction, e.g., being driven crazy in response to other family members, or being driven to suicide	Irreversible self-destruction, e.g., being driven crazy in response to parental role and/or the need to function with child(ren) or other parent, or being driven to suicide

DISORDERS OF DOING HARM TO *OTHERS*

Bottom Right of Chart

***PSYCHOSIS:* DAMAGES OTHERS' ABILITY TO FUNCTION IN THE ORDINARY EVERYDAY WORLD**	**MARITAL DISORDERS**	**FAMILY DISORDERS**	**PARENTING DISORDERS**
	Damages ability of spouse to function in the ordinary everyday world	**Damages ability of other family members to function in the ordinary everyday world**	**Damages ability of child(ren) and/or other parent to function in the ordinary everyday world**
Incapacitates and destroys ability to function	Extreme incapacitating and destroying of spouse's ability to function	Extreme incapacitating and destroying of other family members' ability to function	Extreme incapacitating and destroying of children and/or other parent's ability to function
Irreversible destruction of others—e.g., murdering other, driving other to suicide or murder	Irreversible destruction of spouse—e.g., murdering spouse, driving spouse to suicide or murder	Irreversible destruction of other family members—e.g., murdering others, driving others to suicide or murder	Irreversible destruction of children and/or other parent—e.g., murdering children and/or other parent, driving children and/or other parent to suicide or murder

PART TWO: PERPETRATORS, ACCOMPLICES, BYSTANDERS, AND VICTIMS, AND TRYING NOT TO BE ANY OF THEM

In the following sections, we look in somewhat greater depth at the everyday manifestations of each of the role choices of *perpetrators*, *accomplices*, *bystanders*, or *victims*—and, if at all possible, trying to be none of these. Again we will refer to manifestations of these roles on the societal level, especially in the horrendous genocides that pulverized nearly 300 million people in the twentieth century,[7] but then we will try to move on to how these roles are lived out in our plain everyday human lives, and also in the inner worlds of our own minds.

Primo Levi, an Italian scientist and Holocaust survivor who captured the respect and sympathy of many people for the decency and straightforwardness with which he reported his suffering in Auschwitz, also saw the ultimate meanings of Auschwitz for *ordinary everyday life*:

> Levi was deeply committed to the task of giving testimony about the Nazis' deeds in order to warn us of the sinister danger that Auschwitz represents. Levi went far beyond testimony to engage in an ambitious project of constructing a usable, post-Auschwitz ethics based on "ordinary virtues." Unlike the classical heroic or saintly virtues required for an ideally good life, these are centered on the ordinary life of marriage, family, home, work, and production. Levi's ethical attention was focused on those virtues that are available to everyone and that typically act on a small scale.[8]

Perpetrators

In a sense, little more needs to be said about the *perpetrators* than we have already said, including the observation that many of them experience considerable joy and comfort in their "jobs." They are the actual architects, project directors, and working staff creating horrors in this world such as genocide. It also behooves us to be very aware that this is a role that does not go wanting for players when the opportunity arises. The history of our human race is that enormous numbers of people are available to be perpetrators of the destruction of life on a grand scale, in many cases unhesitatingly, and as just noted, often with obvious considerable satisfaction and joy.

Nonetheless, it is also true that the perpetrators distribute themselves along a complex continuum. There are those who are manifestly sadistic, such as those Eric Fromm called necrophiliacs, or lovers of death.[9] There are those who in political terms subscribe to an ideology and who become so consumed with the idealism and evident truth of their chosen ideology that they believe in taking their loyalty to an extreme—and find joy in doing so. It is their ideology *über alles* that for them justifies taking the lives of anybody who stands in the way of their total truth.[10] There are obviously also many people who rejoice and/or are emboldened to act out their awaiting pull of evil sadism by the "justification" of an ideology that has come their way.

There are others who are not necessarily openly sadistic or inspired believers, but instead obedient, conformist, and pragmatic. They want to do as they are told. They want to be on the winning side. They want to do as most people are doing. A British playwright, C. P. Snow, portrayed so well in a stirring drama, *Good*,[11] how there are expedient people who are seeking to advance, who allow their "career opportunities" to lead them toward the rewards and success that are available to perpetrators in their society, and then also get turned on to the joys of their power. Sadly, there are an enormous number of people who do what they are told to do—they are represented by the two-thirds of the subjects that Stanley Milgram identified in his classic experiments of people who did whatever the experimenter told them to do *just because* he said so.[12] Other perpetrators are people who strive to be the superiors and leaders in a system. Being on top and feeling superior to others is crucial to their feeling good. Power is what interests them, and they take advantage of any structure or situation that empowers them to lord it over others.[13]

To our astonishment, we have learned that the perpetrators who are drawn to the tasks of destroying other people primarily because they are so involved in seeking power for themselves include many physicians. These physicians transform their roles from healers to killers, utilizing the rationalizations of medical imagery to justify their killing as if it is a device for removing some diseased aspect of society and thereby healing society.[14] While they define their killing procedures in medical language as if they were healing the body of society, what is really driving these physician killers is an unstoppable drive toward megalomaniac superiority along with their surrender to the instinct of destruction that lies waiting as a part of all of us.[15]

Freud saw the mind organized around two opposing forces: the life drives, Eros, and the death drives, Thanatos. The dialectical conflict between these runs deeply through all human experience and behavior. Eros promotes the creation of life and creativity; Thanatos aims to break down and destroy life and, in Freud's words, "to lead organic life back into the inanimate state."[16]

In a fascinating exchange of correspondence between Albert Einstein and Sigmund Freud, Einstein wrote in a letter dated April 29, 1931: "I greatly admire your passion to ascertain the truth—a passion that has come to dominate all else in your thinking. You have shown with irresistible lucidity how inseparably the aggressive and destructive instincts are bound up in the human psyche with those of love and the lust for life. At the same time, your convincing arguments make manifest your deep devotion to the great goal of the internal and external liberation of man from the evils of war."[17]

Who are the perpetrators? In everyday business life, perpetrators are the men and women who step on everybody to make it to the top. They are the supervisors, superiors, managers, and employers who rule with an imperious and heavy hand, and have no compunctions about reneging on obligations to workers, terminating other people's gainful employment, or blocking qualified people's opportunities for advancement.

In everyday family life, perpetrators include family members who dominate other members of the family and/or the family group as a whole, essentially for the satisfaction of having power over other(s). They have little real concern in response to signs of distress in others. As parents they intend to be in charge of their children and to have them serve their needs no matter the cost to their children. Such domination can be organized with ostensibly great charm and can be delivered in the name of caring, love, and responsibility. The parent may be a grandly positive figure, such as a munificent father and husband who gives monies and supplies with great generosity, or a super-mother who gives all of herself and more to her family. Yet concealed within the magnanimity is an unrelenting demand for power. As we saw earlier, sometimes this demand for power is evidenced further in a decided and even extreme reluctance to receive supplies or any form of emotional support from others. Sometimes the power is evidenced in a vengeful bookkeeping of demands to be compensated and repaid for all that one has given. The quest for power is obviously in the service of self-interest, and there are also other needs, such as to be at the center of things, that can be involved. Psychological and psychiatric observations abound of parents who are self-involved and out for their own ambitions in life. Psychiatrist Alice Miller described parents whose emotional tyranny and demandingness force the child to be the parent's emotional slave in whatever life functions.[18] Often the parents are unable to see and experience the child and their needs even in dire situations. One woman recovered in therapy a memory of having an asthma attack as a child and knocking pleadingly on the bedroom door of her rich parents' Long Island home, but her parents refused to open the door.

We also spoke earlier about the most concealed perpetrators in family life, who disguise themselves in a calm demeanor no matter what tragedy or pressure is taking place. If, for example, there is a child who is showing serious emotional problems, this kind of parent remains quite composed with the school, police, and mental health authorities—while the second parent may be tearing their hair out in upset. Although this description in essence describes an ultimate bystander rather than a perpetrator, in no few cases this calm, unresponsive parent is, in fact, unconsciously also a prime instigator of the problem. Ostensibly more mature and nicer than everybody else, this parent is "passing the buck" of worry and coping to the next parent, keeping that parent upset enough for the two of them, so to speak, and at the same time cueing the child to keep up the troublemaking. People close to these concealed perpetrators get enraged, but often find little support from others because the perpetrator in these people is so concealed—a form of what M. Scott Peck called "People of the Lie."[19]

To sum up, if and when one has the privilege to look inside the inner minds of perpetrators, one finds sadistic, cruel people, but also people who have a self-serving, narcissistic interest in their own comfort, pleasure, and material gain, including the satisfaction of advancement in a hierarchy—reminiscent of the observations of psychologist Gustave Gilbert[20] at the Nuremberg Trials, who observed the high-ranking

Nazis had two overwhelming characteristics: narcissism and driving ambition. For many perpetrators it is not that they want to hurt others, let alone kill them; what matters to them is that they advance in their system of hierarchies. Seeking power and superiority over others is the end-all and be-all of one's goals. The other—whether spouse, child, business associate, sportsmate, or schoolmate—is not recognized as valuable in the beauty of *their* being, and there is no appreciation of the legitimacy of another person's power for themselves. Many perpetrators show a distinct lack of feeling or empathy for the suffering or the basic needs of other human beings—here too reminiscent of a large figure in the Holocaust, the master administrator of murder, Adolf Eichmann, having no feeling for people as *human beings*, because people were for him *things* or *objects* to be sorted and dispensed.[21] *Every one of us knows these people, and every one of us has parts of us that might make us into one of these people if we let these parts of our minds gain control of our personalities.*

Accomplices

Obviously, the *accomplices* carry a greater responsibility than bystanders for contributing to the actual destruction wrought by the perpetrators. Like bullies who hold the victim while the perpetrator punches them out, the accomplices help make the destruction possible.

In the Holocaust and other genocides, the accomplices are the myriads of people who make the entire convoluted system work. The guards who made sure none of the victims escaped the clutches of the actual killers were accomplices, even if any given one of the guards in his own right may not have killed anyone. The railroad employees who moved Jews to the concentration camps were accomplices. So were even the ordinary merchants who delivered food supplies to the concentration camp, if they knew what was going on. The manufacturers, engineers, chemists, technicians, truck drivers delivering supplies, and whoever else from the plants that produced the Zyklon-B gas that was used in the gas chambers were certainly accomplices. Even the supporting secretarial staff at the offices of the companies that created the gas chambers and mass ovens were bona fide accomplices, because they knowingly sent out the documents for the construction and maintenance of the machinery of mass killing. We have deeply disturbing records of the bids to the Nazi government that were made by engineering companies for these disgusting projects.[22]

The famed and beloved Catholic priest and Trappist monk, Father Thomas Merton, wrote a powerful and moving poem titled, "Chant to Be Used in Processions around a Site with Furnaces." In it he makes brilliant use of the above accursed bids and their testimonies to human beings' relentless quests for power.

> They got the contract and with faultless workmanship delivered very fast goods.
>
> "For transporting the customers we suggest using light carts on wheels a drawing is submitted"[23]

Father Merton concludes apropos ongoing events in our world, "'Do not think yourself better because you burn up friends and enemies with long-range missiles without ever seeing what you have done.'"[24]

A creative Israeli playwright, Wim Van Leer, used a company manufacturing the crematoria for the Nazis as the setting for a play that includes a Jewish worker whose life is saved for a while working for the company, including his being used eerily as a model victim to measure the dimensions of the equipment being constructed.[25] In the Holocaust, some of the Jewish kapos, or appointed block leaders, tragically were also accomplices. Some of the kapos were killed after the war by their fellow prisoners or were subsequently brought to trial in Israel (among the kapos there was a wide spectrum of behaviors ranging from manifest sadistic Nazi-type behaviors to efforts at protective leadership roles and actions to save fellow Jews as much as possible).[26]

The roles of accomplices range over a wide continuum, which begins far away from the scenes of the perpetration, where people in a sense are unaware—though in truth they generally do know but may make themselves believe they do not know—that they are contributing to a machinery of destruction. Further examples of accomplices who were removed from the actual concentration and death camps in the Holocaust would include public relations experts who created the magnificent heraldry that Hitler used to propel himself to hypnotic popularity among the German people. So were the cooks, bakers, garbage men, electricians, plumbers, and whoever in Berlin who kept the government of the Third Reich going in a world in which the Jews were disappearing daily to their fates of death. They were all accomplices in degrees for all that they may have pretended even to themselves to have nothing to do with the policies of their society.

Obviously some accomplices are paid handsomely for their work while others are not paid much at all. Obviously some feel they have no choice but to go along with a regime that might harm them if they don't cooperate, while others know that they have the option not to play a contributing role in the destruction. The moral continuum extends from various degrees of responsibility to exoneration or understanding of the choice to be an accomplice, but the underlying moral choice in all cases is basically the same—*within the range of possibility how much does one agree to help the killers and destroyers or not?*

In everyday life too, we see many accomplices doing harm to others. At all levels of business or professional life, when serious injustice is done to a fellow worker, there are co-workers who know that their colleague(s) is (are) being abused and who even assist directly in the abuse. Many of these workers will execute whatever roles are imposed on them. The same scenarios take place in all walks of life—business, government, medicine, academia, and educational systems, even sports. In all walks of life, there are people who follow the dictates of controlling persons who are doing harm to others. They do the bidding of the leaders unquestioningly and promote their own safety and self-interest by serving the people in power.

Olympic officials agreed to remove Jewish runners from participating in the 1936 Olympics in Berlin in cooperation with the prevailing antisemitism of the host Germans, who were already under Hitler's rule.[27]

In family life, there are members of the family who clearly assist other members of the family to implement their domination and tyranny. Examples of accomplices to persecution in family life include a parent who joins the other parent in punishing a child overly severely, or who actively allows the other parent to engage in physical or sexual abuse, or to insult and degrade a child. Even children can be accomplices to persecution, such as when one or more siblings join in dominating or ganging up on one of the children who is designated the victim (see the intended fate of the biblical Joseph!), or even in ganging up on a parent or both parents.

Accomplices in family life also include a spouse or children who accept gifts given by a seemingly generous donor in return for obedience and cooperation with the nastiness and unfairness of the donor to others. Some children will accept an unfair share of an inheritance at the expense of other siblings in return for cooperating with and serving the egotistical demands of the parent who is pulling the purse strings. For all that accomplices can plead, even in their own minds, that it wasn't they who pulled the trigger, accomplices are obviously the Devil's helpers.

Bystanders

Bystanders by definition have been looked upon by many people as innocents who were trapped by fate into witnessing evil actions they did not initiate or assist and did not have the sense, ability, or courage to do something. More probing analyses of bystanders nonetheless raise questions whether in *some* cases they really could have done something to stand up against evil, and how by doing nothing active they actually allowed, facilitated, or supported the evil. *The very choice to do nothing* can also be a choice of a policy position to enable evil to prevail.

Implicit in many a choice to be a bystander—sometimes even observably so—is a kind of joy in seeing another person hurt or destroyed, based perhaps on a kind of relief that another person is suffering what one fears to suffer oneself, or a kind of cynicism that this is the way it always is and so be it as long as it is a fate that befalls others and not oneself. I have sometimes used the biblical story of Abraham's intended sacrifice of Isaac as an example. Indeed, some classical rabbinical legends have it that Sarah, wife of Abraham, knew that Abraham was taking their son Isaac to Mount Moriah to kill him as a sacrifice to God, but she said nothing.[28]

In everyday business life, bystanders to evil are seen when colleagues stand by in utter silence and watch a fellow worker being abused or unfairly transferred, demoted, or fired. Many times bystanders succumb to a state of mind in which they do not let themselves see and know the injustice that is being done. The bystanders are the managers and employers who do not take the risks of challenging the power of the bosses and the system that is treating others viciously.

❖ A longtime dedicated and capable salesman for a big food company is peremptorily dismissed at age sixty-one, or four years before his retirement and pension are due to come into force—in a system where there is no accumulation of credits for the many years he worked. The other sales executives accept management's right to do as it sees fit, and his fellow employees do not stand up for him. The employee who has been forced out is stunned and sickened by his dismissal. In the ensuing years he ages very rapidly and falls chronically ill.

In family life, bystanders are members of the family who stand by passively, as if unknowingly, without reacting to the domination and tyranny of others—for example, a parent who remains passive in the face of their spouse abusing, rejecting, or persecuting one or more children. The bystander ignores possible opportunities for intervention in the situation such as challenging their mate to stop hurting the child, or at least personally extending additional emotional protection and support to the child. Whatever the problems in family life, one can at least try to take a helpful and meaningful stand—for example, doing everything to stop the other spouse from drinking, taking charge to stop a child from taking drugs, or fighting to regain parental control over a teenager's abusive domination of a family. Siblings, too, can be bystanders when they stand by without reacting to obvious rejection or persecution of a brother or sister. I have seen many people suffer serious guilt feelings in later years over having taken the coward's easy way out of not reacting to what they really did see happening to others in their family. A clear-cut example of being a bystander in family life is a parent who fails to offer an involved caring leadership to stem a child's emotional disturbance.

In a study of the roles of parents in the development of *subsequent* manifest mental instability or illness, Pnina Blitz showed how in cases where the disturbance could be identified as rooted primarily in the destructiveness of one of the parents toward that child, the other parent in a majority of cases was found to have remained a passive bystander who allowed the emotional damage to take place.[29]

Years ago, I wrote an impassioned plea for the use of family therapy for mobilizing the second parent in such situations to take a role, intervene, and stand up to protect and fight for the beleaguered child.[30] It was clear to me that here is a major tool for saving any number of children from being victims (which sadly I myself had to employ in my personal life in one aspect of my parenting). But a fair number of my mental health colleagues criticized me, even severely, for creating additional conflicts in the family rather than finding a peaceful way to unite the parents in common good cause. Personally, I believe there are frequent enough instances where one parent is so committed to evil, for whatever reason of seeking power or seeking to exploit a child emotionally for the parent's own mental economy, that even the most talented therapists have no possibility of correcting these parents and redirecting them to more positive ways of taking care of their children. Therefore, the only viable option that remains is the possibility of mobilizing the *other* parent to love and protect the beleaguered child and to undertake as positive a fight as possible to stop or minimize the destructiveness of the first parent.

John Darley[31] conducted a quixotic study at the prestigious Princeton Theological Seminary, a Christian seminary, with students who were studying the subject of the Good Samaritan. The students were told that they needed to tape a sermon on the subject of the Good Samaritan at the campus studio and were given a time for their taping. On their way to the studio, the students encountered a dupe who acted injured and called out for help. The question was how many students of the Good Samaritan would stop to help the man in trouble. To add further irony and understanding, half of the students had been told they were late for their studio time and needed to rush if they didn't want to lose their turn and half were not. Yes, the ones rushing in their self-interest were less often helpers. *To be a bystander in effect can be a kind of accomplice to the perpetrators. Many times it can work to allow and assist the perpetration of destruction.*

Victims

There remains one more dramatic role for us to consider: the would-be *victims.* Surprisingly, victims, too, play certain roles in the dramas of the destruction of the gift of life along with the perpetrators, accomplices, and bystanders. Of course, many, probably most, victims in this world do *not* choose their fates but are selected by the whirls of fate to be unwillingly victimized by others. It is both wrong and immoral in any way to blame the millions of people in this world who have been overpowered by destruction wreaked by strong and ugly forces. Nonetheless, *some* cases of victims do involve some degree or kind of availability to be victims, such as a failure of the potential victim to take precautions against being selected, or being unnecessarily available to be victimized, or being unprepared to defend oneself, or sometimes even an "asking for it." It would be intellectually and scientifically corrupt not to recognize a victim's enabling role for what it is when that is what is happening.

In general, an important and quite marvelous question we need to ask is, who are the people who do *everything* to fight back against being victimized if at all possible, versus those who are too paralyzed, frightened, cowered, or passive to try to protect themselves? In the case of children, already at young ages there is an amazing difference in some children who are much too available to succumb to being victims and suffer terrible defeats in their lives, versus some children in whom some wonderful natural force of pride and integrity rises up and stimulates them to fight against being victimized. I personally do not know how to understand these marvelous choices by these children, but I admire and love them so much. To this day I am not sure whether a fight for life such as these children put on derives from an intrinsic inner spirit like some other aspects of temperament with which a child is born; how much is taught, developed, and reinforced by influences in a child's environment; and how much is a spiritual gift that rises within a "soul." I do know that major differences in spirit do exist, and to this day I do not know of a psychological theory or model that explains or predicts who these warriors for survival are, but they take one's breath away in admiration. As a therapist, I try my best to evoke the fighting spirit for life that lies latent in children and have seen some wonderful outcomes, although the other sad side of this truth is that there are also children who fail to respond to my therapy or to the efforts of other helpers and educators in their lives, or even to constructive efforts by their parents who want them to be stronger, and in the mystery of the nature of their personalities these children themselves *choose* to be victims. Some young people get "hooked" into finding joy and satisfaction in being treated by their family and community as weak and incompetent. *Frighteningly and sadly, giving up becomes their way to "win" and even to feel good (in feeling bad).*

Again I want to state that people who commit suicide by definition are victims, but they also are perpetrators because they are literally taking the life of a person, albeit their own. Admittedly, in the face of their tragedy it takes a leap of thinking to consider or call them perpetrators of evil. (Remember I exclude from this discussion all cases where suicide is chosen in the face of terminal illness or disaster, torture, or oppressive conditions. I am referring to ordinary situations of what are obviously severe life stresses for the victim, but where objectively there is reason to judge that there was enough life left that hope and positive coping were viable options, yet the person chooses to kill themselves.) Notwithstanding our sympathy with the tragedy of the victim, even under great emotional stress the act of suicide is an internal philosophical *choice* that bespeaks one's basic orientation to life. For the suicider, life is not inviolate, holy, sacred, and to be protected. Suicide may well be seeking relief from overwhelming pain, but it is at the same time also a philosophical choice that ending life is a legitimate way of gaining a desired outcome.

Many other everyday behaviors, which are far removed from direct suicide, are also enactments of a readiness to suffer harm to oneself. In ordinary life, there are many "losers" who we know or sense are helping others to victimize them. Again I emphasize that I am very aware of the dangers of blaming victims unfairly and unkindly for their bad fates, which they do *not* bring on themselves. But I am also aware that a political exaggeration has developed in mental health where it is considered politically incorrect to identify objectively any roles or partial roles that *some* victims do play in seeking, soliciting, creating, or enabling their problems, and I believe that it is important for psychiatry and psychology to re-create an objective approach to seeing these situations as they really are and not surrender objectivity to pressure groups who mistakenly feel they are protecting the honor of victims by censoring all awareness of any of their contributing roles when they are present.

Thus some people lose their jobs by virtue of their performing less well than they could have or as a result of damaging their interpersonal relationships on the job, and one senses that they somehow needed and even wanted unconsciously to do themselves in. The victims in business include those who take their dismissal from a position without protest or fighting back against the insult of their termination, in some cases notwithstanding available possibilities of support from a union or possible legal help. Other people damage their health by failing to care for themselves, or by adopting known health-damaging habits such as smoking or eating unhealthfully, driving recklessly, handling weapons carelessly, or exposing themselves knowingly to damaging materials such as asbestos, dark and damp locations, or excessive radiation. Millions of people engage in various behaviors of excess that are obviously self-damaging.

There are also many ways to put oneself into a bad emotional state. The cultivation and management of one's emotional control is an important arena of life in which we are called on to manage our lives. One can deprive oneself of sleep for days on end, or stay constantly revved up to a level of disturbing turbulence, or stay violently enraged, or succumb to chronic brooding. One can also put all of one's eggs into a single basket of a specific profession or vocation and be swallowed up in a unidimensional way of life with too little exposure of oneself to other experiences or to meaningful relationships with people, and then there comes a point where one finds oneself very alone and disconnected.

Self-destructive behaviors go against the grain of a natural wisdom that tells us they are not good for our lives, but too many people do not respond to this wisdom. There are so many ways of doing oneself in, some slowly and some more rapidly. Some adults and children take the physical, sexual, and/or emotional abuse that is meted out to them as their fate and have little to no impulse to fight back or attempt to escape. Victims also include people who are on the "take" and agree to receive "rewards" from others at the expense of their freedom, personal power, and capacity for initiative; for example, children who accept unlimited indulgence from their parents at the expense of not developing more of their own natural individuality and pride in their own self-sufficiency.

Of course, in family life, only in a few cases is the actual life of a person at risk in quite the same immediate and brutal ways that are the case in an actual fascist state such as the Nazi world or several Communist dictatorships that were no less (in several cases even more) killers than Hitler. But so much of the *quality* of peoples' lives is very much at stake in everyday family life. Here is the story of a family and the respective roles of perpetrator, accomplice, bystander, and victim, where virtually everybody paid a huge price, including one who actually gave up his life and committed suicide.

❖ She was an enticingly seductive woman who produced such a fascinating flow of her emotional production that any number of her children, if not all, fell completely in love with her. The father—the mother's husband—had long since eliminated himself from being a significant figure in the family. His role was to be an *as if* person—as if significant, but not really so. He was a seemingly competent man who devoted himself to work and fervent religious practice, but he was a shadow appendage to his wife, and in no way did he figure as a meaningful presence in the lives of any of his children. On the contrary, he was the quintessential accomplice who allowed his wife to dominate seductively the lives of all the children.

The terrible price of the children's enticement by their mother was that they lost many parts of their own inner freedom to define themselves. The children grew up as if capable and successful in the atmosphere of indulgent nurturance that mother poured on them so long as they were hers, but inside themselves they were basically shaky. Although for many years they were ostensibly successful in their studies, military service, and setting up families, in truth they were unable to enjoy the seemingly considerable successes of their lives.

When the time came to marry, none of the children felt capable of really holding their mates for themselves because they felt themselves truly lovable and deserving. Instead they believed—like their mother—that their mates owed it to them to be possessed by them unconditionally, but unlike their mother they failed to captivate their mates, and soon there were major developments of disloyalty including sexual betrayals and decisions to divorce. Slowly but surely, three of the four adult children were estranged from their spouses who betrayed them or left them, and one of the adult children committed suicide—leaving behind several young children.

The emotional perpetrator in this case was clearly the seductive controlling mother (although she too suffered tragically), and the emotional bystander (to a degree of being an accomplice) in this case was the father, precisely because he did nothing to give his children strength. It was interesting that in the wake of the tragedy of the one adult child's suicide, at least one of the siblings suffered deeply, as if having been an accomplice. This brother feared he hadn't done enough to save his brother when he saw that his brother was in emotional turmoil, when in fact he did attempt to give all that he knew how to give of himself to his brother in a vain effort to help. The children were the victims, in a general sense unwittingly and without choices, yet in another sense also participating in their being victimized because they did not fight back against their mother's overcontrol of them and her seductive claims of power over them.

Conclusion: Standing Up against the Ruination of Life

Surprising as it seems, there is a common bond that exists between perpetrators, accomplices, bystanders, and those victims who make themselves too available, and that is they do not value and cherish life and protect it at all costs. All are too available to harm and destroying life.

A Fascist Mind is naturally available to initiating behaviors that lead to the ruination of life. The chain of destructiveness can begin with the fact that a Fascist Mind strongly insists on a single outcome and broaches no interference with that outcome. Ultimately, Fascist Mind thinking lends itself to a belief that anyone and anything that stands in the way of the desired goal needs and deserves to be eliminated and possibly even exterminated. A Fascist Mind is so taken with a joy of being superior to others and having power over others that it delights in going to war against its external and internal enemies.

A Democratic Mind abhors the destruction of life. It makes choices and sets goals that are life-enhancing and protecting of life, and is careful that the pursuit of its goals not justify utilizing ugly means to achieve the goal that in their own right will do harm to life. For then the most precious of all will have been lost. With the exception of cases where the principle of self-defense against evil and freedom from tyranny are really involved, whatever the goals and however worthy they are all become meaningless when innocent human life is destroyed in vain.[32] By definition, a Democratic Mind calls for maximum life opportunity for everyone and celebrates battling for life.

PART THREE: (THE BIBLICAL) *JOB* FIGHTS BACK AGAINST TRAGEDY AND TOTAL DISASTER

In this section we will look at possible psychotherapeutic help for victims of terrible serious losses, pain and illness, privations of all sorts, and also known oncoming unnatural death. These are *Job*-like people, following the biblical figure of *Job*. They are in big trouble.

Who knows? My own judgment is that in the overall course of life many—perhaps even a majority—of human beings have to endure some *Job*-period(s) in their lives—whether a terrible premature loss of one or more loved ones, discomforting and life-threatening injury or illness, the unfolding of a disaster such as earthquakes, typhoons, meteors, infectious epidemics, or historical processes such as revolution, the rise of fascist government, dictatorship, inquisitions, pogroms and massacres, wars, and genocide. Life gets rough. For many people it becomes overwhelmingly terrifying, painful, and disillusioning, and as we know, ultimately it is naturally downright fatal for everyone.

In truth this section on *Job* is an "impossible" one to write. For there are obviously so many times in life when a victim is so devastated and destroyed that they have no real chance to fight back, neither in spirit nor in action against the oppressor. For example, when we stand at the gravesides of tragic victims of atrocity, massacre, and genocide, where the victims literally had no chance to fight back for themselves, we can only grieve and protest their fates after the fact, when there is nothing we can do to bring them back. Similarly, on the more prosaic level of our individual lives, there are many irreparable situations where the wisest path is to yield to our oncoming death in as spiritually wholesome a way as possible. It is also heartbreaking to see loved ones and friends in unbearable agonies over their bodies, minds or primary relationships—losing power to a degenerative illness, terminally ill with cancer, worried about a child on serious drugs, alone or facing the breakup of a marriage and/or family—and often enough an unfathomable torture of a combination of these.

However, the brighter side of *Job*-conditions is that there also are situations, even of persecution and atrocities, where there *are* possibilities of fighting back against a perpetrator, and it is an ennobling and wonderful function of free and healthy people to "take up arms" on their own behalf.

- If I am in a concentration camp, I pray that I will join or initiate an underground revolt.
- Given genocidal persecution of my people, I pray that I will take every step to hide out as cleverly as possible and not submit myself sheepishly to imprisonment and execution.
- Given a period of hostile occupation of my land and denial of the democratic rights of my people, I pray that I will make every effort to join or will take the initiative to create a local underground that fights back for freedom.
- If my own government turns fascist and persecutory (and I think this happens periodically to democratic governments, too), I pray that I will fight back.

It would seem that it is so much simpler to fight back against threats and traumas in our own *everyday lives* than against the devastating destructiveness at the hands of fearsome military, police, or terrorist powers. Yet, strangely enough, even in these "simple" situations it is often very hard, and these too also require thrusts of real courage to stand up and fight.

- If I am being exploited, manipulated, or pushed around insultingly by an employer, I pray that I will find ways to carry myself in dignity and fight back as capably and wisely as possible.
- If I am being dominated and pushed around by a member of my family—my spouse, a dominating parent, a nasty sibling, or (as also happens too often) a child of mine, I pray that I will develop wise and effective power for stopping the domination.
- If a person whom I love and need very much suffers a fatal accident or illness, I know that I will mourn them deeply and heartbreakingly, but I pray that I will come to terms with the reality and if possible develop meaningful alternative relationships.

  Without at all minimizing the shock, worry, and sadness when a person becomes ill or disabled, there are nonetheless some positive measures that it may be possible to take. In general these include steps to take better care of oneself and insofar as possible to seek the best possible help from competent physicians and medical centers.
- If I am sick, I want *both* to yield to the situation's reality and at the same time to fight back in all ways possible for better health and, if possible, for a cure.

Often enough people get pounded by a sequence of events in their lives that places them in what I am calling a *Job*-position. The *Job*-like positions—based on the biblical character who lost *everything* in his life—are hells. In the Bible, *Job* was a rancher who was the father of ten children and renowned for being a pious man. A skeptical angel, Satan, calls for a test of *Job* to prove whether he is really sincere in his faith or is simply responding gratefully to the wealth God has given him. God gives Satan permission to unleash on *Job* a series of catastrophes ranging from economic disaster to the deaths of his children. *Job* responds to his travails in submission to God: "The Lord gave, and the Lord hath taken away; blessed be the name of the Lord" (*Job* 1:21). When God remonstrates with Satan for drawing *Job* into a needlessly brutal experiment, Satan nonetheless argues for a further test. Again with God's permission, Satan now inflicts on *Job* "evil boils," or a painful skin disorder. Finally, *Job*'s wife urges him to "bless God," the paradoxical meaning of which is to curse God (see further explanation of this "bless" shortly), but he refuses. *But I am in favor of the wife's advice.*

The story and image of *Job* naturally become a guiding paradigm for all of us who have to cope with great losses, disasters, or illnesses—the endless evils that are done to human beings by and in the course of life.[33] Like all helping professionals, I of course have seen any number of people in the depths of their misery—a multi-millionaire industrialist who literally lost all his wealth and did not have money with which to hold together body and soul; a grieving parent who lost a beloved child to a cruel and premature death; a sick terminal patient who knew that death lay ahead in just a matter of time. Granted, even these illustrations are different from one another in the degree of finality of each situation. In theory the poor millionaire can become a millionaire once again, although he will have to start from scratch and his prospects the second time around may be as limited as those of most of us. Coming to terms with one's own imminent death or with the loss of a loved one are much more ultimate *Job*-like conditions,[34] and of these two examples people say the runaway "winner" in grief and pain is when one loses a child. Nonetheless, there is a good deal in common in all deeply difficult situations of bad fates, all of which are awesome and terrifying.

I suggest that recognizing the utter rottenness and unfairness of what is happening to us rather than submitting totally to a god's will or to fate—and fighting back in one's soul, and if possible in practical ways—may give some victims greater strength and endurance. This is as true for situations of unintentional, random, hellish pieces of bad luck as it is for the agonizing but more understandable suffering brought on by identifiable conditions such as war, terrorism, epidemics, the collapse of an economy, and more.

The alternative of yielding and accepting bad fates also has its real advantages. The decided advantage of yielding and accepting one's bad fate is that it brings many people comfort and quiet. When a theological concept of accepting god's will is invoked, there is the possibility of a mental experience of peacefulness and being carried away by angelic spirits that take one away from oneself and one's suffering. And in some cases, the quieting may in fact release potential forces for healing and overcoming that were locked up in the prior focus on one's pain.

On the other hand, blindly yielding and accepting one's bad fate is all too commonly a gateway to passivity and surrender. There are many situations where a spiritual regrouping and counterattack can be effective, and it is a huge mistake not to fight back.

Unexpected *Job*-situations that fall on us from seemingly "nowhere" are obviously demoralizing. They evoke feelings of self-pity and also self-accusations that somehow one has brought rotten outcomes on oneself, perhaps also as if they are intrinsically deserved by us. To suffer the blows of evil as if this is one's fate, and perhaps even one's deserved fate, is much more debilitating than to know that one is being unfairly persecuted and victimized, and to fight back, beginning inwardly, in protest and anger. To be angry at whatever and whoever is attacking us and/or at the forces and context that are doing us harm can be somewhat heartening and strengthening of a victim's endurance. It can be good for one's health—doctors have always observed which patients fight back for themselves and which patients let illness conquer them. It is also a firmer basis for organizing a battle against evil if and when there is a known perpetrator who is doing the harming.

My judgment is that we do best if we *combine* yielding to a bad result with fighting back—if only in protest, better yet in practical steps that just might change that unchangeable reality. (Personally, I've had a few brushes with life-threatening or less final but also ostensibly incurable disabilities where I have nonetheless succeeded in finding help—some conventional, some unconventional—and recovering.)

I am, of course, aware that encouraging people to fight back—and especially to "bless" the gods—is unacceptable theologically to some people. I apologize that unintentionally we are stepping on some people's sensitivities and opposing some official religious doctrines. There is one religious tract after another that interprets the story as it is written, that *Job* was a good God-fearing man who did not succumb to the agony of his situation and protest to God even when *Job*'s wife says to him, "Bless God." For many believers, protests that condemn or curse God are telltale blasphemy. Many traditional interpreters of the Bible actually condemn Job's wife, the poor woman, for being cruel and evil both to God and to her husband.

On the other hand, there remain a few clerics who do say she was a compassionate woman who felt badly for her husband and was trying to release him from his agony (to get it over with). We need to know that the meaning of the Hebrew is both *Bless* and *Curse*—an intriguing dialectic where the same word is understood to contain within it two contradictory options.

When I treat *Job*-people, I attempt to help them *both* to yield to the truth of what has taken place and certainly to grieve, but then to get angry and to fight back as strongly as possible for as full a life as may still be achieved. In effect I join *Job*'s wife's advice to "bless God" in both senses of the word—to accept reality *and* to protest as a basis for reenergizing and redefining the legitimacy of one's existence. My proposed theology is to combine yielding genuinely to the travail that is happening with courageous and wise fighting for a better life. Even in the face of a truly unchangeable/incurable situation, a measure of anger at one's lousy fate—along with letting go to the reality—may help a person feel stronger in their tragedy. The concepts of yielding and protesting sound completely contradictory of one another and will be mocked in conventional and politically correct thinking, but they are in fact dialectical complements. It is possible to yield and fight at the same time.

I am reminded of two other biblical stories in the Old Testament. The first is again Abraham's readiness to obey God to go and slaughter his son Isaac in sacrifice—

though here there is a happy ending because God rescinds his order in time, but the fact remains that Abraham was ready to obey. The second story is that of Yiftach, who took a vow that if he came back alive from battle he would sacrifice the first living thing he saw on his return, and that turns out to be his own daughter. Here he actually completes the task of killing her, and she herself is understanding and acquiescent that absolute loyalty to God comes first. (One of our lovely granddaughters, age ten, chose this story as the theme of a composition for school and praised the good man for being true to his word. She was then shaken when Grandma and I both criticized Yiftach for his slavishness and most of all for his arch-evil action. After thinking through Grandma and Grandpa's critiques, she changed her mind.)

I do not intend to call for any reduced loyalty to religious practices, but I see literal interpretations of these stories as teaching human beings the kind of absolute loyalty that we see in murderous ideological movements, whether sponsored by a church or by a political movement, and I have no hesitation in saying these are wrong. I have no doubt that creative theological authorities can create interpretations of these stories as metaphors that are turned into injunctions for serving life.

Similarly, if you look at popular Western thought about anger, including many mental health articles about anger, you will find that the prevailing advice is to control your anger and get rid of it because it isn't good for you. At the same time, *some* notable intellectuals through the ages, like Aristotle, have recognized that "[t]he man who is angry at the right things and with the right people, and further, as he ought, when he ought, and as long as he ought, is praised."[35] The author whose article cited this quote from Aristotle continues in her own voice about contemporary Western society: "Today, many of us see anger as a negative emotion that doesn't serve any purpose. In one study that asked participants about anger, 28 percent of respondents said that their anger was inappropriate, because anger is generally harmful or useless. Yet, as with most things, Aristotle is right. Anger can be good for you because it's designed to protect us, our relationships, and our way of seeing the world. In the everlasting battle between right and wrong, the bodily effects of anger are meant to tell us that something is wrong."[36]

There are *some* authoritative voices in the field of mental health who also have recognized that the emotion is natural and that some degree of expression of it can be healthy. But almost always such recognition is directed to telling whoever it is that angers us that we are angry and why, which is a very good idea when possible and when done correctly, but there are many cases where it is not possible. We are then left with a huge question of what to do with the anger inside of us in the many, many situations where one cannot possibly talk out anger with others—for example, situations where a parent has died or lives in another country, and in the many situations where the other simply is unavailable to any sharing of such emotions.

I think that releasing angry fantasies, and appreciating one's democratic freedom to do so in one's mind, can help a great deal. Yet rarely if ever have I seen an application in the literature of using imagination and guided association to go "all the way" with one's anger at one's enemies in our own minds, but to be careful to do so in a spirit and goal of accepting and releasing our anger in order for us to become quieter and stronger. The proper goal of experiencing anger in our minds is not to become agitated. In fact, being connected to such feelings of anger is important in order for us to gain better control of our anger, and certainly not to execute in actions the fantasies that we are releasing in our minds.

A document of the American Psychological Association that begins with acknowledging that anger is natural nonetheless is a clear example of the prevailing advice not to feel anger too much:

> Anger can be a good thing. It can give you a way to express negative feelings, for example, or motivate you to find solutions to problems. But excessive anger can cause problems. Increased blood pressure and other physical changes associated with anger make it difficult to think straight and harm your physical and mental health.
>
> What You Can Do? Controlling anger before it controls you: Anger is a normal, usually healthy emotion we all experience. But when anger gets out of hand, it can cause problems at home and at work. There are ways you can get control of your anger, instead of letting it control you.[37]

I will return in this chapter to the subject of imagining anger virtually, and how it helps one release tension and also stay nonviolent in one's actions. But right now the major point is to establish the importance of fighting back against bad fates as much as possible. To submit, yield, and acknowledge the bad blows of our fates is necessary, but it should not be a basis for giving up. There should not be abject acceptance and surrender, which increase a person's passivity, weakness, inability to cope, and defeatism, and turn off one's vitality. The various religions and spiritual philosophies that teach people *only* to yield to their fates and to trust in prayers for a miracle of a possible redemption and recovery that will never exist, do not appeal to me as sufficiently enlivening a person who is already down. I believe and thus recommend to *Job*-people in my clinical practice to combine acceptance of the reality, including prayerful acceptance of what has happened with expression and ritualization of one's grief with as little denial as possible of the damage that has taken place and is due to take place, with good healthy doses of being angry at one's bad fate. *Arise Jobs of the world and "bless" your gods!*

Whether it is the gods or blind winds of fate or chance that have gone out of our control and done horrors to us, I recommend getting angry. It's not very different than saying "Shit!" when a plank of wood smashes down on one's foot (which I don't think is vulgar or obscene). In the terrible larger *Job* situations, I recommend holding the anger accessible for some time, and of course channeling it to whatever constructive efforts to fight back may be possible.

Again I note respectfully that for those who need a theology that is entirely tranquil and not messy, and therefore want only to reach a state of saintly acceptance of whatever happens to them, the idea that *Job* fights back in spirit is likely uncomfortable and even morally distasteful; and again I say that I mean no rudeness nor to argue theology with those who adopt this kind of faith, but I cannot agree with them. I think that reconciliation with a tragedy that happened and/or may be going to happen is more genuine if one engages one's also God-given power to protest and even to blaspheme the sources of one's lousy fate. One has to search creatively for every possible way of fighting back that comes to mind. There is time enough for the final acceptance and reconciliation with a reality that cannot be changed after doing one's fight and after the script is fully finalized—at least then one knows one hasn't skipped over any possible alternatives for helping oneself.

A then-older friend of mine, a devout Christian and a distinguished attorney who I respected deeply, suffered a stroke and began to recover physically in his rehabilitation. He was deeply demoralized by his disability, and even more so when his law partners pushed him to leave the firm. He asked me if I could help him. I taught him to be angry and was delighted to see him do a wonderful job of it. The business and professional results were that first he negotiated a generous financial settlement with his partners, and then promptly went and opened a new law office on the same block as his old firm. I cheered for him heartily.

The overall psychological sequences of natural responses to loss and threat have been traced by many therapists. The paradigmatic sequence includes an initial reaction of shock—even to a possible point of stupor or paralysis, which is perfectly normal in response to the impact of a crushing blow or loss; deep sadness, regret, and grieving; stirrings of a powerful anxiety that bespeaks a rumbling of a power that is seeking to come back alive and emerge from the bowels of one's misery; then rushes of strong and even torrential anger at the fate one has endured, where the anger is hardly a mean-spirited response but a cry and protest of an energetic desire for the maximum gift of the wonder of life (a big-small example of such energy is the terminal patient who fights to keep alive until a loved one arrives to say goodbye), and finally acceptance of one's fate.

What is desired in the end is an integration of one's reality—accepting what is unchangeable, with sadness over it, but also with a maximum fighting back on behalf of everything one yet dare hope for in one's life. It is a symphonic orchestration of yielding to loss along with a courageous battle.[38]

Conclusion: The Therapist's Job Is to Help Job to Accept and to Fight Back

These are situations where there is no choice, and acceptance of a sad reality represents the bravest possible response to a rotten situation. We have all seen people who are terminally ill who have gone humbly and courageously, with incredible grace, to their end, enjoying so many of the moments of the remainder of their lives with a profound appreciation of the very essence of the simplest remaining functions. I appreciate their response and honor their dignity and bravery.

In truth, I love more the sequence of experiences in psychotherapy of *Job*-people for those who can yet hope to correct a lot in their lives. In all cases, it is a profound privilege to be present for people in whatever stage of their *Job*-process, for they indeed need and can benefit from the presence of another human being. As a therapist,

I in turn grieve the losses and great pain people endure, and I have become fairly good at yielding to sad realities. At the same time, as a therapist I am also on the alert, looking for possible ways to protest and fight back for whatever improvement may be possible, and I admit that I love this fighting most, let alone there is a strong part of me that is furious at the hell and injustice so many people are sent to suffer, and I am only glad I am so furious.

Now that I am an old person myself, I have a further challenge on my hands—to yield to my own approaching ending, yet fight to prolong my life as much as possible but no longer with any illusion that I just might "beat it" all the way. I am fighting to accept the truth of what's coming and at the same time to savor all that I still enjoy being in the present. *Wish me luck.*

I am impressed at how inevitably life seeks to restore itself. As the rumblings of shock and pain subside, people move to regroup their remaining capacity for experiencing life. A choice clearly emerges between being a broken, despondent person with no hope versus bringing together all that one can do and being grateful for each and every piece of the life force one can experience and celebrate. A choice emerges between surrendering to disability and misfortune (which I would also note becomes a giving up and is *not* the same as yielding and accepting) versus rising to the occasion to work and fight in any possible way for a maximum of possible health and life. It is my privilege to try to help people with these choices.

Some people need no professional help in their response to major trauma to turn themselves toward striving for the maximum good life possible for them. This includes any number of people who are terminally ill or others who know they are at serious risk of not making it but who carry themselves and conduct their lives with such dignity, graciousness, and even sweetness that they take my breath away. I am in awe of them. I sit at their feet marveling and am deeply touched by their inspiration. At the same time, there are many people who can benefit from a psychotherapist's caring presence and involvement, and from help to fight back in whatever ways possible.

PART FOUR: PSYCHOTHERAPY OF EMOTIONAL VIOLENCE

A Model for Treating Emotionally Expressive Violence

In this section we will look at how some of the violence that befalls many people can be overcome with psychology and stopped. The subject is an important practical issue for practicing therapists who are faced with a great deal of domestic and family violence, as well as in treating people who explode or who become absorbed in revenge in whatever area of their life, such as in their workplace—or also at their helping professional. Symbolically, the underpinning philosophy from which this approach to the treatment of violence is built may also offer some insight and hope for thinking about new cultural directions for checking the addictive power of violence in human affairs in our societies. *God only knows we humans are presently destructive idiots, and we better figure out new ways for reducing violence before it is too late for us on this planet.*

I will present shortly the basic assumption of this model and then a series of "rules." In each case I will describe an actual technique of treatment and then also give the theoretical underpinning from which this approach to stopping and healing violence is constructed. The model I will describe is for treating people who are full of emotional rage. The basic theory rests simultaneously on the two principles of inhibiting and rejecting all violence (except in self-defense) as immoral, and on developing alternative constructive channels for directing anger and violent impulses—because basically they are here to stay in us human animals.

But a critical caveat: The model is not at all applicable to ideological violence. The only advice I can give there is that, if we want to keep our heads, we should stay far away from ISIS types!

The basic rationale of this model is that violence fundamentally is rooted in very natural processes in human beings. Man is not simply only a goody-goody darling who becomes corrupted by life. He is by nature's construction genuinely and deeply (instinctively) both good and bad, and the life experiences he undergoes impact on his built-in machinery for both directions of being human—one humane and the other violent and destructive. There is a huge span of natural violent impulses that includes our desires to express our feelings of anger and rage—anger as a rush of the need for self-expression and self-assertion; anger as a response to frustrations of needs, such as an unsatisfied need to make contact with objects of our sexual desires or intended love; anger at not being recognized and/or advanced in our lives, say at work; and, of course, anger in response to convictions (which may or may not be objective) that one must fight back against another's aggression in self-defense. Any one or more of these and other natural drives and mechanisms can be at the core of eruptions of violence. Anger and violence are basically very *human*, but then we make a mess of expressing them too violently or intensely and in inappropriate ways that do unnecessary harm.

The present model develops a way of treating and managing violence that issue from bursts of aggressive emotions in hurt, desperate, and angry people. These emotionally expressive eruptions of violence occur in the home and community and also in professional mental health, social service, and medical service settings. These are the everyday domestic violence that social workers, police officers, and other authorities such as school officials are called on to stop, limit, and prevent.

Scientific understanding of different types of violence can make it possible to develop more effective responses and interventions to manage and prevent much of this violence. With proper training, professionals should be able to make rapid distinctions as to the type or cause of ongoing, incipient, or potential violence and then make appropriate responses to that type. As in many types of emergency and stress situations, the more personnel are trained in well-defined methods of coping, the more likely they are to be effective in preventing or at least reducing the violence.

Table 7.2. Basic Principles in the Treatment of Emotionally Expressive Violence

	ACCEPTING THE NATURALNESS OF IMPULSES INCLUDING VIOLENCE	CONTROLLING DESTRUCTIVE VIOLENCE	CHANNELING VIOLENCE CONSTRUCTIVELY
01	Accepting the naturalness of violent impulses and desires.	Rejecting as immoral all acts that actually do violence to other human beings (except in clear-cut physical self-defense).	Channeling the energies of aggression and violence toward workable solutions of the conflict and resolving legitimate reality needs.
02	Accepting the naturalness of respect for human life.	Paradoxically, one also must take care not to be led to excessive violence in the name of protecting life!	Using power and violence for genuine peacebuilding as nonviolently as possible.
03	Expressing some anger and rage to people at whom these feelings are directed, but without violence.	Controlling expressions of anger for appropriate timing, intensity, and style.	Using anger to build relationships and arrive at solutions of problems.
04	Learning to experience and enjoy anger freely in inner fantasies and thoughts.	Limiting and pacing inner experiences of anger so as not to flood the personality, and clear knowledge that the goal of the fantasies is to discharge impulses and not to act them out.	Channeling the energy of one's inner freedom to fantasize aggression to help bear tensions in life, and to return to engage real problems and conflicts as effectively as possible.
05	Identifying needs and demands whose frustration is generating anger and violence.	Maintaining a practical goal of trying to satisfy objective needs so that one is not pushed to violent emotions and behaviors.	Conveying to another party a clear feeling of wanting to "do business" together effectively from a position of strength.

06	Acknowledging underlying wishes for self-expression and assertiveness, as well as desires to engage in meaningful relationships that are hidden in expressions of anger and violence.	Try to translate violence into self-assertiveness and efforts to create meaningful relationships.	Where possible, and not out of weakness, reaching out to offer new opportunities to "do business" with one's enemies.
07	Appreciating the conviction that one must attack in self-defense draws urgently on a natural primordial violence for self-defense that in itself is wholesome, but it is important to know that the conviction that one is being threatened is often wrong.	Knowing many perceptions of being in danger are inherently incorrect, it is important to go as slowly as possible before invoking violence in self-defense.	Testing carefully the validity of claims of self-defense before responding; including knowing that we are all prone to major distortions of feeling that we are under severe attack when we are not, and that we often feel under greater threat than is really the case. (*See 08 below*.)
08	Experiencing that one must respond to the threats of violence of the other with even greater strength.	It is important to develop a policy that seeks to limit sequences of escalation, including the capacity to initiate overtures of peace and de-escalation.	Testing the objective reality of urges to defend oneself, and carefully developing opportunities for unilateral initiatives at peace; renewing possibilities for negotiation and new initiatives of communication and cooperation on common tasks.

Source: Created by the author.

Where This Model Does Not Apply

I will emphasis once again: Central to the model is the recognition of the naturalness of violent *impulses*, which in large part are to be respected, but decisively differentiating these impulses from doing any *actual* harm and causing real physical damage and destruction to other human beings, which is understood to be wrong and must be stopped.

We have said clearly that the model is not applicable to ideological violence, such as terrorism including dread suicide bombers—although very occasionally there are exceptions here too, where it may prove possible to make what might be called *human* contact with the aggressor and thereby to call out a potential for decency and for honoring a nonviolent ideal in the would-be killer. Very occasionally there are heartwarming instances when a would-be aggressor is recalled from within themselves not to take human life.

A striking example took place in Israel in June 2002 when a young Palestinian woman on the way to detonate herself in a suicide bombing of civilians remembered that she had been taught as a child not to take life. Arien Ahmed, then twenty, skipped a lecture on marketing (not murdering—ha, ha) at Bethlehem University to carry out a suicide bombing. The news report in the *New York Times* comments in a way that is strikingly reminiscent of our concept of how the Fascist mind gets caught up in whatever it believes must be done and can't let go: "A chain of events was dragging her down with a speed that left her frozen, unthinking." However, this young woman did change her mind. "'I look at the sky,' Ms. Ahmed recalled . . . as she described a kind of awakening. 'I look at the people.' She said she remembered a childhood belief 'that nobody has the right to stop anybody's life.' Ms. Ahmed, a rare exception among suicide bombers, turned back.[39]

But the point remains nonetheless that overall there are any number of situations in which this model does not apply. One less dramatic set of situations is where violence is employed in efforts to manipulate financial and other material gains,[40] or outright psychopathic and criminal situations of violence for personal gain. The committed criminal whose life occupation includes violence as a standard working tool is not susceptible to the techniques discussed here. More likely he will laugh you down.[41] The overall point is that people who are violent in order to gain material benefits cannot be treated by psychological or relationship and emotional tools, but instead require clear structural definitions and legal responses to their efforts to manipulate people and societal systems.

This approach also does not relate to instances of violence based on drug abuse and addiction or to the criminality associated with drugs. Violence that is induced by drugs has increased in certain Western societies, and many treatment institutions report that such conditions do not respond even to time-honored management techniques for psychotic and other emotionally uncontrolled people.[42]

On the larger stages of society, nonviolence movements have produced instances of great leaders and movements that have transformed the very history of their societies for the better (e.g., Gandhi[43] in India and Martin Luther King in the United

States[44]). There are small and large examples of incidents of violence that have been averted by nonviolent interventions.[45] A. Paul Hare,[46] for example, reported on the organized work of the *Shanti Sena* in India, a group that would go out to confront the building momentum of religious-ideological violence by calling on people to respect human life.

However, it remains a truth of life that in a large number of situations it is futile to put out ethical-psychological calls to morality to committed ideologues or in the face of mounting collective violence.

An American physician in Israel named Baruch Goldstein, who was widely known for how much he went out of his way to care for his patients devotedly and sympathetically, executed a terrifying mass murder of unarmed Arab men, women, and children who had come to pray at a historic holy site. Goldstein, who himself was shot dead by a soldier, was committed to a fundamentalist fascist ideology of Jewish occupation and domination by Israel.[47]

The Basic Assumptions: The Naturalness of Violent Emotions and the Naturalness of Respecting Life

The purpose of psychotherapeutic and social science strategies should not be to suppress *all* aspects of violence, but to differentiate between *constructive* expressive functions of violence and *destructive* consequences of doing violent damage to people. We define destructive consequences as doing actual bodily harm to another human being (not including self-defense in military and other security situations). We define constructive expressive functions of violence as the venting of anger, rage, and protest and the communication of needs to release emotional pressure and to bring about desired changes within a system of relationships with other people or institutions. The first and major principal technique of treatment for stopping emotionally based violence is to confirm for clients that their violent emotions are natural and will be listened to, but that violent acts that harm others physically are inhuman, unethical, immoral, and wrong.

Violent feelings must be genuinely understood to represent and serve desirable, natural functions—and in my opinion too many overly "positive psychotherapists" refuse to know this.[48] Because violent emotions are powerful and because they inherently tend to excess and are easily subject to processes of contagion, there is naturally a high level of danger that angry emotions will fan into acts of destructiveness. The solution, however, is not to outlaw or reject angry emotions, but to teach proper channeling and control of the natural emotions in a firm ethical framework of disallowing actual violent acts against people. Moreover, it needs to be recognized that there are times of a clear-cut need for self-defense when violent actions are necessary, lifesaving, and life-serving and therefore justified. At the same time, violent acts that are not in true self-defense are defined unambiguously as acts against life and in violation of a universal ethical imperative to respect life.[49]

How does a therapist apply these principles? How does the therapist treat a raging, emotionally wrought person—who sometimes is armed with a knife or gun, who sometimes is rampaging through the therapist's office turning over furniture, and who sometimes is openly threatening to kill the therapist? I have had the "pleasure" of all of these experiences and have never been injured—though I know all too well there is no guarantee either for me or for other therapists who adopt this technique.

The technique of treatment is that the therapist first tells the patient the two principles—there can be no violence because it is wrong, and yes, you'll get help expressing anger and having it heard meaningfully.

As you might imagine, rarely is the therapist able to sit with professional decorum behind a desk when they are getting this "package of psychological medicines" across. So many such scenes are high-wire-living dramas. They typically have the therapist on their feet, speaking spiritedly, sometimes even yelling. In all cases it is important for the patient to feel and know that the therapist is not afraid. When a patient has threatened me personally, I almost automatically react by coming up close to him—in a sense "putting my face into his."

"You're not going to touch me, now or ever. If you make one move to harm me, I'll call the police. You know it's wrong to harm another person's body. But I will definitely help you to have your anger heard and to get you the best possible help with what you're angry about." This is how I spoke to a bright, handsome playboy attorney who had been sent for treatment because he was hitting his wife and then threatened to kill me.

The therapist says these things passionately, vividly, and as much as possible in the language and natural cultural style of the client. This treatment is an ultimate "joining" of the therapist and patient—rooted in and inspired by the basic value of safe living.

A Proposed Checklist for the Treatment of Emotionally Based Violence

I have put together here a kind of checklist (see rules 1–8 in the coming pages with accompanying explanation of theory) for therapists of the guidelines that I propose as the basis for therapists' interventions to violent and potentially violent people whose violence wells up from their emotions.

Many psychotherapists are at a loss about how to deal with violence, say in family life, other than in situations where the violent person comes to therapy explicitly for help with "anger management." At times this is their own genuine wish, and at other times it is treatment required by legal authorities or a showdown demand by the family. There is little to no training in most clinical courses on what to do about immediate eruptive and threatening situations of family violence, and little to no training about responding to an eruption of violence in the treatment situation itself, beyond preparations to call for help from security people in a hospital or large clinic or the police. Where there is material appearing in the professional literature, it generally focuses on collaboration with law enforcement and/or addresses broad-based educational efforts to reduce later violence, and not so much directly on specific prevention and treatment of violence in the immediate present.[50] A recent book published by the American Psychological Association gives the overall opinion: "With so many answers to the question 'What makes a person violent?' there is surprisingly little insight into 'How do we prevent violence?"[51] The method of treatment of acute eruptions of emotional violence that is proposed here is essentially new, although it was published in the professional literature many years ago but without a noticeable impact,[52] and I hope this presentation will be helpful to more psychotherapists.

Rule 1

Desires to do harm to another human being in themselves are natural. However, unless there are circumstances where there is objective justification of self-defense, doing overt violence to others violates another natural imperative that human beings must respect, protect, and sustain life.

Theoretical Underpinning: Differentiating between natural *wishes* to harm others and actual or overt *acts* of violence is a developmental experience that generally reaches some clear-cut crystallization around ages three to four in a child's life. However, clinical observations of a wide variety of people demonstrate that this differentiation is *not* learned by many individuals in our society—especially by decent and overly tender people as well as by people committed to using brawn and physical power to get their way, but also by many people who received no training in this principle in their childhood and are simply not ready to deal with rage when it wells up inside of them. When a person does not internalize this differentiation, there are consequent disturbances throughout life. One common example for good people can be undue feelings of responsibility for the death of someone whom one has not harmed in a real way—and especially if the other person was the object of one's unconscious anger (note that the anger "simply" can be at someone we loved who has left us by dying). Another common example is the belief that if one is angry, there is no alternative but to "settle the score" and take overt action against the object of one's anger.[53]

In my experience, even in the very heat of the distress and rage of people who are emotionally agitated, say at a wrong they feel was done to them, it often is possible to respect the rage and whatever objective needs are related to that rage while insisting on the wrongness of any actual violence to whomever—one's spouse, lover, a child, parent, neighbor, community official, and so forth. Clinically, there is generally genuine relief at being guided and limited away from acting out overt violence. In my judgment, inwardly many people very much desire to protect life if only they can be helped to do so. Although they may be on the verge of allowing their also-natural violent impulses to overpower their instinctive sense of the validity of life, their inner voice calling for decent humanness remains.

Rule 2

There is also a natural desire in human beings not to be destructive of other living beings, so that it is natural for many people who experience a need to be violent to experience considerable fear of their violence and a desire to restrain themselves from causing any real harm to others' lives.

Theoretical Underpinning: To say the least, the story of basic human nature is complex. Human nature includes *both* strong instincts for violence and primary instincts to protect life against violence. It need hardly be belabored that most human beings are haunted by fears of themselves falling victims to the violence of others and want to protect their lives, but, although not often recognized, there is for many people a powerful generalization to the validity and legitimacy of the existence of other human beings' lives as well. For many people there are also religious and ethical backgrounds that have taught them and left deeply imprinted images inside their minds and hearts to value not being destructive to others. Additionally, in my judgment, there is also a natural existential base inside the human soul that calls for a reverence for life—including a wish to be "whole" or in tune with existence and nature. This wellspring of respect for life is a natural part of the basic "software" of Mind very much alongside other quite contradictory "defaults" that enable the human animal to fight and destroy, certainly when a need for self-defense is experienced, as well as for territorial conquest and exhilaration.

There is considerable evidence that a fear of doing harm to others is a powerful force in the human mind, and that it is possible to call this instinct forth in the management and treatment of a good deal of emotionally expressive violence. The wish not to hurt others at times can be psychologically more definitive and pressing than fears of being harmed. Psychoanalytic studies of various mental illnesses, such as by Robert Searles,[54] demonstrate that over and above people's fears of being victims to others, the fear of victimizing others is sufficient to justify for some number of people a flight into mental illness, including suicide (death to themselves) as an alternative over their possibly acting out to destroy others. We described earlier in the book that many times the choice to be psychotic can be understood from this point of view—in effect a decision to neutralize oneself by going crazy so as to be unable to wreak destruction on others.

Surprising as it is, I have had experiences that show that this model can work both in instances of outright mental illness or organic brain damage. Evidently, for all that such patients obviously have real problems in impulse control, they are still people subject to the lawfulness of human desires to curb oneself from being destructive if helped to do so. However, once again it must be stressed that this model does *not* relate to violence that is rooted in ideological doctrines or otherwise legitimated by a collective process.

The cross-cultural studies of Lawrence Kohlberg[55] speak to a universal developmental sequence of psychoethical constructs in the human mind, which reaches its highest level of development in a natural appreciation of the validity and sacredness of all life. Similarly, the thrust of many humanistic, religious, and psychological evocations of man's spiritual nature attest overwhelmingly to the naturalness of oceanic feelings of joy and reverence for life as a powerful natural force alongside the naturalness of impulses to destroy others. Again it cannot be emphasized strongly enough that we are referring to the workings of passions and emotions in people so long as they have not been subject to systematic education in an ideology of violence, in which case the sorry record of human nature is that people who are destructive in the name of and at the instruction-command of an ideology more than likely lose whatever contact they once had with caring for other people. Here is a clinical example of this therapy:

❖ He was an American sailor with a long history of violence against his wife and also against Navy personnel (at one time he was sent to jail for hitting his Navy social worker). I told him that he cannot continue to be violent to his wife. He replied threateningly, tough ruffian that he was: "You know I can kill you first of all."[56]

I purposely moved my chair in closer, put my face in to his, and repeated the mantra intensely and confidently: "You know it's wrong to hurt a human being. I will help you with your anger at your wife or anyone else, but you can't harm people, not me or anyone." The sailor's body heaved as he broke into sobs and put his head in my arms. The treatment was happily effective in this case, and the sailor gave up his style of violence.

Whether violence is aimed at a family member, a professional in mental health, social service, or a medical setting, people in one's workplace, or at random victims in the community, the first and major message that we need to deliver in the very heat of the confrontation with the looming violence of the enraged person is that they must have deeply felt reasons for their rage, but that they also know it is intrinsically wrong to do real physical harm to another human being. As noted earlier, this message needs to be delivered with strong conviction, often with considerable emotion, and in a language that is drawn from or "friendly" to the language-culture of the potentially violent person—even at a gut level or in everyday standard "profanity." (A colleague social worker, herself unmarried, criticized me years ago for talking to a truck driver patient about his sex life in elegant upper-class science language instead of in his everyday street language. I am forever grateful to her.)

❖ A teenager was referred for therapy by his high school not only because he was doing poorly in school, but because he exuded a frightening aura that seemed to say he could be dangerous. I soon learned that this boy was well advanced in his preparations to commit mass murder at a local shopping mall. He had already stockpiled most of his ammunition and was rehearsing detailed fantasies—plans for his climactic event in this world, which included shooting the local chief of police dead and then himself being shot dead by the police.

Happily—it seemed miraculous—he responded to the therapeutic intervention and put a halt to his terrible plan. In fact, a touching experience of

> intimacy blossomed between us. I remember him saying to me, "You need to be careful." When I asked him why, he explained, "I'm afraid you could get hurt by bad people because you're too good a person." Before his contact with me ended, this "dumb," almost "unable to read" (according to his school) young man gave me a gift of a quite sophisticated academic book that he had purchased about the Nazi SS.

Simply telling a person to stop being violent leaves them no room for their violent feelings and does not offer them the promise of any alternative outlet. There is an enormous difference between only telling a violent husband that he has no right to beat up his wife, and telling him that he is obviously terribly angry and that the therapist wants to help him with his rage, but that he himself also knows deep in his heart that it is basically wrong to do actual physical violence to another human being. The intervention combines an acceptance of the thrust of the aggression emotions with a braking and limiting of the acting out of actual violence.

Again, the very fact that the therapist feels reasonably organized and confident about handling a crisis with the possibility of violence in itself serves to quiet the situation. When a therapist responds with panic and indecision, it is human nature that the panic excites even more reactive cruelty on the part of the person threatening violence. But when the therapist is emotionally and authoritatively in charge, the therapist's leadership helps the person who threatens to be out of control to organize themselves.

Once the immediate danger of violence has been successfully broken, the therapist is obligated to continue with providing the client the promised outlet for their anger. The goal of treatment now becomes to enable statements of rage, protest, and need—first of all in the person's actual relationships with the people or community agencies at whom they are fuming. If the therapist feels the anger is objectively justified, the therapist may also even take further steps to "represent" or support the patient's demands—for example to a government agency.

A fascinating paradox that deserves to be noted is that there are often times when there is a personal or collective conviction to act in order to protect others, and the undue violence is applied in the name of saving life. The same goes for self-defense. In all instances of violence purportedly for a good cause, there needs to be a rigorous checking of the nature and extent of the violence that is being applied, so that the ultimate outcome will not be an intensification of harm to human life.

Rule 3

In our interpersonal relationships, there are a great many possibilities for expression and clarification of feelings and confrontations with others that are alternatives to violence.

Theoretical underpinning: There are constructive ways for discharging many violent feelings against others in interpersonal relationships, including expressing what one feels authentically, but doing so wisely. This is especially true in intimate and personal relationships, but also in other situations where one has no choice but to deal with difficult people, including bureaucrats or official personnel who exert a real degree of power, and realistically one must be careful about how to express one's anger and complaints to these people who have such real power.

The social science literature teaches us that good communication of feelings often opens the doors to discharging angry and violent tensions so that there is less need for actual violence, and that good communication helps people to arrive at proper solutions of their problems. In many situations clear, firm clarification of what one feels will lead to a quieting down of rage and an effective correction of an abuse. In the area of marriage, George Bach was perhaps the first to pioneer recommendations and guidelines to couples ("the intimate enemy") on how to fight out conflicts.[57] Much of the literature on healthy self-assertion, creative aggression, and constructive marital fighting in effect is dedicated to helping people avert the possibility of violence by giving them healthy outlets for their aggressive feelings.

Obviously, in many cases people who become violent feel that there is no point in communicating, or that they have already tried and hit a dead end. The question then becomes whether even then people can be counseled and trained to go back to communicate in words their anger and rage more than they thought possible, and indeed it turns out that this is often possible. There are surprisingly effective ways of delivering even difficult messages by paying careful attention to the timing of what is said, controlling the intensity, and choosing a wise and appropriate style of expression. We have learned in family therapy that promiscuous expression of rage generally is not helpful, and on the contrary often leads to more disturbed relationships or to further breakdown of the relationship. But there are ways of expressing anger clearly and forthrightly yet not provocatively, and without cueing an interest in escalating to a more bitter struggle. Speaking one's anger with wisdom can provide a great deal of emotional release and can result in improving some relationships even in very difficult situations.

There are also intriguing symbolic ways of gaining control over a person who has gathered too much power and control over us. A delightful example—which I have had the pleasure of staging in family therapy sessions and witnessing more than once—is when the son of a tyrannical father dared to put his arm around his feared father and spoke to him purposely, with a deliciously designed casualness, about a triviality such as what a nice day it was. Intriguingly, though such a choreography of taking charge in a situation where historically the son has always been fearful and angry seems trivial, the son's self-assertion literally changed the power structure of the tyrannical relationship before my eyes. It is real fun. I have come to enjoy very much therapy sessions in which planned "choreographies" of major changes in relationship status are rehearsed in preparation for the real performance.

❖ He literally had not spoken to his tyrannical father for several years before he came for therapy. Breaking off the relationship with his father had helped this thirty-year-old man feel somewhat stronger, but he still did not feel really equal to his father or adequate as a man.

When the father put out messages to his son that he was interested in a reconciliation, we planned for a series of therapy sessions for the two of them together. If you've ever been frightened by an overwhelming father figure, you know how awesome the thought of placing yourself on an equal footing to such a tyrannical man can be.

The son and I literally rehearsed like one rehearses for a play. "Go up to your father, look him in his eyes, and place your arm on his shoulder. You'll then say to him: 'Dad, thank you for coming to this session. I appreciate it very much, and I hope we can get closer together and speak openly to one another.'" P.S. The "show" went off as planned successfully.

Rule 4

There are also surprisingly less well recognized possibilities for effectively releasing angry feelings in the privacy of one's own mind in many situations when it is not desirable or possible to express emotions to others.

Theoretical underpinning: What is least recognized, and in fact is not even really known by many psychotherapists and therefore is used much too infrequently by too many of them, is that even before attempting direct confrontation, there is a surprisingly unrecognized freedom of the human mind to engage in and enjoy release of anger for oneself through active fantasies of anger at others. This technique can also save many a day when it remains absolutely impossible to speak of one's anger directly with the other—because the other person is far away, or has died, or is totally not amenable to conversation.

❖ She was an overseas college student from Europe who was rapidly decompensating toward a psychotic state. When I learned of her bitter disappointment and anger at her parents, we "simply" brought them into the office using the wonderful old Gestalt psychology techniques of imagining them in two empty chairs. She told them what she was feeling! In fact, because they weren't really there, and after we had reviewed carefully that expressed emotions were in no way equivalent to real actions, she told them her anger "with no holds barred." It took only a few sessions for this young woman to come down from her incipient psychotic state.

I have sent major executives and professionals into situations that objectively do not allow for expression of criticism and anger and instructed them to savor consciously their fantasies of rage and violence against whomever. The result has been, in many cases, that they even enjoyed otherwise impossible situations instead of the misery of their suppressed rage. In fact, the joke is that in some of the situations in which they had previously suffered, their pleasure in experiencing fantasies of rage led them to enjoy such a good feeling that they radiated a kind of vitality and joy that unexpectedly led to more positive responses toward them from the very people they hated and feared, and a strangely unexpected chain of positive interaction was set in motion.

❖ A minister who was a dried-up, overly serious man came to therapy at his wife's urging because his mind was bursting with sexual urges, and because he felt perennially small and unrecognized, including by his church superiors. Each year he would be visited briefly by an archbishop who generally responded to him with a patronizing indifference and routinely turned down his requests for a raise. Now, armed by therapy with a newfound freedom in his mind for all his "bad impulses," and with a newly developing attractiveness and charm, he won the real praise of his superior as well as a good raise. Was he ever happy and proud of himself.

In family life, too, there are many situations where it is possible to learn to be powerfully angry inside one's own mind and to savor hating in one's private fantasies during times that it is inappropriate and would be destructive to go for direct expression of anger toward one's family members.[58] There are so many situations where one cannot actually convene a family for real family therapy. When I would ask students whether they could imagine ever inviting their parents to family therapy, at least half would reply, "No way. They wouldn't hear of it."

Rule 5

Violence, many times but not all times, is often a plea for the solution of problems and needs.

Theoretical underpinning: It is foolhardy and a common mistake of well-intended liberal people to "understand" the needs of violent people too much. This error has led to absurdities of thinking of how to appease the Hitlers and other dangerous leaders, and also to huge errors in personal relationships with ruthless people. But it is true that violence often is a result of frustrated needs and desires. If a therapist can help a person to translate violent feelings into efforts to clarify and work through an issue with the person(s) toward whom the violence is directed, the energy that threatens to explode in raging and possible dangerous violence may be re-directed into self-assertion and positive communication. For example, a person who is out of work, or a person whose need for respect and dignity has been humiliated, is more prone to eruptive violence. Recognizing the need, worry, hurt, or humiliation is a key to preventing much violence, especially if recognizable help is also extended to solve the realistic problems and prevent their recurrence.

Rule 6

There are times when violence is a cry of a desire for self expression, and contact and friendship with the hated and hateful other. The welling up of violence can come from an inability to acknowledge desires to get closer. Often it is too painful to think of what one really wants because there is little expectation of being able to win a positive response. The violence becomes an effort both to make contact with the unreachable lost object and to end the pain of being rejected once and for all.

Theoretical underpinning: Frustrated wishes to express oneself, make contact and be accepted underlie much violence, including "classic" violent attacks by spurned lovers. Similarly, marginalized youths who really wish to be accepted into the mainstream of society turn instead to delinquency and violence. Recognizing needs for acceptance can be made a basis for treatment interventions both for individuals and groups. For example, there have been marvelously effective interventions that have successfully brought violent youth groups back into the mainstream of their society by respecting them and offering them bona fide roles in society.[59]

Rule 7

The feeling that one is in danger of being destroyed by the other springs readily to the human mind. As a result, we are also in danger of being propelled into being violent against those whom we incorrectly perceive as being out to harm us. Individuals and groups must learn to test the legitimacy of claims of self-defense before acting on them.

Theoretical underpinning: Archetypal universal laws of life tell all living creatures that it is legitimate to kill someone in self-defense if the other person is about to kill you. In traditional Judaism, for example, there is an explicit rabbinical injunction: "If someone is coming to kill you, anticipate and kill him first." Unfortunately, in addition to correct perceptions of threats of violence, human beings are highly vulnerable to distorted exaggerations of other people's violent intentions, as well as to outright projections of their own violent wishes onto others. The result is that there are many times when people sincerely experience themselves under life-threatening attack and respond with violent actions out of genuine feelings of self-defense when, in fact, the objective circumstances do not warrant their violence.

Rule 8

Violence often develops as a culmination of a series of escalations in which each party experiences itself responding in self-defense to a previous assault until finally one or both parties pass another point of no return and commit to further violence.

Theoretical underpinning: Whether in intimate relationships or in broader patterns of relationships between peoples and nations, any unilateral renunciation of strength, such as unilateral disarmament by one country, leaves one exposed to the ruthlessness of others who are in fact bent on destruction and will *not* respond even to the most generous gestures for peace.[60] Peace researcher Alan Newcombe[61] argued that the best strategy is to remain strong and organized for one's self-defense while *at the same time* taking initiative toward inviting a reciprocal renunciation of force by the other party. It is important to know (dear committed peace-loving liberals, take special note) that unless there is already reason for basic trust in the character and principles of the others, there is no guarantee that a peace policy will necessarily lead to reciprocal measures toward peace. The only way to peace and nonviolence is to take risks to offer to end all violence sincerely, though from a position of strength where one is prepared to fight again if the peace offer is met with unrelenting violence. In an individual's personal relationships, too, one needs to develop a moral conviction to be able to renounce all violence even as one remains committed to standing up for oneself and one's needs in nonviolent strength and dignity.

The Utilization of Police against Violence to Health and Social Work Professionals: Pros and Cons

Here I will switch over from psychotherapy of emotion-derived violence to the alternative of surviving the eruption long enough to be able to call in the police. Obviously, the machinery one thinks of first in managing just about any violence in the community is that of the police. However, there are many situations where the police response in a tough "law and order" manner proves to be *more* inciting of violence, not only between the original parties to the conflict but also toward the police themselves, who report high statistics of police injuries when they intervene toughly. In everyday violence situations, when police themselves use violence for the solution of conflict, they often unwittingly encourage more violence. One reason is that they are often challenging masculine or prideful ("macho")-type responses, and the larger reason is "simply" that violence invites violence, and also that violence is a model to be copied in further violence.

In an impressive report, psychologist Morton Bard[62] told of training policemen in New York to respond to domestic violence and fights in ways where the police were trained to be careful not to provoke the counter-aggressive needs of people. On arrival at the scene of family violence, the policemen would be careful to address members of the family respectfully and understandingly as opposed to the traditional tough, "What's going on in here?!" The police would then seek to create an atmosphere of respectful consultation. They would thoughtfully put down their nightsticks, remove their caps and jackets, and otherwise let it be known that they were there to help stop the violence through getting people to talk out their angry feelings and help them control themselves not to be violent. The approach proved remarkably helpful not only for containing the violence within families, but also for reducing violence toward the police—the incidence of injuries of policemen responding to violence in these situations dropped remarkably.

In dealing with criminals, there have been many observations that some policemen themselves tend to identify with certain dimensions of criminality and violence-making. In any number of cases there are police who engage in excesses of violence against criminals, and as life would have it, against any number of innocent people who have been mistakenly taken to be criminals. In other words, calling in the police in some sense can be calling for more rather than less violence. It is important that police who are called to violent situations be trained and prepared to present themselves as agents of violence reduction rather than punishers of violence.

In some successful cases of treatment of violent clients, I have been able to plan *with* the violent person present with his spouse or family how they—the spouse or children—will call the police if there is ever any violence. I emphasize that we are planning this painful step together precisely because we do *not* want there ever to be a need to call the police, and that what we really want is a genuine and uncompromising decision to be nonviolent and self-controlled.

So far it has been my experience that *if* we succeed in couple or family therapy in winning over the violent person to an agreement that the police will be called if he becomes violent, it has not been necessary to call the police. I rehearse with the couple or family, as in a play, the actual phone call to the police. These rehearsals characteristically evoke a tense kind of laughter, but are conducted in full seriousness and with repeated respectful statements of the hope that no such situation will ever take place in the people's lives.

❖ In one case, the agreement was even extended by the potentially violent husband to a commitment that *he* himself would call the police against himself. I think he really meant it, although he never had to put himself to the real test. In my practice over the years, other than with one jilted suitor who burned his girlfriend's car and threatened me, her therapist, the police never needed to be called by anyone. However, on a number of occasions I have called the police to request that they take away a firearm from a person (who had the proper permit) for fear of possible violence.

There certainly are clients with histories of repeated violence where no interventions will work to stop domestic violence. In these instances it certainly should be clear that the police will be called if there is any further violence. Police also need to be called in runaway emergency situations where serious violence is already taking place or is clearly imminent, and no agreement for stopping the violence can be reached.

There is another way to use police, and that is to introduce them in advance into a situation that is simmering with a potential for violence. Families or community agencies that historically have been the scenes of repeated violence will do well to make prior arrangements with the local police for how best to call on them in emergencies to get immediate help and what the interventions will be. In some cases I have succeeded in bringing in police to a case by arranging for a person who was threatening to be violent, or who had already been violent, to be summoned to the police where he was sternly advised in advance that there would be a strong police response to any violent behavior should it take place. However, there have also been cases where I wanted to use this procedure, but it was not possible to gain the cooperation of police officials who did not understand the important preventive role they could serve. There is also the possibility of bringing in an attorney to represent symbolically a judge and the judicial system, where the attorney in effect plays the role of a judge who sternly reminds a potentially violent person of the shame and punishment that await people who are violent. Although I have wanted to, I have never gotten to use this technique.

Violence as Representative of Family Dynamics

Family therapy has also helped make it very clear that a considerable number of violent events are better understood in terms of the network of family or other intimate relationships in people's lives. The issue of rage at family members and intimates is often at the center of the agenda in the management and treatment of violence, even when the violence is directed at other people. In no small number of cases, the effective management of violence-prone people is best done through bringing in various family members and conducting much of the treatment in family or couple sessions where angry feelings are brought into the open for clarification and negotiation as much as possible. Family members can also be mobilized to become spokespersons for the demand not to be violent. Family intervention is especially indicated when it is a child or youth who is violent.

"We don't want you getting into trouble this way."

"We are against you bringing weapons to school and planning mob fights."

"We don't want you to be the last angry man on the sports field who gets thrown out of the games."

Using Natural Anger and Healthy *Mental* Violence for Good Living without Hurting Anyone: The Wonderful Ultimate Democracy of Our Own Mind

Everywhere in life the problems of violence are enormous, and so far largely beyond the reach of most societies' available systems for control. The huge problems of war, terrorism, and genocide are the lots of man everywhere, and to date overwhelmingly defy solution. In addition, there is so much deadly small-scale violence that plagues peoples' everyday lives. In so many places all over the world, people wake up daily to face undue allotments of violence in their homes, on the streets they walk—even at the sports events they frequent, where rival fans set upon one another as if they are deadly enemies—and at the hands of their police and governments. Many people are the *victims*, and many other fellow human beings are the *victimizers* (perpetrators or persecutors).

Yet this has also been an era of an important beginning understanding of violence in the social sciences. Although we are still far away from being able to deliver solutions to the larger-scale problems, it is my judgment that we have a solid base of knowledge-building from which to proceed to a variety of techniques to remove, reduce, or manage some of the violence done by individuals in our lives.

Because I value this technique so much and believe it is the best solution for the huge number of situations where we cannot or dare not talk out our anger with others, and also because I am aware that most mental health clinicians are not trained in this concept, here I want to repeat and expand on ideas that were introduced earlier about feeling and imagining anger in order to reduce anger and to develop even greater control inwardly against possible violent actions. The technique for good living I describe involves the pleasure of releasing angry feelings within one's own mind with a certainty of not doing any harm to another person.

I have often said to patients that the ultimate bastion of democracy into which we can retreat safely, even under many conditions where our freedoms to act publicly are suppressed, is the grand privacy of our own minds. So long as my strength of will and contact with my true self are intact in my own mind, I can think *anything* I want to, about anyone and any institution, and I can do my thinking in the ways that are most genuinely rewarding for me.

When I am making love to my wife, I can create any silent scenario that increases my power and pleasure. I can, without being in any way unkind, imagine myself possessing her in whichever ways are pleasing to me; I can imagine a different sexual activity than the one we are actually doing and thus enhance my experience of what we are doing with one another; I can substitute another woman for her in my mind, or generate a group sex scene. (Obviously, all of the above can be restated the same way for the woman making love to her husband.)

To the best of my knowledge, *moderate* though even quite regular use of such fantasies long ago received seals of approval from psychotherapists and sexologists—so long as these devices are exercised responsibly, which means not too extensively (I generally recommend to patients no more than 10 percent of the time), and certainly not as templates for planning to transform these *fantasy* tonics of the sexual spirit into *actual* behaviors.

There are many difficult life situations that can be solved in this way. A person who fantasizes—and *enjoys* the fantasizing—their authentic feelings and "gets out" all that they want to express generally feels better; feeling better not only reduces personal anxiety and oppression but, intriguingly, often facilitates far better performance in the very real world that one had feared so badly.

Of course, there are many circles and groups where these ideas are treated as licentious and sacrilegious and are officially forbidden (in my experience with a resulting greater degree of acting out in these communities or a depression of sexual vitality and pleasure).

It is good to at least have the notion of naturalness of diverse sexual fantasies enunciated in the sexuality and mental health literature, but this is far less the case when it comes to fantasies of angry feelings. The prevailing motif, even in mental health circles, is that you are disturbed or immoral or dangerous if you think and fantasize bad things happening to others, and especially if you fantasize yourself being the agent of delivering these aggressive blows.

I believe the opposite is true. Again, the "bad" fantasies should be modulated within boundaries of time (not too much) and intensity (not to be experienced as uncontrollable), and most of all the fantasy work should be dedicated to a purpose of releasing and reducing anger, along with ensuring there will be no actual ugly actions.

Thus, when I am forced to perform in a business or professional situation where I choose to agree that I must button my lip and not show or act on any of my "negative" feelings of dissatisfaction, disagreement, protest, anger, revenge, or what have you, I nonetheless can give full voice *inside my own mind* to all the feelings I would have wanted to express in the real world. Moreover, in my mind I can enrich and supplement the scripts and scenes I would have wanted to act on in reality, and turn them into fantasies of far more colorful and expressive escapades that I can enjoy over and over.

❖ One attorney who agonized fearfully over having to appear in a public situation with the head of the bar association, whom he hated, learned in therapy how to imagine happily that he had stripped the distinguished "head of the bar" stark naked in front of everyone. At the time of the reception, he found himself laughingly enjoying his fantasy so much that the dreaded public event turned into a delightful experience for him, including the fact that the hated "head of the bar" acknowledged his presence more respectfully than in the past because said attorney was having such a good time that he radiated a winning and attractive manner.

The "trick" is not to use this "medicine" too often, and definitely not bitterly or with increasing rage. A critical goal that the therapist should set for the patient who is instructed in this technique is to work toward reaching an experience of release and satisfaction, and to aim consciously at feeling *less* anger and rage because one is totally at home with the anger one feels. In the total privacy of my mind—indeed the ultimate bastion of my democracy—I am able to exercise every known form of anger, hurt, hate, torture, revenge, murder, and any other atrocity that was not yet mentioned in this atrocious list.

The point needs to be made *ad nauseam* that the actions "taken," meaning imagined, inside the privacy of one's mind, are in no way connected to any actual actions in real life. Imagining actions in one's mind is in no way equivalent to taking the actions being fantasized. On the contrary, the evidence is that for healthy people, exercising freedom of the mind in correctly responsible ways actually provides considerable protection against possible lapses into impulsive, uncontrolled violent actions.

Again I emphasize that *thinking* and *feeling* violently can be used to provide a measure of protection against the dangers of erupting into *actual* violence, and to augment one's energy and resolution to be committed to *non*-violence in one's actual behavior in the real world. I am not unaware of some psychological research that has shown that thinking-imagining violence does increase the readiness to be actually violent. But if such thinking-imagining is accompanied by and framed as an effort to release one's violence without doing any actual violent harm to the hated object, it helps.

- He hated his father for being a brutish, bossy, dominating, tyrannical figure. As a child he remembered lying in bed at night literally fearing his father's gruff return from his day's work. In therapy he learned first to give full verbal bent to his intensely angry free associations of taking revenge on his father, beating him up, even killing him and watching him die with satisfaction. From this work in therapy sessions, it was a logical leap to take the same capacity home and engage in fantasies of murdering his father gleefully as desired and needed. Slowly but surely he perfected his technique, overcoming his fear, guilt, and moral qualms, and then to his amazement and pleasure he began using the technique—silently, of course!—when he was actually visiting with his father. He was now able to engage fully in whatever conversation or interaction with his father while at the same time silently rehearsing—enjoyably!—his inner fantasies.

  The results were spectacular. He began to enjoy himself so much in his inner freedom to be his real self in a perfectly ethical way that he also relaxed to enjoy more and more the nice and interesting parts of his father. The visits between them took on a more relaxed and even jovial character. Over the years the father, who was already respectably retired when this process began, aged and became more dependent on his son, who now thoroughly enjoyed taking care of him as well as continued to take pleasure from their conversations and being together. All along the son continued silently his personal mind exercises of killing his father and enjoying doing so.

  The ultimate moment came when the son was present at his father's terminal illness and death at a ripe old age. He was totally relaxed and devoted as he cared for his father before he died. The son reported now feeling virtually simultaneously a wave of the most exquisite compassion and love for the dying old man, along with a recapping of his silent and pleasureful murdering of his father for all that he had been emotionally cruel to him. The two sets of feelings simply coexisted quietly and validly for him in his heart as he went about caring for his father respectfully and reducing his discomfort as much as possible.

To recap the two areas of living we have visited in respect of current or conventional wisdom in psychology: We saw that freedom for authentic sexual fantasies will be accepted in wider circles (though definitely not by all and certainly not by conservative society), and that the concept of allowing oneself to "tell" one's boss, mate, business colleagues or professional associates unwelcome truths in one's own mind also will be generally honored, although even this technique is not necessarily widely prescribed or recommended; but the notion of cultivating in our minds really horrible, ugly images, similes, and ideas of aggression toward our parents, other members of our family, or other intimates, bosses, colleagues, whoever, will be spurned and rejected by wide circles of mental health practitioners, and again obviously by conservative groups in our society.

Some, perhaps many, mental health professionals may go along with accepting the same angry ideas and feelings as quite human and not deserving of guilt reactions when patients come in and report that they have *unwittingly* experienced such ideas and feelings, certainly in dreams, even in waking fantasies, but many of the same clinicians will object to any notion of therapists *prescribing* such fantasies as elective experiences to be pursued and celebrated by choice. Personally, I believe the method is a highly effective one, and that it is grounded in psychological truth and philosophical integrity.

Intriguingly, one might link the subject to the tradition of telling children fairy tales in which often grim figures and threats and even horrible actions are described. There are many who interpret this seemingly strange custom of exposing children to evil as training for life—among other things to teach children to expect evil and to be able to recognize evil when it comes their way, and to retain a stamina, including keeping hope alive, that they can overcome it.[63]

The concept is also related to many therapy techniques of rehearsal (e.g., how to overcome fears of speaking publicly and other phobias) and to techniques of visualization (e.g., to help improve athletic and other performances, or to overcome disturbing emotional scripts with more constructive alternative fantasies and outcomes). Imagining is also recommended to enhance and enable a creative effort.[64] With specific regard to anger management, the technique is reminiscent of the old punching bag many parents arranged for their children (or for themselves), but here the bag is inside our own minds.

Conclusion: Fighting Emotionally Charged Violence in Real Life and via the Mind

It is rare to find in the psychotherapy literature advice on how to feel and rehearse anger for the purpose of controlling, releasing, and reducing the anger and its possible negative consequences. It is sort of funny that psychoanalytic therapists generally display a good deal of comfort about violent fantasies by patients in dreams or in free associations, but too often tilt their intervention toward a goal of recovering from the anger in order to not experience it further. Similarly, New Age psychologies are all over the place in recommending experiencing and releasing feelings in general, but rarely do so about anger. When anger is the subject, again the focus is generally placed on getting rid of the hot potato more than on releasing it and using it to become a more constructive and less angry person.

We are proposing a surprising dialectical concept: Be angry in your mind to release it and become both a more assuredly nonviolent person and a more positive person. Be angry and hate and go all the way in your fantasies of revenge to ensure being *nonviolent*, to become *less* agitated and *more* constructive in relationships that anger you, and by extension also to other life experiences and relationships. Oh, and put away those meds you were given to reduce your anger and prevent violence. They simply don't "get it."

PART FIVE: PSYCHOTHERAPEUTIC ENGAGEMENT OF EVIL

Psychotherapy and Psychotherapists Need to Take a Moral Stand against Evil

The topic of psychotherapeutic engagement of evil is not exactly a familiar one. The very word *evil* is used relatively rarely in the psychotherapy literature or in circles of therapists. And yet the very same species that is treated daily by psychotherapists is also renowned for its history of gargantuan and endless evils on every level of behavior. Obviously, phenomena of evil also have to be appearing regularly in the practices of therapists, whether they want to know it or not.

Although the subject of evil has precious little professional literature, it is so widespread in life that it cannot really go unnoticed, and we do find some works in psychology and psychotherapy even as the subject never really gets incorporated into the basic knowledge of therapists. Thus a set of several volumes published in 2011 brings together a huge assembly of discussions of evil, including the very correct admonition by several psychologists that therapists often err in sympathizing with an evildoer rather than confronting the person doing harm.[65] So many therapists empathize and sympathize with the "poor client" who arrives in their office without really clarifying what the person has been doing in the real world to other people.

Another major work on evil was published by the American Psychological Association, and its title promises to address psychotherapy of evil but in my opinion does not really do so. The promo of the book advertised in the flagship *American Psychologist* announces correctly that there is far too little in the professional literature about how psychotherapists deal with the "dark side of humanity" in therapy, and does provide some engaging case histories, but it still does not direct us toward a coherent model for psychotherapy of evil.[66] (In the present section we at least take a few stabs (pun intended) at some degree of model building.)

In one of the chapters in the above work, Ronald Miller reports interestingly a famous controversy on the subject of evil between two beloved giants of psychology and psychotherapy, Carl Rogers and Rollo May. Carl Rogers persists in his well-known belief that man is essentially good but warped by social influences as well as bad choices. Rollo May argues that humanistic psychology fosters narcissism and a blindness for evil, and that evil in our culture is also a reflection of the evil in *us*.[67]

Miller himself puts his finger on a core philosophical issue that underlies much of the Rogers-May discussions, "the proposition that psychological theory and practice must be undertaken from a position of complete moral neutrality vis-a-vis the actions of those whom we study or attempt to influence." Miller's position in turn is clear-cut, and I agree with him: "Clinical theory, research, and practice are, whether explicitly or implicitly, exercises in moral and ethical reasoning and judgment, and . . . in making these judgments explicit and open to dialogue within psychology we can work far more effectively for the greater good"[68]

Arnold Lazarus is a well-known clinician who has done outstanding work in what he defined as "multi-modal therapy" that focuses on "seven interactive processes . . . behaviors, thoughts, feelings, sensory reactions, mental images, interpersonal relationships, and biological factors."[69] In a chapter in which he proposes to write about the treatment of evil, this fine clinician and theorist of therapy brings only one case example, and it turns out to be a person who regards *herself* unfairly—pathologically—as evil when she isn't, and the therapist's task, of course, is to heal her self-condemnation. But that is not a contribution to our understanding of how to treat evil.[70]

Lazarus writes that very few of his clients in treatment over the years were perpetrators of evil—the vast majority were victims. This makes sense insofar as many a perpetrator is a tough macho (of either gender) kind of person and not likely to be asking for help from another human being. But one also wonders whether Lazarus, and so many other clinicians, was also alert to finding out whether and how much his clients were hurting somebody else in their lives, and not only being hurt thenselves.

We also wrote earlier about the excellent contribution of M. Scott Peck's important, touching, and impressively best-selling book on *People of the Lie.*[71] Peck's contribution to identifying/naming hidden evil is monumental. But when the time comes for Peck to discuss treatment of the disorders of evil that he has so sensitively defined, we lose the previously rational, learned, psychodynamically oriented therapist to a flight into the shamanic and occult as Peck offers us nothing less than a method of religious exorcism as the solution he genuinely believes in for evil people. I definitely respect the creation of ceremonial spiritual pageantry for treatment of different ethnicities and faiths (see, for example, the discussion earlier of a case of SUNDS). I know that symbolic group processes have powerful healing and corrective effects on many disorders of the mind and being. But I cannot accept a proposal of exorcism as a scientific healing process other than for indigenous members of a faith or culture that teaches belief in such a ritual.[72]

The big problem is just whom are we going to be asked to treat. Some People of the Lie do show up in therapy, most often in a family therapy organized by someone else in the family, and it is crucial that the therapist know how to diagnose them and addresses the therapy correctly to them in their hiding places. Therapy may be helpful in some of these cases but definitely not in all—evil people are typically characterized by resolute and absolute resistance to correction and instruction.

I see-remember a long parade of openly degrading and abusive spouses and parents, and a long parade of power-seeking people in the community, academia, and government whom I have seen clinically. Many of them were dragged by other people in their lives, often with meaningful results, but also perhaps more often without any tangible benefit. Then I see before me in my mind's eye a terrible assembly of devoted sadists and terrorists, past and present, such as Saddam Hussein, Pol Pot, Arafat, and leaders of Hamas, Talaat, Stalin, Hitler, bin Laden, and now the leaders of the Islamic State (ISIS)—an endless number of people who have joyed in genocidal mass murder of unarmed men, women, and children. I don't see *any* of these people signing up—neither for exorcism nor for psychotherapy. Moreover, were serious evildoers to agree to meet with a therapist, I can think of very few references in our psychotherapy literature that will guide us to know how to treat them.

Obviously, psychotherapy is not by any stretch a full answer to evil. However, psychotherapy can be one tool that fits *some* situations of evil. In addition, once we learn to recognize evil more clearly, the further understanding gained from contacts with the minds and souls of evil people may contribute to new thinking about critical treatment tools for stopping violence. Moreover, psychotherapeutic research may also contribute to solutions at a societal level, such as legal procedures, legislation, and the development of new institutions such as the emergence of the remarkable Truth and Reconciliation processes.[73]

The observations that follow on the treatment of evil address treatment of those people who are still within the reach of a psychotherapeutic process. Some will come on the basis of an order by a court, or at the direction of an authority in their lives whom they accept, such as a clergyman or a doctor; some will be genuinely responsive to an insistent demand by their spouses and families to undergo a genuine review of their destructive actions; and a very few will respond to loving pleas to correct themselves and seek help.

The suggestions for treatment that are made here represent the limited development of the field of psychotherapy for addressing evil, perhaps even to the point of constituting an absurdity, because for the most part the methods and interventions proposed can be applied only to evil people who agree to participate in a therapeutic process and remain within the reach of influence of other people. We cannot prescribe psychotherapy for those who are so far out of reach that they are irretrievably committed to destruction of others, and we need to admit that there are many such people in the sad veil of tears of this world. (I will note here that an interesting aspect of psychotherapy for many good people is to help them grow beyond a childish and naive belief in justice and human goodness. We wish their goodness were not so naive.)

On the level of groups, ideologies, and nations, the execution of evil obviously is enmeshed in many other systems of human experience, including guiding folk images of power and destruction in a given culture, economics, politics, media influences, military strategy and ambitions, health and ecological processes, the roles of leaders, and more.[74] It cannot be our goal in this book to engage in the search for means to bring peace to this world—although many of us hope that in the long run of civilization the concepts of decency and correction of wrongs that we develop in psychotherapy will also become influences on the players in larger systems of human behavior.

Evil for me refers to doing avoidable harm to life by taking away from people, ourselves or others, the opportunity to live one's lives in safety as free people. It pertains both to doing harm to oneself—*being hard on oneself, being unfair to oneself, destroying oneself,* as well as to doing harm to other people—*being insensitive, unfair, cruel to others or destroying others.* However, since in a democratic philosophy there is seemingly a greater right for individuals to elect to mess up their own lives, the word *evil* generally is reserved more to refer to actions that are imposed on other persons whom one has far less or no right at all to harm. Personally, I prefer to put the weight of definition on the harming of life in general rather than on who is the victim, although I too feel the greater moral evil of taking out one's nastiness and worse on others.

Facing Evil for What It Is: Identifying Patterns of Destructive Forces Both Against Us and By Us

A basic theme that emerges from a relatively wide range of religious, philosophical, and also some psychotherapeutic literature is that both the *reality* of evil all about us in human life and the *potential* of evil within every one of us need to be met with greater consciousness and awareness.[75]

Evil is everywhere in human life including in the actions of people we are inclined to see as "good people." T.S. Eliot observed that "[m]ost of the evil in this world is done by people of good intentions." Mahatma Gandhi identified "Seven Deadly Sins" that lurk in the lives of human beings who did not necessarily set out with evil intentions.

The Seven Deadly Sins are:

Wealth without work
Pleasure without conscience
Science without humanity
Knowledge without character
Politics without principle
Commerce without morality
Worship without sacrifice[76]

There are endless observations of the universality of evil in many sources of human culture. Thus a Christian theological statement:

> We all have the knowledge of Good and Evil: Because Adam and Eve ate the fruit from the tree of the knowledge of good and evil (Genesis 2:17), the law is in our hearts. We can decide what is morally right and what is not. However, we are inclined to follow the evil side because sin is inherent in us.[77]

As we have noted, in a number of religious cultures the idea of harboring angry thoughts is frowned upon seriously. A distinct polarity is established between bad feelings and good feelings and the believer is exhorted to rise to a wholesome capacity to entertain only good feelings. See for example in the *New Testament*:

> 23 Your hearts and minds must be made completely new, 24 and you must put on the new self, which is created in God's likeness and reveals itself in the true life that is upright and holy. 26 If you become angry, do not let your anger lead you into sin, and do not stay angry all day. 27 Don't give the Devil a chance.[78]

On the other hand, there are also any number of religious sources where anger is recognized as valid, such as by several of the biblical prophets who themselves are openly angry at the erring people of Israel. There are also some religious sources that embrace anger as natural and wholesome and lay the emphasis on how and to what purpose the anger is directed. Thus the Baha'i, a small but worldwide faith with many beautiful emphases on the sacredness of human life and democracy, has a concept that "[i]n creation there is no evil, all is good . . . all the natural qualities of man constitute the capital of life." The trick is *how* these qualities are used. If they are tapped to advance human life, they are a fulfillment of our god-given potential; if they are used to destroy life, they constitute evil.[79]

Thus, too, a parable that a rabbi, Harold Schulweis, attributes to the founder of Hasidism:

> The disciples of the Baal Shem Tov, the founder of Hasidism, tell of a dream he had. In the dream, the very incarnation of the Evil Impulse appears in the form of a sinister heart. The Baal Shem Tov seizes the heart and pounds it furiously. He would destroy evil and redeem the world. As he pummels it, he hears an infant's sobbing emitted from the heart. He stops beating it. In the midst of evil is a voice of innocence; there is goodness entangled in evil.[80]

Recognizing Evil for What It Is

Perhaps the strongest contribution psychotherapists can make at this point is to help people identify evils to which they are being subjected. The earlier one admits this awareness, the more careful and resolute one can be. The clearer one recognizes evil for what it is, the more capably and powerfully one can respond. Thus, how often do spouses (it used to be largely females, but today it is more and more often also men who are victimized by women's power) fail to recognize the extent of ugliness and spiritual corruption in their mate and fail to confront or limit the other? How often do workers fail to recognize that they are being exploited by manipulative and exploitative bosses and/or work systems and do not seek means to stand up to them?

Any number of victims "refuse" to recognize they are being abused—be it by a spouse, employer, government, church, or ideological movement. Thus, how many devoted, well-intentioned communists simply could not tolerate the emerging information about Stalin as a mass killer (note sadly how popular Stalin is to this day in Russia)? Similarly, how many believers and devotees of an ineffective and even damaging mental health treatment—for example, lobotomies, or even individual psychotherapy when there is an exploitative therapist or when a therapist issues an absolute injunction against seeing other family members—stay locked into submitting to that system? The recognition of evil as a natural part of the human condition can help provide a frame of reference for many people who are victims to come to terms with the reality of the evils that befell them, both personally or as members of collectives.

First of all, accepting the reality of evil as something in nature, which was not assigned purposely and specifically to them as if they personally really deserved the suffering they endured, can help some people to reduce their traumatization and go on living more effectively. Second, recognizing another person's evil for what it is can provide a basis for strengthening people to guard against and fight back against being victims. Moreover, informing people that they are hurting others may give *some* perpetrators *who really do not want to be destructive to others* the opportunity to correct themselves and stop doing harm.

One lady proposed a definitive methodology for identifying evil: "If 9 out of 10 grandmothers selected from 10 respective cultures can agree it is evil, then it's evil. Cut it out."[81] The recognition of evil can provide an inspirational entry into spotting one's own potential for evil, and addressing it and containing it.

As noted, a very common error in a great many individual and family psychotherapies is that many evildoing people are not seen for who and what they are. Instead efforts are made through traditional techniques to invite the people who are doing harm to life to speak of their hurt, losses, and yearnings in a vain hope that they will then be transformed into socially positive and constructive creatures. A related common error in psychotherapy is to treat evil people respectfully and generously, avoiding confrontation, provocation, or aggression, with the expectation that they will respond quid pro quo to the decency offered them. There are many such evildoing participants in therapies who know how to carry themselves with seeming aplomb and courtesy, and in effect sit and mock their naive, innocent, and essentially impotent therapists as well as their victims. On a metaphoric level, in their unconscious experience if not consciously, they enjoy a triumph of their power over their naive, innocent therapists who don't know enough about people and life to know that there are people who should *not* be approached with a belief in their kindness and goodness, but who need to be confronted with what they are doing and pushed authoritatively, including by invoking authorities such as protective care services or the police when appropriate, to stop their doing harm to others.

The Case of the Brother Who Stole Several Millions from His Brother

❖ He was the younger brother and lifelong business partner of his older brother. The older brother had greater emotional flair and business ability, and was the senior partner of the two. He generated great wealth for himself and also considerable though less wealth for his younger brother.

The younger brother had his "successful" ways, too. In his everyday manner, the younger brother was ostensibly a gentleman, courteously correct to a fault, and to his credit with few pretensions or public displays of power-seeking, but also annoyingly taciturn, a man of few words with a suggestion of a sardonic and even sadistic humor playing through his relatively few words. In his business dealings he used a distinctly maddening style in which he delighted setting people up in situations in which they expected certain things of him—he would even enter into contractual definitions of these expectations—but then he would strike like a snake with a twisted redefinition of the terms and conditions of the agreement. In many cases people were then left with a choice of renegotiating the situation to save whatever they could of their investment and limit their losses, or enter into costly and energy-consuming litigation, or suffer their losses. One can say these clients were driven "crazy" by this man who delighted in being their crazy-maker.

The older, more successful brother knew of his younger brother's doings, and even laughed at them as if they were spoils he was willing to leave for his underdog brother to somehow make up for his being the lesser of the two of them. So long as the victims were not people in whom the senior brother-partner was interested, and so long as the deals that were spoiled did not really make a dent in the overall balance sheet of their multimillion dollar operation, the little brother was allowed his diet of victims.

There came the day that the victim turned out to be the older brother himself—in spades. Given their family connection and assumed loyalty to one another, and the gratifications derived from being a Mr. Big who didn't have to bother with detail work, the older brother regularly turned over many of the papers of financial dealings to the younger one, who in any case had far less to do with clients than his more charismatic older brother. Over time the two of them cornered the market on a series of major office buildings and lots in their city. The properties had been ostensibly purchased as equally owned by each of the brothers. Year after year the properties were duly reported as such in each of their respective and various corporate tax returns. But then one amazing day when the whole portfolio of their buildings came up for review, it became clear that the younger brother had *never* registered his older brother's name on any of the deeds for the properties. He had left himself as the sole legal owner of all of them! The older brother remained with no financial resources! (Everything he did own was lost to claims against him, and in his great hubris he had never even set aside a penny in any protected personal account.)

After making an "unsuccessful" try at suicide, the older brother entered therapy. The therapist succeeded in getting the younger brother to provide some (though not exactly generous) financial support for his now destitute older brother, and therapy also succeeded in helping the shell-shocked older brother to come to terms with the reality of what had happened. In time the therapy even laid a foundation for a degree of renewed relationship between the two brothers and their families—the first ice-breaking conversation between the two brothers was in a long-distance telephone call which was negotiated and scheduled by the therapist for the older brother to call the younger from the therapist's office.

The Denial of Evil versus Recognition and Acknowledgment

Evil augments its power by a combination of the perpetrators' concealment and the innocence and denial of evil's existence by the victims. Those who have been emotionally abused or rejected should at least have the advantage of *knowing* what has happened to them, and having the evil that was done to them recognized consensually by others in their lives. To have suffered a damnable curse of deep rejection, condemnation, or invalidation of one's essential value, and then also to have that harm denied, leads to the most perplexing, prolonged, and bitter symptoms of despair, depression, and self-invalidation of the victim.

Parental messages in particular have an enormous power for confirming or weakening a child's confidence in their living. What parents really feel toward a child shapes the mental health and illness of children for the many forthcoming years of their lives—although I have also seen brave people who were cursed-rejected by their parents who fight their way back successfully to a decent self-love. Any number of clinicians have observed that there are parents who harbor inner wishes and expectations that a child be incompetent, troubled, damaged, or even die and that these messages are central in fomenting serious psychiatric disorders in children.[82] One intriguing implication for therapeutic practice is that there is a huge therapeutic power waiting to be tapped if and when parents develop the ability to acknowledge to their children the harm they have done and apologize sincerely.

❖ I witnessed such a dramatic scene even with a severely autistic child who at the time did not speak. In the months following his mother's apology to him, there was an enormous growth spurt, and one cannot help but consider the possible contribution of the parent's acknowledgment to the child as a major spur to that growth.[83]

People who tend to be "innocents" often are caught unaware by nastiness, scheming, malevolence, power manipulations, and outright destructiveness and are more available victims in all the worlds of family life, work, community, and society. Thus innocent people may not understand why they feel so badly in a work situation where there are evil leaders who degrade workers and stalemate their possible advancement. The worker may try desperately to curry the favor of the evil leaders or the evil system, and only when repeated evidence makes it clear that good efforts lead to no change for the better and the machinery for insulting workers and keeping them down continues or even intensifies, do they allow themselves to realize that the people in charge at their work are really bad and/or that an objectively harassing structural situation is pressing down on them.

As is well known, fascist killers engage in torture and commit genocidal murders in contexts of self-justification: the French Revolution led to a bloodbath in the name of *liberté*, *egalité*, and *fraternité*; the Nationalist Socialist Party sought glory for its racial and national heritage by eliminating the inferior peoples who sully it; Communists have eradicated tens of millions of people in the name of socialist equity; a variety of churches have persecuted their non-believers, heathen, and infidels.

Of course, being able to recognize evil being done to us should not be an excuse for skipping past the acknowledgement of *one's own evil* to others. In therapy, it is the therapist's task—responsibility and privilege—to identify evil behaviors from all sources for what they are, and to help the people who are consulting him to call things what they really are—both about others and about themselves.

There are also many victims who know quite clearly they have been deeply hurt, and even with all our devoted efforts to help them cannot recover their will and fight for life.

Unfortunately, not all victims of evil can be helped. Some experiences of evil are so overwhelming that people cannot recover. This has been true of some Holocaust survivors, for example. Their capacities for trust of human beings and for hope were shattered permanently.

❖ A man who had been a teenage survivor of the Holocaust told me in therapy, "The worst thing about the Holocaust was that I could no longer believe in human beings." Although he survived, moved to Israel (which he loved deeply), and built a lovely family, he never was able to work gainfully again. Whenever he went to work, he would set off a bitter conflict, causing his employers not to be able to trust him. Although his relationship with me was genuinely respectful and warm (and good contact has been maintained over the years even after completion of the failed therapy), he never gained the ability to work successfully. Finally, because of his chronic inability to build trusting and calm work relationships, he quit working altogether.

For those who are the victims of hidden evil by others, the response to clarification of the evil is often a dramatic mixture of intense anxiety and deep relief and elation at being freed to know the truth.

For those who themselves must become accountable for the grave hurt and harm they are doing to others, the response in therapy is often one of intense resistance, at worst even efforts to dismiss the therapist or render them impotent to continue, but there are times when this resistance nonetheless can be tapped constructively to help a person acknowledge the dread part of themselves that has been hurting others, which they have been denying.

Still often enough in this world of tears, the best efforts can fail. Here is a case that embodies both a constructive lessening of evil behavior but then a grand finale of evil triumphant.

❖ A brother/business partner was confronted by a therapist with his repeated expressions of deep disrespect to his brothers with whom he shared the management of a complex multimillion dollar business. His standard language included recurring references to their imbecility and incompetence, whether in his conversations with them or in speaking about them to others. At work he would seize almost happily on every possible evidence of real failures on their part and add them to his growing dossier of "proofs" that they were basically incompetent.

In his therapy the degrading brother denied that there was any aspect in his personality that sought to celebrate his brothers' failings and to take advantage of the weakness they showed as a personal triumph. The therapist confronted him with quotation after quotation in which he placed himself above his brothers—for example, "It is obvious to everyone that if either of them died or both of them, this company would continue successfully, but if I were to die, in a matter of weeks this corporation would dissolve." At first his reaction was to become violently enraged at the therapist. However, to his credit, over a period of time he did agree to the therapist's advice that he stop saying many of the nasty phrases he was using to his brothers. He forced himself instead to adopt a style of relative friendliness and courtesy. In time, he seemed to relax some of the underlying projections he placed onto his brothers and also began to see them as more capable.

Yet, sadly, there was still to come a day when this brother slyly manipulated his way to become the major owner of the company in which they all had been equal partners, and now his superiority was an incontrovertible fact of life.

Meeting Evil and Responding to It with Firmness and Power

Therapy involves mobilizing all the forces that are available to confront, limit, and overcome the evildoers if at all possible. Innocents who do not recognize evildoers for what they are may pay with far more than their pocketbooks for not taking all possible steps to overcome and defeat the persons doing them harm. Therapy can be potentially helpful for victims and potential victims to work on what to do in responding to evil attacks and threats on their existence, or in response to attacks against other people for whom they care, or to evil threats against the community and society in which they live and want to protect.

I do not believe that evil should be met with niceness unless there is very good reason to believe decency can possibly help the perpetrator to turn over a new leaf. The revered pacifist, A.J. Muste, is reported to have said that if he had met Hitler, he would have loved him.[84] I deeply disagree. I would pray instead for the foresight and courage to shoot the Hitlers of our world. Many kinds of evil "simply" have to be fought hard and toughly. In personal relationships too, there are people who are mean, harmful, and dangerous to other living creatures and who will not change their ways even if approached with the best intentions, and they have to be stopped in their tracks.

Intriguingly, the great Albert Ellis—whose basic work on "rational-emotive therapy" I referred to earlier with the greatest respect—is reported to have gone in the same wrong direction as Muste. I have never seen this myself in Ellis's writings or heard him say this in the several lectures of his that I attended, but Arnold Lazarus is adamant in his criticisms of Ellis for taking a sanctimonious position about the great evildoers of humanity and saying that he did not hate them, but rather that he hated what they did. He quotes Albert Ellis, "Hitler, Stalin, Genghis Khan are never bad people and if you condemn them you are going to condemn yourself when you are bad."[85] Lazarus continues for himself:

> There is a point at which deeds of horror transcend the line of thought that the deed should be separated from the person. For instance, I contend that the doctors in Nazi death camps who performed atrocious and inhuman operations on people in the name of scientific investigation were unspeakable evil individuals.[86]

Like it or not, at every level of human organization there are regularly needs for authoritative interventions to put a stop to harassment, abuse, and violence. On the societal level there are many situations that would benefit from international forces to stop potential ethnic cleansing and genocide. On the community level, we may need to call in police to break up potential massacres, such as a looming massacre in a school or a would-be terrorist plot. On the family level, overt physical and sexual abuse often require authoritative legal intervention. Similarly, even when there is no physical abuse, intense emotional abuse may require the intervention of authorities such as the requirement of supervision by a court or by social workers who remove children or even adults from a family home.

The task of the psychotherapist is to bring to light clearly and sanely what is *really* going on in a family or relationship, including seeing the unpleasant truths we wish were not so, such as parents who hate a child and/or abuse a child; or siblings who want to trample a brother or sister, whether in an ugly mad race for an inheritance, fierce competitiveness in business, or sometimes even in sexual competitiveness for a sibling's spouse; or children who couldn't care less for a parent, no matter how aged or in need of help they are, or who only want to speed up gaining control of their parents' assets; and on and on.

Many perpetrators will *not* go away and stop doing harm to their victims even when challenged and exposed. The task of the therapist is to get the facts out in the open, strengthen the victims, and to help neutralize the perpetrator as much as possible. There are also times when the therapist needs to exclude someone who is coming to therapy sessions from making a mockery of psychotherapy. In the course of a presentation on formulating a psychodynamic diagnosis and treatment plan in short-term therapy, psychiatrist James Mann[87] noted that there are certain people who are so clearly evil that they cannot be treated by any of the conventional methods that we have. It was his recommendation that once identified, such people should be excluded and dismissed from any therapy effort.

There are also happier times when perpetrators *can* be influenced to stop harming others, and there are cases where the victims can be helped to fight successfully the evil being done to them. Along with the therapist's first task of identifying and calling the evil actions what they are, the therapist's task is to assist their patient(s) to call forth their natural resources and their will to fight back, and help them formulate a strategy for fighting back against the evil. This means moving the therapy from the time-honored position of commiserating with hurt, loss, and emotional injury to an activist position of mobilizing protest and anger against people who are hurting the patient, and helping to plan the most effective counterattacks possible in the given circumstances.

In those cases where the evil issues from the patient(s) themselves, it means that the therapist moves from the time-honored tasks of commiserating and identifying with the patient and understanding their point of view to a "moral therapeutic analysis" of how the patient is doing immoral and harmful things to other people and needs to stop doing the harm.[88]

Family therapy can be especially helpful in working with perpetrators of harm in the family. The family therapy constitutes a prearranged group structure for meeting with perpetrators and trying to work with them. It also offers a structure for the victim to meet with other members of the family who may be able to help. Note that family therapy need not include the full family group. It is a concept for creating different forums for meeting different members of a family in whatever subgroups, such as a husband and wife, or a given parent with a specific child, also even for individual sessions with a specific member of the family that focus on relationships in the family.[89]

❖ In the second year of family therapy for a sixteen-year-old boy who had made a very serious suicide attempt a year earlier, the boy was signaling newly emergent desires to grow and become a more healthy person. For many years, this boy had treated himself as a self-indulgent, pleasure-loving, tension-escaping free spirit, and thus had also missed out on developing normal school skills, and especially skills for taking examinations.

Given his new readiness to learn, the therapist asked the parents to arrange for private tutoring in which the youngster would be given systematic practice and immediate feedback on his performances on tests in the subjects for which he was preparing to take matriculation examinations. Yet months went by with the father subtly sabotaging the process and failing to engage a tutor, and then unexpectedly the father announced that he was ending the therapy for the boy and all of them.

In the showdown that now took place, the therapist gave the father the critical feedback that he was reluctant to have his son gain new strength for himself because it served the father's unconscious purpose to keep the boy weak, and also served his need for living proof that his wife had failed to bring up a healthy child, so that he could enjoy blaming her and feeling superior to her.

"Why do you think that you set your mind not to understand the importance of getting the tutor I asked you to get for your son, and then you let yourself go so far as to think of stopping a therapy that is obviously working for him?" the therapist asked the father in a climactic session in the presence of his wife and son.

"I didn't realize that I was holding him back," said the father, "and I don't think I want to hold him back, but it's like in many other things, I get so lazy," he replied.

"Yes, you take the lazy way out, including not using your talents to be a better father," said the therapist. "In this way you contributed to your son learning the pattern of escapism and fleeing all tension and challenges until ultimately he went so far as to run away from life itself when he attempted to commit suicide."

The father yielded and hired a tutor and allowed the therapy to continue to its normal conclusion. Over time the youngster qualified in his matriculation examinations, graduated high school, and was successfully inducted into the army. It was a proud day when he came dressed in his handsome new uniform to say goodbye to the therapist.

Fighting back against the evil of others should not be taken as an excuse for avoiding confrontation of one's own weaknesses or contributing in any way to being victimized. Nor should it be an excuse for not accepting the reality of one's bad luck and plain not succeeding in the normal competition of life. On the other hand, not to be able to spot the truth that others are exploiting us and doing us harm will augment unjustified neurotic feelings of unworthiness and being a failure.

❖ He was a capable and ambitious young academic who was hired for his first position by a prestigious university. He poured his whole self into his beginning work in teaching and research, and on the whole did very well, including showing very clear signs of a good potential for developing into a prominent researcher. However, unbeknownst to him, the department had hired him on the basis of special three-year funding by the government for encouraging new scientific talent, and there was never any intention nor a structural possibility of retaining him once these funds were used up.

At the end of the second year, he received verbal and written advisories from the chair of the department that his work was not sufficiently satisfactory for him to be considered a candidate for continuing on a tenure track a year later, and that it would be in his best interests to begin looking for other work.

Needless to say, the young academic was crushed and fell into a combination of hurting, self-criticism, and attempts to appease and renegotiate with the chairperson and seniors in the department. He did not allow himself to realize that there was nothing that he had done, nor anything that he could do to rectify the purely cold-blooded exploitation of him and the total indifference of the seniors in the department to the shame and hurt they were causing him.

When he was helped to put together the truth of the abuse done to him, he not only stopped his self-effacing efforts at appeasing the evil people, but also began to draw more energy for himself. He moved into being able to experience an appropriate anger at the seniors of his department, and he also successfully organized himself to apply secretly for a fine alternative position at another university where years later he rose to become a professor and chairperson of the department.

Giving Evil People Alternative Positive Ways to Act, and Showing Them How to Be More Decent

We have acknowledged that we are not treating the Hitlers, Khoumeinis, or heads of Islamic State. They do not perceive that they need help, nor would they allow us to approach them. Sadly, we are currently unable to prescribe psychotherapy for those who are irretrievably committed to the destruction of others. People who choose to act malevolently, and those who have already run up a record of vicious victimization of others and have tasted more than a little blood (so to speak or actually), are hardly likely to participate in therapeutic rechanneling of their behavior. Even many of the people who are significantly evil but who will agree to come for a period of time to therapists will spurn our efforts to join with them and create a sincere therapeutic alliance, and will turn away from authentic clarification of the harm they are doing to others.

Nonetheless, whenever we are granted an opportunity to work with an evil person about the harm they do to others, we can try to help and sometimes succeed, and we also can try to learn more about the nature of evil so that we can contribute to new knowledge about containing evil.[90]

Where possible, the ideal therapeutic goal is to transform evil actions against other people into positive alternatives. When this is possible, therapists and patients together truly experience a heartwarming triumph of good over bad, and the transformative experience will take on historical milestone meanings for people that will inspire them (and perhaps others) for years to come.

Understandably, such transformations are more likely when the evil actions originated from an unintentional, unconscious process that grew out of dynamics that were beyond the reach of the person doing harm. In some cases, evil actions develop out of legitimate aggressive impulses, which need and deserve to be expressed, but which become runaway processes of harming the other because of a lack of knowledge of how to pace and master the expression of the aggression, and not because there was a real desire to cause serious or permanent harm to another. Sometimes evil can be seen more as continuing the suffering a person experienced in their own past, which they now continue unconsciously by transferring or redirecting their suffering against their current victim. Thus, a man who was beaten in his childhood may push his wife around insultingly even though he loves her a great deal, because unconsciously he now needs to be the one beating the other up. He really needs to be tough, but he also needs to learn how to achieve the strength he needs without it being at another person's expense. Similarly, parents who themselves were unnourished, rejected, or manipulated in their childhoods, who wish to do better by their own children but are literally unknowing and unable to deliver a warmth they themselves never enjoyed, can set in motion a tragic and disastrous chain of psychopathological development in a child—up to and including psychosis, and as we have seen in the views of some therapists, also autism, and then be genuinely shocked and alarmed to see their child deteriorating. When mobilized in a family therapy process, many of these parents will give a great deal of themselves to arrest and correct the serious damage that they really do not want to occur to their child's development. Some parents are able to achieve in therapy an authentic inner dialogue with their memories of how they too were frozen out as children and denied warmth. Seeing the catastrophic impact on the child, these parents mobilize themselves caringly to renounce their evil and recommit themselves to being nurturing parents.[91]

Many family cutoffs and even incidents of family violence in their origins are rooted in legitimate and necessary waves of anger and hatred that arise in people's natural emotional machinery and then erupt in overt violence. As we have been emphasizing, in therapy it is possible to teach a great many people that while their aggressive *feelings* are legitimate, their overt *acts* of harmful violence to the other person are not. The therapist teaches people that they will be happier with themselves as decent people if they commit themselves to learning how to control the flow of their anger and give it expression in legitimate communication, including intense displeasure and anger, but not in acts of actual violence that do harm to the physical being of the other.[92] As previously reported, clinical experience shows that even people who are bona fide psychiatric patients with poor impulse control can be brought down from states of agitated threats of violence, and even to give up weapons they are holding, to recommit themselves to a therapy process that will seek real justice for their angry feelings but without their doing overt harm to people.

Another group of situations where it may be possible to guide people who are doing harm to others into a constructive orientation is where a collusive unit within a family, such as two parents or two siblings or even a total family group, have conspired on the basis of an unconscious collusion to scapegoat, injure, or punish a family member (Ivan Nagy's work on uncovering the map or ledger of ethical balances in families is very relevant here).[93] Insofar as the therapist is able to break up the collusive unit and win over someone(s) in the family to the cause of seeking justice for the victim, a good deal of help for the person being harmed is likely, beginning with the moral support of finally having somebody on their side.

❖ The seventy-year-old father had gotten into trouble financially in his business. He and his wife appealed to their son and daughter-in-law to lend them money by taking a reverse mortgage on their home. The middle-age couple did so, even gladly, to help their elders. Throughout this period, the parents continued to live in their own home, which they owned. Unfortunately, the father was unable to rescue his business, and the new funds went down the drain as well. The younger generation now asked the parents to sign their (the parents') home over to them (at least as of the time of their deaths in the future), but the father absolutely refused to do this. So now the children no longer had a home! A desperately tense and angry situation developed in the family.

A family-wide intergenerational family therapy session was called that included the parents, the middle-age couple, and other siblings. The therapist clarified the history of the problem and put forward an explicit definition of how the parents had exploited the younger couple and owed them compensation. The therapist's clear statement succeeded in enlisting the agreement and support of the previously silent seventy-year-old mother. She now abandoned her formerly collusive role with her husband and took a heroic stand that unless her husband agreed to sign over the title to their home to their son and daughter-in-law, she would in fact leave him—notwithstanding their long-term marriage, his and her ages, and also his heart condition. In a dramatic turnabout, the legal transfer of title to the young couple was executed in the immediate days following the intergenerational family session.

Accepting the Naturalness of Anger and Its Potentially Constructive Energy

Again I offer the opinion that there are many (far too many) instances where therapists attempt to help people put aside and stop their anger. Many therapists treat anger as intrinsically immature and disturbed and as an inappropriate way to try to release pent-up frustrations. The preferred goal of therapy then becomes knowing more clearly when one is frustrated and about what, and to devote one's energies to resolving and removing the frustration without becoming angry—obviously not a bad idea in itself—but when the anger is real the translation into frustration is an escape from reality. In truth many of these therapists dislike anger and are afraid of it. Admittedly, their intentions likely are good, and they want a cleaner and nicer world, but they are not facing the fact that the real world in which we live, at every level of human experience, is continually unjust, provocative, and evokes considerable anger. The preferred truth is to know how to channel these angry feelings so that they do not contribute to destruction but instead contribute to the improvement of relationships and life situations.

First, anger can be released constructively, as we have described, in one's own mind, enjoying—*yes, enjoying*—the imaginative versions of expressing our anger, as well as by sublimating and transforming our anger into resolutions and strategies for bringing about a better reality. Secondly, anger can provide a healthy basis for confronting people and situations who are doing us harm, and challenging them to stop or act with better self-control. Our angry feeling are a major source of our energy and power. Indeed they are dangerous and can heat up to destructive explosions, but "engineered" correctly and channeled healthily they can be the basis for much-improved health, improved relationships, and, surprising as it may be, even increased love. (Intriguingly, once one frees one's anger, it may be possible to see the other in a new and even lovable light).

Limiting and Containing Evil that Cannot Be Fought and Confronted

Finally, regrettably, we need to face the many times when evil *cannot* be fought and overcome. Yet in these situations, too, there may still be a number of steps that can be taken to contain the spread of the evil and the extent of its influence. Again the first therapeutic task is recognition that ugly and harmful actions are afoot.

Thus there are tyrannical parents whose behavior cannot be modified in therapy—even if for a period of time they ostensibly agree to participate in family therapy. Many times therapists will have no choice but to advise children to leave or reduce contact with one or both such parents. There are *Job* situations where one is doomed to be humiliated and exploited, and no amount of competence or goodwill, self-assertion, or politicking will change the situation. If one can get away from such a position, it is wise to do so, but so long as one cannot, there are ways in which to build an inner repertoire of greater strength, at least through the use of healthy inner aggression against the sources of insult. And there are many situations where one must fight back by calling in authorities. Continuing a case referred to earlier:

❖ A woman had broken up with her lover of some years, and he responded with rage and ominous acting out of violence—he burned her car, stalked her, and threatened more violence. She was in terror and felt helpless. The therapist counseled her to call the police, but she felt too terrified and weak and couldn't bring herself to do it. She told the therapist that she also believed that her ex-lover was secretly stalking her outside when she came to her therapy sessions. In the course of one therapy session, the phone rang and it was the lover. He growled ominously at the therapist that unless the woman returned to him, she would end up getting hurt and so would the therapist. The therapist responded—in his patient's presence—with unmistakable power and definiteness.

"If you ever call her again, or if I so much as see you near my office, you will end up in jail that day! I don't want to hear of one more threat from you to me or to your ex-girlfriend, or I guarantee that I will personally arrange for you to be picked up and jailed and that they will throw away the key!" The man left the country almost immediately thereafter and was not heard from again.

The concept of containing evil includes instructing people to stop their evil actions to others even in those situations when they are not yet able to really overcome their inner dynamics of wanting to hurt and mistreat the other person.

❖ A teenager showing psychotic symptoms was on the verge of being hospitalized. In the course of the family therapy that sought to avoid the hospitalization, an incident developed where the boy spoke back rudely to his father and the father went crazy and smashed some of the boy's possessions.

Years before, this father too had suffered a period of sudden immobilization at work following a narcissistic injury. Without his knowledge, his son's current breakdown was reminiscent to him of his own period of being paralyzed, and his fury at his son's impotence was the thrust of rage both at his own impotence as well as at his own father—the boy's grandfather—who had very much sought to keep all of his sons much less competent and potent than he was so that he could rule the roost and revel in his superior feelings. It was far too early in therapy to help the father learn what his blind rage was about and how it could be genuinely corrected from inside of him. But it was not too early in therapy to tell the father that he must commit himself to containing any and all of his violent emotions no matter how pressing and natural his violent feelings appeared to him, so that he could help his son to control the violence that also blew up in the youngster's disturbed mind.

Of course, there will also be many times when the psychotherapeutic modality will *not* succeed in limiting and containing ongoing emerging evil. The therapist's sad acceptance of such limitations and failings is an intrinsic part of the role of a helping professional.

❖ He said of himself that he was incredibly self-destructive. Although he suffered from a serious level of diabetes, more than once he had indulged himself in dangerous "sweet-outs" that led to violent physiological reactions and the necessity for stabilizing medical procedures, if not lifesaving ones. In this and other respects too, he described himself as forever walking a tightrope, playing against falling to the beckoning death, which he dared to take him—excitedly yet also fearfully. In his work he had caused himself to be demoted from a high position by making sure to convey to his superiors that he was not up to the tasks required, and yet he was adroitly successful in gaining another lesser position in the same organization rather than causing them to let him go entirely. His whole pattern of a "Russian roulette life" had grown out of a series of truly massive losses that had taken place one after the other. At this point, his entire small family was gone and he was totally alone in life, titillating himself with his daredevil style and awaiting his ultimate big fall into oblivion.

With all of this, he wanted to have a baby. He was not married. He was going with a girl whom he described disparagingly and almost with repugnance as far below him in many of her intellectual qualities. According to his description, she was basically unable to stand up responsibly for her actions and for her errors and limitations, but instead created a pseudoself (similar to his pseudoself of daredevil confidence) by propping herself high in an aura of pseudoperfection. Although he obviously did not respect her, he liked the fact that she depended on him and adored his charismatic brilliance and emotional vibrancy, and he loved commanding her as if she were his slave, let alone that he was attracted to her pseudoself as a mirror of his own.

Since he wanted a baby, and she was the only port of call in his life who would accept him, he planned to use her for that purpose. Although unmarried, they reported to a fertility clinic as a married couple. Therapeutic efforts to dissuade the man from any and all of his high-wire behaviors were unsuccessful. One day he disappeared from therapy.

CONCLUSION: THE DEMOCRATIC MIND STRIVES FOR BASIC DECENCY

The subjects of psychotherapy of violence and evil are of the greatest importance, and in my opinion badly neglected in the clinical training of therapists and in the professional literature. The Democratic Mind affirms that psychological health includes the maintenance of a basic respect, equality, wholesomeness, and integrity both in one's management of one's own life and in relationships with one's family and other human beings, while a Fascist Mind embraces the fact that life is a jungle where one can abuse people and/or seek to gain one's ends at whatever expense to life.

Traditionally, psychology and psychiatry are very much concerned with all forms of self-destruction, but incredibly less so—up to actual omission—of harm done to others. There has been only a limited recognition of the common underlying process in harms done to oneself and to others, that both are renunciations and attacks on life itself, and that the caring for life is a key issue in understanding and treating both sides of the disorder.

This concept of goodness both to oneself and to others calls for a paradigmatic shift in much of professional psychology and psychiatry from a kind of self-centered or narcissistic involvement with a given human being's ability to function without being disturbed, crazy, and dysfunctional to looking at relationships both with one's own self and with other human beings through a lens that measures the extent to which a person is facilitating, supportive, and creative in the true sense of generating life and protecting life either and both for oneself and others.[94]

I believe this is a more noble, and at the same time a more down-to-earth and true-to-life basis for psychological and psychiatric diagnosis and treatment that fits everyday observations of human beings as to who is emotionally responsible and effectively healthy and who is not—not only in relation to oneself but in relation to the impact one has on other people with whom one is connected.

Psychological and psychiatric disturbance is to be diagnosed when one cultivates despair, sorrow, and incompetence either in oneself or in others, including one's spouse, family group, children, or spouse-partner in parenting, also business associates, students, neighbors, other members of one's community, or plain other people in this world whom a person has the power to influence.

In respect of the practicalities of managing violence based on surges or intensities of emotions, we have proposed an active method of psychotherapy in which the therapist speaks very humanly, and as much as possible in the client's culture-language, and says, "You know it's wrong to hurt people's bodies, but I will help you with your anger—expressing it and getting it to work for you." Note that it is the synergy-combination of the two "medications" together that make it work. Either one alone falls flat.

We also recommend for daily living the use of one's mind as the ultimate bastion of democracy, to fantasize even the worst aggression at our hated others, but to do so with a resolute knowledge that no violent acts are to be committed, and with the explicit intention of enjoying release of one's rage and the goal of reducing our anger by accepting it.

In respect of the treatment and management of evil, we have emphasized most of all learning to recognize evil so as to better be able to stand up to it, preferably through measures to contain it, but at the least to be able to experience an inner anger and conviction that gives us greater strength to endure. We also have given a special emphasis on the ability to identify hidden evil for what it is. Evil needs to be met head-on firmly and contained as much as possible. Psychological health is loving life, supporting life, and not doing harm to life!

> The world is a dangerous place to live, not because of the people who are evil, but because of the people who don't do anything about it.[95]
>
> —*Unknown*

> If only it were so simple! If only there were evil people somewhere insidiously committing evil deeds, and it were necessary only to separate them from the rest of us and destroy them. But the line dividing good and evil cuts through the heart of every human being. And who is willing to destroy a piece of his own heart?[96]
>
> —*Alexander Solzhenitsyn*

> The prophecy that our great leader Uthman Ibn 'Affan, may Allah be pleased with him [made] in the year 35 or 36 of the Hijra has come true. He made this prophecy when the wild mob that came from distant regions of the kingdom, from Egypt and Iraq, entered his home, having decided to kill him.
>
> "If you kill me, you put the sword to your own neck, and then Allah will not lift it from you until the Day of Resurrection . . . and Allah will never remove discord from amongst you."
>
> They murdered him, and their murder of him was tantamount to the crushing of the symbol of consensus in the [Islamic] nation, and the violation of its sanctity, and the tearing to shreds of the garment of awe and reverence. . . . With this deed, they transgressed all bounds and trampled all that is sacred. And indeed, we see after that deed how . . . throughout Islamic history to this day . . . those same evil spirits returning with different masks, garb, and forms, using a new language with diverse tongues, holding implements of destruction which are capable of more destruction and more widespread damage.
>
> Collective rage is a . . . hidden evil against which reasonable people must unite. . . . This can be [accomplished] only by wisdom, prudence, knowledge, honesty, and frankness. It's either this or clear deterioration.[97]
>
> —*Al-Tayyib Salih*

NOTES

1. Berson, Deane Shore (1994). Evil counsel. *Jerusalem Post*, March 30. The writer is identified as a psychiatrist in private practice in Colorado Springs, Colorado.

2. This model for identifying and categorizing doing harm in family relationships was developed jointly by Israel Charny and Pnina Blitz as "an extension of Charny's 1986 model for a revised psychiatric classification which includes both disturbances to self and doing harm to others" that was reported earlier in an article in *Psychiatry* in 1986 titled "Genocide and mass destruction, *op. cit.* The expanded model was then presented for the first time in Blitz, Pnina (1993). *Parental Collusions in Destructiveness towards a Child as a Cause of Subsequent Psychiatric and Emotional Disturbance.* Master's thesis, at the Bob Shapell School of Social Work, Tel Aviv University. The model was subsequently revised further and presented once again in Charny, Israel W. (1996). Evil in human personality. In Kaslow, Florence (Ed.). *Handbook of Relational Diagnosis and Dysfunctional Family Patterns.* Hoboken, NJ: Wiley-Interscience, 484–485.

3. Herman, Judith Lewis (1992). *Trauma and Recovery, op. cit.*; Trepper, Terry S. and Barrett, Mary Jo (1989). *Systemic Treatment of Incest, op. cit.*; Barrett, Mary Jo and Fish, Linda Stone (2014). *Treating Complex Trauma: A Relational Blueprint for Collaboration and Change.* New York: Routledge. See also Scaer, Robert (2005). *The Trauma Spectrum: Hidden Wounds and Human Resiliency.* New York: Norton.

4. Rhode, David and Chivers, C.J. (2002). The jihad files: Qaeda life in Afghanistan. *New York Times*, reprinted in the *International Herald Tribune*, March 18.

5. The story was reported in *International Herald Tribune*, April 1, 2002, fuller citation not available. There have been many reports since of the "instruction in terror" that took place in the London mosque. See Coll, Steve and Glasser, Susan B. (2005). In London, Islamic radicals found a haven. *Washington Post*; *BBC News* (February 7, 2006). Mosque raid findings revealed. As Masri is convicted of race hate crimes, police have revealed details of a raid on north London's Finsbury Park Mosque in 2003; Sherwell, Philip and Barrett, David (May 19, 2014). Abu Hamza trial: London cleric found guilty on terror charges by US jury. Jury takes less than two days to find radical Islamic preacher guilty on terror and kidnapping charges. *The Telegraph*.

6. Glover, Jonathan (1999). *Humanity: A Moral History of the Twentieth Century.* London: Jonathan Cape.

7. This figure is given by R.J. Rummel as a conservative or mid-range estimate of the dead. Can we possibly encompass-experience the scope and meaning of such a number?

8. The quotation is from a review of two books about Primo Levi by David H. Jones (2002). *Holocaust and Genocide Studies*, 16(3), 427–431 (quotation on p. 427). The two books are Gordon, Robert S.C. (2001). *Primo Levi's Ordinary Virtues: From Testimony to Ethics.* Oxford: Oxford University Press; and Homer, Frederic, D. (2001). *Primo Levi and the Politics of Survival.* Columbia: University of Missouri Press.

9. "By necrophilia is meant love for all that is violence and destruction; the desire to kill; the worship of force; attraction to death, to suicide, to sadism; the desire to transform the organic into the inorganic by means of 'order.' The necrophile, lacking the necessary qualities to create, in his impotence finds it easy to destroy because for him it serves only one quality: force." Fromm, Erich (1997). *On Being Human.* New York: Bloomsbury Academic.

10. *Deutschland über alles* (Germany above all) was the title of the German national anthem and the rallying cry of the Nazis. Lyrics for the song were written in 1841 by Hoffmann von Fallersleben to a Haydn melody as a call for German unification. For a broad discussion of ideology and violence, see Fox, Jonathan (2012). Religion and Violence. Chapter in *An Introduction to Religion and Politics: Theory and Practice.* New York: Routledge, 121–133.

11. Taylor, C. P. (1981). *Good* (a play). First staged by the Royal Shakespeare Company at the Donmar Warehouse in September 1981. The play is frequently staged around the world.

In *Good*, a liberal German professor is favored by the Nazis because of his writings on the biology of unfitness for life. He joins the SS, rises in rank, and becomes progressively corrupted, but continues to think of himself as a good man.

12. Milgram, Stanley (1974). *Obedience to Authority, op. cit.*

13. Philip Zimbardo wrote in a retrospective view of his Stanford Prison Experiment: "Good people can be induced, seduced, initiated into behaving in evil (irrational, stupid, self-destructive, antisocial) ways by immersion in 'total situations' that can transform human nature in ways that challenge our sense of the stability and consistency of individual personality, character, and morality. It is a lesson seen in the Nazi concentration camp guards; among the destructive cults, such as Jim Jones Peoples Temple or more recently by the Japanese Aum cult; and in the atrocities committed in Bosnia, Kosovo, Rwanda, and Burundi, among others. Thus any deed that any human being has ever done, however horrible, is possible for any of us to do—under the right or wrong situational pressures." Zimbardo, Philip G.; Maslach, Christina; and Haney, Craig (2000). Reflections on the Stanford Prison Experiment: Genesis, transformations, consequences. In Blass, Thomas (Ed.). *Obedience to Authority: Current Perspectives on the Milgram Paradigm, op. cit.* (quotation on p. 206).

14. Lifton, Robert Jay (1986), *The Nazi Doctors, op. cit.* See also Seidelman, William E. (1999). Medicine and the Holocaust. In *Encyclopedia of Genocide, op. cit.*, 412–414. Many people are not aware that vicious "Mengele-type medical experiments" in the name of scientific research were carried out earlier in the 1930s in Manchuria by the Japanese. See the feature story accompanying the above entry in the *Encyclopedia of Genocide*: Japanese Unit 731—Dread medical experiments that preceded the Nazis, 413.

15. See also an example of advice on how to apply this concept in everyday life: How recognizing your death drive may save you—your death drive is out to destroy you. Tame it. Berry, William (2011). *Psychology Today* website. http://www.psychologytoday.com/blog/the-second-noble-truth/201110/how-recognizing-your-death-drive-may-save-you. Retrieved on December 14, 2014.

16. Freud, Sigmund (1991). The Ego and the Id. In *On Metapsychology—The Theory of Psychoanalysis.* Albert Dickson (Ed.). Harmondsworth, Middlesex: Penguin. Originally published 1923.

17. Einstein, Albert with Nathan, Otto and Norden, Heinz (Eds.) (1988). *Einstein on Peace.* With a foreword by Bertrand Russell. New York: Random House Value Publishing (page for quotation not known).

18. Miller, Alice (1981). *Prisoners of Childhood: The Drama of the Gifted Child and the Search for the True Self.* New York: Basic Books (originally published in German as *Das Drama des begabten Kindes*, 1979. Frankfurt am Main: Suhrkamp Verlag.)

19. Peck, M. Scott (1983). *People of the Lie, op. cit.* In my experience, many mental health professionals are too frightened for their own skins to diagnose such parents forthrightly, especially if the parent is an affluent or influential person. One of the impressive aspects of M. Scott Peck's book are his descriptions of viciousness and deadly sabotage by otherwise nice-looking and competent people.

20. Gilbert, Gustave (1950). *The Psychology of Dictatorship, op. cit.*

21. Kulcsar, I. Shlomo (1978), *op. cit.* In Chapter 6 several references are given to a historic examination of Eichmann by the Kulcsars.

22. Here are some excerpts from commercial bids for the contracts for gas chambers from the accursed Nazis as reported by Harry H. Shapiro in the *Philadelphia Jewish Exponent*, March 29, 1968, as cited in Charny, Israel W. (1982). *How Can We Commit the Unthinkable? Genocide: The Human Cancer, op. cit.*, 185:

The Nazis ran closed bids for the construction of the gas chambers:

1. A. Tops and Sons, Erfurt, manufacturers of heating equipment: "We acknowledge receipt of your order for five triple furnaces, including two electric elevators for raising the corpses and one emergency elevator."
2. Vidier Works, Berlin: "For putting the bodies into the furnace, we suggest simply a metal fork moving on cylinders."
3. C.H. Kori: "We guarantee the effectiveness of the cremation ovens, as well as their durability, the use of the best material and our faultless workmanship."

23. Merton, Thomas (1962). Chant to be used in processions around a site with furnaces. In McDonnell, Thomas P. (Ed.), *A Thomas Merton Reader.* New York: Harcourt, Brace & World, 404–406 (reprinted from earlier publication in *The Catholic Worker*, date not given). This is an amazingly moving poem.

24. *Ibid.*

25. Van Leer, Wim (1964). *The Final Solution* (a play). (Originally titled *D.R.P. 861731*, performed for the first time on November 3, 1964, at the Wimbledon Theatre, Wimbledon, England.)

26. There were good and bad kapos in the nightmare world of the concentration camps, including kapos who were evil to some inmates even as they saved the lives of other inmates. The subject is an extraordinarily complex one. It is also one level of larger questions about Jews who played other roles as functionaries under the Nazis, such as the Jewish police in the ghettos, or the members of governing councils in ghettoes—the *Judenrat.* See Trunk, Isaiah (1972). *Judenrat [The Jewish Councils in Eastern Europe Under Nazi Occupation].* New York: Macmillan. See about postwar trials of councilmen and ghetto police in Bayzler, Michael and Turkheimer, Frank M. (2014). *Forgotten Trials of the Holocaust.* New York: New York University Press, 548–569.

27. Jewish Virtual Library. The Nazi Party: The Nazi Olympics August 1936. https://www.jewishvirtuallibrary.org/jsource/Holocaust/olympics.html. Retrieved March 24, 2015.

28. Charny, Israel W. (1973). And Abraham went to slay Isaac, *op. cit.*

29. Blitz, Pnina (1993), *ibid.* Blitz's study showed that when one parent was destructive to a child, 20 percent of their spouses or the second parent did not help the child "at all," and another 34 percent were described as helping the child "very little," together a total of 54 percent who can be described as playing the roles of bystanders. Unfortunately, too, the good news of second parents who did help the child "a great deal" was limited to 16 percent; for the remaining 30 percent no information was available.

30. Charny, Israel W. (1972). Parental intervention with one another on behalf of their child: A breaking-through tool for preventing emotional disturbance. *Journal of Contemporary Psychotherapy*, 5(1), 19–29.

31. Darley, John M. and Batson, C. Daniel (1979). "From Jerusalem to Jericho": A study of situational and dispositional variables in helping behavior." *Journal of Personality and Social Psychology*, 27, 100–108.

32. When a suicide bomber exploded in Tel Aviv on July 18, 2002, a problem seemed to arise because the wounded included a good number of illegal aliens who were not legally entitled to medical and social services. The mayor of Tel Aviv, Ron Huldai, promptly announced on Israel Radio: "A human being is a human being is a human being because he is a human being. Every resident of Tel Aviv will receive full treatment as needed. This is our Jewish tradition." Ron Huldai, mayor of Tel Aviv in interview on Israel Radio, July 18, 2002.

33. See among others Kahn, Jack with Solomon Hester (1986). *Job's Illness: Loss, Grief and Integrations—A Psychological Interpretation.* London: Gaskell; Kutz, Ilan (2000). *Job*

and his "doctors": Bedside wisdom in the book of *Job*. *British Medical Journal*, 321(7276), 1613–1615; Renik, O. (1991). The biblical book of *Job*: Advice to clinicians. *Psychoanalytic Quarterly*, 60(4), 596–606; Golan, Naomi (1981). *Passing through Transitions*. New York: Free Press.

34. Two classic works on the psychology of death and grieving are Kubler-Ross, Elisabeth and Byock, Ira (2014). *On Death and Dying: What the Dying Have to Teach Doctors, Nurses, Clergy, and their Own Families*. New York: Scribner Reprint Edition; Kubler-Ross, Elisabeth and Kessler, David A. (2014). *On Grief and Grieving: Finding the Meaning of Grief through the Five Stages of Loss*. New York: Scribner Reprint Edition.

35. Aristotle, cited by Edmonds, Molly (June 24, 2008). Can getting angry be good for you? HowStuffWorks.com. http://science.howstuffworks.com/life/good-anger.htm. Retrieved December 15, 2014.

36. Edmonds, Molly, *ibid*.

37. American Psychological Association. Topics/Anger (website—no date). http://apa.org/topics/anger/index.aspx. Retrieved December 15, 2014.

38. See Minow, Martha (1998). *Between Vengeance and Forgiveness*. Boston: Beacon.

39. Bennett, James (2002). Rash of new suicide bombers showing no pattern or ties. New suicide attackers are rising untrained from anger of the street. *New York Times*, June 21, A1, A10 (quotation from page A1).

40. In Israel, for example, for a long time there was considerable confusion between the social worker's role in welfare agencies as a counselor and as an allocator of financial resources, with the result that there were many instances of threats and actual violence against caseworkers in an effort to extort monies. Once these roles were separated and financial grants were made by clerks working with a series of clear-cut legal definitions of eligibility, violence against social workers dropped considerably. Marks, Emanuel (2013). *The Social Context of Violent Behaviour: A Social Anthropological Study in an Israeli Immigrant Town*. New York: Routledge (originally published in 1976). Around the same period (the 1970s), other studies of violence in social welfare offices in Israel came to a similar conclusion, that a majority of instances of violence were essentially efforts to gain payoffs from the social welfare bureaucracy. More recently a majority of instances are reported to be protests against social work rulings regarding child custody. Gravé-Lazi, Lidar (May 13, 2014). Welfare Ministry report: Increase in violence against social workers. *Jerusalem Post*. The common denominator in all instances is that violence is used to get a desired goal, even if it is also an emotional outburst.

41. It is of some interest that beyond the classic picture of a cold-blooded and perhaps even charmingly conscienceless psychopath whose attitude is to "rip off" everything he can, there have been some studies that have shown that deep down within the dynamic processes of psychopaths there may remain reachable traces of hurt and being abandoned, and a corresponding potential for developing some degree of real relationships with people and society. Insofar as this is true, there may be a very few situations for managing and treating psychopaths where it could be possible to re-contact their remote but real potential for humanness, and what is presented here could be relevant. However, for the most part we have learned that almost all psychopaths require very decisive police-action responses.

Two classic works on treatment of psychopaths are Linder, Robert (1976). *The Fifty Minute Hour: A Collection of True Psychoanalytic Tales*. New York: Bantam Books; McCord, William and McCord, Joan (1964). *The Psychopath: An Essay on the Criminal Mind*. New York: Van Nostrand. In more recent times too, there are a surprising number of publications and initiatives to improve the treatment of psychopaths. See the description of the work of David Bernstein, a psychologist in the Netherlands, written by van Vinkeveen, Hans (October 23,

2012). "Some Psychopaths Can Be Treated." *Maastrict University Magazine*; Salekin, Randall T.; Worley, Courtney; and Grimes, Ross D. (2010). Treatment of psychopathy: A review and brief introduction to the mental model approach for psychopathy. *Behavioral Sciences and the Law*, 28, 235–266. See also The Aftermath: Surviving Psychopathy Foundation, http://aftermath-surviving-psychopathy.org/.

42. When I presented a workshop on the management of violence at the University of Rochester Medical School-Strong Memorial Hospital in 1994, a physician who works with drug addicts insisted that he has good success applying the model that follows to drug addicts as well. I regret that under the circumstances of the workshop, I did not succeed in recording this physician's name so as to be able to credit him for this remark. Since I myself have no experience with this clinical population and have not heard or read otherwise, I still have to leave my disclaimer that the model is not to be expected to be applicable to this population, but I'd be delighted if this is not so.

43. Gandhi, Mohandas K. (1961). *Non-Violent Resistance* (Satyagraha). New York: Shocken.

44. King, Martin Luther (2003). *A Testament of Hope*. New York: Harper One Reprint Edition (originally published in 1976). Global Corporate.

45. Sharp, Gene (1973). *The Politics of Nonviolent Action*. Three-volume set: *Power and Struggle—Part One*. Boston, MA: Porter Sargent; Sharp, Gene (1973). *Part Two: The Methods of Nonviolent Action*. Boston, MA: Porter Sargent; Sharp, Gene (1973). *Part Three: The Dynamics of Nonviolent Action*. Boston, MA: Porter Sargent, 447–902.

46. Hare, A. Paul (1978). Dealing with collective violence [with examples from India and Kent State]. In Charny, Israel W. (Ed.). *Strategies against Violence: Design for Nonviolent Change*. Boulder, CO: Westview Press, 257–279. See also Hare, A. Paul and Blumberg, Herbert (Eds.) (1969). *Nonviolent Direct Action: American Cases; Social-Psychological Analyses*. Washington, D.C.: Corpus Books; Blumberg, Herbert; Hare, Paul; and Costin, Anna (2007). *Peace Psychology: A Comprehensive Introduction*. Cambridge: Cambridge University Press; and MacNair, Rachel M. (2008). Review of Blumberg, Herbert et al., *Peace Psychology, ibid., Political Psychology*, 29(5), 798–901.

47. Goldstein killed 29 and wounded 125 Moslems in what is known as the Cave of the Patriarchs massacre. *Tablet Magazine*. http://tabletmag.com/scroll/163725/lunch-with-baruch-goldstein-one-year-before-the-hebron-massacre.

48. As noted, only relatively few psychologists conceive of anger not only as natural—that is only too obvious—but as potentially healthy; and if they do, the application is generally addressed to expression of anger interpersonally and rarely to the legitimacy and desirability of using and enjoying one's anger in one's mind. One striking exception in the field of mental health was the beloved and respected Donald Winnicott, who described the naturalness—yes inevitability—of anger and even hate (his word) in every intimate relationship beginning with the mother-child relationship. Indeed, Winnicott advises that in meaningful depth therapy, it is desirable to reach a point where the patient experiences and expresses hate to the therapist, and vice versa as well! The purpose is to learn how to experience hate within an overall loving relationship. Nonetheless, Winnicott, too, calls for appropriate expression of these feelings more than developing the subject of savoring them in one's mind. See Winnicott, Donald W. (1949). Hate in the counter-transference, *op. cit.* Note that this article was subsequently reprinted many times. See also later in this chapter the discussion of the attitudes of psychologists to evil.

49. Philosopher Immanuel Kant's basic opposition to war and violence is known and clear, but then there are varying understandings of whether and how Kant made room for violence under certain circumstances, which become the exceptions to nonetheless continuing the overall basic rule. One scholar, David Colclasure, writes: "What at first glance seems to be a categorical rejection of warfare in fact opens the possibility of justifiable wars that go beyond mere self-defense. Kant's defense of human dignity and its protection, I contend, provides the impetus for this line of argument." Colclasure, David (2011). Just war and perpetual peace: Kant on the legitimate use of political violence. In Elisabeth Krimmer and Patricia Anne Simpson (Eds.) (2011). *Enlightened War: German Theories and Cultures of War from Frederick the Great to Clausewitz.* Woodbridge, UK: Boydell & Brewer, 241–257.

50. Miller, Anna (2014). Psychologists are leaders in a growing field: A threat assessment, working with law enforcement and security professionals to prevent violence before an attacker strikes. *APA Monitor on Psychology*, 45(2), 37—40.

51. Shaver, Philip R. and Mikulincer, Mario (Eds.) (2011). *Human Aggression and Violence: Causes, Manifestations, and Consequences.* Washington, DC: American Psychological Association. PsycINFO Database Record © 2012 APA.

52. Charny, Israel W. (1967). The psychotherapist as a teacher of an ethic of nonviolence. *Voices: The Art and Science of Psychotherapy*, 3(1), 1–24.

53. Philosopher Lionel Rubinoff developed at length the difference between aggressive wishes and actual violence in his treatment of the "pornography of power": Rubinoff, Lionel (1978), In nomine diaboli. The voices of evil. In Charny, Israel W. (Ed.). *Strategies against Violence, op. cit.*, 34–67. Of course there is no doubt that unchecked rumination of anger and planning and rehearsal of violence precede and become inducers of violent actions. Thus research in three London schools showed that "male street gang affiliates who think continuously about provoking negative events and situations have the greatest tendency toward displaced aggression against innocent others . . . angry rumination can provide an opportunity for revenge planning and fantasizing, as well as justifying the anger that a person feels . . . the desire and motivation for revenge is maintained, prolonged or exacerbated." (http://www.sciencedaily.com/releases/2012/07/120712092429.htm. The published research can be found in Vasquez, Eduardo A.; Osman, Sarah; and Wood, Jane L. (2012). Rumination and the displacement of aggression in United Kingdom gang-affiliated youth. *Aggressive Behavior*, 38, 89–97. A key difference in our point of view is that the fantasy of aggression is expressly *for the purpose of releasing and overcoming the aggressive feelings* and that is why it lays a basis for reducing and overcoming the prospects of actual violence.

54. Searles, Harold F. (1960). *The Nonhuman Environment, op. cit.* See also Charny, Israel W. (1967). The psychotherapist as a teacher of an ethic of nonviolence, *op. cit.*, where clinical illustrations are presented of the treatment of violent patients, including psychotic and brain-damaged patients, based on this differentiation between angry *feelings* and actual violent *actions.*

55. Lawrence Kohlberg's theory of moral development proposes that individuals pass through moral stages from the concrete to the abstract. Kohlberg, Lawrence (1963). The development of children's orientation toward moral order: I. Sequence in the development of moral thought. *Vita Humana*, 6(1–2), 11–33; Kohlberg, Lawrence (1966). Moral education in the schools: A developmental view. *The School Review*, 74(1), 1–30; Kohlberg, Lawrence (1968). The child as a moral philosopher. *Psychology Today*, September, 2(4), 24–30; Van Voorhis, Patricia (2010), Kohlberg, Lawrence: Moral Development Theory. In Francis T.

Cullen and Pamela Wilcox (Eds.). *Encyclopedia of Criminological Theory*. Vol. 1. Thousand Oaks, CA: Sage, 508–513.

There have been a number of empirical studies that have given strong support to Kohlberg's theory. Thus a recent study reports confirmation of: "the construct validity . . . and the stages and levels in Kohlberg's theory" (quotation on p. 165): Söderhamn, Olle; Bjørnestad, John Olav; Skisland, Anne; and Cliffordson, Christina (20111). Construct validity of the Moral Development Scale for professionals (MDSP). *Multidisciplinary Health*, 4, 165–170.

56. The session was videoed! but it turned out something was wrong with the camera. I do have a video recording of another session with this same man and his wife a year later when he was showing definite signs of a resolve to end his violence, and the focus in this session was on identifying the unconscious complicity of his beaten wife cueing him to hit her! It made an excellent teaching video for many years.

57. Bach, George R. and Wyden, Peter (1969). *The Intimate Enemy, op. cit.* See earlier in the book others who have contributed meaningfully to the subject of marital fighting, including Israel Charny, Lori Gordon, and Daniel Wile.

58. See the discussion of this use of one's mind later in the chapter in "The Wonderful Ultimate Democracy of Our Own Mind."

59. A classic work on resocializing delinquents is that of August Aichorn, who was not averse to befriending and being with delinquent youth before they could be reached via more traditional psychotherapeutic interventions. Aichhorn, August (1951). *Wayward Youth*. London: Imago (first published in German in 1925: *Verwahrloster Jugend Wien: Internationaler Psychoanalytischer Verlag*). For an interesting introduction, see the "Digest" by Robert Shaw Davidlane, August 1, 2009, at http://www.childrenwebmag.com/articles/key-child-care-texts/wayward-youth-by-august-aichhorn.

60. The dean of genocide studies in the world for many years was sociologist Leo Kuper at UCLA. In his book on polarization between peoples (based on four cases in Africa), Kuper captures better than any other writing I have seen how such conflicts inevitably escalate into reciprocal excesses not only of war but of savage mass murder. He described the interaction of "two antagonist groups with incompatible and irreconcilable interests, rendering inevitable the resort to violence. In its extreme form, polarization is marked by mounting violence and atrocious holocaust." The process is "embedded in the structure of society, in the nature of the situation, in the concepts of authority, and in the exigencies of the struggle." Kuper, Leo (1977). *The Pity of It All: Polarisation of Racial and Ethnic Relations*. London: Duckworth; Minneapolis: University of Minnesota Press (quotations on pp. 128 and 139).

61. Newcombe, Alan (1978). "Lovemate": A personal and international foreign policy for peace. In Charny, Israel W. (Ed.). *Strategies against Violence, op. cit.*, 3–18.

62. Bard, Morton and Zucker, Joseph (1976). *The Police and Interpersonal Conflict: Third Party Intervention Approaches*. Washington, DC: Police Foundation; Bard, Morton (1970). *Training Police as Specialists in Crisis Intervention*. Washington, DC: U.S. Department of Justice, National Institute of Law Enforcement and Criminal Justice.

In surveying contemporary Internet literature on police intervention in domestic violence, I find the greater number of publications involve training police in proper arrest procedures and protection of victims. In one way this is entirely understandable and justified given what we know today about the dire extent of serious violence and murder in family situations. But it loses the part of how police themselves can be contributing to the violence. It is only in a smaller number of cases that we find training programs that are directed at what Bard achieved in training the New York City police to shrink crisis situations and reduce violence, with the result also that there were far fewer injuries to the police. The following is an example of such contemporary training: CPI-Crisis Prevention Institute [Milwaukee, WI] (no date given). De-escalation Tips, http://www.crisisprevention.com/Resources/Knowledge-Base/De-escalation-Tips.

63. See Chainani, Soman (2013). *The School for Blood and Evil.* London: Harper Collins. This is a book for children that faces the necessity of a child to choose between good and evil.

64. See Dilts, Robert (website, no date). Harnessing the Imagination. NLP Article of the Month, http://www.nlpu.com/Articles/artic16.htm.

65. Ellens, J. Harold (2011). *Explaining Evil.* Three-volume set. *Volume One: Definitions and Development; Volume Two: History, Global Views, and Events; Volume Three: Psychology, Religion, and Spirituality*. Santa Barbara, CA: ABC Clio.

66. Bohart, Arthur C.; Held, Barbara S.; Mendelowitz, Edward; and Schneider, Kirk J. (2016) (Eds.). *Humanity's Dark Side: Evil, Destructive Experience, and Psychotherapy*. Washington, DC: American Psychological Association, 213–236.

67. Miller, Ronald B. (2013). Deny no evil, ignore no evil, reframe no evil: Psychology's moral agenda. In Arthur C. Bohart, et al., *ibid.*, 213–236. The original papers by Rogers and May are: May, Rollo (1992). The problem of evil: An open letter to Carl Rogers; and Rogers, Carl (1992). Reply to Rollo May. In Ronald B. Miller (Ed.) (1992). *The Restoration of Dialogue: Reading in the Philosophy of Clinical Psychology*, 314–316. Washington, DC: American Psychological Association.

68. Miller, *ibid.*, 214

69. Lazarus, Arnold A. (2013). The ubiquity of evil—and multimodal cognitive treatment of its effects. In Arthur C. Bohart et al. (Eds.). *Humanity's Dark Side, ibid.*

70. Lazarus, *ibid.*, 162

71. Peck, M. Scott (1983). *People of the Lie, op. cit.*

72. It is interesting to note Peck's stipulation of a necessary element for construction of the exorcist "surgery," that a group of true believers must be gathered to do the process. Of course, recruiting true believers and indigenous peoples will only cover a segment of the world's population of evildoers. I nonetheless suggest that we take to heart a beautiful metaphoric implication of Peck's insistence, namely that psychotherapists also need to be "true believers" in a person's or family's capacity to overcome (but not in every case) and be sincerely committed to the task of fighting evil if we are going to have any chance of being effective.

73. The task of truth and reconciliation commissions is to bring to light past wrongdoing in an atmosphere of correction and conciliation. The basic concept is not restricted to governments and can be applied to ideological movements, groups promoting prejudice, and to individuals in re the harm done by one person to another. The first truth commission is reported to have been formed in Uganda in 1974. The most famous is the South African Truth and Reconciliation Commission that was created after the transition from apartheid by President Nelson Mandela and Archbishop Desmond Tutu. More than thirty nations are reported to have utilized the truth commission model, including Peru, Ghana, East Timor, and Sierra Leone. The key to the truth and reconciliation process is a concept of "restorative justice," which differs from the customary "retributive justice." The goal is to heal rather than punish. This is done by revealing all the facts in a process where both victims and perpetrators are free to speak. Sharing of pain, acknowledgement, public mourning, and forgiveness are the methods of healing.

74. Chirot, Daniel; and Seligman, Martin E. P. (Eds.) (2001). *Ethnopolitical Warfare: Causes, Consequences, and Possible Solutions.* Washington, DC: American Psychological Association.

75. See among others Browning, Christopher (2013), *Ordinary Men, op. cit.;* Charny, Israel W. (1982), *How Can We Commit the Unthinkable? Genocide: The Human Cance*r, *op. cit.*; Girard, René (1977). *Violence and the Sacred.* Baltimore: Johns Hopkins University Press; Mowrer, O. Hobart (1961). *The Crisis in Psychiatry and Religion, op. cit.*

76. Mahatma Gandhi's writings, philosophy, audio, video, and photographs. www.mkgandhi.org/mgmnt.htm. Retrieved January 2015.

77. Christianity (website). http://christianity.stackexchange.com/questions/28598/does-the-bible-contain-a-definitive-explanation-of-morality. Retrieved January 5, 2015.

78. New Testament Bible (Web site). Ephesians, Chapter 4, selection from What the Bible says about violence, anger, jealousy, arguments, and living in peace with each other. http://www.broadcaster.org.uk/section2/transcript/violence1.htm. Retrieved January 5, 2015.

79. Baha'i International Community (no date given). On Good and Evil. http://info.bahai.org/article-1-4-0-9.html. Retrieved November 14, 2014.

80. Schulweis, Harold. In Quotes about Good and Evil. Goodreads (website). http://www.goodreads.com/quotes/tag/good-and-evil?page=6. Retrieved January 5, 2015.

81. Quoted from Williams, Lynda. http:// www.goodreads.com/quotes/ tag/good-and-evil?page=6.

The grandmotherly principle reminds me of the statement by psychologist Arnold Lazarus: "Evil is a deliberate action that harms an object or a creature. The intent to do harm is its essence . . . One of the most famous phrases in the entire history of the [U.S.] Supreme Court was in reference to 'obscenity': 'I may not be able to define it, but I know it when I see it,' coined by Justice Potter Stewart in 1964. Perhaps the same may be said of evil." Lazarus, Arnold A. (2013). The ubiquity of evil—and multi-modal cognitive treatment of its effects, *ibid.*, 157, 158.

82. Anthony, E. Jarvis and Benedeck, Therese (1970). *Parenthood: Its Psychology and Psychopathology.* Boston: Little, Brown; Charny, Israel W. (1980). Why are so many (if not really all) people and families disturbed? *Journal of Marital and Family Therapy*, 1980, 6(1), 37–47. Roth, Dina (1994). Personal communication. Two unpublished studies at Hadassah Hospital, Mount Scopus, Hebrew University of Jerusalem, of parental expectations in teenage obesity and teenage suicide attempts. Roth was then psychiatrist in charge of an adolescent ward at Hadassah Hospital.

83. Charny, Israel W. (1980). Recovery of two (largely) autistic children through renunciation of maternal destructiveness in integrated individual and family therapy, *ibid.*

84. Alfred Hassler, longtime executive secretary of the pacifist organization Fellowship of Reconciliation, recorded on the occasion of his retirement some of his thoughts about pacifism, in which he emphasized the centrality of the pacifist's compassion, humility, and understanding, no matter what the circumstances. Hassler refers to his predecessor, world-renowned A.J. Muste, who once said, "If I can't love Hitler, I can't love." Says Hassler, "You can't get anywhere with it unless you realize that love means understanding and compassion. Then it opens up. Compassion, not in the sense of lessening your opposition to what Hitler was doing, but compassion for a man who clearly had suffered terribly, who was terribly distorted, who had so little real happiness and joy." An interview with Alfred Hassler, *Fellowship*, September 1974 (quotation on p. 8). To this day, repeatedly, the same concepts of forgiveness and compassion—and eradication of hate, revenge, and even violence in self-defense—are promoted by many "good people" and is considered religious doctrine by any number of Christians and other faiths.

85. Heery, Myrtle. An Interview with Albert Ellis. Hypnosis Alliance. https://www.hypnosisalliance.com/articles/An%20Interview%20With%20Albert%20Ellis%20PHD%20-%20Myrtle%20Heery.pdf. Retrieved March 23, 2017. Cited by Lazarus, Arnold A. (2013). The ubiquity of evil—and multi-modal cognitive treatment of its effects. In Arthur C. Bohart et al. (Eds.). *Humanity's Dark Side, ibid.*, 160.

86. Lazarus, Arnold A. (2013), *ibid.*

87. Mann, James (1973). *Time Limited Psychotherapy*. Cambridge, MA: Harvard University Press; Mann, James and Goldman, K. (1983). *A Case Book in Time Limited Psychotherapy*. New York: McGraw-Hill; Shefler, Gaby; Dasberg, Haim; and Ben-Shakhar, Gershon (1995). A randomized controlled outcome and follow-up study of Mann's time-limited psychotherapy. *Journal of Consulting and Clinical Psychology*, 63(4), 585–593.

88. There aren't too many publications in the psychotherapy literature on working to identify and expose moral defects in patients and seeing psychotherapy as a major opportunity for helping them rise above themselves and correct these defects. One quiet and thoughtful discussion of this issue is Aponte, Harry J. (2002). Spiritually-sensitive psychotherapy. In Florence W. Kaslow and Robert F. Massey (Eds.). *Comprehensive Handbook of Psychotherapy, Volume 3, Interpersonal/Humanistic/Existential*. New York: Wiley, 279–302.

89. Once an absolute no-no, the concept of working with subgroups in families became widely accepted and is addressed in the writings of many of the greats of family therapy, such as Salvador Miunchin, Ivan Boszormenyi-Nagy and James L. Framo, Luciano L'Abate, and more. One explicit discussion of the subject is found in the excellent work on object relations therapy: Scharff, David E. and Scharff, Jill (2004). Exclusion or inclusion of subgroups. In *Object Relations Family Therapy*. Lanham, MD: Rowman & Littlefield, 152–154.

90. There are scattered reports of successful therapy of evil people. Robert Lindner's unforgettable works in the mid-twentieth century include *The Fifty-Minute Hour: A Collection of True Psychoanalytic Tales, op. cit.* This is a classic in the field, but one has a hard time generalizing from his work to therapy to be done in a "normal" office (Lindner saw his patients in a prison setting with its built-in boundaries, let alone that his clients were serious psychopaths).

Carl Goldberg gives us more recently a series of case descriptions and also formulates on the basis of these cases an explanatory model of "the primary factors that explain serious violence," which "when found together adequately explain why as adults they fail to develop a capacity for emotional connectedness and mutuality with others [and] instead, they become involved in destructive behavior." The five "toxic factors" that he identifies in raising children who will prove to be violent are "shame vulnerability; benign neglect; inability to mourn; linguistic difficulties expressing feelings; and witnessing significant people who behave as if rageful anger is a legitimate means for dealing with frustration and conflict." He further identifies five "secondary factors": "parental seduction; heavy exposure to media violence; identification with a philosophy of superiority; conceptual inability to understand death as a permanent event; and family conspiracy." Goldberg, Carl (2000). *The Evil We Do: The Psychoanalysis of Destructive People*. Amherst, NY: Prometheus (quotations on pp. 213, 212, 222).

91. Two cases of autism were successfully treated from a point of view of identifying the parents' destructive wishes to the child and then renouncing them and apologizing to the child. Charny, Israel W. (1980). Recovery of two (largely) autistic children, *ibid.*

92. Bach, George R. and Wyden, Peter (1969). *The Intimate Enemy, ibid.*

93. Boszormenyi-Nagy, Ivan and Spark, Geraldine, M. (1973). *Invisible Loyalties, op. cit.*

94. See, among others, Buber, Martin (1963). *Pointing the Way*. New York: Harper; Friedman, Maurice S. (2002). *Martin Buber: The Life of Dialogue*. New York: Routledge (4th edition) (original publication 1960).

95. Quotation is widely attributed to Albert Einstein, but no source is found, and there are scholars who dispute the authenticity of the source.

96. Cited in a Unitarian-Universalist Blog, posted July 22, 2016 (no author given). "Who is Willing to Destroy a Piece of Their Own Heart?" In *Another Possibility*, https://revgretchenhaley.wordpress.com.

97. Middle East Media Research Institute (MEMRI) (April 30, 2004, No. 704). Sudanese Scholar on Murder and Violence in Early Islam. Cited and translated from the London Arabic language daily, *Al-Sharq Al-Awsat*. *©1998-2017, The Middle East Media Research Institute All Rights Reserved. Materials may only be cited with proper attribution.*

8

Author's Voice: What Is Going to Happen to All of Us? What Can I Do in My Time?

Theodor Adorno is known for his statement, "There can be no poetry after Auschwitz" (in German: *Nach Auschwitz ein Gedicht zu schreiben, ist barbarisch).*[1]

Robert S.C. Gordon, a major reviewer of the work of Primo Levi, reported that Levi reformulated Adorno's dictum that there can be no poetry after Auschwitz by saying, "After Auschwitz there can be no poetry except poetry after Auschwitz."[2]

Much of this concluding chapter of the book is a kind of poem, or rap, or free association, though not exactly a pleasant one with a climactic happy ending. Instead of a neat inspiring climax to the "symphony," the music ends in a discomforting though haunting discord that is simultaneously jarring but also, I think, in its own way even beautiful.

This chapter is organized in a distressing counterpoint of dialectical truths, but even the happier side of the dialectic leads us to grim views of our future. One prepublication reader characterized it as a "rhetorically loose, almost free associative style," which unnerved him, but he also added that it was "engaging writing" that succeeds in conveying the "substance, depth, and truth of your life perspective and worldview"—with which he says he fully agrees but at the same time doesn't like.

One can also characterize this chapter in the language of psychotherapeutic techniques as "therapist self-disclosure," a technique that is very honored by many therapists for its contribution to an authentic and more egalitarian relationship between therapist and patient, but treated with great reservations by many others who feel that it reduces the stature and potential effectiveness of the therapist.[3]

PART ONE: SUMMING UP A LIFE'S THINKING

I am lucky. I came into an Age of Hope immediately following the end of the horrors of World War II. I was then a teenager moving into the marvelous journey of shaping my young adult self, leaving home for college (with the additional luck that I had to support myself). So many of us, especially young people, believed a new wisdom was in the offing and would prevail, and that science would now advance us to a far better world.

Granted, utterly terrible things had happened in the world. The twentieth century was a monstrous serial killer en large:

- World War I with its senseless killing of millions of people;
- The Armenian Genocide of Armenians along with their co-victims, the Assyrians, Yezidis, Greeks, and still other non-Muslim/non-Turkish people;
- The indescribable inferno of World War II and its utter threat of a super-brutal madman (Hitler) and two super-mad totalitarian regimes (Nazi Germany and Japan) heading to take over the world (and to add a totally bizarre note, the victory over them that was enabled by still another super-madman-regime (Stalin) fighting with the Allies, who were committed to a more democratic civilization (poor Stalin had no choice about on which side to fight after his greedy mad "buddy" Hitler betrayed their alliance—fortunately we can count on fascists to war insanely against one another);
- And during World War II, with its terrifying toll of 20 million civilians, the unparalleled Holocaust of the Jewish people, and here too, a number of co-victims, including the Roma (Gypsies), homosexuals, Soviet POWs, Jehovah's Witnesses, and mentally limited and disabled people defined as "unfit for life." *Hooray indeed to our civilization! The Holocaust was a disgusting showpiece of our science, engineering, and organization!*
- And (God help us), in bringing the war against Japan to a close, a new super WMD (weapon of mass destruction) was unleashed that has become an omnipresent marker of the unlimited "genius" of man to create more and more mega-weapons. This morning I heard of a nuclear bomb that is fifteen times the power of the bomb rained on Hiroshima/Nagasaki-and more in coming.

So how could I possibly consider myself lucky to have been born into such an era? First of all, the above events were obviously committed by the has-been elders of my time, and I felt that certainly my generation was going to be different.

Second, like all kids of all generations, I didn't *really* feel the suffering and losses all around me. I knew they were wrong and I was appropriately and respectfully sad, but it didn't really break my naturally selfish-kid heart. Moreover, my inner defense of denial of death (a universal defense mechanism that has us all living out an ultimate lie throughout most of our lives) held strong (this notwithstanding my own very terrible loss and sadness for my young mother who took ill with cancer when I was six and died when I was fourteen).

But the most beguiling was that we—mankind—surely had learned from our tragedies, and surely our exciting new wisdom in psychology and philosophy (my two primary intellectual loves) and in all areas of science and learning were now on a surefire path to improvement of the human race and human destiny. Life was aliveness, hope, enthusiasm, and confidence in our new era on Earth (it too to last immortally, of course).

I always knew that as people aged and came closer and closer to their oncoming death (which is the position I am in today), that a pessimism and a deep sadness and irony about life grew, and I literally swore to myself that I would be careful not to fall into that boat. When he was young, King Solomon (the lucky guy with a thousand women) authored a magnificent and erotic love song, the *Song of Songs*. When he was a comfortable and wise middle age, he wrote the enlightening *Proverbs* with excellent insights: "There is evil in everything that happens under the sun: the same destiny overtakes all. The hearts of men are full of evil and there is madness in their hearts while they live, and afterward they join the dead." He gave advice for life: "He that diggeth a pit shall fall into it"—translated, "Whatever you sow you will reap." When he was old, he authored the powerful, perplexing perspective, *Ecclesiastes*, in which he proclaimed, "Life is meaningless and futile, all is fleeting."

I knew that Solomon was somehow right in his judgments of our real human condition, but I also knew that he was just another old man who apparently "could no longer get it up," and I swore that I would guard against becoming a pessimistic, nihilistic old man.

Now at this late stage of my life, I cautiously think that the not exactly optimistic judgments I've arrived at are scientific and evidence-based and not my geriatric pessimism, though I also know I am doing the old age thing. Happily, to this day I am having a very fun life and enjoying myself greatly. I am convinced that Solomon got it right not simply because of the decline of old age, but also out of the breadth and wisdom of old age (I have never heard that Solomon revoked his earlier love songs).

Many basic things have changed fundamentally in our world over the ages. There are no longer illusions about a basic goodness of man. There are no longer doubts about how millions of human beings engage in destroying life—and of course how millions are destroyed. There is no doubt that human beings are insanely devoted—in every way and on every level—to gaining power over others. There is no doubt about how greedy and insatiable people are given whatever opportunities they find in every possible economic system. There is no doubt that planet Earth is a speck of a speck in an unfathomably limitless universe that we don't understand one bit.

There is no doubt that we stupid Homo sapiens are ruining our Earth and bringing on our own destruction. Moreover, by nature itself our planet is on its way to dissolution and nonexistence, let alone that there is considerable danger we will be prematurely terminated by meteors, climate changes, or bioevolutionary threats to life. Man, have we ever been humbled and reduced to microscopic sub-sub-particles.

So I was lucky to have been born into a brief period of history in which there was hope and belief in a more humane future. Despite Solomon's and other wisdoms, I was born into an era of continuing denial of man's intrinsic evil and went for it. Now it seems immoral for me to have enjoyed such an optimism that was made possible by denial. Paradoxically, in my life I have become personally well known as a psychotherapist who aims at working with existential truth even when it is painful, and as a genocide scholar I am known, and have been honored internationally, as a researcher and avid opponent of genocide denial. Oh well, this is not the first time in my life that I am confronted with my own hypocrisy.

Where then do I end up in my spiritual journey and in my attempts at a science-based understanding of man's nature? It has been so hard to get to this point, but I confess it now looks crystal clear to me: Man is both good and evil.

- Both constructing and destroying life are innate drives rooted in evolutionary survival and constitute the basic equipment with which we come in to the world.
- Over the long haul, I can count on so many human beings to come forth as life helpers—graciously, generously, wisely, humanely.
- Over the long haul, I also can count on so many human beings to come forth as destroyers of life—power-crazed and imperious, who save their own fearful skins by lording it over other people's pain and disasters.

Moreover, to my eternal confusion, the above are *not* divided absolutely between different people, so that at any given point I cannot be totally certain who is on which team. Granted there are some people who are largely expert and devoted to the one or the other, but overall there are both sides in all of us, and one can never be sure of what's coming at us (nor smugly sure about how decent we ourselves are going to be in future situations).

For all humans there develop a series of critical life choices between goodness (life construction) and badness (life destruction). Often enough the choice is extremely complex and doesn't admit a simple-minded solution, but overall the differentiation between protecting life and destroying life is quite clear.

I believe that each of us has in us a capacity to choose caring for life and that this should be the ultimate goal of education, culture, religion, also science—in fact all pursuits of life. If the battle of choices were to be restricted to the level of individuals, my prediction is that we will still lose many a human life unnecessarily and wrongly, but overall I believe that life building would win out.

Unfortunately, so much of the drama is played out on collective levels of groups, institutions and organizations, societies, religious faiths and movements, nations, economic ideologies, and political ideologies. By definition some of these (too damned many) will be utterly fascist and destructive. By definition some of these (too damned many) will put together huge powers of destruction and not have the slightest reservation about unleashing the murders of millions of people. So on a collective level I am *very* pessimistic—I expect the worst for any numbers of millions of us.

OK, OK, hold on. Of course I know the great American rule of ending the movie happily, or at least ambiguously, and I am also happy to take note that by now there are a large number of wonderful collective efforts to save and advance life. But unfortunately, at any given moment one stinking bomb will bring about a more definitive conclusion than any of these wholesome, admirable efforts. Still, the efforts to build and protect life give us opportunities to do saving work so long as we exist.

At any given moment in my life, this is where I have to be—

- Working hard for the lifesaving outcomes I can influence;
- Praying for the best for as many of us as possible;
- But also, unfortunately, accepting the existential realities that will include my own certain death, and the deaths of so many of my loved ones before and after me.

A CASE TO THE POINT

❖ Here is a case example of how deep in the hearts-minds of many (but not all!) people there sits a "natural ethic" of "Thou shalt not kill" (special care has been taken not to identify the subject of this case): An eighty-five-year-old man in a country outside the United States that is home to different competing ethnicities was asked by a visiting (American) relative about his experience fighting in a war more than sixty years ago when he was nineteen years old. There is little question that in the concepts of Thomas Aquinas this war qualified as a "just war" to protect innocent lives, but over the years historical research has made it clear that the "just" army also engaged in a number of vicious massacres of civilians—I call such killing "genocidal massacres."

The visitor knew that his relative had seen combat in one area where solid proof has emerged of such killings. "Did you see any of the massacres?" he was asked.

"Yes," he replied. "In fact one day my 'buddy,' who I knew from primary school, 'simply' shot and killed fourteen civilians including one lady who was shielding her old mother, and he shot the old mother as well." The eighty-five-year-old man then burst out crying inconsolably for what seemed like an interminable time. He told his visiting relative that he had never spoken of the event and that he had never cried through all sixty-plus years until now.[4]

Today I am giving you a choice
between good and evil,
between life and death.
If you obey the commands of the Lord …
then you will prosper
and become a nation of many people….
If you refuse to listen you will be destroyed
- I warn you here and now.
-Deuteronomy 30

PART TWO: CAN WE REALLY ACHIEVE A DEMOCRATIC MIND?

Can We Really Achieve a Democratic Mind?

No, of course not	***Yes, of course, it can be done***
A huge lie defines every part of our life every day and all the time—a feeling—illusion that we will live forever.	The key is cultivating a genuine appreciation and commitment to the sacredness of life.
This illusion controls everyone, even those who intellectually sort of know that our life is on a "rental" that comes to an end. The reason for our denial-dissociation from really experiencing the fact that each one of us is going to die is not only the obvious wonderful desire we naturally have to live on and not die. There is more to it on a very basic level of our machinery for human experiencing:	It's a matter of evolution, just as Homo sapiens stopped cannibalism, and just like people incorporating medical-scientific information about how to take care of ourselves and live longer.
It simply is not possible for a living human being to experience that they will no longer experience anything, that there will be a flat line and nothingness.	A lot of people like the idea of living longer and healthier, and many (though not all) have a sense that we are all in a challenging process together and are ready to protect one another's right to life.
How can I who am alive possibly experience that I won't be alive anymore? Freud and Einstein, someone please, will you explain how Existence cannot possibly experience Nonexistence?	*While I am around, I like feeling alive. My life feels interesting, fun, meaningful.*

So we spend our lives lying to ourselves that we will always be alive, but we also know from the very first beat of life, like all living creatures do deep inside, that our life is set on an unknown time frame. The time is definitely coming that we will run out of time.

We not only continue our basic lie to ourselves, but we have an additional job to do, and that is to deny any knowledge of our lie and not speak of the end ever coming.

Man, is our world ever buzzing with incredible activities to "prove" that we are immortal.

We prove we are alive through magnificent creative works in art, literature, music, science, engineering, architecture—in so, so many fields.

We bring children to life and invest them with a certainty of being our redeeming continuers.

We also lose ourselves completely in powerful belief systems, ideologies, and causes that of course are defined as eternal truths.

Worst of all, we lay down a trail of blood evidence. Everywhere on our planet we kill huge masses of people—unbelievable hundreds of millions of victims. In each case it is we who decide who lives and who dies—for we are the gods of life and death. Obviously we will give our own selves only life. Therefore, we will never die.

Democratic Mind prefers scientific thinking over ignorance, or taking actions blindly, or acting on the basis of superstitions. It does not give an orgiastic total rapture and certainty that fascist thinking does, but the latter prove fatal before very long, and democratic thinking slowly but surely adds more and more to life. For many people it enables solid feelings of wisdom and decency.

Pluralism is accepted and celebrated on many levels. In our own minds we accept with interest and pleasure the fact that a wide variety of thoughts and impulses are constantly flowing through our minds, including an enormous number that we are committed never to act on in our actual behavior because they would do real harm to living people. Sexual feelings, for example, are enjoyable and tone us up energetically, but even those of us with a good, healthy attraction to other people should not run around betraying our basic love and commitment to our true love relationship—it may be fun, but it is an attack on feelings of belonging and security and brings on too much pain.

We also enjoy pluralism in our society. We respect the colors and forms of many different peoples, the pageantry, folklore, and customs of many different ethnicities, and the differing faiths of so many religions, and at no point do we adopt or allow others to adopt any position of superiority over others.

The healthy release of aggressive feelings in our minds or in constructive clarifications of our anger with the other will get us through many a difficult day with its distasteful conflicts in our family and work life. Both techniques can be used to discharge tension and to tone up our inner strength. At the same time, it is highly recommended that we not actually kill all the people we would want to in our inner emotions.

In *everything* we do, no matter how "good" we try to be, the urge to feel powerful pushes up from inside of us. Everyone wants to be on top—successful at whatever, recognized, running the show, calling the shots (although strangely some of us also call the shots by emphasizing how much we can't do and insist on welfare and that others support us).

Little, little children do it in their games in kindergarten. Kids in grade school poke away at one another, beat up some kids or exclude and ostracize others. Society creates dozens of constructive outlets for competition, but even these are soon contaminated by a driving passion to beat others down and come out top dog. Get it out of your blood in healthy sports? Fans in stadiums beat the shit out of one another. Brilliant doctors sabotage one another's careers, even surgeries (did you hear the one of the doctor who hid a liver because he didn't get to do the transplant surgery?).

How many once genuinely nice people become haughty kings and Jezebel queens? Not to speak of the warlords and oligarchs who run so much of our world imperiously and tragically.

As of early 2016, so many national rulers and heads of state are in advanced stages of the "power sickness." Think, how many national leaders seek to kill off everything that breathes an independent spirit? See especially how these include democratically elected leaders.

In one country critical journalists die mysterious deaths, in another thousands of journalists, writers, and even police, military, and judges are carted to jails. Even in the United States, a struggle has emerged

Most obviously we do not plan or commit genocidal murders.

However difficult, we take a democratic position and oppose any ideology or movement that is totally taken with itself as the messianic redeemer of mankind. It is especially difficult for many of us to stand up to the as if celestial powers of fundamentalist beliefs—there are so many absolute ideologies in the world, and literally billions of people who find their safety in their certainty. The Democratic Mind is careful not to oppose or insult a religion, but at no point compromises with the principle that no group is entitled to place itself over all other people, and certainly not to dominate, attack, and destroy their respective "infidels."

The lives of all human beings are sacred.
Life, our breathing-being-experiencing, is all we have.
If you are a fundamentalist who is seeking celestial immortality by hurting others, be aware that the celestial judges may rule against you. A fundamentalist system inherently is based on disqualifying any number of human beings, and you too can yet find yourself among the disqualified.[1]

On the level of the individual, it really is possible to expand more and more one's Democratic Mind—to repair, empower, and invigorate one's gratitude and joy in life. It takes an honest audit of oneself.

As one deepens the ability to process these questions honestly, there is an advanced level where a person can also ask themselves:

What are the ways in which I really am hurting myself and/or hurting others? where the effects will explode and show at a later date?
In what ways am I hurting myself?
In what ways am I hurting other people in my life?

between plutocracy and populism versus time-honored American values of democracy and equality. Tribal and terrorist leaders all over the world are insane with seemingly god-given rights they give themselves to kill off millions of people.

And yet, despite it all, in the vaunted fields of psychology and psychiatry for understanding human behavior, there are few to no definitions of the corruption of the "power sickness."
There is no religious faith or government system in the world, or for that matter any philosophy, that has ever really succeeded in stopping man's rottenness.

So can we really achieve a Democratic Mind?

At the level of individuals, too many human beings cannot. They are too busy escaping from themselves. They deny that they too will die, and in truth they also deny the preciousness of life for themselves and for others. They escape from freedom, responsibility, joy, and love

At the level of the collective, just look around the world. Just as biological illnesses sprout endlessly and we go from different conditions to newly vicious horrors and who knows what will be coming next. so too the genius of mass killing unfolds with ever more powerful weapons of mass destruction. *This way, please, to the gas chambers, nuclear explosions, holocausts, biological illnesses, chemical deaths, or dissolution by laser rays.*

Thus for individuals:

- Am I going to have a heart attack because I have been living like a couch potato?
- Is my spouse going to walk out on me because I have been crude and nasty?
- Are my children going to fail in school because I took them too much for granted?

Thus, in our relationship to our society:

- Have I been an accomplice or even a silent bystander to serious corruption in my work?
- Do I go along passively with censorship of free speech and free thinking? (I took an undergraduate course in political science during the McCarthy years, and not once did my instructor even mention McCarthy and what was happening in the United States.)

- When authorities order me to do unconscionable things, do I obey? Thus, in the military when a commander orders the killing of unarmed civilians, do I resist the illegal order? Do I follow Professor Stanley Milgram's orders at a respectable lab in Yale University to shock people severely and put their lives at risk when they give the wrong answers in an experiment? (Of course, in the actual experiment the victims were actors and were never really shocked.)

PROGNOSIS: SO WHAT WILL BE?

It's hopeless. The pace of human destructiveness outperforms progress by far.

Human beings are crazy, addicts, losers, mean-spirited, violent. Just look at the data!

Nature itself sends us many, many messages that the destiny of all forms of life and even the existence of planetary bodies is death and dissolution. Obviously one would hope for as healthy and long a life as possible until the inevitable arrives. But nature doesn't let up. It sends us an infinite number of life-destroying challenges in the course of our lives—the who knows when collisions of celestial bodies, enormously powerful eruptions of earthquakes, tsunamis, tornados, solar disturbances, climate crises, famine, continuous eruptions of killer illnesses like AIDS, Ebola, or new genres of lethal flus, on top of all the bitter medical hells that human beings suffer so far—cancer, ALS, Parkinsons, and so on *ad infinitum*.

Moreover there is an endless number of "diseases of social violence" that we humans develop, induce, and prolong. Which of these do you "prefer": prostitution of weapon industries, war, transnational terrorism, genocides (of whatever sizes), or simple plain old everyday murders?[3]

It may well be that the natural terror that we feel about all of the above plays a huge role in how we human beings rush toward our deaths stupidly, wantonly, and cruelly. But even when we are lucky enough to have good safe lives, every one of us is "doomed." In truth,

There's room for lots of hope. Many more individuals are becoming committed to respecting life.

Certainly millions of individuals can walk a beautiful path to become more of their better selves—to themselves and to other people.

Slowly but surely a great many improved institutions have come into being in our world, including a degree of world governance through the United Nations, the World Health Organization, the International Criminal Court, international agencies for human rights and refugees, regional organizations like NATO, and more. Yet many of these agencies are deeply flawed, and the process of their development and other structures of world governance await much-needed improvement—if and when there is sufficient will. There is so much to be done, such as creating machinery for world governance of "failed states" and the creation of an international peace army. (See the *Encyclopedia of Genocide* for a proposal of an International Peace Army that includes three interlinked armies, Medical, Military, and Societal Governance and Rebuilding Community.[2])

Decent people can only give the best they can, and hope against the odds that a sane world will emerge before an apocalypse.

If you're lucky, you get a lot of good years of beautiful living. There are so many delicious experiences in life: memorably tasty and nutritious food; feeling good physically and emotionally; building marvelous buildings, inventing and creating new beautiful ideas, things, and methods in whatever of the huge range of human activity; the pleasures and self-renewal of different sports; spectator pleasures at movies, theatres, sports events (also all that is going on in real

we are living out our existence on a "death row." It's enough to make human beings feel and act crazy.	life fascinatingly before every one of our noses); passion, sensuality, and sexuality; and the capstone of love of so many people who are dear to us, and, if we are fortunate, in our development of widening circles of caring for other human beings, our society, our planet, and our species.[4]
The Democratic Mind doesn't really have a chance.	*Every one of us can grow into a much better and healthier person if we work at it.*
It is all bigger than we are. Our very species may be on the way out, but let us do the best we can.	It's true that millions are suffering, but there are also millions who feel they have meaningful, rewarding lives.
Live as well as you can and as decently as you can for however long you can.	Live as well as you can and as decently as you can for however long you can.

CONCLUSION

The least I can do is to try to do my best for life, both individually for myself and in whatever I can do for others in our common destiny.

1 See the murderous battles not only between defined separate religious groups but also between different streams of belief in the same religion! Thus, in the world of Islam today, battles between Shi'ites versus Sunnis versus Islamic State dominate life more than the battles against out-and-out infidels who do not follow Mohammed, like the Christians and, of course, the eternally damned Jews.

2 Charny, Israel W. (1999). International Peace Army. Encyclopedia *of Genocide, op cit.*, 649–653.

3 A small but growing number of intellectuals and scholars are coming to the conclusion that a good deal of mass murder is derived not from ideological motivations but from a side of our humanness we have most wanted to deny, a built-in readiness to kill for the sake of killing, so to speak. Thus, Thomas Friedman explains evil in a "comic book–type conversation" between Batman and his helper: "Because he thought it was good sport. Because some men aren't looking for anything logical, like money. They can't be bought, bullied, reasoned, or negotiated with. Some men just want to watch the world burn." Friedman, Thomas L. (October 4, 2014). ISIS, Boko Haram and Batman. In*ternational New York Times.*

4 Lanagan, Robert (2014). Review of Grosz, Stephen (2013). "A Life Worth Living": A Review of the Examined Life: How We Lose and Find Ourselves. New York: Norton. In Psychotherapy, 51(2), 322–323 (quotation on p. 322). In a review of the book, Robert Lanagan of the William Alanson White Institute in New York explains that the concept of the examined life is developed against the background of Socrates's statement that "the unexamined life is not worth living"—a statement that led to Socrates being put on trial for his life.

"Is God willing to prevent evil, but not able? Then he is not omnipotent.
Is he able, but not willing? Then he is malevolent.
Is he both able and willing? Then whence cometh evil?
Is he neither able nor willing? Then why call him God?"

—*Epicuris (341–270 BC)*

"The angel of death is a sorry figure
Who does not know how to play with words
And to celebrate life"

—*T. Carmi (translated from the Hebrew)*

NOTES

1. Theodor Adorno was a German philosopher and sociologist who was particularly active immediately following World War II, including his participation in the epical book, which for some years was considered the most significant work in psychology at the time, on the authoritarian personality. Adorno, Theodore W.; Frenkel-Brunswik, Else; Levinson, Daniel J.; and Sanford, R. Nevitt (1950). *The Authoritarian Personality*. New York: Norton.

2. Robert S.C. Gordon is a professor of modern Italian culture. See Gordon, Robert S.C. (2001). *Primo Levi's Ordinary Virtues, op. cit.* The somewhat inspiring revision of Primo Levi's statement is cited by a reviewer of Gordon's book, David H. Jones, in *Holocaust and Genocide Studies*, 2002, 16(3), 427–431 (quotation on p. 428).

3. Sadighim, Sherry (2014). The big reveal: Ethical implications of therapist-self disclosure. *Psychotherapy Bulletin*, 49(4), 22–27. This excellent balanced article provides a perspective of the possible benefits and drawbacks of therapist self-disclosure. See also Barnett, J. E. (2011). Psychotherapist self-disclosure: Ethical and clinical considerations. *Psychotherapy*, 48(4), 315–321; Gibson, Margaret F. (2012). Opening up: Therapist self-disclosure in theory, research, and practice. *Clinical Social Work Journal*, 40(3), 287–296; Peterson, Zoe D. (2002). More than a mirror: The ethics of therapist self-disclosure. *Psychotherapy: Theory, Research, Practice, Training*, 39(1), 21–31.

4. Personal communication to me from the American relative, who is also a practicing mental health professional whom I know very well, as I do the ex-soldier. I was very touched by the story, and also could not help but think of a new variation of the concept of PTSD, which I now call PTESD = Post Traumatic Ethical Stress Disorder. I think this kind of guilt and sensitivity is somewhat consoling in a world that produces so much viciousness, although I dare not forget the huge number of genocidal killers in so many of our different cultures who show no regret at all.

Appendix

The following materials are reprinted from Charny, Israel W. (2017). *A Democratic Mind: Psychology and Psychiatry with Fewer Meds and More Soul:*

1. A Special Invitation to Cognitive-Behavioral Therapists (CBT)
2. Prescriptions for a Free and Democratic Mind
3. Worksheet: Basic Processes in Different Methods of Psychotherapy

A SPECIAL INVITATION TO COGNITIVE-BEHAVIORAL THERAPISTS (CBT)

The author wishes to convey very clearly to the many colleagues and departments that today insist only on "evidence-based therapies" that there is no direct conflict between the concepts presented in this book and CBT. There are different levels of experiencing, and it is my conviction that it is wise and helpful to our clients/patients in many cases to employ both sets of techniques together.

The prevailing mode of psychotherapy today in the United States is clearly cognitive behavioral therapy (CBT). This is an approach to therapy that attempts with considerable success to be anchored in empirical information, and aims with considerable success at relieving symptom distress and reducing the suffering of many patients. But CBT is also accompanied by and linked to a broader philosophy, which I believe constitutes the prevailing current politically correct attitude toward emotional and mental disorders: People with virtually all human conditions and differences are to be honored as they are, and patients are to be guided to self-acceptance without "tough love" or other deep therapist-patient relationship-touching techniques that aim at elevating functioning and are intended to facilitate meaningfully deep character and relationship changes.

I definitely *do* practice CBT techniques in the therapy I practice. On a typical day this week, I taught a patient how to regain control over her breathing, which had gotten out of whack ("I feel like I can't breathe," she said in panic); taught a patient how to use breathing techniques in order to fall asleep or resume sleeping after waking up in the middle of the night; instructed a couple to schedule units of structured conversation in which each one shares what is going on in his (her) life and then the spouse is to convey his (her) understanding (though not necessarily agreement); and designed for another patient a daily exercise in which he is to attempt in his fantasy to be angry and even to hate his mother, who devoted all of herself and more to her "genius son," who ended up so pleasured that he is deprived of much of his natural vitality and stamina for standing up to life. My beloved psychoanalyst so many years ago would not have offered me any of the above or anything remotely similar in the way of immediate help and direct active techniques for relief of the considerable pain that I suffered.

My own original training was essentially in psychoanalysis and as an alternative in Rogerian non-directive therapy, and then it was with awe and gratitude that I met up with the first works of the great Albert Ellis on "Rational-Emotive Therapy." Ellis gave me new tools for real help in urgent situations, such as for a college kid who was on the edge of psychosis but had to and wanted to go back to college in another city to begin the fall semester. I also had the pleasure of being in personal contact with Ellis a number of times, and indeed referred several of my difficult patients (in Philadelphia) to him (in New York) for his more expert help. So I am hardly a stranger or antagonistic to CBT.

Yet I have adopted another kind of philosophy of treatment where, whenever possible, the therapy aims at fighting off renunciations of power and achievement by patients who are giving up on themselves—for example, capable people who are looking to stop their education because of learning difficulties; marital spouses who are heading uncritically to terminate a marriage (and family) because they are currently miserable, but the marriage still has potential for decency and pleasure, or conversely, spouses who surrender to deadness in their marriage but could do better; and even *some* choices of alternative sexual lifestyles by people who then ask for therapy and it becomes clear that they essentially are running away from the pain of heterosexual intimacy, rather than their being naturally among the many people whose psychosexual development intrinsically is pointed in another direction.

For me, many psychotherapies are profound invitations not only to symptom relief but to very meaningful growth of character, spirit, and healthy interactions in relationships. I see no contradiction between the two goals of providing relief and encouraging growth—although of course I am very aware of the significant technical issue that providing relief very quickly can inhibit what might have been a process of deeper engagement of a person with themselves. I believe in a therapy that aims as much as possible at egalitarian experiences with others, banishing prejudice at others who are different than we are in whatever ways, eschewing all violence, and basically living a life where one is good to oneself and decent and good to others—and enjoys living for all its inevitable downs.

To my CBT colleagues; that is, therapists, clinics, and departments that have fully adopted a CBT-only approach, I extend an invitation to read this book openly, if possible without rancor, to disagree with me vigorously, but to be open to a possible contribution from my way of thinking and experience.

PRESCRIPTIONS FOR A FREE AND DEMOCRATIC MIND

1. Organization of Diversity and Complexity
   Take an active coping position in organizing and running your own mind and life. Search for the best ways to deal with problems, including efforts to overcome problems that can be solved along with being ready to yield to unchangeable adversity. Address life's realities as complex and multifaceted, so that you question from the outset any proposals of total and absolute solutions as possibly offering more than can be fulfilled.
2. Acceptance of Uncertainty, Process, Possibility, and Creative Anxiety
   Give up certainty in favor of maps of reality based on scientific evidence of probabilities (including also uncertainty) and concepts of process and change. Accept and enjoy anxiety and uncertainty as spurs to creative thinking and efforts.
3. Open-mindedness to Information, Questioning, and Use of Scientific Method
   Keep yourself open to new information, including especially evidence that contradicts your current ways of thinking and doing things. Be prepared to discard tried-and-true and favored ideas in the face of new evidence. Look for solutions that can be tried out, tested, and revised over time.
4. Freedom, Respect for Dissent, and Responsibility to Make Choices
   Keep in touch with your own mind, and exercise your own real choices. Have the courage to be wary of authority and not to be automatically obedient or blindly conformist to the dictates of authority, certainly when your own basic moral principles are deeply violated. Be especially careful not to join a bandwagon or populist mindset.
5. Sharing Power, Respect and Basic Equality, with Checks and Balances against Excessive Power
   Be aware in yourself of strivings for superiority and power of one part of your personality over the rest of you—for example, a demand for pleasure at any cost—and be aware of strivings for superiority and power over others. In both cases, renounce excessive power in favor of cooperative structures and egalitarian relationships. Create checks and balances in your own mind against the absoluteness of any impulse, idea, or ideology, and seek an interplay with the

critical thinking and critical evaluations of yourself and your ideas by your own self and by others.

6. Nonviolence, Conflict Resolution, and Seeking Peace
   Renounce violence to your own self and/or to other human beings. Commit yourself to the holiness of life, to protecting your own and others' lives, and to nurturing health and a good quality of living for yourself and for others.
7. Acceptance of Responsibility for Doing Harm to Self and Others
   When you do end up harming yourself or others, make every effort to acknowledge the harm you are doing. Whenever you are able to do so, take responsibility for the harm you have done to yourself or to others, and make whatever corrections or compensation possible. Above all, take greater responsibility for stopping further harm and destructiveness.

WORKSHEET: BASIC PROCESSES IN DIFFERENT METHODS OF PSYCHOTHERAPY

	at the core of all therapy: THE HELPING RELATIONSHIP					
THERAPY PROCESS and GOAL EXISTENTIAL EXPERIENCES	Expressive: Release of Emotional Concerns, Personal Narrative	Psychoanalytic, Psychodynamic: Insight and Transference Work	Cognitive: Correction of Mind Paradigms	Behavioral: Correction of Behavior Patterns	Family, Systemic: Treating Hurts and Anger, and Upgrading Relationships	Existential: Accepting Life Realities, and Learning Best Use of Natural Equipment
Desire, Ambition						
Anxiety						
Loss						
Incompetence						
Fulfillment						
Anger, Hate						
Violence						
Longing, Love, Loyalty						
Limitation,Decline, Death						

Bibliography

Adler, Alfred (1917). *Study of Organ Inferiority and Its Psychical Compensation: A Contribution to Clinical Medicine*. New York: Nervous and Mental Disease Publishing.

Adler, Alfred (1924). *The Practice and Theory of Individual Psychology*. New York: Harcourt Brace.

Adler, Alfred (1932). *Individual Psychology and Its Results in the Practice and Theory of Individual Psychology*. New York: Harcourt Brace.

Adorno, Theodore W.; Frenkel-Brunswik, Else; Levinson, Daniel J.; and Sanford, R. Nevitt (1950). *The Authoritarian Personality*. New York: Norton.

Aichhorn, August (1951). *Wayward Youth*. London: Imago.

American Psychiatric Association (2013). *DSM-5, Desk Reference*, 324.

Amundson, Jon; Stewart, Kenneth; and La Nae, Valentine (1993). Temptations of power and certainty. *Journal of Marital and Family Therapy*, 19(2), 111–123.

Ansbacher, Heinz, L. and Rowena, R. (Eds.) (1964). *The Individual Psychology of Alfred Adler: A Systematic Presentation in Selections from His Writings*. Paperback originally published in 1956. New York: Harper Perennial.

Anthony, E. Jarvis and Benedeck, Therese (1970). *Parenthood: Its Psychology and Psychopathology*. Boston: Little, Brown.

Aponte, Harry J. (2002). Spiritually-sensitive psychotherapy. In Florence W. Kaslow and Robert F. Massey (Eds.). *Comprehensive Handbook of Psychotherapy, Volume 3, Interpersonal/Humanistic/Existential*. New York: Wiley, 279–302.

Arendt, Hannah (1969). *Eichmann in Jerusalem: A Report on the Banality of Evil*. New York: Viking (original work published in 1963).

Arieti, Silvano (1955). *Interpretation of Schizophrenia*. New York: Basic Books.

Arieti, Silvano (Ed.) (1961). *American Handbook of Psychiatry*, 3rd edition. New York: Basic Books, 419–454.

Askenasy, Hans (1978). *Are We All Nazis?* Secaucus, NJ: Lyle Stuart.

Bach, George R. and Wyden, Peter (1969). *The Intimate Enemy: How to Fight Fair in Love and Marriage*. New York: Morrow.

Bard, Morton and Zucker, Joseph (1976). *The Police and Interpersonal Conflict: Third Party Intervention Approaches*. Washington, DC: Police Foundation.

Bar-On, Dan (1981). *Legacy of Silence* (1991). Cambridge, MA: Harvard University Press.

Barrett, Mary Jo and Fish, Linda Stone (2014). *Treating Complex Trauma: A Relational Blueprint for Collaboration and Change*. New York: Routledge.

Bass, Ellen and Davis, Laura (1988). *The Courage to Heal: A Guide for Women Survivors of Sexual Abuse*. Revised 20th anniversary edition 2008. New York: Collins Living.

Baum, Steven K. (2008). *The Psychology of Genocide: Perpetrators, Bystanders and Rescuers*. Cambridge: Cambridge University Press, 237.

Bayzler, Michael and Turkheimer, Frank M. (2014). *Forgotten Trials of the Holocaust*. New York: New York University Press, 548–569.

Beck, Aaron T. (1976). *Cognitive Therapy and the Emotional Disorders*. New York: International Universities Press.

Beck, Aaron T.; Rush, A. John; Shaw, Brian F.; and Emery, Gary (1979). *Cognitive Therapy of Depression*. New York: Guilford.

Bell, Norman and Vogel, Ezra E. (Eds.) (1987). *A Modern Introduction to the Family*. New York: Free Press, 628–649.

Berenbaum, Michael (Ed.) (1990). *A Mosaic of Victims: Non-Jews Persecuted and Murdered by the Nazis*. New York: New York University Press.

Berke, Joseph H.; Pierides, Stella; Sabbadim, Andrea; and Schneider Stanley (Eds.) (1998). *Even Paranoids Have Enemies: New Perspectives on Paranoia and Persecution*. New York: Taylor & Francis.

Bettelheim, Bruno (1967). *The Empty Fortress*. New York: Free Press.

Blumberg, Herbert; Hare, Paul; and Costin, Anna (2007). *Peace Psychology: A Comprehensive Introduction*. Cambridge: Cambridge University Press.

Bohart, Arthur C.; Held, Barbara S.; Mendelowitz, Edward; and Schneider, Kirk J. (Eds.) (2016). *Humanity's Dark Side: Evil, Destructive Experience, and Psychotherapy*. Washington, DC: American Psychological Association.

Braginsky, Benjamin M.; Braginsky, Dorothea D.; and Ring, Kenneth (1969). *Methods of Madness: The Mental Hospital as a Last Resort*. New York: Holt, Rhinehart and Winston.

Brotto, Lori A. and Barker, Meg (Eds.) (2015). *Mindfulness in Sexual and Relationship Therapy*. New York: Routledge.

Brown, Emily M. (2001). *Patterns of Infidelity and Their Treatment*. New York: Routledge.

Browning, Christopher (2013). *Ordinary Men: Reserve Police Battalion 101 and the Final Solution in Poland*. New York: HarperCollins (original publication 1992).

Chainani, Soman (2013). *The School for Blood and Evil*. London: Harper Collins.

Charny, Israel W. (1971). Normal man as genocider: We need a psychology of normal man as genocider, accomplice or indifferent bystander to mass killing of man. *Voices: The Art and Science of Psychotherapy*, 7(2), 68–79.

Charny, Israel W. (1972). *Marital Love and Hate: The Need for a Revised Marriage Contract and a More Honest Offer by the Marriage Counselor to Teach Couples to Love and Hate, Honor and Dishonor, Obey and Disobey*. New York: Macmillan.

Charny, Israel W. (1972). Parental intervention with one another on behalf of their child: A breaking-through tool for preventing emotional disturbance. *Journal Contemporary Psychotherapy*, 5(1), 19–29.

Charny, Israel W. (1973). And Abraham went to slay Isaac: A parable of killer, victim and bystander in the family of man. *Journal of Ecumenical Studies*, 4(3), 304–318.

Charny, Israel W. (1980). Recovery of two (largely) autistic children through renunciation of maternal destructiveness in integrated individual and family therapy. In Lewis R. Wolberg and Marvin. L. Aronson (Eds.), *Group and Family Therapy 1980*. New York: Brunner/Mazel, 250–281.

Charny, Israel W. (1980). Why are so many (if not really all) people and families disturbed? *Journal of Marital and Family Therapy*, 1980, 6(1), 37–47.

Charny, Israel W. (1982). *How Can We Commit the Unthinkable? Genocide: The Human Cancer*. Foreword by Elie Wiesel. Boulder, CO: Westview Press.

Charny, Israel W. and Fromer, Daphna (1990). A study of the readiness of Jewish/Israeli students in the health professions to authorize and execute involuntary mass euthanasia of "severely handicapped" patients. *Holocaust and Genocide Studies*, 5(3), 313–335.

Charny, Israel W. and Fromer, Daphna (1990). The readiness of health profession students to comply with a hypothetical program of "forced migration" of a minority population. *American Journal of Orthopsychiatry*, 1990, 60(4), 486–495.

Charny, Israel W. (1992). *Existential/Dialectical Marital Therapy: Breaking the Secret Code of Marriage*. New York: Brunner/Mazel. E-book in press, Routledge, 2018.

Charny, Israel W. (1992). "Catering and not Catering Affairs." In *Existential/Dialectical Marital Therapy, ibid.*, 220–244.

Charny, Israel W. and Fromer, Daphna (1992). A study of attitudes of viewers of the film "Shoah" towards an incident of mass murder by Israeli soldiers (Kfar Kassem, 1956). *Journal of Traumatic Stress*, 5(2), 303–318.

Charny, Israel W. and Parnass, Sivan (1995). The impact of extramarital relationships in the continuation of marriages. *Journal of Sex and Marital Therapy*, 21(2), 100–115.

Charny, Israel W. (1996). Evil in human personality. In Kaslow, Florence (Ed.). *Handbook of Relational Diagnosis and Dysfunctional Family Patterns*. Hoboken, NJ: Wiley-Interscience, 484–485.

Charny, Israel W. (1999). *Encyclopedia of Genocide*. Associate editors: Rouben Adalian, Steven L. Jacobs, Eric Markusen, Marc I. Sherman, Samuel Totten. Forewords by Bishop Desmond Tutu and Simon Wiesenthal. Santa Barbara, CA: ABC-Clio.

Charny, Israel W. (2006). *Facism and Democracy in the Human Mind*. Lincoln, NE: University of Nebraska Press.

Charny, Israel W. (2007). *Fighting Suicide Bombing: A Worldwide Campaign for Life*. Westport, CT: Prager Security International (quotation on pp. 24–25).

Charny, Israel W. (2016). *The Genocide Contagion: How We Commit and Confront Holocaust and Genocide*. Lanham, MD: Rowman & Littlefield.

Charny, Israel W. (In Press, 2017). *A Democratic Mind: Psychology and Psychiatry with Fewer Meds and More Soul*. Lanham, MD: Rowman & Littlefield.

Chirot, Daniel; and Seligman, Martin E. P. (Eds.) (2001). *Ethnopolitical Warfare: Causes, Consequences, and Possible Solutions*. Washington, DC: American Psychological Association.

Churchill, Ward (1997). *A Little Matter of Genocide: Holocaust and Denial in the Americas 1492 to the Present*. San Francisco: City Light Books.

Clarkin, John F.; Yeomans, Frank E.; and Kernberg, Otto F. (2006). *Psychotherapy for Borderline Personality: Focusing on Object Relations*. Washington, DC: American Psychiatric Association.

Clarkin, John F.; Levy, Kenneth N.; Lenzenweger, Mark F.; and Kernberg, Otto F. (2007). Evaluating three treatments for borderline personality disorder: A multi-wave study. *American Journal of Psychiatry*, 164(6), 922–928.

Cocks, Geoffrey (1985). *Psychotherapy in the Third Reich: The Göring Institute.* New York: Oxford University Press.

Colclasure, David (2011). Just war and perpetual peace: Kant on the legitimate use of political violence. In Elisabeth Krimmer and Patricia Anne Simpson (Eds.) (2011). *Enlightened War: German Theories and Cultures of War from Frederick the Great to Clausewitz.* Woodbridge, UK: Boydell & Brewer, 241–257.

Darley, John M. and Batson, C. Daniel (1979). "From Jerusalem to Jericho": A study of situational and dispositional variables in helping behavior." *Journal of Personality and Social Psychology*, 27, 100–108.

Dearey, Melissa (2014). The Banality of Evil: Genocide, Slavery, Holocaust, War. In *Making Sense of Evil: An Interdisciplinary Approach.* London: Palgrave Macmillan, 186–204.

Dicks, Henry V. (1972). *Licensed Mass Murder: Socio-Psychological Study of Some SS Killers.* London: Heinemann.

Einstein, Albert with Nathan, Otto; and Norden, Heinz (Eds.) (1988). *Einstein on Peace.* With a foreword by Bertrand Russell. New York: Random House Value Publishing.

Ellens, J. Harold (2011). *Explaining Evil.* Three-volume set. *Volume One: Definitions and Development; Volume Two: History, Global Views, and Events; Volume Three: Psychology, Religion, and Spirituality.* Santa Barbara, CA: ABC Clio.

Ellis, Albert (1962). *Reason and Emotion in Psychotherapy* (originally published in 1962). Secaucus, NJ: Carol Publishing Group.

Ellis, Albert and Harper, Robert, A. (1961). *A Guide to Rational Living.* Upper Saddle River, NJ: Prentice-Hall.

Ellis, Albert and Harper, Robert A. (1968). *A Guide to Successful Marriage.* Hollywood, CA: Wilshire.

Ellis, Albert (1987). The impossibility of achieving consistently good mental health. *American Psychologist*, 42, 364–375.

Feinstein, Adam (2010). *A History of Autism: Conversations with the Pioneers.* New York: Wiley-Blackwell.

Fox, Jonathan (2012). Religion and Violence. Chapter in *An Introduction to Religion and Politics: Theory and Practice.* New York: Routledge.

Freud, Sigmund [1952–1974]. *The Complete Works of Sigmund Freud.* (24 volumes). London: Hogarth.

Freud, Sigmund (1991). The Ego and the Id. In On *Metapsychology—The Theory of Psychoanalysis.* Albert Dickson (Ed.). Harmondsworth, Middlesex: Penguin.

Friedman, Maurice S. (2002). *Martin Buber: The Life of Dialogue.* New York: Routledge.

Fromm, Erich (1941). *Escape from Freedom.* New York: Farrar & Rinehart.

Fromm, Erich (1964). *The Heart of Man: Its Genius for Good and Evil.* New York: Harper and Row.

Fromm, Erich (1997). *On Being Human.* New York: Bloomsbury Academic.

Fromm-Reichmann, Frieda (1959). *Psychoanalysis and Psychotherapy: Selected Papers.* Edited by Dexter M. Bulard. Chicago: University of Chicago Press.

Fulbrook, Mary (2012). *A Small Town Near Auschwitz: Ordinary Nazis and the Holocaust.* Oxford: Oxford University Press.

Gajzago, Christine and Prior, Margot (1974). Two cases of "recovery" in Kanner syndrome. *Archives of General Psychiatry*, 31(2), 264–268.

Gandhi, Mohandas K. (1961). *Non-Violent Resistance* (Satyagraha). New York: Shocken.

Gardner, Richard A.; Sauber, S. Richard; and Lorandos, Demosthenes (Eds.) (2003). *The International Handbook of Parental Alienation Syndrome: Conceptual, Clinical and Legal Considerations*. Springfield, IL: Charles C. Thomas.

Gernsbacher, Larry Morton (1985). *The Suicide Syndrome: Origins, Manifestations and Alleviation of Human Self-Destructiveness*. New York: Human Sciences Press.

Gilbert, Gustave M. (1979). *The Psychology of Dictatorship: Based on an Examination of the Leaders of Nazi Germany*. Westport, CT: Greenwood (original publication New York: Ronald Press, 1950).

Girard, René (1977). *Violence and the Sacred*. Baltimore: Johns Hopkins University Press.

Glover, Jonathan (1999). *Humanity: A Moral History of the Twentieth Century*. London: Jonathan Cape.

Golan, Naomi (1981). *Passing through Transitions*. New York: Free Press.

Goldberg, Carl (2000). *The Evil We Do: The Psychoanalysis of Destructive People*. Amherst, NY: Prometheus.

Goldhagen, Daniel Jonah (1996). *Hitler's Willing Executioners: Ordinary Germans and the Holocaust*. New York: Knopf.

Gordon, Lori H. (1990). *Love Knots: How to Untangle those Everyday Frustrations that Keep You from Being with the One You Love*. New York: Dell.

Gordon, Lori (1997). *If You Really Loved Me*. Palo Alto: Science and Behavior.

Gordon, Lori with Frandsen, Jon (1999). *Passage to Intimacy: Key Concepts and Skills from the Pairs Program which has Helped Thousands of Couples Rekindle their Love*. New York: Fireside Books.

Gordon, Robert S.C. (2001). *Primo Levi's Ordinary Virtues: From Testimony to Ethics*. Oxford: Oxford University Press.

Gottman, John (1999). *The Marriage Clinic: A Scientifically Based Marital Therapy*. New York: Norton Professional Books.

Gottman, John (2011). *The Science of Trust: Emotional Attunement for Couples*. New York: Norton.

Gottman, John with Joan Declaire (2001). *The Relationship Cure: A Five-Step Guide for Building Better Connections with Family, Friends, and Lovers*. New York: Crown.

Gottman, John with Julie Schwartz Gottman (2008). *And Baby Makes Three: The Six-Step Plan for Preserving Marital Intimacy and Rekindling Romance After Baby Arrives*. New York: Three Rivers Press.

Gottman, John with Nan Silver (1999). *The Seven Principles for Making Marriage Work*. New York: Three Rivers Press.

Gottman, John and Silver, Nan (2012). *What Makes Love Last: How to Build Trust and Avoid Betrayal*. New York: Simon & Schuster.

Green, Hannah (1992). *I Never Promised You a Rose Garden*. New York: St. Martin's Press [original publication 1964].

Gross, Jan Tomasz with Gross, Irena Grudzinska (2012). *Golden Harvest: Events at the Periphery of the Holocaust*. New York: Oxford University Press.

Harari, Yuval Noah (2011). *Sapiens: A Brief History of Humankind*. London: Harvill Secker.

Hart, William (2004). *Evil: A Primer: A History of a Bad Idea from Beelzebub to Bin Laden*. New York: Thomas Dunne Books.

Hayes, Steven C.; Follette, Victoria M.; and Linehan, Marsha M. (Eds.) (2011). *Mindfulness and Acceptance: Expanding the Cognitive-Behavioral Tradition*. New York: Guilford.

Herman, Judith (1997). *Trauma and Recovery: The Aftermath of Violence: From Domestic Abuse to Political Terror.* New York: Basic Books.

Hertlein, Katherine M.; Weeks, Gerald R.; and Gambescia, Nancy (Eds.) (2015). *Systemic Sex Therapy*. 2nd edition. New York: Routledge.

Hinton, Alexander Laban (1996). Explaining the Cambodian genocide in terms of psychological dissonance. *American Anthropologist*, 98(4), 818–831.

Homer, Frederic, D. (2001). *Primo Levi and the Politics of Survival.* Columbia: University of Missouri Press.

Honig, Albert M. (1972). *The Awakening Nightmare: A Breakthrough in Treating the Mentally Ill.* Rockaway, NJ: American Faculty Press.

Honig, Albert M. (2001). *Hard Boiled Eggs and Other Psychiatric Tales: The Rebirth of the Psychotherapy of Severe Mental Illness.* Doylestown, PA: North Street Publishers.

Horney, Karen (1937). *The Neurotic Personality of Our Time.* New York: Norton.

Horney, Karen (1942). *Self-Analysis.* New York: Norton.

Horney, Karen (1946). *Are You Considering Psychoanalysis?* New York: Norton.

Howarth, Glennys and Leaman, Oliver (Eds.) (2001). *Encyclopedia of Death and Dying.* New York: Taylor & Francis.

Hufford, David J. (1982). *The Terror that Comes in the Night.* Philadelphia: University of Pennsylvania Press.

Huntington, Samuel P. (1996). *The Clash of Civilizations and the Remaking of World Order.* New York: Simon and Schuster.

Kaffman, Mordecai (1981), Paranoid disorders: The core of truth behind the delusional system. *International Journal of Family Therapy*, 3(1), 29–41

Kaffman, Mordecai (1981). Paranoid disorders: The interpersonal perspective. *Journal of Family Therapy*, 3, 21–30

Kaffman, Mordecai (1983). Paranoid disorders: Family sources of the delusional system. *Journal of Family Therapy*, 5(2), 107–116.

Kaffman, Mordecai (1985). Twenty years of family therapy in Israel. *Family Process*, 24(2), 113–27.

Kaffman, Mordecai (1981). Monoideism in psychiatry: Theoretical and clinical implications *American Journal of Psychotherapy*, 35(2), 235–243.

Kahn, Jack with Solomon Hester (1986). *Job's Illness: Loss, Grief and Integrations—A Psychological Interpretation.* London: Gaskell.

Kant, Immanuel (1797). *The Metaphysics of Morals.* Cambridge: Cambridge University Press, 1991.

Kaplan, Helen S. (1974). *The New Sex Therapy.* New York: Brunner-Mazel.

Karon, Bertram P. and Vandenbos, Gary R. (1981). *Psychotherapy of Schizophrenia: The Treatment of Choice.* Lanham, MD: Rowman & Littlefield.

Kelley, Douglas M. (1961). *22 Cells in Nuremberg: A Psychiatrist Examines the Nazi Criminals.* New York: Greenberg (original publication in 1947).

Kelman, Herbert C. and Hamilton, V. Lee (1989). *Crimes of Obedience: Towards a Social Psychology of Authority and Responsibility.* New Haven: Yale University Press.

Kernberg, Otto (1975). *Borderline Conditions and Pathological Narcissism.* New York: Jason Aronson.

King, Martin Luther (2003). *A Testament of Hope.* New York: Harper One Reprint Edition (originally published in 1976).

Kohlberg, Lawrence (1963). The development of children's orientation toward moral order: I. Sequence in the development of moral thought. *Vita Humana*, 6(1–2), 11–33.

Kohlberg, Lawrence (1966). Moral education in the schools: A developmental view. *The School Review*, 74(1), 1–30.

Kohut, Heinz (1977). *The Restoration of the Self.* New York: International Universities Press.

Kohut, Heinz (1984). *How Does Analysis Cure?* Edited by Arnold Goldberg. Chicago: Chicago University Press.

Krell, Robert and Sherman, Marc I. (Eds.) (1997). *Medical and Psychological Effects of Concentration Camps on Holocaust Survivors.* Volume 4 in Series*: Genocide, A Critical Bibliographic Review.* New Brunswick, NJ: Transaction.

Kubler-Ross, Elisabeth and Byock, Ira (2014). *On Death and Dying: What the Dying Have to Teach Doctors, Nurses, Clergy, and their Own Families.* New York: Scribner Reprint Edition.

Kubler-Ross, Elisabeth and Kessler, David A. (2014). *On Grief and Grieving: Finding the Meaning of Grief through the Five Stages of Loss.* New York: Scribner Reprint Edition.

Kulcsar, I. Shlomo; Kulcsar Shoshanna; and Szondi, Lipot (1966). *Adolf Eichmann and the Third Reich.* Springfield, IL: Charles Thomas.

Kulcsar, Shlomo I. (1978). De Sade and Eichmann. In Israel W. Charny (Ed.). *Strategies against Violence: Design for Nonviolent Change.* Boulder, CO: Westview, 19–33

Kunz, George (1998). *The Paradox of Power and Weakness: Levinas and an Alternative Paradigm for Psychology.* New York: State University of New York.

Kuper, Leo (1977). *The Pity of It All: Polarisation of Racial and Ethnic Relations.* London: Duckworth; Minneapolis: University of Minnesota Press.

Laing, R.D. (1960). *The Divided Self: An Existential Study in Sanity and Madness.* Harmondsworth: Penguin.

Laing, R.D. (1967) *The Politics of Experience and the Bird of Paradise.* Harmondsworth: Penguin.

Laing, R.D. (1970). *Knots.* London: Penguin.

Laing, R.D. (1971). *The Politics of the Family and Other Essays.* London: Tavistock.

Laing, R.D.; Esterson, A.; Cooper, D.G.; and Laing, R.D. (1965). Results of family-orientated therapy with hospitalized schizophrenics. *British Medical Journal*, 2(5476), 1462–1465.

Laing, R.D. and Mullan, B. (1995). *Mad to be Normal: Conversations with R.D. Laing.* London: Free Association Books.

Lasch, Christopher (1991). *The Culture of Narcissism: American Life in an Age of Diminishing Expectations.* New York: Norton.

Latane, Bibb and Darley, John M. (1970). *The Unresponsive Bystander.* New York: Appleton-Crofts.

Le Bon, G. (1903). *The Crowd: A Study of the Popular Mind.* London: F. Unwin. (Translated from the French.)

Lee-Chai, Annette Y. and Bargh, John A. (Eds.) (2001). *The Use and Abuse of Power: Multiple Perspectives on the Causes of Corruption.* Philadelphia, PA: Psychology Press, 41–55.

Lemkin, Raphael (1944). *Axis Rule in Occupied Europe.* Washington, DC: Carnegie Foundation for International Peace.

Lewis, Sinclair (1935). *It Can't Happen Here.* New York: Doubleday Doran.

Lidz, Theoodore; Cornelison, Alice R; Fleck, Stephen; and Terry, Dorothy (1957). The intrafamilial environment of schizophrenic patients: II. Marital schism and marital skew. *American Journal Psychiatry*, 114(3), 241–248.

Lifton, Robert Jay (1967). *Death in Life: Survivors of Hiroshima.* New York: Random House.

Lifton, Robert Jay (1973). *Home from the War: Vietnam Veterans—Neither Victims nor Executioners.* New York: Simon & Schuster.

Lifton, Robert Jay (1979). *The Broken Connection: On Death and the Continuity of Life.* New York: Simon and Schuster.

Lifton, Robert Jay (1986). *The Nazi Doctors: Medical Killing and the Psychology of Genocide.* New York: Basic Books.

Lifton, Robert Jay and Markusen, Eric (1990). *The Genocidal Mentality: Nazi Holocaust and Nuclear Threat.* New York: Basic Books.

Linder, Robert (1976). *The Fifty Minute Hour: A Collection of True Psychoanalytic Tales.* New York: Bantam Books.

Linehan, Marsha M. (1993). *Cognitive Behavioral Therapy of Borderline Personality Disorder.* New York: Guilford Press.

Linehan, Marsha M. (1993). *Skills Training Manual for Treating Borderline Personality Disorder.* New York: Guilford Press

Linehan, Marsha M. (2000). The empirical basis of dialectical behavior therapy: Development of new treatments versus evaluation of existing treatments. *Clinical Psychology: Science and Practice*, 7(1), 113–119 (quotation on p. 114).

Linehan, Marsha M. (2003). *Getting Through a Crisis Without Making It Worse: Crisis Survival Skills: Distracting and Self-Sooth.* New York: Guilford

Linehan, Marsha M. (2003). *From Suffering to Freedom: Practicing Reality Acceptance.* New York: Guilford

Livingstone, David (2011). *Less Than Human: Why We Demean, Enslave, and Exterminate Others.* New York: St. Martins.

Lorenz, Konrad (1966). *On Aggression.* New York: Harcourt, Brace & World.

Luborsky, Lester; Diguer, Louis; Seligman, David A.; Rosenthal, Robert; Krause, Elizabeth D.; Johnson, Suzanne; Halperin, Gregory; Bishop, Monica; Berman, Jeffrey S.; and Schweitzer, Edward (1999). The researcher's own therapy allegiance: A "wild card" in comparisons of treatment efficacy. *Clinical Psychology: Science and Practice*, 6(1), 95–106.

Mann, James and Goldman, K. (1983). *A Case Book in Time Limited Psychotherapy.* New York: McGraw-Hill.

Mann, Michael (2000). Were the perpetrators of genocide "ordinary men" or "real Nazis"? Results from fifteen hundred biographies. *Holocaust and Genocide Studies*, 14(3), 331–366.

Marks, Emanuel (2013). *The Social Context of Violent Behaviour: A Social Anthropological Study in an Israeli Immigrant Town.* New York: Routledge.

Masters, William H. and Johnson, Virginia C. (1970). *Human Sexual Inadequacy.* Boston: Little Brown.

Masterson, James F. (1976). *Psychotherapy of the Borderline Adult: A Developmental Approach.* New York: Brunner/Mazel.

May, Rollo (1992). The problem of evil: An open letter to Carl Rogers; and Rogers, Carl (1992). Reply to Rollo May. In Ronald B. Miller (Ed.) (1992). *The Restoration of Dialogue: Readings in the Philosophy of Clinical Psychology*, 314–316. Washington, DC: American Psychological Association.

May, Rollo (1998). *Power and Innocence.* Originally published in 1972. New York: Norton, 94–95.

McCord, William and McCord, Joan (1964). *The Psychopath: An Essay on the Criminal Mind.* New York: Van Nostrand.

Merton, Thomas (1962). Chant to be used in processions around a site with furnaces. In McDonnell, Thomas P. (Ed.), *A Thomas Merton Reader.* New York: Harcourt, Brace & World, 404–406.

Merton, Thomas N. (1967). A devout meditation in memory of Adolf Eichmann. Reprinted in *Reflections.* Merck, Sharp & Dohme, 1(3), 21–23.

Miller, Alec L.; Rathus, Jill H.; and Linehan, Marsha M. (2006). *Dialectical Behavior Therapy with Suicidal Adolescents.* New York: Guilford.

Miller, Alice (1981). *Prisoners of Childhood: The Drama of the Gifted Child and the Search for the True Self.* New York: Basic Books.

Millon, Theodore (2011). *Disorders of Personality: Introducing a DSM/ICD Spectrum from Normal to Abnormal.* New York: Wiley.

Minow, Martha (1998). *Between Vengeance and Forgiveness.* Boston: Beacon.

Minuchin, Salvador. (1974). *Families and Family Therapy.* Cambridge MA: Harvard University Press.

Minuchin, Salvador; Rosman, Bernice L.; and Baker, Lester (1978). *Psychosomatic Families: Anorexia Nervosa in Context.* Cambridge, MA: Harvard University Press.

Minuchin, Salvador, and Fishman, H. Charles (1981). *Family Therapy Techniques.* Cambridge, MA: Harvard University Press.

Munder, Thomas; Brütsc, Oliver; Leonhart, Rainer; Gerger, Heike; and Barth, Jurgen (2013). Researcher allegiance in psychotherapy outcome research: an overview of reviews. *Clinical Psychology Review,* 33: 501–511.

Napier, Augustus Y. and Whitaker, Carl A. (1978). *The Family Crucible: The Intense Experience of Family Therapy.* New York: Harper & Row.

Newcombe, Alan (1978). "Lovemate": A personal and international foreign policy for peace. In Charny, Israel W. (Ed.). *Strategies against Violence, op. cit.,* 3–18.

Nietzsche, Friedrich (2003). *Beyond Good and Evil: Prelude to a Philosophy of the Future.* London: Penguin.

Ogden, Gina (Ed.) (2015). *Extraordinary Sex Therapy: Creative Approaches for Clinicians.* New York: Routledge.

Oliner, Samuel P. and Oliner, Pearl M. (1992). *The Altruistic Personality: Rescuers of Jews in Nazi Europe.* New York: Simon and Schuster.

Olson, David H.; Sprenkle, Douglas H.; and Russell, Candyce S. (1979). Circumplex model of marital and family systems. 1. Cohesion and adaptability dimensions, family types, and clinical applications. *Family Process,* 18(1), 3–28.

Palazzoli, Mara Selvini (1977). *Self-Starvation: From Individual to Family Therapy in the Treatment of Anorexia Nervosa.* New York: Jason Aronson.

Palazzoli, Mara Selvini et al. (1978). *Paradox and Counterparadox: A New Model in the Therapy of the Family in Schizophrenic.* New Brunswick, NJ: Transaction.

Perec, George (1988). *W or the Memory of Childhood.* Boston: David R. Godine.

Raimy, Victor (1975). *Misunderstandings of the Self.* San Francisco: Jossey-Bass.

Rapoport, Anatol (1974). *Conflict in Man-Made Environment.* Baltimore: Penguin Books (quotation on p. 73).

Redfield, James (1994). *The Celestine Prophecy: An Adventure.* New York: Bantam.

Reich, Wilhelm (1990). *Character Analysis.* New York: Farrar, Straus, and Giroux (original published in German 1933, and English translation 1945).

Resnick, H.L.P. (Ed.) (1968). *Suicidal Behaviors: Diagnosis and Management.* New York: Little Brown & Company.

Rheingold, Joseph C. (1964). *The Fear of Being a Woman*. New York: Grune & Stratton.

Rheingold, Joseph C. (1967) *The Mother, Anxiety, and Death*. New York: Little Brown.

Rogerson, Mark D.; Gottlieb, Michael C.; Handlesman, Mitchell M.; Knapp, Samuel; and Younggren, Jeffrey (2011). Nonrational processes in ethical decision making. *American Psychologist*, 66(7), 614–523.

Rosenthal, Rovik (Ed.) (2000). *Kfar Kassem: Myth and History*. Tel Aviv: Hakibbutz Hameuchad Publishing House (Hebrew).

Rubinoff, Lionel (1978). In nomine diaboli. The voices of evil. In Charny, Israel W. (Ed.). *Strategies against Violence*, 34–67.

Rummel, R.J. (1997). *Power Kills: Democracy as a Method of Nonviolence*. New Brunswick, NJ: Transaction Publishers.

Rummel, R.J. (1999). *Statistics of Democide: Genocide and Mass Murder since 1900*. New Brunswick, NJ: Transaction.

Sanua, Victor D. (1983). Infantile autism and childhood schizophrenia: Review of the issues from the sociocultural point of view. *Social Science and Medicine*, 17, 1633–1651.

Sanua, Victor D. (1984). Is infantile autism a universal phenomenon? An open question. *International Journal of Social Psychiatry*, 30(3), 163–177.

Sanua, Victor D. (1986). The organic etiology of infantile autism: a critical review of the literature. *International Journal of Neuroscience*, 30(3), 195–225.

Sanua, Victor D. (1989). Studies in infantile autism. *Child Psychiatry and Human Development*, 19(3), 207–227.

Sanua, Victor D. (1990). Leo Kanner (1894–1981): The man and the scientist. *Child Psychiatry and Human Development*, 21(1), 3–23.

Saul, Leon (1956). *The Hostile Mind: The Sources and Consequences of Rage and Hate*. New York: Random House.

Saul, Leon (1972). *Psychodynamically Based Psychotherapy*. New York: Science House.

Scaer, Robert (2005). *The Trauma Spectrum: Hidden Wounds and Human Resiliency*. New York: Norton.

Scharff, David E. and Scharff, Jill (2004). *Object Relations Family Therapy*. Lanham, MD: Rowman & Littlefield.

Searles, Harold Frederick (1986). *Collected Papers on Schizophrenia and Related Subjects*. London: Karnac.

Sechehaye, Marguerite (1951). *Symbolic Realization: A New Model of Psychotherapy Applied to a Case of Schizophrenia*. New York: International Universities Press.

Sechehaye, Marguerite (1951). *Autobiography of a Schizophrenic Girl*. New York: Grune and Stratton.

Sechehaye, Marguerite (1956). *A New Psychotherapy in Schizophrenia: Relief of Frustrations by Symbolic Realization*. New York: Grune and Stratton.

Seikkula, Jaako and Olson, Mary E (2003). The open dialogue approach to acute psychosis: Its poetics and micropolitics. *Family Process*, 42(3), 403–418.

Seligman, Martin, E.P. (1974). Depression and learned helplessness. In Raymond J. Friedman and Martin M. Katz (Eds.). *The Psychology of Depression: Contemporary Theory and Research*. Washington, DC: Winston-Wiley.

Seligman, M. E. P. and Csikszentmahalyi, M. (2000). Positive psychology: An introduction. *American Psychologist, Special Issue on Happiness, Excellence, and Optimal Human Functioning*, 55(1), 5–14.

Shapiro, David (1974). *Neurotic Styles* (originally published 1965). New York: Basic Books.

Shapiro, David (1989). *Psychotherapy of Neurotic Character*. New York: Basic Books.

Sharp, Gene (1973). *The Politics of Nonviolent Action*. Three-volume set. *Part One: Power and Struggle. Part Two: The Methods of Nonviolent Action. Part Three: The Dynamics of Nonviolent Action*. Boston, MA: Porter Sargent.

Shaver, Philip R. and Mikulincer, Mario (Eds.) (2011). *Human Aggression and Violence: Causes, Manifestations, and Consequences*. Washington, DC: American Psychological Association.

Sheleff, Leon Shasholsky (1978). *The Bystander: Behavior, Law, Ethics*. Lexington, MA: Lexington Books.

Spinelli, Ernesto (2000). *Interpreted World: An Introduction to Phenomenological Psychology*. London: Sage.

Spinelli, Ernesto (2001). *The Mirror and the Hammer: Challenging Orthodoxies in Psychotherapeutic Thought*. Thousand Oaks, CA: Sage.

Sprenkle, Douglas H. and Olson, David H. L. (1978). Circumplex model of marital systems: An empirical study of clinic and non-clinic couples. *Journal of Marriage and Family Counseling*, 4(2), 59–74.

Stanley, Scott M. and Blumberg, Susan L. (2010). *Fighting for Your Marriage: A Deluxe Revised Edition of the Classic Best-Seller for Enhancing Marriage and Preventing Divorce*. 3rd edition. San Francisco, Jossey-Bass.

Stannard, David E. (1992). *American Holocaust: Columbus and the Conquest of the New World*. New York: Oxford University Press

Strous, Rael D. (2006). Hitler's psychiatrists: healers and researchers turned executioners and its relevance today. *Harvard Review of Psychiatry*, 14(1), 30–37.

Sullivan, Harry Stack (1947). *Conceptions of Modern Psychiatry*. Washington, DC: William Alanson White Foundation.

Sullivan, Harry Stack (1953). *The Interpersonal Theory of Psychiatry*. New York: Norton.

Tamarin, George R. (1980). *Studies in Psychopathology*. Kennewick, WA: Turtledove Press.

Taylor, C. P. (1981). *Good* (a play). First staged by the Royal Shakespeare Company at the Donmar Warehouse in September 1981.

Totten, Samuel and Parson, William S. (Eds.) (2012). *Centuries of Genocide: Critical Essays and Eyewitness Testimony*. 4th edition. New York: Routledge.

Trepper, Terry S. and Barrett, Mary Jo (1988). *Systemic Treatment of Incest: A Therapeutic Handbook*. New York: Psychology Press.

Trunk, Isaiah (1972). *Judenrat [The Jewish Councils in Eastern Europe Under Nazi Occupation]*. New York: Macmillan.

Twenge, Jean M. and Campbell, W. Keith (2009). *The Narcissism Epidemic: Living in the Age of Entitlement*. New York: Simon and Schuster.

Ullman, Leonard P. and Krasner, Leonard (Eds.) (1965). *Case Studies in Behavior Modification*. New York: Holt, Rinehart & Winston.

Van Leer, Wim (1964). *The Final Solution* (a play). (Originally titled *D.R.P. 861731*, performed for the first time on November 3, 1964, at the Wimbledon Theatre, Wimbledon, England.)

VandenBos, Gary R. (2007). *APA Dictionary of Psychology*. 1st edition. Washington, DC: American Psychological Association.

Vogel, Ezra F. and Bell, Norman W. (1960). The emotionally disturbed child as the family scapegoat. *Psychoanalytic Review*, 47, 21–42.

Volkan, Vamik (1988). *The Need to Have Enemies and Allies: From Clinical Practice to International Relationships*. Dunmore, PA: Jason Aronson.

Waller, James (2007). *Becoming Evil: How Ordinary People Commit Genocide and Mass Killing.* 2nd edition. New York: Oxford University Press.

Wallerstein, Judith S. and Kelly, Joan B. (1980). *Surviving the Breakup: How Children and Parents Cope with Divorce.* New York: Basic Books.

Wallerstein, Judith S. and Blakeslee, Sandra (1989). *Second Chances: Men, Women, and Children a Decade after Divorce.* New York: Ticknor & Fields.

Weeks, Gerald R. and Treat, Stephen R. (2001). Treating the extramarital affair. In *Couples in Treatment: Techniques and Approaches for Effective Practice.* New York: Routledge, 226–263.

Wernick, Uri (2016). *Nietzschean Psychology and Psychotherapy: The New Doctors of the Soul.* Lanham, MD: Lexington Books.

Wertham, Fredric. (1966). *A Sign for Cain: An Exploration of Human Violence.* New York: Macmillan.

Whitaker, Carl and Bumberry, William M. (1988). *Dancing with the Family: A Symbolic-Experiential Approach.* New York: Brunner/Mazel.

Wiesel, Elie (1964). *The Town Beyond the Wall.* New York: Atheneum.

Wile, Daniel B. (1981). *Couples Therapy: A Nontraditional Approach.* New York: Wiley.

Wile, Daniel B. (1988). *After the Honeymoon: How Conflict Can Improve Your Relationship.* New York: Wiley.

Winnicott, D.W. (1950). Some thoughts on the meaning of the word democracy. In *Home is Where We Start From: Essays by a Psychoanalyst.* New York: Norton, 239–259.

Wolfgang, Marvin E. (Ed.) (1966). *Patterns of Violence. Annals of the American Academy of Political and Social Science*, 364(1).

Wouk, Herman (1952). *The Caine Mutiny.* New York: Doubleday.

Wynne, Lyman C.; Ryckoff, Irving M; Day, Juliana; and Hirsch, Stanley I. (1958). Pseudo-mutality in the family relations of schizophrenics. *Psychiatry*, 21, 205–220.

Zillmer, Eric A; Harrower, Molly; Ritzler, Barry A; and Archer, Robert P. (1995). *The Quest for the Nazi Personality: A Psychological Investigation of Nazi War Criminals.* New York: Lawrence Erlbaum/Routledge.

Zimbardo, Philip G.; Maslach, Christina; and Haney, Craig (2000). Reflections on the Stanford Prison Experiment: Genesis, transformations, consequences. In Blass, Thomas (Ed.). *Obedience to Authority: Current Perspectives on the Milgram Paradigm.* Mahwah, NJ: Lawrence Erlbaum, 193–238.

Index

About the Author

Israel W. Charny is an American and Israeli who is widely known in the United States, Europe, and Israel as a leader in both family therapy and genocide studies and prevention. In both cases his work is anchored in his continuing clinical practice and professional leadership as a clinical psychologist and family therapist. He is well known as founder and first president of the Israel Family Therapy Association, a past president of the International Family Therapy Association, and a cofounder and past president of the International Association of Genocide Scholars. In 2011 he was honored with a Presidential Prize by the president of Armenia "in recognition of his decades-long academic work and activities contributing to international recognition of the Armenian Genocide and his researches of denials of genocides." He has written a good deal about marriage and family therapy, including two books, *Marital Love and* Hate, 1972, and *Existential Dialectical Marital Therapy: Breaking the Secret Code of Marriage*, 1992. Three of his previous books have been awarded "Outstanding Academic Book of the Year" by the American Library Association: *Genocide: A Critical Bibliographic Review*, editor, 1988; *Encyclopedia of Genocide*, editor, 1999; and *Fascism and Democracy in the Human Mind*, 2006. A recent book, *The Genocide Contagion: How We Commit and Confront Genocide*, 2016, has won the "Spirituality and Practice Book Award." The present book, *Psychotherapy for a Democratic Mind: Treatment of Tragedy, Intimacy, Violence, and Evil*, follows an earlier book also by Lexington Books, *A Democratic Mind: Psychology and Psychiatry with Fewer Meds and More Soul.* The present book *applies* the concept of a Democratic Mind to actual diagnosis and treatment of many relationship disorder and psychiatric conditions, old and new, recognized and unrecognized.